Orofacial Growth and Development

World Anthropology

General Editor

SOL TAX

Patrons

CLAUDE LÉVI-STRAUSS
MARGARET MEAD
LAILA SHUKRY EL HAMAMSY
M. N. SRINIVAS

MOUTON PUBLISHERS · THE HAGUE · PARIS
DISTRIBUTED IN THE USA AND CANADA BY ALDINE, CHICAGO

Orofacial Growth and Development

Editors

ALBERT A. DAHLBERG
THOMAS M. GRABER

MOUTON PUBLISHERS · THE HAGUE · PARIS
DISTRIBUTED IN THE USA AND CANADA BY ALDINE, CHICAGO

General Editor's Preface

While teeth — often the first-discovered traces of early man — have played an important role in our understanding of hominid evolution, many general anthropologists are not aware of the other important problems of human biology which this book addresses. It is relatively easy to observe significant phenotypic characteristics of teeth and to preserve them in dental casts for careful study. This possibility greatly benefits the study of human variations, especially in differentiating genetic factors from those which are cultural and environmental. Moreover, since variations in the growth and development of teeth and associated facial characteristics affect a person's health, their study is important to both the science and practice of medicine and dentistry. Hence the importance of a book that brings together recent data on these problems. It is the result of a symposium immediately preceding — and occasioned by — the IXth International Congress of Anthropological and Ethnological Sciences, which was attended by large numbers of scientists from the socialist and capitalist industrialized countries, as well as from the ex-colonial parts of the world.

Like most contemporary sciences, anthropology is a product of the European tradition. Some argue that it is a product of colonialism, with one small and self-interested part of the species dominating the study of the whole. If we are to understand the species, our science needs substantial input from scholars who represent a variety of the world's cultures. It was a deliberate purpose of the IXth International Congress of Anthropological and Ethnological Sciences to provide impetus in this direction. The *World Anthropology* volumes, therefore, offer a first glimpse of a human science in which members from all societies have played an active role. Each of the books is designed to be self-contained; each is an attempt to update its particular sector of scientific knowledge and is written by specialists from all parts of the world. Each volume should be read and reviewed individually as a separate volume on its own given subject. The set as a whole will indicate what changes are in store for anthropology as scholars from the developing countries join in studying the species of which we are all a part.

The IXth Congress was planned from the beginning not only to include as many of the scholars from every part of the world as possible, but also with a view toward the eventual publication of the papers in high-quality volumes. At previous Congresses scholars were invited to bring papers which were then read out loud. They were necessarily limited in length; many were only summarized; there was little time for discussion; and the sparse discussion could only be in one language. The IXth Congress was an experiment aimed at changing this. Papers were written with the intention of exchanging them before the Congress, particularly in extensive pre-Congress sessions; they were not intended to be read aloud at the Congress, that time being devoted to discussions — discussions which were simultaneously and professionally translated into five languages. The method for eliciting the papers was structured to make as representative a sample as was allowable when scholarly creativity — hence self-selection — was critically important. Scholars were asked both to propose papers of their own and to suggest topics for sessions of the Congress which they might edit into volumes. All were then informed of the suggestions and encouraged to re-think their own papers and the topics. The process, therefore, was a continuous one of feedback and exchange and it has continued to be so even after the Congress. The some two thousand papers comprising *World Anthropology* certainly then offer a substantial sample of world anthropology. It has been said that anthropology is at a turning point; if this is so, these volumes will be the historical direction-markers.

As might have been foreseen in the first post-colonial generation, the large majority of the Congress papers (82 percent) are the work of scholars identified with the industrialized world which fathered our traditional discipline and the institution of the Congress itself: Eastern Europe (15 percent); Western Europe (16 percent); North America (47 percent); Japan, South Africa, Australia, and New Zealand (4 percent). Only 18 percent of the papers are from developing areas: Africa (4 percent); Asia-Oceania (9 percent); Latin America (5 percent). Aside from the substantial representation from the U.S.S.R. and the nations of Eastern Europe, a significant difference between this corpus of written material and that of other Congresses is the addition of the large proportion of contributions from Africa, Asia, and Latin America. "Only 18 percent" is two to four times as great a proportion as that of other Congresses; moreover, 18 percent of 2,000 papers is 360 papers, 10 times the number of "Third World" papers presented at previous Congresses. In fact, these 360 papers are more than the total of ALL papers published after the last International Congress of Anthropological and Ethnological Sciences which was held in the United States (Philadelphia, 1956).

The significance of the increase is not simply quantitative. The input of scholars from areas which have until recently been no more than subject matter for anthropology represents both feedback and also long-awaited theoretical contributions from the perspectives of very different cultural, social, and historical traditions. Many who attended the IXth Congress were convinced that anthropology would not be the same in the future. The fact that the next Congress (India, 1978) will be our first in the "Third World" may be symbolic of the change. Meanwhile, sober consideration of the present set of books will show how much, and just where and how, our discipline is being revolutionized.

The numerous Congress sessions on physical anthropology, human biology, and hominid evolution have resulted in many volumes which will interest readers of this book — particularly those volumes on the adaptation of the species through time to many different environments and to shifts in demography, which in turn have effected nutritional, social, and psychological differences that have medical implications.

Chicago, Illinois   SOL TAX
August 25, 1976

Preface

A symposium designed to synthesize aspects of growth, development, genetics, and dental anthropology related to the craniofacial region was held August 30 and 31, 1973, at the University of Chicago at the invitation of the Department of Anthropology and of the Zoller Memorial Dental Clinic. The dates of the sessions were chosen as a convenience for those individuals who planned to attend the meetings of the IXth International Congress of Anthropological and Ethnological Sciences the following week.

This volume includes most of the papers presented at those sessions plus some additional ones that had been submitted to the IXth Congress itself.

The symposium was organized by Albert Dahlberg and Thomas Graber who also acted as moderators at the panel discussions that followed each of the two days of presentations. The first two subject sessions on growth and development were discussed by the Graber-led panel of Walker (University of Michigan), Moyers (Columbia University), McNamara (University of Michigan) and Koski (University of Turku, Finland). The sessions included a wide range of discussions from the ultrastructure of cells and tissues of teeth and Meckel's cartilage to the biodynamics and descriptions of the growth forces of craniofacial structures.

The second day was devoted to two sessions, genetics and dental anthropology. The genetics session included varied approaches of statistics, variance, chromosomes, congenital evidences, and experimental designs. This was followed by population-tooth-trait and craniofacial analyses. Dahlberg moderated the panel and audience participation.

The panel included Garn (University of Michigan), Lundström (Karolinska Institute School of Dentristry, Sweden), Kirveskari (University of Turku, Finland), Mayhall (University of Toronto, Canada), and Hylander (Duke University).

Lively participation ensued on the part of the audience, who challenged definitions of populations, techniques, and concepts, and contributed to understanding the recent ideas about the functions, mechanisms, and genetics of the subjects that were discussed.

Appreciation is expressed especially to Phyllis Flattery and Robert Cederquist for much detailed editorial work in the preparation of this volume.

ALBERT A. DAHLBERG
THOMAS M. GRABER

Table of Contents

Introduction

ALBERT A. DAHLBERG and THOMAS M. GRABER

This volume contains papers that were presented at the Symposium on Oral Growth and Development and Dental Anthropology during the IXth International Congress of Anthropological and Ethnological Sciences. The sessions were held at the University of Chicago at the invitation of the Department of Anthropology and the Zoller Memorial Clinic with support from the University, the Kenilworth Dental Research Foundation, Albert A. Dahlberg, and Thomas M. Graber. The latter two were responsible for the program and acted as co-chairmen.

The sessions were divided into three broad subjects: growth and development; genetics; and dental anthropology and population studies.

GROWTH AND DEVELOPMENT

The sessions on growth and development included papers by K. Koski, G. Walker, S. Rosenstein and B. Jacobson, S. Molnar, H. Droschl and T. Graber, and R. Biggerstaff.

In craniofacial biology the concept of "growth centers," with their independent potential for bone growth (specifically the condylar cartilage and the synchrondoseal cartilages of the cranial base), has long been a subject of controversy. Koski provides a lucid discussion of the importance and nature of these cartilages. He reviews his extensive research on subcutaneous and intracerebral transplantation of condylar and cranial base cartilages in the rat. Koski rejects the idea of the supremacy of craniofacial cartilages and the theory that these cartilages play a major role as genetically determined leaders in craniofacial growth.

Walker discusses the progress of the cephalometric atlas of cranio-facial morphology which he, together with W. M. Krogman and J. Harris, among others, is preparing. Their data will be based on large population samples of North Americans, including blacks and Indians. They will also include relatively large samples from the South Pacific (Maoris and Tongans), an isolated population from the Amazon (the Peruvian Cashinahua), samples of Nubian children, a group of Sioux Indians, and a sample of pre-Hellenic skulls from the island of Crete. Walker also discusses two methods of defining "normality" in human craniofacial form, both the clinical and the statistical approach. In order to avoid subjective or individual preferences inherent in the first method, they have preferred to take an approach based upon statistical population sampling.

Rosenstein and Jacobson present the philosophy of their early treatment of congenital cleft lip and palate malformations. Their approach involves early maxillary orthopedics and allows molding of the maxillary arch segments after lip closure. This is followed by stabilization of the segments by means of the well-known autogenous bone graft. Rosenstein and Jacobson have extensive records on about one hundred patients and are beginning to obtain data for long-term evaluation of the procedures. The results, which would hardly have been conceivable in the past, are very favorable with occlusions and arch forms.

Molnar discusses his research on variations in microstructure of primate teeth. It has already been noted that interglobular dentin occurs more frequently in man and pongids than in cercopithecoid monkeys. Molnar's work tends to substantiate those earlier observations. He also noted that differences exist between captive and free-ranging primates, which raises questions about the environment and dental development. Environmental influences acting on the developing primate may be evaluated by comparisons of histological tooth sections taken from different populations.

Droschl and Graber present a histological investigation on mutual response to heavy continuous orthopedic force on the maxilla of *Saimiri sciureus* monkeys. The sutures that were studied were the zygomatico-frontal, zygomatico-maxillary, fronto-maxillary and pterygopalatine. Oxy-tetracycline and Procion red H.8BS were used as *in vivo* bone markers. All the sutures were heavily affected and the orthopedic force produced a widening two or three times greater than normal, and intensive remodeling activity in the sutures was evident. The regular tissue pattern changed to a mixture of precollagen and collagen fibers running in all directions and a great number of active cells. Droschl and Graber discuss whether the changes will be permanent and examine the phenomenon of "catch-up growth" which will determine its clinical significance.

Several hypotheses exist concerning the biological factors which have contributed most to the origin and evolution of the shape of the human mandibular symphysis. Biggerstaff in his article "The biology of the human chin" gives an extensive review of these hypotheses and critically evaluates the data upon which these hypotheses are based. He states a convincing case for Bolk's shifting theory. The differential growth potentials and growth gradients of the alveolar bone and the basal bone of the mandibular body contribute to the importance of this theory. The effect will be that the mandibular alveolar bone and basal bone shift in such a way that the dentition regresses posteriorly while the mental protuberance progresses anteriorly.

GENETICS

Three major contributions to the text on the subject of genetics were made by Lundström, Alvesalo, and Cohen.

As the X-chromosome is much larger than the Y-chromosome, it is assumed that females have more genetic material than males. Lundström reviews the hypothesis of Lyon concerning the effects of this overweight and the effects of the so-called Barr's bodies of the cell nucleus (whereby in each cell only one X-chromosome is active). This hypothesis is partly based on the fact that in abnormal cases with more than two X-chromosomes an increase in the number of Barr's bodies is observed. With three X-chromosomes there are thus two Barr's bodies instead of the normal one. Lundström discusses his findings in his studies of quantitative variations in teeth. He also reviews the studies of sex differences in teeth by Bowden, Goose, Garn, Lewis, Kerewsky, Lundström, Seipel, and Selmer-Olson. While sexual dimorphism might well be due to genes on the Y-chromosome, there is some evidence that genes on the X-chromosome also play a part in tooth size variation. Correlation studies and tooth size are discussed. He believes that the greater variation between dizygotic than between monozygotic co-twins is due in the first place to gene differences between the former with a a direct bearing on the ontogenetic development of teeth and dental arches.

Alvesalo, Osborne, and Kari report that tooth sizes, of 47, XYY males studied were larger than those of normal control males and females. In their article they discuss probable causes for this difference and the influence of one versus two Y-chromosomes on the cell cycle within the developing tooth germ.

Tooth size reduction has been shown to be present in several disorders of prenatal origin. No comparative data have been available. In order to determine the magnitude of crown size reduction in congenital disorders, Cohen, Baum, Garn, Osorio, and Nagy collected odontometric data on 255 subjects representing five different congenital defects: Down's syndrome, hypodontia, cleft palate, prenatal rubella, and congenital syphilis. The crown size profile pattern of the mesiodistal tooth size dimensions were calculated, using Z scores or standard deviation units in comparison with the reference population. Their findings indicate that a gradient of sex similarity in crown size profile pattern exists for the five conditions examined. A hierarchical order of crown size reduction in these groups has been noted as well as several individual syndrome pattern differences.

DENTAL ANTHROPOLOGY AND POPULATION STUDIES

Hylander states that most of the unusual bony features of the Eskimo craniofacial region are especially adapted to generate and dissipate large vertical biting forces. He states further in his article that there is little evidence supporting adaptation to cold in the Eskimo skull. He cites root resorption, dental chipping, fractured crowns, and the mandibular and palatal tori as features often associated with an increase in occlusal or biting force.

The Habbanites are an isolate population living in Israel, differing physically from all their neighbors in many respects. Smith finds three lineages in the group an excellent model for studying differences in tooth morphology. She uses cusp number on teeth, presence or absence of the sixth and seventh cusps and the deflecting wrinkle on lower molarocclusal surfaces and occlusal tubercles in her investigations. Dimorphism is present to only a minor degree in each of two teeth and relatively insignificant compared to interlineage differences. It is suggested that the number of factors responsible for specific traits may be fewer than those which govern tooth size.

Goose uses the data on dentition to compare both morphological characteristics and pathological conditions between the general local Caucasoid population and Chinese living in Liverpool. He finds that inheritance patterns for the dental traits are far from simple. His data add to the store of information on Mongoloid dentitions.

In his article, Hanihara finds dental characteristics of Ainu very similar to those of Japanese and Eskimos, but differing greatly from those of the Caucasoids. He suggests that the biological distance is not great between the Ainu and the Australian aborigine (casts were made in the Yuendumu settlement in Central Australia). He concludes that the Ainu are probably derived from a Mongoloid ancestry as are some neighboring populations such as the Japanese, Eskimos, and American Indians.

A report on French male conscripts gives data on their dentition. The frequency of congenital absence of lateral incisors and third molars is somewhat comparable to that frequency in other modern populations. Le Bot also concludes that some of the differences in the dental arcade have a purely mechanical explanation.

In a full discussion of the dental traits of several Eskimo populations, Mayhall points out that they have taken on a new, and in most cases a detrimental, role in the mastication of food and other cultural usages. This has resulted in diminished efficiency in comminution of food, in speech, and also in a diminished esthetics.

Turner and Scott include a wealth of data on the dental traits of Easter Islanders. This group shows greater tooth similarity with Asians than with any other population. They show greatest dissimilarity to American Indians, a finding which contradicts theories on the peopling of Polynesia from the New World.

The Skolt Lapps, an isolated and inbred population in the north of Finland, become a new source of information on tooth form in Kirveskari's study and analysis of tubercles and eminences on tooth surfaces. He reports in detail on the early literature and on the unusually large incidence of these traits in the Lapp and neighboring populations of the north.

The craniofacial studies of Wainwright Alaskan Eskimos show skeletal similarity with earlier populations of that region. Age differences are reflected in posterior and anterior facial height, according to Cederquist and Dahlberg's analysis of an X-ray report on precontact skeletal material from the Canadian Arctic in which the facial flatness is less pronounced.

Odontoglyphics is a new term suggested by Zoubov in the studies of the variations of the patterns of the human molar masticatory surface. Zoubov outlines the principles of the patterns in the furrow system. He indicates that a body of material of this nature is already in existence, but that treatment of this information, as it relates to ethnic studies remains for another, later, report. A similar study on premolar furrows is also referred to, but is not included here.

Koritzer proposes new terminology and approaches to dental data and cultural relationships.

The problem of morphological changes in human teeth and jaws is discussed by Hylander. He feels that the notion that edge-to-edge bite is due to differential tooth migration is not supported by data. The edge-to-edge bite is in part formed by compensatory condylar growth of the mandible during adult life; continued elongation is associated with a more anterior positioning of the mandibular dentition.

Johnson reports on the specificity and interrelationships of Meckel's cartilage cells in tissue culture and Cotton and Gaines contribute some data on toothless rats.

The treatment of craniofacial biology in the articles included in the volume is comprehensive and thoroughgoing. The authors are leading authorities on the problems of growth and related subjects.

The IXth International Congress proved to be a distinct focal point for scientists from a host of disciplines dealing with man, and this volume is an example of their impact on an important area of genetic, evolutionary, and morphological study.

SECTION ONE

Growth

The Role of the Craniofacial Cartilages in the Postnatal Growth of the Craniofacial Skeleton

KALEVI KOSKI

Once upon a time, and that was only fifteen years ago, all textbook writers, whether anatomists or orthodontists, were repeating the same doctrine: the craniofacial cartilages are like epiphyseal cartilages, if not in structure, at least in function, i.e. they are the most important centers of craniofacial skeleton growth. Presumably, all teachers were teaching the same doctrine, and all students were more or less learning it. Then the "functional matrix" theory was introduced to the craniofacial world (Moss 1960, 1962), and it has never been the same since. There are still those who prefer the old text, without even noticing what has happened during the last fifteen years; but more and more wordings are being changed even in traditionally conservative textbooks.

The functional matrix idea was, as we all know, not really a new, nor a very precise theory. However, by questioning, as it did, the old beliefs, such as the supremacy of the craniofacial cartilages, it stimulated more research, perhaps, than any other idea in the recent history of craniofacial biology. Thanks to that, we now know much more about craniofacial growth than we did fifteen years ago. On the other hand, it is quite obvious that we do not know nearly enough (cf. Dullemeijer 1971, 1972; van Limborgh 1970, 1972; Kremenak 1972); our present knowledge is still limited to a few fragments belonging to a large puzzle, the complete version of which nobody has seen.

The author's investigations have been supported by grants from the Sigrid Juselius Foundation, Helsinki, Finland, and by United States Public Health Service grants D-1434, DE-01793, and HD-00177. I should like to thank Mr. Jarmo Koskinen for his skillful microphotography and Mrs. Sirpa Laakso for her secretarial assistance.

For Plates, see pp. iii–ix, between pp. 330–331.

It is my purpose here to present some findings related to certain fragments and to discuss their possible place in the puzzle.

INVESTIGATIONS

Two cartilages of the craniofacial skeleton, previously considered to be important growth centers, have been studied with special regard to their independent potential for promoting bone growth: the condylar cartilage of the mandible (Koski and Mäkinen 1963; Koski and Mason 1964; Koski and Rönning 1965; Rönning, Paunio, and Koski 1967; Rönning and Koski 1970) and the cranial base synchondroseal cartilages (Koski and Rönning 1969, 1970). The experimental animal has been the rat. Observations have been made on the histology, histochemistry and biochemistry of the cartilages *in situ*, and on dimensional and histological aspects of growth in transplanted specimens. Because detailed reports of the experiments and their results have been published elsewhere, only the main findings will be described here in general terms.

Condylar Cartilage of the Mandible

In situ observations on condylar cartilages of five-day-old rats revealed the following details:

The cartilage as a whole lacks the clear organization so characteristic of long-bone epiphyseal growth plates. The top of the cartilage consists of densely packed small round cells, underneath which is a zone of more ovoid-shaped cells somewhat loosely arranged. The latter zone blends without a clear boundary with the next zone of chondroid and cartilage cells, which in turn is followed by a wide zone of relatively small hypertrophied cells forming about three-fifths of the whole height of the cartilage. Noteworthy is the narrowness of the zone of the true cartilage cells and the scantiness of the matrix throughout. No primary spongiosa comparable to that present in long-bone growth zones is seen here.

An interesting finding was the extent of the Sudan Black stain, indicating the zone of mineralization. This zone covered the whole area of hypertrophied cells. The same situation was observed in the thirteen-day condylar cartilage, in which the different zones were markedly reduced from the five-day dimensions.

Biochemically, the condylar cartilage was found to be low in glycos-
aminoglycans, especially in the acid moiety; the sulphate content of the
condylar cartilage was very low.

Transplantation of the condylar cartilage was done using both subcutaneous and intracerebral sites. The types of transplants studied in
different series were (1) condylar cartilage proper, (2) condylar cartilage with the adjacent immature spongiosa, (3) condylar cartilage with
the adjacent ramus down to the more mature ossified area, and (4)
condylar cartilage with the articular disc (see Table 1 and Plate 1). In
addition, the articular disc alone was also transplanted.

Table 1. Types of condylar-ramal transplants, periods of transplant growth, number of transplanted and recovered specimens

Type	Period	Transplanted	Recovered
Condylar cartilage, subcutaneous	30	22	12
	60	22	14
	90	14	4
Cartilage and immature spongiosa,	30	26	20
subcutaneous	60	36	16
Cartilage and ramal bone,	30	19	18
subcutaneous	60	24	21
	90	18	16
Condylar cartilage, brain	5	14	14
	10	13	13
	15	23	15
	30	9	2
Cartilage and articular disc, brain	5	13	13
	10	18	11
	15	23	12
	30	8	—
Articular disc, brain	5	12	11
	10	12	9
	15	20	15
	30	9	6
		355	242

The condylar cartilages proper, without adjacent bone and disc,
showed relatively little or no increase in size in the direction corresponding to the height of the ramus *in situ*. Their lack of growth was
not dependent on the site of transplantation, nor was it a function of
time, i.e. the increase was not proportional to the period of transplanta-

tion, except during the first ten days or so (see below). In some instances the dimensional increase appeared to have taken place in a direction corresponding to the dorsoventral direction of the condylar cartilage *in situ*.

The inclusion of the articular disc, which at this age is only a thin connective tissue capsule surrounding the condyle, did not affect the dimensional growth of the cartilage transplant.

A short-term experiment involving brain tissue sites revealed a possible explanation for the lack of sustained dimensional growth (Plates 2-3). As early as five days after transplantation, the cartilages, whether plain or with the disc, appeared to be in a state of erosion; this proceeded rather fast, so that after ten days the transplants had no or very few cartilage cells left, i.e. the mitotic zone had been destroyed and the cartilage could not have grown further. A usual finding after the first ten days was an ossicle which more or less resembled the original transplant in its shape.

The findings in regard to the condylar cartilages with some adjacent bone attached contrasted in an interesting way with those described above. The compound transplants, as a rule, increased in size, in some instances considerably; this increase appeared to be somewhat dependent on the transplant's composition inasmuch as the pieces containing only the immature spongiosa did not grow as much as the pieces which included also the more mature ramal bone. In transplants of the latter type the time element came into play: although neither the mean nor the maximum length of transplants showed a consistent trend to increase after thirty days, the minimum length did. Some of the transplants of the larger type reached a size that equaled or even surpassed the length of the corresponding part of the ramus *in situ* at an equivalent age.

An interesting finding in these compound transplants was the resemblance of the microscopic structure with that of the ramus *in situ* (Plate 4). Cartilage persisted in these transplants for the first thirty days, as a rule, but then disappeared gradually, so that after ninety days cartilage cells were rarely seen in the transplants. However, the structure of the cartilage did not quite match that of a normal condylar cartilage because it consisted of patches of hypertrophic cells, surrounded by a matrix which appeared to be in a state of mineralization, and the so-called intermediate zone was missing. The cartilaginous patches were separated by strands of cells running from the mesenchymal cell zone which formed the top of the transplant. The cells in these strands were seemingly undergoing transformation into osteoblasts or perhaps even osteoclasts; both of these cell types were present in abundance farther down in the transplants .

In connection with the study of the significance of the articular disc on the condylar cartilage growth, the disc alone was also transplanted into the brain tissue; the results of this ranged from lumps of fibrous tissue through patches of cartilage to pieces of bone. Here, as in other instances, no attempt was made to ascertain the possible role of cells of the host site in the growth of the transplants.

Cranial Base Cartilages

Histologically the cranial base synchondroses resembled closely epiphyseal growth plates of long bones; in fact, they could be described as two-faced growth plates. While the organization typical of a growth plate was there, the zones of different types of cells were not as wide as in long-bone growth plates, but were about one-half the size of the zones of the latter.

The zone of mineralization, as revealed by the Sudan Black stain, reached through the zone of degenerating cells to the hypertrophied cell area; this observation may have been affected by the narrowness of the cell zones. Alcian Blue and PAS staining was more intensive in the cerebral than in the pharyngeal parts of the cartilages.

Biochemically the cranial base cartilages resembled long-bone epiphyseal cartilages, with some minor differences.

The types of the cranial base cartilage transplants were (1) the synchondroseal cartilages proper, from both sites, (2) the cartilages with some adjacent bone on both sides, from both sites, and (3) the whole cranial base from the occipital foramen to the septosphenoidal junction (see Table 2 and Plate 5).

There did not seem to be any difference in the growth in the subcutaneous transplant sites of the two cartilages. There was a difference, however, regarding the fate of the two main types of transplants; the plain cartilages showed some increase in length in about 20 percent of the instances, while the compound transplants showed no growth, except in three cases (out of 147) in which a barely measurable increase had taken place. Most of the transplants in both groups had either decreased in length or, at best, maintained their original length.

It was a frequent and curious finding that the transplanted cartilages had increased in size in a direction corresponding to the breadth of the cranial base.

Table 2.   Types of cranial base transplants, periods of transplant growth, number of transplanted and recovered specimens

Type	Period	Transplanted	Recovered
Synchondroseal cartilage,			
subcutaneous	2	10	10
	5	17	17
	10	11	11
	15	46	45
	30	44	37
	60	38	34
Synchondroseal cartilage and bone,			
subcutaneous	2	10	10
	5	17	17
	10	11	11
	15	52	42
	30	49	45
	60	52	46
	90	18	16
Synchondroseal cartilage and bone,			
brain tissue	30	166	6
	60		12
Cranial base, subcutaneous	2	10	10
	5	12	12
	10	9	9
	15	11	11
	30	16	15
	60	28	22
		627	438

Regarding the intracerebral transplants, five of the eighteen recovered specimens had increased in size, up to doubling their length, while at the same time decreasing in breadth.

The whole cranial base transplants had mostly decreased in length, and only about one-third of them showed a small amount of growth. This growth did not seem to be correlated with the transplantation time. The interesting finding in this group was that the intrasynchondroseal distance showed a small but time-linked trend toward increase (Plate 6).

Histologically, the cartilage transplants in the subcutaneous sites presented a rather uniform picture, irrespective of their original composition (Plates 7, 8). They were ossicles, mostly, as mentioned above, grown along the breadth axis of the cartilage, and presenting a variably healthy cartilage, plus variable amounts of bone and marrow. The cartilage appeared to have become anteroposteriorly narrower with time. The ossicles were, as a rule, sealed by lamellar bone to the surrounding host tissue. Of special interest was the finding that in many instances the amount of bone on both sides of the cartilage was not equal, as it had been in the original transplanted pieces containing bone. The histology of the whole cranial base transplants was not noticeably different from that seen in the synchondroseal specimens.

The intracerebral transplants presented a variety of histological pictures. Most of them were ossicles consisting of lamellar bone shell filled with normal marrow, but the ones which had increased in length had the cartilage still in a recognizable shape, either in the middle or toward the other end of the transplant, which otherwise consisted of bony tubules filled with marrow tissue (Plate 9).

DISCUSSION[1]

The characteristics of the condylar cartilage of the mandible have been recently elucidated by a number of workers both from the static and dynamic points of view (Blackwood 1966; Greenspan and Blackwood 1966; Duterloo 1967; Folke and Stallard 1967; Rönning et al. 1967; Frommer et al. 1968; Durkin et al. 1969, 1973; Baume 1970a, 1970b; Duterloo and Jansen 1970; Melcher 1971; Durkin 1972; Joondeph 1972; Petrovic 1972; Silbermann and Frommer 1972a, 1972b; Bremers 1973). While some details apparently need clarification, especially with respect to the maturation process in the condyle from the fetal start to adulthood, the essentials of the condylar cartilage are now well known. From the viewpoint of craniofacial growth, the important characteristics of this cartilage during the growth period seem to be that (1) it grows by proliferation of cells, which can hardly be called cartilage cells but are more like mesenchymal cells, and it contains only a small amount of true nonhypertrophied cartilage cells; (2) most of the cartilage at any given time consists of hypertrophied cells; (3) the matrix is scanty and apparently in a state of mineralization through the hypertrophic area at any given time; (4) the architecture does not reveal the growth direction; and (5) the pattern of vascularization at this cartilage resembles that seen at articular cartilages of long bones, and the erosion pattern of the condylar cartilage, involving multinucleated giant cells, is also similar to that of an articular cartilage. Thus, some authors stress the permanently embryonic nature of this cartilage

[1] In this discussion references to the so-called growth centers of the skull are mainly from papers published since 1967; the previous literature was reviewed by the author at that time (Koski 1968).

(Durkin 1972; Durkin et al. 1973), which is similar to articular cartilages and definitely dissimilar to the epiphyseal cartilages which organize themselves into growth plates.

There are aspects in the origin of the condylar cartilage that deserve
attention. While it has been well known that it arises as a secondary
cartilage, separate from the already existing and growing osseous mandible (cf. Duterloo and Jansen 1970), it was only very recently indicated that its development may be dependent on the presence of movement, i.e. articulation (Duterloo and Wolters 1972). This, of course,
would tie the condylar cartilage nicely with the articular cartilages (cf.
Hall 1968). On the other hand, it is conceivable that the bony mandible
acts as an inducer, stimulating the mesenchymal cells to choose the
chondrogenic path of specialization. This explanation would appear to
get some support from the fate of the compound condyle transplants,
in which the cartilage is preserved for much longer periods than when
no bone is attached to the cartilage. There is a slight possibility that the
cartilage in the compound transplants was preserved because these
specimens, due to their large size, were moving in relation to their
host environment, as if they were articulating with the subcutaneous
tissues. This appears unlikely, however, in view of the fact that in
similarly transplanted long bones the articular cartilage soon disap-
pears (Koskinen and Koski 1967). The postnatal interaction between
the mandibular bone and the cartilage, as an example of cellular interactions in postnatal life (cf. Auerbach 1971; Manson 1968), warrants
further study.

The peculiar process of mineralization seen in the condyle has caught
the eye of some investigators (Rönning et al. 1967; Silbermann and
Frommer 1972a; Durkin et al. 1973); the pericellular calcification pattern is like the pattern in early ossification centers of cartilaginous pre-
cursors of bone (Durkin et al. 1973). There may be more mineralization
than endochondral bone formation taking place here. The finding that
the chondrocytes of the condylar cartilage may not be destroyed but assume a new function as chondroclasts or osteoprogenitor cells (Silbermann and Frommer 1972a, 1972b), when considered with similar findings made on different types of cartilage (Holtrop 1964, 1966, 1972;
Crelin and Koch 1967; Bohatirchuk 1969), reinforces the notion that
the specialized connective tissue cells retain their multipotentiality and
are capable of different functions, depending on the environmental
stimuli (cf. Hall 1970; Pritchard 1972; Tonna and Pentel 1972).

There is even recent evidence on the atypical reaction of the condylar
cartilage to biochemical stimuli, when compared to that of epiphyseal

cartilages (Baume 1970b; Rönning 1971); while this may be not surprising in view of the differences in the biochemical makeup (Rönning et al. 1967), the phenomena are still waiting for explanation.

On the clinical side, evidence is accumulating, both from experimental stimulation or inhibition of mandibular growth (Charlier et al. 1969a, 1969b; Joho 1969; Ramfjord and Enlow 1971; Stöckli and Willert 1971; Adams et al. 1972; Elgoyhen et al. 1972; McNamara 1972; Petrovic 1972; Petrovic and Stutzmann 1972) and condylectomies (Sarnat 1971; Pimenidis and Gianelly 1972; Poswillo 1972) that the condylar cartilage is not an independently functioning important growth center of the mandible. It apparently can be affected, especially at a young age, and its disappearance does not *per se* cause great disturbance of growth in the mandible, except locally in the ramus. Considering the relatively loose structural association of the condyle to the ramus, not to speak of the body of the mandible (Moss 1968; Koski 1973), this is not surprising.

Studies of the independent bone-growth-promoting capacity of the condylar cartilage have employed methods of transplantation (Lacroix 1951; Felts 1961) and tissue culture (Fell 1956). These studies (Koski and Mäkinen 1963; Koski and Mason 1964; Koski and Rönning 1965; Rönning 1966; Charlier and Petrovic 1967; Duterloo 1967; Rönning and Koski 1970; Melcher 1971; Duterloo and Wolters 1972; Petrovic 1972) have shown that the condylar cartilage alone is not capable of any sustained bone-growth-promoting existence when it is separated from its normal functional environment. The fact that transplanted condylar cartilages, and, to a very small degree, cultured cartilages, increase in size during the first days, until the proliferative cells are destroyed by erosion and mineralization, is, of course, to be expected. When contrasted to the long-lasting maintenance, indeed a differentiation if necessary, of structure and function as endochondral bone-growth apparatus of transplanted long-bone epiphyseal cartilages (Lacroix 1951; Felts 1961; Koski and Rönning 1966), the dissimilarity is obvious. The fate of transplanted condylar cartilages resembles that of articular cartilages in a nonfunctional environment (Koskinen and Koski 1967).

The maturation stage of the condylar cartilage may be of some importance for its independent growth potential (Rönning et al. 1967; Koski 1971), and it is conceivable that its capacities during the fetal stage are somewhat greater than they are postnatally (cf. Bremers 1973). In view of its structure, it seems hardly likely that it even then would have an independent bone-growth-promoting potential. Regarding the other end of the maturation process, one recent opinion seems to stress the significance of the disappearance of the hyper-trophic cells for the termination of the adaptational period of this cartilage (Durkin et al. 1973). While the idea that the condylar car-tilage is an adaptive cartilage is perfectly acceptable, the adaptive capacity of this or any other cartilage surely must be associated with the proliferative zone and not with the hypertrophic zone of the cartilage.

The condylar cartilage is still seen as an important growth center for the mandible in some texts (Sicher and Du Brul 1970; Scott and Dixon 1972). It is, of course, true that dimensional increase in the con-dylar region is, especially during the fetal and early postnatal growth, of considerable magnitude, and in this sense the condylar area is an important growth site. The term "growth center" was defined by Baume (1961) to mean "places of endochondral ossification with tissue separation force." This, as we have seen, does not apply to the condylar cartilage. However, some investigators still prefer the older view (Baume 1970a, 1970b; Björk 1972; Björk and Skieller 1972), even when their own findings cannot always be properly interpreted to support their opinions. Whether the concept of growth center in Baume's terms, in the light of recent data and theories, is at all mean-ingful is another matter which shall be touched upon later.

After having received little detailed attention previously (Björk 1955; Scott 1955; Baume 1961), the structure and growth of the cranial base synchondroses have interested an increasing number of researchers during recent years (Rönning et al. 1967; Enlow 1968a; Riolo 1970; Dorenbos 1971; Kvinnsland 1971; Melsen 1971; Elgoyhen et al. 1972; Latham 1972; Michejda 1972; Moss et al. 1972; Vilmann 1972).

Summarizing the findings from various studies, it can be stated that the cranial base synchondroses have a microscopic structure very much like the epiphyseal growth plates, with the typical zones of resting, proliferative, hypertrophic, and degenerative cells being readily dis-cernible. This, and the mode of growth, which is through the mitotic activity of true cartilage cells, is in contrast to the situation found in the condylar cartilage. The function of these synchondroses seems to be similar to that of growth plates, i.e. they are involved in typical endochondral bone growth processes. The bipolarity, a natural feature for a synchondrosis, gives these cartilages the look of a Janus-faced growth plate, in which the relative shortness of the cellular columns is most likely associated with a relatively small growth activity (cf. Hansson 1967). This activity may be asymmetrical, i.e. the rates of growth of bone on either side of the cartilages may be of different magnitude. The general textbook label for these cartilages has been and still is that of an important growth center for the cranial base (Weinmann and Sicher 1947; Sicher and Du Brul 1970; Scott and Dixon 1972); the label is accepted without reservation by some investigators (Baume 1968).

Studies on the biochemistry and reactions to agents of biochemical nature (Rönning et al. 1967; Baume 1970b; Rönning 1971) indicate that the cranial base cartilages tend to be similar to epiphyseal growth cartilages, but differ clearly from the condylar cartilages.

Because the cranial base synchondroses are "leftovers" from the primary chondrocranium, the problems of their formation are different from those of the condylar cartilages. It is possible that the cartilaginous model of the cranial base arises as the result of an inductive action of the notochord (Dorenbos 1971; see also Cohen and Hay 1971; Carlson 1973).

While the homology with the long-bone epiphyses is so obvious, the significance of the cranial base synchondroses for the growth of the skull base has been questioned by some authors in the past, although on circumstantial evidence and in a speculative fashion (Ortiz and Brodie 1949; Koski 1960). It is interesting to note that recent authors either join the early doubters (Riolo 1970; Kvinnsland 1971), acknowledge the contribution of periosteal apposition to the dimensional increase of the cranial base (Kvinnsland 1971; Melsen 1971), or stress the role of the synchondroses in the process of flexure of the skull base (Melsen 1971; Michejda 1972; Vilmann 1972). As the cranial base shapes vary among species, so apparently do the extent and mode of action of the synchondroses as well as of the periosteum in the cranial base growth.

The fact that the two synchondroses in the monkey skull base have differing growth patterns, including the timing of growth (Michejda 1972), would seem to agree best with the idea that these cartilages function under environmental stimuli (Moss et al. 1972). The cranial base synchondroses are, both in their structure and their relationship to neutral mass, very much like the so-called neurocentral epiphyses of the vertebrae, which have been found to have an adaptive nature that responds to altered functional stimuli (Karaharju 1967).

The studies on the independent growth potential of the cranial base cartilages are few and, at first glance, somewhat contradictory. In culture, the synchondroseal cartilages have grown at a rate of 80 percent of the *in situ* growth rate; however, this growth has been observed for only eight days, and bone formation in the explants has been almost nonexistent (Petrovic and Charlier 1967). Halves of synchondroses, divided through the resting cell zone, have likewise been found to increase slightly in size as transplants in the brain tissue over a period of eleven days (Dorenbos 1972). Our own findings on the growth of subcutaneous transplants of synchondroseal cartilages have been negative, but some of the transplants in brain tissue have grown, and intersynchondroseal distance in whole cranial base transplants in subcutaneous sites has been noticed to increase.

It is perhaps worth repeating that from the viewpoint of skull growth we should be mainly interested in the bone-growth-promoting capacity of the cartilages under discussion. That mitotic cartilages *per se* are able to increase in size, especially during short periods of time, as explants *in vivo* or *in vitro*, should not surprise anyone. The question again is: are these cartilages capable of sustained endochondral bone promotion when separated from their normal environment? The net conclusion from the experiments so far seems to be that there is no unequivocal proof for the independent bone-growth-promoting capacity of the cranial base cartilages.

Some findings made on synchondrosis transplants seem worthy of special notice. In many of the transplants the development, even if no gross dimensional increase was noticed, was asymmetrical. The endochondral bone formation at the spheno-occipital synchondrosis in man has also been stated to be asymmetrical (Enlow 1968a); if the growth of the cartilage *in situ* has been programmed to be asymmetrical, it can conceivably continue this program for a short period even in a transplantation site. When dimensional growth was evident in transplants, it had mostly taken place in a transverse direction; transversal growth has been noticed in transplanted epiphyseal cartilages (Lacroix 1951), and even the condylar cartilage transplants often increased in a similarly "abnormal" fashion. These transplant behaviors are understandable if we assume that *in situ* there are factors which restrict and direct the growth of these cartilages (see below). Finally, the moving apart of the cartilages in the whole cranial base transplants can be interpreted as a sign of interaction between the bone and the cartilage, but, as we shall see later, other explanations are also possible.

What kind of craniofacial growth theory do the findings related to these two types of cartilages support? Can they be explained by the conceptions which stress the autonomous and pacemaking nature of the craniofacial cartilages (Weinmann and Sicher 1947; Sicher and Du Brul 1970; Scott and Dixon 1972)? Do they support the idea that chondrocranial growth, governed by intrinsic genetic factors, is controlling the desmocranial growth as a source of epigenetic factors (van Limborgh 1970, 1972)? Or are they in better concert with the by now well-known "functional matrix" concept (Moss 1960, 1962, 1971; Moss and Salentijn 1969) with its periosteal and capsular matrices? And what about the explicitly holistic theories, which conceive an organism as composed of members connected mutually in a multifactorial system (Dullemeyer 1971, 1972) or as a self-regulating open hierarchic order of autonomous holons (Koestler 1970)?

Before we try to decide this matter, we should take a look at the status of the cartilage and bone tissues in general.

The cartilage tissue arises from mesenchymal cells, which are apparently multipotential and choose their function and line of specialization according to environmental stimuli (Pauwels 1960; Bassett 1962; Krompecher and Toth 1964; Wurmbach 1967; Lash 1968; Hall 1970; Rodbard 1970; Tonna and Pentel 1972). Although differences exist among the authors as to the nature of these stimuli, they seem to agree, at least, on two factors: compression and hypoxia. When it comes to early development of the craniofacial cartilage mass, the role of neural elements and of the notochord cannot be neglected (cf. Cohen and Hay 1971; Dorenbos 1972; Carlson 1973). It seems obvious that the birth of the cartilage tissue, including the craniofacial cartilages, does not take place under a predominant effect of intrinsic genetic factors (cf. van Limborgh 1970, 1972).

The growth potential, even the bone-growth-promoting potential, of epiphyseal cartilages has been found to be great (Lacroix 1951; Felts 1961; Koski and Rönning 1966). However, there appears to be an agreement again regarding the capacity of these cartilages, indeed of any cartilage, to exhibit and promote directional growth: "Only when cartilage is constrained by connective tissues or bone can it exert orientated forces which determine the direction of bone growth" (Storey 1972; see also Krompecher and Toth 1964; Pritchard 1972); normally, the perichondrial ring apparently restricts the transverse growth of the epiphyseal growth plate (Langenskiöld et al. 1967; Hansson et al. 1972; Hert 1972). Its growth, with respect to both magnitude and direction, is under the influence of the surrounding periosteum, muscles, and ligaments (Hert 1964; Moss 1972); recent evidence for this is furnished by the findings that the epiphyseal growth plates seem to be controlled by the periosteal tension (Crilly 1972), and that the arrested growth of one growth plate is compensated by the increased activity of the other in a long bone (Hall-Craggs 1968; Hall-Craggs and Lawrence 1969).

Bone tissue arises from the same mesenchymal cells as the cartilage tissue, and again under the influence of environmental stimuli. Although *in vitro* studies may indicate that compression and high oxygen tension are involved (Bassett 1962), the former may not be necessary; according to other views, bone tissue arises in loci which have good circulation and are well protected from compression or tension (Wurmbach 1967), and no specific mechanical stimulus exists for bone (Pauwels 1960). The latter opinion derives support from the variety of conditions in which ectopic bone formation has been encountered (cf. Ostrowski and Wlodarski 1971).

It is a fundamental fact that "the skeleton does not grow as a result of growth of bone" (Baer 1971); there is, in contrast to cartilage, no interstitial growth in bone. To cite further, "the skeleton grows as a result of the proliferation of cartilage or connective tissue" and "the osseous tissue is a secondary event, a consolidation" (Baer 1971). The opinion, apparently widely held, that the osseous skeleton would have an inherent morphogenetic potential (Lewis and Irving 1970), is thus based on a misunderstanding of facts. The role of the soft connective tissue for the growth of the bony palate (Kremenak et al. 1967) is but one example of many; on the other hand, it is obvious that the growth potential and bone-producing activities of the connective tissue in sutures, for instance, are not self-controlled (cf. Ryöppy 1965; Isotupa 1972).

As we have seen, the evidence tends to speak against the idea that intrinsic, genetically determined potential is the controlling factor in the growth of cartilage, not to speak of bone. Once the existence and importance of environmental stimuli in chondrogenesis and osteogenesis are accepted, it is rather logical to expect these stimuli to continue to affect the subsequent growth of these tissues. How can the tissues, arising from undifferentiated cells that all carry the same genetic information, acquire their tissue-characteristic potentials? This can hardly happen without, at least, the contribution of cellular interaction, and, most likely, of other extrinsic factors as well.

In this connection it is appropriate to note that the clonal model may well be applicable also to the formation of the skull (Moore and Mintz 1972). However, this would still not suffice to grant the synchondroses full autonomy; as we have seen, the condylar cartilage certainly lacks it. Even if the cartilaginous cranial base were of clonal origin, the asynchronous life histories of the leftover synchondroses clearly indicate that the controlling factors reside outside the cartilage cells.

In the light of the presented evidence, the concept "growth center"

(Baume 1961) does not appear meaningful. When cartilaginous and periosteal-endosteal bone formation and growth are equally controlled by extrinsic factors, the fact that some tissues, e.g., the epiphyseal cartilages, do possess some growth potential of their own, manifestable for some periods outside the normal environment, does not carry any specific weight when we deal with growth *in situ*. The concepts best suited to the factual conditions would be CARTILAGINOUS, PERIOSTEAL, and ENDOSTEAL GROWTH SITES, which serve the process of adaptive growth (cf. Goss 1964).

The question remains: why are the cartilages there?

Everything seems to indicate that the condylar cartilage is there for reasons typical for secondary cartilages: presence of intermittent pressure and movement, and need for rapid growth during early life. In the postnatal period, it is best compared to articular cartilage, although certain differences do exist.

In regard to the cranial base synchondroses the picture is different. These remnants of the chondrocranium can obviously expedite growth for as long as that is needed; note that in man, whose anterior cranial base does not grow after the first few years, the synchondroses in this region ossify very early. But the often overlooked fact is that the synchondroses are bioelastic, pressure-bearing joints (cf. Storey 1972; Vilmann 1972). The need for elastic joints in the cranial base is obvious. This bony region is located amidst several functionally and structurally different vital parts, whose rates and schedules of growth may vary widely: the portions of the brain, the nasopharynx, the oropharynx, the atlanto-occipital joint region, including the prevertebral and postvertebral muscles and ligaments, even the mandible and hyoid bones through their muscular and ligamental connections. The cranial base with its flexible synchondroses is in a strategic position for acting as a balance master for this complexity, and there is one especially important task: the maintenance of the horizontal position of the horizontal semicircular canals, which is a fundamental feature in all vertebrates (cf. Delattre and Fenart 1958; Dullemeyer 1971).

Before returning to the craniofacial growth theories, I shall consider briefly the cartilaginous nasal septum, even though my own studies do not deal with it. The role of this cartilage has been under lively discussion, and two main schools of thought seem to exist: one regards the septum as a main growth center and pacemaker for the upper face (Baume 1961; Latham and Scott 1970; Scott and Dixon 1972), while the other sees it in a passive role (Moss et al. 1968; Moss and

Salentijn 1969). Investigators continue to interpret the results of their experiments in opposite ways (Babula et al. 1970; Stenström and Thilander 1970; Kvinnsland and Breistein 1973). If the cartilaginous nasal septum were indeed a growth center, with intrinsic and autonomous growth potential *in situ*, it would, in view of what we have learned about cartilages in general, be an exception among cartilages. This is unlikely; the septal cartilage, whatever its potential, most likely also functions under the influence of its environment. However, more has to be learned about this cartilage before its full story can be written.

In light of the preceding discussion it is obvious that concepts or theories which assign the craniofacial cartilages a major role as genetically determined leaders in craniofacial growth are not soundly based. The idea of mutual dependency between the components of the craniofacial region has in one form or another been expressed by many students of this area (cf. Scott 1955; Enlow 1968b). Among the comprehensive theories incorporating this view are those of Dullemeyer, Koestler, and Moss.

The "functional matrix" idea of Moss (Moss 1960; Moss and Salentijn 1969) is perhaps the best known of these theories. In its present form, which still leaves something to be desired from the point of view of those who would like to design experiments to test it, it nevertheless, in general terms, is in good agreement with the observations discussed here. As we have seen, the growth activities of the craniofacial cartilages dealt with here can easily be visualized to be under the influence of the periosteal matrix in the first place; what the overruling capsular matrices in each instance are remains an open question.

The self-regulating open hierarchic order (SOHO) theory of Koestler (1970) is an interesting attempt to characterize biological organisms. The hierarchical order of semiautonomous "holons," governed by the system's "canon," seems to be applicable to the structure and functions of the craniofacial area. In Koestler's terms, the synchondroses might then qualify as "holons," whereas the condylar cartilage *per se* would have to be looked upon as a part of a "holon," the nature of which remains obscure. The "holon" concept would seem especially applicable to epiphyseal cartilages, which do show a certain amount of autonomous growth potential.

So far, Dullemeyer (1971, 1972) is the only craniofacial biology theoretician who has attempted to build detailed models of craniofacial relationships that are capable of specific experimental testing. He stresses the dynamic structural totality of animals and maintains that the growth problems can be solved only by paying due attention to the multiplicity and the changes of the interrelationships. From the methodological viewpoint, he considers the comparative approach perhaps more fruitful than the experimental one. Dullemeyer's approach is that of a general biologist, well founded in facts and drawing also from disciplines outside biology; there is no doubt that this approach is useful in studies of craniofacial growth. In Dullemeyer's terms, we have just begun to gather the necessary information, both in the qualitative and the quantitative sense, about the growth phenomena associated with the condylar and synchondroseal cartilages, and we have a long way to go.

Any theory that acknowledges the interrelated nature of craniofacial structures is in agreement with known facts. On the other hand, no theory has been tested enough to be fully acceptable as a comprehensive explanation; in fact, the concepts discussed above include working hypotheses, theoretical models, and pure theories. The student of craniofacial biology is free to make his own choice; he should, however, be aware of the limitations inherent in any and all decisions regarding his research (Dullemeyer 1972).

The role of the craniofacial cartilages, in spite of the numerous studies, is still not clear. The same is true, to an even greater degree, of the growth of the craniofacial skeleton as a whole. The problems still to be studied are innumerable (cf. Moffett 1972; Moss 1972); I shall mention here only the crucial question about the mechanism of information transfer in the process of skeletal growth (cf. Bassett 1972; Moss 1972; Pritchard 1972). The history of science, including the recent history of our own small branch of science, shows that real progress often comes from unconventional departures from the traditional path; this is very likely to happen also in the future in the field of craniofacial biology.

SUMMARY

In the first section I reviewed my studies of transplanted condylar and cranial base cartilages in the rat. The results show that the condylar cartilage lacks an independent bone-growth-promoting potential, while the synchondroseal cartilages may have that potential to some degree.

When data from several sources and on different types of cartilages and of bone are scrutinized, it appears that the question regarding the so-called independent growth potential, i.e. the concept "growth center," is meaningless from the viewpoint of normal skeletal growth. The evidence speaks for an extrinsic control of growth, not only for bones, but also for cartilages. The important task for future research is to unravel the nature of this control. And with respect to theories of craniofacial growth, only those are acceptable which acknowledge the interdependent nature of craniofacial growth phenomena.

REFERENCES

ADAMS, C. D., M. C. MEIKLE, K. W. NORWICK, D. L. TURPIN
  1972 Dentofacial remodelling produced by intermaxillary forces in *Macaca mulatta*. *Archives of Oral Biology* 17:1519–1535.

AUERBACH, ROBERT
  1971 Inductive tissue interaction in mammalian development. *Journal of Dental Research* 50:1382–1384.

BABULA, WALTER J., GARY R. SMILEY, ANDREW D. DIXON
  1970 The role of the cartilaginous nasal septum in midfacial growth. *American Journal of Orthodontics* 58:250–263.

BAER, M. J.
  1971 In *Cranio-facial growth in man*. Edited by Robert E. Moyers and Wilton M. Krogman, 288. Oxford: Pergamon.

BASSETT, C. ANDREW L.
  1962 Current concepts of bone formation. *Journal of Bone and Joint Surgery* 44-A:1217–1244.
  1972 A biophysical approach to craniofacial morphogenesis. *Acta Morphologica Neerlando-Scandinavica* 10:71–86.

BAUME, L. J.
  1961 Principles of cephalofacial development revealed by experimental biology. *American Journal of Orthodontics* 47:881–901.
  1968 Patterns of cephalofacial growth and development. *International Dental Journal* 18:489–513.
  1970a Cephalofacial growth patterns and the functional adaptation of the temporomandibular joint structures. *Transactions of the European Orthodontic Society 1969:* 79–98.
  1970b Differential response of condylar, epiphyseal, synchondrotic, and articular cartilages of the rat to varying levels of vitamin A. *American Journal of Orthodontics* 58:537–551.

BJÖRK, ARNE
  1955 Cranial base development: a follow-up X-ray study of the individual variation in growth occurring between the ages of 12 and 20 years and its relation to brain case and face development. *American Journal of Orthodontics* 41:198–225.
  1972 The role of genetic and local environmental factors in normal and abnormal morphogenesis. *Acta Morphologica Neerlando-Scandinavica* 10:49–58.

BJÖRK, A., V. SKIELLER
1972 Facial development and tooth eruption. *American Journal of Orthodontics* 62:339–383.

BLACKWOOD, H. J. J.
1966 Growth of the mandibular condyle of the rat studied with tritiated thymidine. *Archives of Oral Biology* 11:493–500

BOHATIRCHUK, Г. P.
1969 Metaplasia of cartilage into bone: a study by stain historadiography. *American Journal of Anatomy* 126:243–254.

BREMERS, L. M. H.
1973 "De condylus mandibulae in vitro." Doctoral dissertation, Catholic University, Nijmegen.

CARLSON, EDWARD C.
1973 Intercellular connective tissue fibrils in the notochordal epithelium of the early chick embryo. *American Journal of Anatomy* 136: 77–90.

CHARLIER, J.-P., A. PETROVIC
1967 Recherches sur la mandibule de rat en culture d'organes: le cartilage condylien a-t-il un potentiel de croissance indépendant? *L'Orthodontie Française* 38:119–128.

CHARLIER, J.-P., A. PETROVIC, G. LINCK
1969a La fronde mentonnière et son action sur la croissance mandibulaire. Recherches expérimentales chez le rat. *L'Orthodontie Française* 40:99–109.

CHARLIER, J.-P., ALEXANDRE PETROVIC, JEANNE HERRMANN-STUTZMANN
1969b Effects of mandibular hyperpulsion on the prechondroblastic zone of young rat condyle. *American Journal of Orthodontics* 55:71–74.

COHEN, ALAN M., ELIZABETH D. HAY
1971 Secretion of collagen by embryonic neuroepithelium at the time of spinal cord-somite interaction. *Developmental Biology* 26:578–605.

CRELIN, E. S., W. E. KOCH
1967 An autoradiographic study of chondrocyte transformation into chondroclasts and osteocytes during bone formation in vitro. *Anatomical Record* 158:473–484.

CRILLY, R. G.
1972 Longitudinal overgrowth of chicken radius. *Journal of Anatomy* 112:11–18.

DELATTRE, A., R. FENART
1958 La méthode vestibulaire. *Zeitschrift für Morphologie und Anthropologie* 49:90–114.

DORENBOS, JACOB
1971 "Craniale synchondroses." Doctoral dissertation, Catholic University, Nijmegen.
1972 In vivo cerebral implantation of the anterior and posterior halves of the spheno-occipital synchondrosis in rats. *Archives of Oral Biology* 17:1067–1072.

DULLEMEYER, P.
1971 "Comparative ontogeny and cranio-facial growth," in *Craniofacial growth in man*. Edited by Robert E. Moyers and Wilton M. Krogman, 45–75. Oxford: Pergamon.
1972 Methodology in craniofacial biology. *Acta Morphologica Neerlando-Scandinavica* 10:9–23.

DURKIN, JAMES F.
1972 Secondary cartilage: a misnomer? *American Journal of Orthodontics* 62:15–41.

DURKIN, JAMES, JOHN HEELEY, J. T. IRVING
1973 The cartilage of the mandibular condyle. *Oral Sciences Reviews* 2:29–99.

DURKIN, J. F., J. T. IRVING, J. D. HEELEY
1969 A comparison of the circulatory and calcification patterns in the mandibular condyle in the guinea pig with those found in tibial epiphyseal and articular cartilages. *Archives of Oral Biology* 14: 1365–1371.

DUTERLOO, H. S.
1967 "In vivo implantation of the mandibular condyle of the rat." Doctoral dissertation, Catholic University, Nijmegen.

DUTERLOO, HERMAN S., DONALD H. ENLOW
1970 A comparative study of cranial growth in *Homo* and *Macaca*. *American Journal of Anatomy* 127:357–368.

DUTERLOO, HERMAN S., HENK W. B. JANSEN
1970 Chondrogenesis and osteogenesis in the mandibular condylar blastema. *Transactions of the European Orthodontic Society 1969*: 109–118.

DUTERLOO, HERMAN S., JOHANNA M. WOLTERS
1972 Experiments on the significance of articular function as a stimulating chondrogenic factor for the growth of secondary cartilages of the rat mandible. *Transactions of the European Orthodontic Society 1971*: 103–115.

ELGOYHEN, J. C., R. E. MOYERS, J. A. MC NAMARA JR., M. L. RIOLO
1972 Craniofacial adaptation to protrusive function in young rhesus monkeys. *American Journal of Orthodontics* 62:469–480.

ENLOW, DONALD H.
1968a *The human face*. New York: Hoeber.
1968b Wolff's law and the factor of architectonic circumstance. *American Journal of Orthodontics* 54:803–822.

FELL, HONOR B.
1956 "Skeletal development in tissue culture," in *The biochemistry and physiology of bone*. Edited by Geoffrey H. Bourne, 401–441. New York: Academic Press.

FELTS, W. J. L.
1961 In vivo implantation as a technique in skeletal biology. *International Review of Cytology* 12:243–302.

FOLKE, L. E. A., R. E. STALLARD
1967 Cellular kinetics within the mandibular joint. *Acta Odontologica Scandinavica* 25:437–489.

FROMMER, J., C. W. MONROE, J. R. MOREHEAD, W. D. BELT
    1968   Autoradiographic study of cellular proliferation during early
            development of the mandibular condyle in mice. *Journal of
            Dental Research* 47:816–819.
GOSS, RICHARD J.
    1964   *Adaptive growth.* London: Logos.
GREENSPAN, J. S., H. J. J. BLACKWOOD
    1966   Histochemical studies of chondrocyte function in the cartilage of
            the mandibular condyle of the rat. *Journal of Anatomy* 100:615–
            626.
HALL, B. K.
    1968   In vitro studies on mechanical evocation of adventitious cartilage
            in the chick. *Journal of Experimental Zoology* 168:283–306.
    1970   Differentiation of cartilage and bone from common germinal cells.
            Journal of Experimental Zoology 173:383–394.
HALL-CRAGGS, E. C. B.
    1968   The effect of experimental epiphyseodesis on growth in length of
            the rabbit's tibia. *Journal of Bone and Joint Surgery* 50-B: 392–
            400.
HALL-CRAGGS, E. C. B., C. A. LAWRENCE
    1969   The effect of epiphysial stapling on growth in length of the rab-
            bit's tibia and femur. *Journal of Bone and Joint Surgery* 51-B:
            359–365.
HANSSON, LARS INGVAR
    1967   Daily growth in length of diaphysis measured by oxytetracycline
            in rabbit normally and after medullary plugging. *Acta Orthopae-
            dica Scandinavica,* supplement 101.
HANSSON, LARS INGVAR, SVEN-ARNE AHLGREN, ANDERS LINDSTRAND
    1972   Deposition of oxytetracycline in perichondral ossification in rab-
            bit. *Acta Orthopaedica Scandinavica* 43:461–468.
HERT, JIRI
    1964   Regulace rustu dlouhych kosti do delky. *Plzensky Lekarsky
            Sbornik,* supplement 12:5–132.
    1972   Growth of the epiphyseal plate in circumference. *Acta Anatomica*
            82:420–436.
HOLTROP, MARIJKE E.
    1964   "Enchondrale verbening in muizeribben." Doctoral dissertation,
            University of Leiden.
    1966   "The origin of bone cells in endochondral ossification," in *Calci-
            fied tissues.* Edited by H. Fleisch, H. J. J. Blackwood, and M.
            Owen, 32–36. Berlin–Heidelberg: Springer.
    1972   The ultrastructure of the epiphyseal plate II. The hypertrophic
            chondrocyte. *Calcified Tissue Research* 9:140–151.
HOYTE, D. A. N.
    1971   "The modes of growth of the neurocranium: The growth of the
            sphenoid bone in animals," in *Cranio-facial growth in man.*
            Edited by Robert E. Moyers and Wilton M. Krogman, 77–105.
            Oxford: Pergamon.

ISOTUPA, KAUKO
1972   Alitsariinijuosteet kokeellisessa kallon kasvun tutkimuksessa [Alizarin trajectories in experimental studies of skull growth]. *Proceedings of the Finnish Dental Society* 68: supplement II.

JOHO, JEAN-PIERRE
1969   Changes in form and size of the mandible in the orthopaedically treated *Macacus irus* (an experimental study).*Transactions of the European Orthodontic Society 1968*: 161–173.

JOONDEPH, DONALD R.
1972   An autoradiographic study of the temporomandibular articulation in the growing *Saimiri sciureus* monkey. *American Journal of Orthodontics* 62:272–286.

KARAHARJU, ERKKI O.
1967   Deformation of vertebrae in experiment scoliosis. *Acta Orthopaedica Scandinavica*, supplement 105.

KOESTLER, ARTHUR
1970   Beyond atomism and holism: the concept of the holon. *Perspectives in Biology and Medicine* 13:131–154.

KOSKI, KALEVI
1960   Some aspects of the growth of the cranial base and the upper face. *Odontologisk Tidskrift* 68:344–358.
1968   Cranial growth centers: facts or fallacies? *American Journal of Orthodontics* 54:566–583.
1971   "Some characteristics of cranio-facial growth cartilages," in *Cranio-facial growth in man*. Edited by Robert E. Moyers and Wilton M. Krogman, 125–138. Oxford: Pergamon.
1973   Variability of the cranio-facial skeleton. An exercise in roentgencephalometry. *American Journal of Orthodontics* 64:188–196.

KOSKI, KALEVI, LAURI MÄKINEN
1963   Growth potential of transplanted components of the mandibular ramus of the rat. I. *Suomen Hammaslääkäriseuran Toimituksia* 59:296–308.

KOSKI, KALEVI, KARL E. MASON
1964   Growth potential of transplanted components of the mandibular ramus of the rat. II. *Suomen Hammaslääkäriseuran Toimituksia* 60:209–217.

KOSKI, KALEVI, OLLI RÖNNING
1965   Growth potential of the transplanted components of the mandibular ramus of the rat. III. *Suomen Hammaslääkäriseuran Toimituksia* 61:292–297.
1966   Pitkän luun rustoisen pään siirrännäisen kasvupotentiaalista rotalla. *Suomen Hammaslääkäriseuran Toimituksia* 62:165–169.
1969   Growth potential of subcutaneously transplanted cranial base synchondroses of the rat. *Acta Odontologica Scandinavica* 27:343–357.
1970   Growth potential of intracerebrally transplanted cranial base synchondroses in the rat. *Archives of Oral Biology* 15:1107–1108.

KOSKINEN, LEENA, KALEVI KOSKI
1967   Regeneration in transplanted epiphysectomized humeri of rats.

American Journal of Physical Anthropology 27:33–40.
KREMENAK, CHARLES R., JR.
1972   Circumstances limiting the development and verification of a
        complete explanation of craniofacial growth. *Acta Morphologica
        Neerlando-Scandinavica* 10:127–140.
KREMENAK, CHARLES R., WILLIAM C. HUFFMAN, WILLIAM H. OLIN
1967   Growth of maxillae in dogs after palatal surgery: I. *Cleft Palate
        Journal* 4:6–17.
KROMPECHER, ST., L. TOTH
1964   Die Konzeption von Kompression, Hypoxie und konsekutiver
        Mucopolysaccharidbildung in der kausalen Analyse der Chondro-
        genese. *Zeitschrift für Anatomie und Entwicklungsgeschichte* 124:
        268–288.
KVINNSLAND, STEINAR
1971   The sagittal growth of the foetal cranial base. *Acta Odontologica
        Scandinavica* 29:699–715.
KVINNSLAND, STEINAR, LIV BREISTEIN
1973   Regeneration of the cartilaginous nasal septum in the rat, after
        resection. *Plastic and Reconstructive Surgery* 51:190–195.
LACROIX, P.
1951   *The organization of bones.* London: Churchill.
LANGENSKIÖLD, A., T. RYTÖMAA, T. VIDEMAN
1967   An autoradiographic study with ³⁵S-sulphate on the growth in
        diameter of epiphyseal cartilage in rabbits. *Acta Orthopaedica
        Scandinavica,* supplement 106.
LASH, JAMES W.
1968   Chondrogenesis: genotypic and phenotypic expression. *Journal of
        Cellular Physiology* 72 (Supplement) 1:35–46.
LATHAM, R. A.
1972   The sella point and postnatal growth of the human cranial base.
        American Journal of Orthodontics 61:156–162.
LATHAM, R. A., J. H. SCOTT
1970   A newly postulated factor in the early growth of the human
        middle face and the theory of multiple assurance. *Archives of
        Oral Biology* 15:1097–1100.
LEWIS, E. A., J. T. IRVING
1970   An autoradiographic investigation of bone remodelling in the rat
        calvarium grown in organ culture. *Archives of Oral Biology* 15:
        769–776.
MANSON, J. D.
1968   *A comparative study of the postnatal growth of the mandible.*
        London: Kimpton.
MC NAMARA, JAMES A., JR.
1972   *Neuromuscular and skeletal adaptations to altered orofacial func-
        tion.* Ann Arbor: Center for Human Growth and Development,
        University of Michigan.
MELCHER, A. H.
1971   Behaviour of cells of condylar cartilage of foetal mouse mandible
        maintained in vitro. *Archives of Oral Biology* 16:1379–1391.

MELSEN, BIRTE
1971 The postnatal growth of the cranial base in *Macaca rhesus* analyzed by the implant method. *Tandlaegebladet* 75:1320–1329.

MICHEJDA, MARIA
1972 The role of basicranial synchondroses in flexure processes and ontogenetic development of the skull base. *American Journal of Physical Anthropology* 37:143–150.

MOFFETT, BEN C.
1972 A research perspective on craniofacial morphogenesis. *Acta Morphologica Neerlando-Scandinavica* 10:91–101.

MOORE, W. JAMES, BEATRICE MINTZ
1972 Clonal model of vertebral column and skull development derived from genetically mosaic skeletons in allophenic mice. *Developmental Biology* 27:55–70.

MOSS, MELVIN L.
1960 Functional analysis of human mandibular growth. *Journal of Prosthetic Dentistry* 10:1149–1159.
1962 "The functional matrix," in *Vistas of orthodontics*. Edited by Bertram S. Kraus and Richard A. Riedel, 85–98. Philadelphia: Lea and Febiger.
1968 Functional cranial analysis of mammalian mandibular ramal morphology. *Acta Anatomica* 71:423–447.
1971 "Ontogenetic aspects of cranio-facial growth," in *Cranio-facial growth in man*. Edited by Robert E. Moyers and Wilton M. Krogman, 109–124. Oxford: Pergamon.
1972 New research objectives in craniofacial morphogenesis. *Acta Morphologica Neerlando-Scandinavica* 10:103–110.

MOSS, MELVIN L., BERTRAM E. BROMBERG, IN CHUL SONG, GILBERT EISENMAN
1968 The passive role of nasal septal cartilage in mid-facial growth. *Plastic and Reconstructive Surgery* 41:536–542.

MOSS, MELVIN L., MARY-ANN MEEHAN, LETTY SALENTIJN
1972 Transformative and translative growth processes in neurocranial development of the rat. *Acta Anatomica* 81:161–182.

MOSS, MELVIN L., LETTY SALENTIJN
1969 The capsular matrix. *American Journal of Orthodontics* 56:474–490.

ORTIZ, MANUEL HIGINIO, ALLAN GIBSON BRODIE
1949 On the growth of the human head from birth to the third month of life. *Anatomical Record* 103:311–333.

OSTROWSKI, KAZIMIERZ, KRZYSZTOF WLODARSKI
1971 "Induction of heterotopic bone formation," in *The biochemistry and physiology of bone* (second edition). Edited by Geoffrey H. Bourne, volume two, 299–336. New York and London: Academic Press.

PAUWELS, FRIEDRICH
1960 Eine neue Theorie über den Einfluss mechanischer Reize auf die Differenzierung der Stützgewebe. *Zeitschrift für Anatomie und Entwicklungsgeschichte* 121:478–515.

PETROVIC, ALEXANDRE G.
1972 Mechanisms and regulation of mandibular condylar growth. *Acta Morphologica Neerlando-Scandinavica* 10:25–34.

PETROVIC, ALEXANDRE, JEAN-PAUL CHARLIER
1967 La synchondrose sphéno-occipitale de jeune rat en culture d'organes: mise en évidence d'un potentiel de croissance indépendant. *Comptes Rendus Hebdomadaires des Séances de l'Académie des Sciences*, series D 265:1311–1513.

PETROVIC, A., J. STUTZMANN
1972 Le muscle ptérygoidien externe et la croissance du condyle mandibulaire. Recherches expérimentales chez le jeune rat. *L'Orthodontie Française* 43:271–283.

PIMENIDIS, M. Z., ANTHONY A. GIANELLY
1972 The effect of early postnatal condylectomy on the growth of the mandible. *American Journal of Orthodontics* 62:42–47.

POSWILLO, D. E.
1972 The late effects of mandibular condylectomy. *Oral Surgery, Oral Medicine and Oral Pathology* 33:500–512.

PRITCHARD, JOHN J.
1972 The control or trigger mechanism induced by mechanical forces which causes responses of mesenchymal cells in general and bone apposition and resorption in particular. *Acta Morphologica Neerlando-Scandinavica* 10:63–69.

RAMFJORD, SIGURD P., RANDALL D. ENLOW
1971 Anterior displacement of the mandible in adult rhesus monkeys: long-term observations. *Journal of Prosthetic Dentistry* 26:517–531.

RIOLO, MICHAEL LYNN
1970 "Growth and remodelling of the cranial floor: a multiple microfluoroscopic analysis with serial cephalometrics." Unpublished Master's thesis, Georgetown University, Washington D.C.

RODBARD, SIMON
1970 Negative feedback mechanisms in the architecture and function of the connective and cardiovascular tissues. *Perspectives in Biology and Medicine* 13:507–527.

RÖNNING, OLLI
1966 Observations on the intracerebral transplantation of the mandibular condyle. *Acta Odontologica Scandinavica* 24:443–457.
1971 Alterations in craniofacial morphogenesis induced by parenterally administered papain. *Suomen Hammaslääkäriseuran Toimituksia* 67: supplement III.

RÖNNING, OLLI, KALEVI KOSKI
1970 The effect of the articular disc on the growth of condylar cartilage transplants. *Transactions of the European Orthodontic Society* 1969:99–108.

RÖNNING, OLLI, KEIJO PAUNIO, KALEVI KOSKI
1967 Observations on the histology, histochemistry and biochemistry of growth cartilages in young rats. *Suomen Hammaslääkäriseuran Toimituksia* 63:187–195.

RYÖPPY, SOINI
  1965   Transplantation of epiphyseal cartilage and cranial suture. *Acta Orthopaedica Scandinavica*, supplement 82.

SARNAT, BERNARD G.
  1971   Surgical experimentation and gross postnatal growth of the face and jaws. *Journal of Dental Research* 50:1462–1476.

SCOTT, JAMES H.
  1955   Craniofacial regions. *Dental Practitioner* 5:208–214.
  1958   The cranial base. *American Journal of Physical Anthropology* 16:319–348.

SCOTT, JAMES HENDERSON, ANDREW DERART DIXON
  1972   *Anatomy for students of dentistry* (third edition). Edinburgh and London: Churchill and Livingstone.

SICHER, HARRY, E. LLOYD DU BRUL
  1970   *Oral anatomy* (fifth edition). St. Louis: Mosby.

SILBERMANN, MICHAEL, JACK FROMMER
  1972a The nature of endochondral ossification in the mandibular condyle of the mouse. *Anatomical Record* 172:659–668.
  1972b Vitality of chondrocytes in the mandibular condyle as revealed by collagen formation. An autoradiographic study with ^{3}H-proline. *American Journal of Anatomy* 135:359–370.

STENSTRÖM, STEN J., BIRGIT L. THILANDER
  1970   Effects of nasal septal cartilage resections on young guinea pigs. *Plastic and Reconstructive Surgery* 45:160–170.

STOREY, ELSDON
  1972   Growth and remodeling of bone and bones. *American Journal of Orthodontics* 62:142–165.

STÖCKLI, PAUL W., HANS G. WILLERT
  1971   Tissue reactions in the temporomandibular joint resulting from anterior displacement of the mandible in the monkey. *American Journal of Orthodontics* 60:142–155.

TONNA, EDGAR A., LEON PENTEL
  1972   Chondrogenic cell formation via osteogenic cell progeny transformation. *Laboratory Investigation* 27:418–426.

VAN LIMBORGH, J.
  1970   The control of the morphogenesis of the skull. *Studieweek 1970*: 7–29.
  1972   The role of genetic and local environmental factors in the control of postnatal craniofacial morphogenesis. *Acta Morphologica Neerlando-Scandinavica* 10:37–47.

VILMANN, HENNING
  1972   Osteogenesis in the basioccipital bone of the Wistar albino rat. *Scandinavian Journal of Dental Research* 80:410–421.

WEINMANN, JOSEPH P., HARRY SICHER
  1947   *Bone and bones*. St. Louis: Mosby.

WURMBACH, HERMANN
  1967   Wirksame Kräfte beim Wachstum, der Formgestaltung und der Gewebsdifferenzierung. *Acta Anatomica* 66:520–602.

The Development of a Cephalometric Atlas of Craniofacial Morphology

GEOFFREY F. WALKER

In the course of preparation of a craniofacial atlas, it was necessary to define certain objectives and to ask ourselves questions related to the practical applications of the atlas. It was intended not only to provide a statistically adequate description of the craniofacial form of the American child but also, in its form and text, to be useful to clinicians in the assessment of normality or abnormality in patients seeking diagnosis and treatment.

If the atlas is to be representative of the supposedly normal child, and of practical significance in recognizing or defining the abnormal, then several questions come to mind, such as:

1. When considering facial form, what is "normal?"
2. What are the essential differences between normal and "abnormal?"
3. Are differences of race, sex, and age significant?

The definition of normality in human affairs is a difficult one, and depends to some extent on whether one approaches it from a clinical or a statistical viewpoint; the former approach tends to be very subjective, whereas the latter depends mainly on the population surveyed and the sampling methods used.

THE CLINICAL APPROACH

Let us first consider the clinician's approach. The question of whether his patient is "normal" in craniofacial form and development is a problem that occurs daily, and his usual yardstick for evaluation is based on what we may call his "clinical experience," and not on sets of tables or diagrams. Clinical experience may be described as the impressions accumulated by observing and treating a comparatively large number of patients. It has value insofar as it creates a subjective sense of what is the average, or most common, set of conditions which are acceptable to the clinician's group or profession.

In the practical situation, the main difficulty arises from the subjective nature of the evaluation. In assessing facial form and "harmony," no doubt we all have our own personal criteria of the range from poor to excellent. A case in point is the judging of beauty queens — I would be surprised if many viewers of these television marathons did not differ quite strongly from the judges in their evaluation of the final winner. Biases or preferences of a similar nature may tend to influence our assessment, and thus our treatment plan, for many of our patients. One practitioner may prefer relatively vertical, or orthognathic, faces and be dedicated to aligning a dentition to "textbook perfection." Others may accept some degree of bimaxillary protrusion as aesthetically preferable, and I suspect that the editors of *Vogue* magazine prefer this type of face for fashion models. Practitioners dedicated to the "nonextraction" concept of orthodontic treatment may be required by the biological discrepancies between tooth size and jaw size to accept some degree of bimaxillary protrusion, and even mild dental crowding. Thus the current state of the art indicates that there is a lack of agreement in the profession on what constitutes the normal or even acceptable. In fact, the range of variation of what is "normal" or even "clinically acceptable" is uncomfortably wide, and may not bear a sound relationship to the craniofacial statistics of the population from which our patients emerge.

THE STATISTICAL APPROACH

Largely because of these subjective or individual preferences, we have preferred to take the statistical or population sampling approach. This has both advantages and disadvantages. Probably the greatest advantage is that a large population sample may be obtained, and as long as the sampling method is taken into account, sufficiently accurate and representative measurements may be gathered. Projects to gather statistical data of facial form have been carried out many times and in various places. Direct measurements of facial form of many hundreds of children were made by the late Milo Hellman between 1921 and 1935 (Hellman 1922, 1927, 1932, 1935). Photographs of heads and faces have value in assessing form and have been one of the recording methods of anthropologists for many years. At present, taking accurate measurements from photographs of the human body presents many difficulties. Some interesting new methods in photogrammetry are emerging, but the state of the art is not sufficiently advanced for it to be a universal tool.

A more useful method of recording the hard tissues of the skull was Pacini's application of X rays to anthropology (1922). In that work he described the taking of standardized lateral X rays of the head. This approach was considerably improved when special headholders (cephalostats) were proposed in 1931. One of these was designed and made in Cleveland and became known as the Broadbent-Bolton cephalostat (Broadbent 1931); another was designed by Hofrath in Germany (Hofrath 1931). Since 1931 many thousands of cephalometric X rays have been taken for diagnostic and research purposes. For example, craniofacial data on non-Europeans have been reported by Björk (1950), who compared prognathism in Swedes and African Bantu. A set of measurements (the Downs analysis) was applied to three ethnic groups by Cotton, Takano, and Wong (1951), who studied twenty Negro, twenty Nisei, and twenty Chinese children. Haralabakis (1954), also using Downs' measurements, studied a population sample of Greeks and inferred that their facial pattern differs from other populations similarly studied. Craven (1958) reported a study of Australian aborigines, as did Brown (1965).

From these investigations it becomes obvious that racial and individual variation exist, and what could be considered average for one population may differ significantly in another. For example, Oriental populations tend to have a shorter maxillary component than do many Europeans, together with a lower average interincisal angle, and thus have a tendency to bialveolar protrusion. Therefore some dental protrusion could be considered more "normal" in Orientals than in Europeans. Davies (1956) also considers Class III malocclusions to be relatively more frequent among the people of Pukapuka.

To provide the profession with more objective criteria of the range of variation of various populations requires the measurement of a large sample of people and their cephalograms. To this end Dr. W. M. Krogman, Dr. James Harris, and I have applied ourselves over a period of more than twenty-five years. Our data banks now contain comparatively large samples of North Americans, including North

American blacks and North American Indians. The main effort has been to obtain cephalograms of American white children, as these comprise the largest population pool from which our patients come. For comparative purposes we have reasonably large samples from the South Pacific (Maoris and Tongans), an isolated population from the Amazon (the Peruvian Cashinahua), generous samples of Nubian children, a group of Sioux Indians, and a sample of pre-Hellenic skulls from the island of Crete.

NEW RETRIEVAL AND ANALYTICAL TECHNIQUES

Analyzing this large collection of data required the application of efficient methods of quantification, storage, and retrieval, plus powerful statistical techniques. This objective was gained by developing a computer-oriented system of coding, storing, and retrieving the information which has been previously described (Walker 1967, 1972; Walker et al. 1971; Walker and Kowalski 1972a). Essentially, the cephalogram is reduced to a mathematical model or map of carefully defined points, and these are digitized or scanned and stored in the computer memory. From this data base we may retrieve the pattern or shape of the skull or any segment thereof, as well as any linear, angular, or area measurements. As the data base is inherently consistent, it becomes possible to group or average any desired sets of measurements, or even to produce an average shape or pattern from a large sample of individuals.

This computer-based technology was used in the preparation of our population standards which will become the atlas of craniofacial morphology of American children. The first cephalograms were collected in 1948 at the Philadelphia Center for Research in Child Growth (now the W. M. Krogman Center for Research in Child Growth). The cephalograms used in the atlas are from some 10,000 children of both white and black families. Many of the children were measured at annual intervals, so that growth information as well as craniofacial form could be analyzed.

The system of population sampling was not entirely random. The children of five schools were examined, and those with a history of severe illness, high caries incidence, noticeable malocclusion, or facial disharmony were eliminated from the study. Thus the upper and lower ends of the variance spectrum were to some extent "trimmed" to leave what was inferred to be the more average or "normal" child. A set of physical measurements was taken using spreading calipers and anthropometers to record facial and body dimensions. Height and weight were measured and reported (Krogman 1970). Upper and lower dental casts were made, and skull shape and dimensions were recorded on X-ray film using a Bolton-Broadbent cephalometer. Both lateral and posterior-anterior films were taken for the children at each visit. Many children were measured only once or twice, but several hundred continued for from four to ten visits. Thus the data comprising the atlas could be called a mixed longitudinal sample and should be interpreted with this in mind. The main effect would be to reduce the overall variance of the population sample, so that the standard deviations and percentile rankings should be considered as conservative, and biased toward a clinically selected "normal." For clinical evaluation of orthodontic patients this may have more value than a population atlas randomized to include a representative sample of all types of malocclusions and other craniofacial disharmonies.

The author can foresee some scientific and clinical value in developing a series of atlases. One should contain children of clinically acceptable craniofacial harmony, such as the atlas currently being prepared. A second should be a larger and more randomized cross-sectional sample of the population, including representative numbers of those with and without craniofacial disharmonies. This second sample could then be divided into subgroups, one with "optimal" Class I occlusions, another with Class III malocclusions, and a third from the opposite end of the spectrum, that is, a group with so-called Class II malocclusions. If the original randomized sample were sufficiently large, then it should be possible to carry out even further subgroupings, by clinical or statistical criteria, to provide Class II division II subgroups, etc. Although the average orthodontist is reasonably confident that he can clinically classify his patients, our experience, using metrical and statistical criteria, is that patients present all manner of individual variations, and that facial harmony and disharmony are composed of a spectrum or range of measurements which do not "cluster" or correlate into neat little packages.

Thus, to return to our opening questions, our current definition of "normal" is a clinically biased sample with severe abnormalities eliminated, the remainder being quantified and averaged to form a diagram representing a particular age, sex, and race. Examples of these for American white girls are shown in Figure 1 and for Tongan (Polynesian) girls in Figure 2.

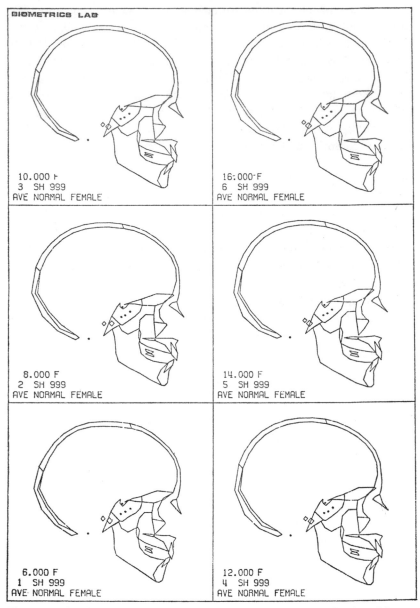

Figure 1.   Craniofacial averages of normal American white girls, 6 to 16 years

The diagrams shown are the average measurements of relatively large samples (circa 100) in each group. Thus we have approximately 100 white girls from 11.5 to 12.5 years averaged to form the 12-year-old "norm." Once again, the reader should be cautioned against

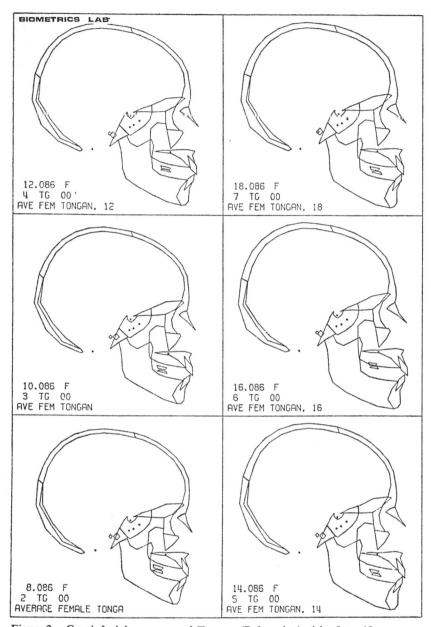

BIOMETRICS LAB

12.086 F
4 TG 00·
AVE FEM TONGAN. 12

18.086 F
7 TG 00
AVE FEM TONGAN. 18

10.086 F
3 TG 00
AVE FEM TONGAN

16.086 F
6 TG 00
AVE FEM TONGAN. 16

8.086 F
2 TG 00
AVERAGE FEMALE TONGA

14.086 F
5 TG 00
AVE FEM TONGAN. 14

Figure 2.   Craniofacial averages of Tongan (Polynesian) girls, 8 to 18 years

taking this "norm" too literally. It merely represents the central tendency, or average of distribution of measurements. An example of a variable distribution (in this case the ANB angle of some 113 boys from 12 to 14 years) is shown in Figure 3. All these measurements are presumably within a "normal" range, although for convenience in the clinical evaluation we would tend to consider those in the zone between plus and minus one standard deviation (approximately 68 percent of the entire sample) as being the "most normal." Hence, normality is relative. It depends on the population, the sampling method, and the area under the curve which is acceptable to the practitioner.

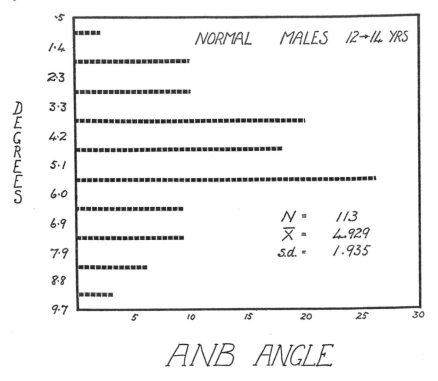

Figure 3.   Distribution of ANB angle in normal American white boys, 12 to 14 years old

Thus it seems that we are almost back to our original subjective evaluation — but not quite. We now have reasonably good criteria of population measurements, their change through time, and the variation and distribution of most required parameters, such as jaw size and position, facial proportions, facial angles, incisal relationships, and so on.

The average value of the ANB angle (Downs' alveolar point A to Nasion to Downs' alveolar point B) and its distribution is interesting and has been previously reported (Walker and Kowalski 1972b), as have other angles used in the Steiner analysis (Kowalski and Walker 1972). It appears that the measurements from the general population do not always match the subjective "preferences" of the clinician. For example, the ANB angle showing a population average of 5°, with a range from 0° to almost 10°, is significantly different from the usually recommended 2°. If 2° is taken as the "normal" yardstick, then most of the American children may be classified as being well above average for this dimension, and thus possibly diagnosed as having a Class II skeletal deformity and in need of orthodontic treatment.

The atlas being prepared from large population samples reveals a number of these differences from currently accepted norms and will, hopefully, initiate a constructive evaluation of our concepts of normality and of our treatment objectives.

REFERENCES

BJÖRK, A.
  1950   Some biological aspects of prognathism and occlusion of the teeth. *Acta Odontologica Scandinavica* 9(1):140.

BROADBENT, B. H.
  1931   A new X-ray technique and its application to orthodontia. *Angle Orthodontist* 1(2):45–66.

BROWN, T.
  1965   "Craniofacial variations in a Central Australian tribe." Unpublished Master's thesis, University of Adelaide, Adelaide, Australia.

COTTON, W. N., W. S. TAKANO, W. W. WONG
  1951   The Downs analysis applied to three other ethnic groups. *Angle Orthodontist* 21:213–220.

CRAVEN, A. H.
  1958   A radiographic cephalometric study of the Central Australian aboriginal. *Angle Orthodontist* 28:12–35.

DAVIES, G. N.
  1956   Dental condition among the Polynesians of Pukapuka 1. General background and the prevalence of malocclusion. *Journal of Dental Research* 35(1):115–131.

HARALABAKIS, H.
  1954   Familial resemblances in craniofacial osteology as revealed by cephalometric X-rays in Greek families. Abstract in *American Journal of Orthodontics* 43.

HELLMAN, M.
  1922   Studies on the etiology of Angle's Class II malocclusion manifestations. *International Journal of Orthodontics and Oral Surgery* 7(3):1–20.

1927   The face and occlusion of the teeth in man. *International Journal of Orthodontics and Oral Surgery* 13:921–945.
1932   An introduction to growth of the human face from infancy to adulthood. *International Journal of Orthodontics and Oral Surgery* 18(8):777.
1935   The face in its developmental career. *Dental Cosmos* 77(7/8):1–25.

HOFRATH, HERBERT
1931   Die Bedeutung der Röntgenfern und Abstandsaufnahme für die Diagnostik der Kieferanomalien. *Fortschritte der Orthodontik* 1:232.

KOWALSKI, C. J., G. F. WALKER
1972   The use of incisal angles in the Steiner cephalometric analysis. *Angle Orthodontist* 42:87–95.

KROGMAN, W. M.
1970   Growth of head, face, trunk, and limbs in Philadelphia white and Negro children of elementary and high school age. *Monographs of the Society for Research in Child Development,* Serial number 136, 35(3).

PACINI, A. J.
1922   Roentgen ray anthropometry of the skull. *Journal of Radiology* 3:230, 322, 418.

WALKER, G. F.
1967   Summary of a research report on the analysis of craniofacial growth. *New Zealand Dental Journal* 63:31–38.
1972   A new approach to the analysis of craniofacial morphology. *American Journal of Orthodontics* 61:221–230.

WALKER, G. F., R. GRAINGER, W. S. HUNTER, R. LEDLEY, F. WESTERVELT
1971   "New techniques in processing and handling growth data," in *Craniofacial growth in man.* Edited by W. M. Krogman and R. E. Moyers, 315–331. Oxford: Pergamon.

WALKER, G. F., C. J. KOWALSKI
1972a Computer morphometrics in craniofacial biology. *Journal of Computers in Biology and Medicine* 2:235–249.
1972b Use of angular measurements in cephalometric analyses. *Journal of Dental Research* 51:1015–1021.

SECTION TWO

Development

Early Maxillary Orthopedics and Osteoplasty in Cleft Lip and Palate and Their Effects on Facial Growth

SHELDON W. ROSENSTEIN and BAILEY N. JACOBSON

Controversy as to the explanation of the growth of the skull does not limit itself only to its morphogenesis. Strong differences of opinion are still in evidence as to how the entire cranial complex grows after birth (Enlow 1968; Moss 1962; Scott 1956; Sicher 1952). Further complicating the problem is the need to introduce, extraneously and relatively early, surgical reduction of a congenital facial anomaly such as cleft lip and palate. Because any surgery adds a new dimension (variable) to the overall growth assessment, any surgical procedure considered debatable, or even controversial, bears close scrutiny.

For the orthodontic clinician, congenital malformation, for all practical purposes, means cleft lip and palate. It becomes obvious, too, why cleft lip and palate has been singled out for such intensive study and habilitative effort by the medical and dental professions. It is a very common congenital anomaly, and the malady of direct concern to the dentist because of its location. Then, too, it can be quite severe with resultant long-term facial growth alteration and denture mutilation. It is the relevant one in terms of treatment. Because the Veau Class III (unilateral, complete cleft of lip, ridge, and palate) and Class IV (bilateral, complete) render incomplete the integrity of the maxilla and break it into segments, either unilaterally or bilaterally, they appear to be the culprits as far as growth is concerned. In our society we must close the lip and palate surgically, thereby introducing extraneous factors early in life which can and do have a bearing on growth. Cleft lip and palate, then, offer an opportunity to help explore more fully some of the pertinent theses regarding the development of the skull.

For Plates and Figures, see pp. xi–xx, between 330–331.

This article will concern itself with the Veau Class III and Class IV types of facial cleft only.

VEAU CLASS III

At present two schools of thought would appear to have evolved about the management of the maxillary segments in complete unilateral clefts. One is composed of those who would do nothing early in infancy, and would confine orthodontic treatment to the classic procedures available, i.e. arch alignment and reduction of crossbites in the primary dentition and eventual full comprehensive treatment in the permanent dentition. This, augmented at an even later date with permanent prosthetic restoration, has been the conventional approach of choice for many. Here, early surgical procedures are kept to a minimum, essentially only lip and palate closure. Those of this persuasion feel justified in maintaining the status quo for a number of reasons. First, they feel that early procedures are unnecessary and unwarranted, and really do not offer that much benefit in the long run (Ross 1970). Secondly, because all Class III cases do not necessarily present identically (i.e. wide and narrow arch form, high and low septum attachment, minimal and maximal deviation of the greater segment from the midline, and marked and minimal hypoplasia of tissue), all unilateral, complete cases will not necessarily end up with crossbite and segment collapse, or even growth attenuation. Thirdly, if additional surgical procedures are introduced early, over and above the necessary lip and palate closure, adverse consequences can ensue relative to maxillary growth. In other words, surgical undermining for a graft might well additionally hinder growth in a maxilla already struggling to keep up (Robertson and Jolleys 1968).

The other approach to this problem finds favor with those who, in addition to the aforementioned procedures, would attempt to do something additional and early. The reasoning here would seem to be a need on the part of these individuals to improve upon what has usually been obtainable previously. Our group subscribes to this latter view. We have not been fully happy with what we have obtained in the past. We know that a certain percentage of these children present not only dental crossbites, but even true segment collapse to an extreme degree. We feel, too, that a lack of bony base over which to move teeth in the past has been a real problem, and the ectopic eruption of teeth further complicates the picture. Our goals of function, esthetics, and stability have quite often not been fully realized.

The procedures which we advocate have been fully described in the literature (Rosenstein and Jacobson 1967). This is our approach to the problem in our institution. We claim no panaceas, nor do we think it is THE only approach. It is AN approach and carries with it a definite sequence of procedures. In essence, it consists of:

1. The placement of an intraoral prosthesis prior to lip closure.
2. Guided molding of the arch segments after lip closure.
3. Stabilization of the segments by means of autogenous bone grafts.
4. Retention of the prosthesis until palatal closure.

We are generally finished with our early infant procedures by fifteen to eighteen months of age.

Two major avenues of legitimate investigation and concern should now be mentioned. First, following the sequence of procedures advocated, do early maxillary orthopedics and osteoplasty do any harm, and secondly, do these procedures do any good? In reference to the first question, we do not really know yet. It is still too early for final judgment. The oldest of our series of close to a hundred patients is now only seven and one-half years of age. However, we can observe these children as they are growing and begin to formulate some thoughts. Last year one of our graduate students studied a series of ten non-cleft lip and palate children, ten Class III clefts with no bone grafts, and ten Class III clefts with bone grafts. Each child was five years of age, plus-or-minus three months (Wachs 1972). After extensive cephalometric measurement (after the method of Cobin) and computer analysis, it was determined that there was no significant size difference in the maxillary area between any of the samples. To date, cephalometrically, none of our children present with Point B in the mandible ahead of Point A in the maxilla (Figure 1).

Now, do we do any good? Again we cannot give a definite yes or no at this time; it is too early. However, as these children grow, and we see them daily, we tend to feel that we are obtaining occlusions and arch forms which were hardly conceivable before.

One of our cases is now seven and one-half years of age and has been followed for the longest period of time using this sequence of procedures. Maxillary-mandibular relationship appears to be very acceptable as shown in Plate 1.

In another instance we have followed a young boy with a Veau Class III for over six and one-half years. He has had the sequence of procedures which we advocate, and in addition we have proceeded with a first phase of orthodontic treatment to see if we could specifically move a tooth in or around a bone-graft area. The accompanying illustrations show this case from birth (Plate 2) through the alignment of the primary dentition (Plate 3). When compared to a "standard" from the Bolton Case-Western-Reserve growth study (Figure 2), both the mandible and maxilla appear to be within the normal range, and there is no growth attenuation (Bolton et al. i.p.).

At present there are some clinical groups who would abandon these procedures because of obvious failings (Jolleys and Robertson 1972; Rehrmann et al. 1970) in their samples, and some who still continue the procedure (Wood 1970; Rosenstein et al. 1972). Jolleys and Robertson make the statement that the graft contributed to the retardation in growth and actually can prevent growth. Yet, in the same city, Wood and Robinson feel that the graft brings the detached segments under the growth mechanism of the nasal septal cartilage and therefore encourages the middle third of the face to grow as one unit. Another authority accounts for the conflicting reports by stating that the critical variable may be the surgical procedure utilized in closing the palate, not necessarily the placement of the graft (Ross 1970).

With mention of the nasal septal cartilage, one brings into account one of the theories prevalent today regarding growth of the skull and the contribution of the nasal septum to this growth. Of the three pertinent theories advanced today relative to the morphogenesis of the skull (Sicher 1952; Moss 1962; Scott 1953), perhaps the one least familiar to clinicians is the one advanced by the late J. H. Scott of Belfast (1953). Van Limborgh's (1970) recent interpretation of Scott's thesis is of interest, and can be paraphrased in the following manner. Scott assumed that intrinsic growth-controlling factors are present only in the cartilage and periosteum of the skull. He felt that growth of the sutures was secondary and dependent upon extrasutural influences. The cartilaginous parts of the skull are seen as centers of growth; thus he poses the "primacy of the cartilage." Growth of the sutures is regulated in part by growth of the synchondroses, and in part by growth of structures adjacent to the skull. In this way, growth of the skull itself would be properly coordinated and keep up with growth of other structures.

VEAU CLASS IV

The aforementioned thoughts by Scott appear to be directly applicable in the case of complete bilateral cleft and freely mobile premaxilla. Burston (1959) pointed out that perhaps the principal factor in the early development of the middle third of the face is "... the cartilaginous intraorbital nasal septum." He believes that the septum, an enormous structure during fetal development, continues to play a most important role into the first few years of postnatal life. At this time the septum is almost completely intrafacial and extends posteriorly to the basisphenoid region. After birth the intrafacial portion of the septum becomes progressively ossified from the mesethmoid superiorly and the cartilaginous portion proceeds anteriorly to become the definitive nose (Figure 3). The septum, because of its close overall relationship to the maxilla anteriorly, provides a continuing separation of the sutures joining the maxilla to the remainder of the cranial complex, and this allows for normal growth. He goes on to state that when the septum is not bound down or confined to the maxilla, as in the case of the bilateral complete cleft of the lip, ridge, and palate, the bony lateral components can easily drop behind the unencumbered septum in both the anteroposterior plane and to some degree in the vertical.

Attempts to validate this thesis have led to contradictory results. Investigators working on different animals have come to conclusions that the septum does and does not (Moss 1968) primarily contribute to the growth of the head. In fact, and as a corollary to the theory of primacy of the cartilage and intrinsic growth factors of the periosteum advanced by Scott (1953), Hellquist (1972) recently reported that the effect of extensive periosteal resection on facial skeleton growth is considerable in the rabbit, but practically negligible in the guinea pig, and that the difference may be tentatively explained by differences in the skeletal and vascular anatomy of the maxilla. In essence, he advances the possibility of species difference.

The clinically important aspect of all this, according to Burston (1959), is that, immediately postpartum, this growth potential of the septum is very great and continues to be so until the child reaches two or three years of age, or the time that the intrafacial portion of the septum ceases to exert influence.

The treatment approaches to date, in attempting to reduce this apparent bony dysplasia, are many and varied and include extraoral traction, intraoral traction, placement of intraoral plates, and surgical excision of a portion of the septum. As enlightened as these attempts might appear, they all undoubtedly leave something to be desired. It is to the credit of the investigators and those reporting that no one claims complete conquest of this problem.

Our approach to bilateral complete cases is to construct an intra-oral prosthesis and place it before lip surgery. The lip is then closed and when segments are in favorable approximation, through the molding action of the repaired lip (Plate 4), they are surgically stabilized with autogenous bone grafts. This is what we routinely attempt to do in bilateral cases.

On very rare occasions, we have found it necessary to section the vomer and recess the premaxilla. The sectioning is done a considerable distance posterior to the prevomerine suture region. The single criterion for this procedure is the decision on the part of the surgeon that closure of the lip would be technically difficult or even impractical in the face of a premaxilla positioned extremely far forward. Therefore, this is generally done at the time of lip closure; it must be emphasized that this is not a routine procedure and has been done only in selected cases (Monroe et al. 1970).

In judging both resultant esthetics and bony relationships, two regions in the sagittal plane are utilized. One is intraoral, and the assessment is made through diagnostic study casts and serial lateral cephalometric radiographs of hard-tissue relationship. The other, admittedly subjective, is extraoral, and is an evaluation of the soft-tissue profile. Final judgment cannot and should not be made until at least the circumpubertal growth of all of these children has been realized, and all secondary surgical procedures have been considered. On the surface, a long-term follow-up of these procedures would appear to offer greater understanding of the role of the septum.

Three interesting cases will now be presented wherein septum setback was done. They are interesting, we feel, because though they are bilateral complete clefts of the lip, ridge, and palate (Veau Class IV), and all have had the septum section, the results to date differ somewhat.

The first case (Plate 5) was originally seen at the hospital at birth in 1955, and has been previously reported (Monroe et al. 1970). The young woman is now eighteen years of age. Septum setback was done and at eleven years of age she had a revision of the columella and orthodontic treatment. No bone grafts were placed in the maxilla. The gross facial deformity and attenuation of growth, alluded to by some, has failed to materialize.

Though the second case (Plate 6) was treated in a very similar manner to the previous one (the same surgical procedures — both primary and secondary — no maxillary bone grafts, the same sequence of procedures, the same surgeon, and the same orthodontist), the esthetic results are different. At age eleven years nine months, after a revision of the columella and orthodontic therapy, though the occlusion is acceptable, one must point out that skeletally the maxilla has fallen behind the mandible and Point B is slightly ahead of Point A. This is the only case of our sample thus far that presents as such.

The last case (Plate 7) to be discussed is a twelve-year, nine-months-old boy. He has had a septum setback and bone grafts to the maxillary alveolar ridges. He is, at present, about to begin his orthodontic treatment. The anteroposterior relationship of the maxilla and mandible to each other and to the cranial base can be seen to be entirely different from that of the previously shown cases. Point A is substantially forward of Point B, and it would appear that the maxillary bone grafts have not attenuated growth.

These three cases would certainly seem to offer some room for reflection. We do not routinely section the septum — only in extreme situations. When we do, with the technique described, we do not have growth attenuation in the middle third of the face; yet, in the one case just presented it can apparently happen. Why? Apparently it would seem that our knowledge of just how the premaxilla grows, and our ability to predict to what extent, is not yet complete.

In cases followed for a number of years we have observed premaxillae which have failed to increase in size and appear attenuated and nondescript. Though no surgery other than lip closure is done in the immediate area in the form of setback or graft placement, the premaxilla just does not grow. On the other hand, in the same given situation, we have seen the premaxilla increase far in excess of what we would consider normal size. This increase in dimension is such that, though the lateral maxillary segments are in good relation to the lateral mandibular segments and buccal occlusion is good, the premaxilla is still blocked out and far too large (Plate 8). Thus, the management of the protruding premaxilla still poses a distinct challenge for us.

SUMMARY

We have presented one congenital anomaly, cleft lip and palate, along with innovative and somewhat controversial approaches to it. These patients can also have inherent jaw malrelationships over which is superimposed their cleft lip and palate problem. Are the lateral bony segments hypoplastic to begin with? One author quantifies this lack of tissue in the bilateral complete cleft to be on the average about 27 percent (Huddart 1970). Are they in turn positioned more posteriorly than in a patient without cleft lip and palate? If we accept the probability of a lack of tissue in the child with a complete cleft of the lip and palate, would it not seem reasonable that early septum and arch alignment and autogenous bone grafting can help attain a more stable maxilla in good relationship to the mandible, without fear of growth attenuation? There are differences in techniques which can and do influence results. If some investigators obtain results, then there should be no condemnation of the basic principle or overall concept of this treatment because of individual inaccuracies and failures.

REFERENCES

BOLTON, W. A., B. H. BROADBENT, W. GOLDEN
   i.p.   *Cephalometric standards for Caucasian male and female.* Cleveland: Case Western Reserve University Press.

BURSTON, W. R.
   1959   Treatment of the cleft palate. *Annals of the Royal College of Surgeons England* 25:225.

DAHLBERG, ALBERT A.
   1965   Evolutionary background of dental and facial growth. *Journal of Dental Research* (supplement) 44:151–160.

ENLOW, D. E.
   1968   *The human face; an account of the postnatal growth and development of the craniofacial skeleton.* New York: Harper and Row.

HELLQUIST, R.
   1972   Facial skeleton growth after periosteal resection. *Scandinavian Journal of Plastic and Reconstructive Surgery* (supplement) 10. Stockholm.

HUDDART, A. G.
   1970   Maxillary arch dimensions in bilateral cleft lip and palate subjects. *Cleft Palate Journal* 7:139–155.

JOLLEYS, A., N. R. E. ROBERTSON
   1972   A study of the effects of early bone grafting in complete clefts of the lip and palate — five-year study. *British Journal of Plastic Surgery* 25:229–237.

KREMENAK, C. R., W. C. HUFFMAN, W. H. OLIN
  1970   Maxillary growth inhibition by mucoperiosteal denudation of palatal shelf bond in noncleft beagles. *Cleft Palate Journal* 7: 817–825.
MONROE, C. W., *et al.*
  1970   Surgical recession of the premaxilla and its effect on maxillary growth in patients with bilateral clefts. *Cleft Palate Journal* 7: 784–793.
MOSS, M. L.
  1962   "The functional matrix," in *Vistas in orthodontics*. Edited by B. S. Kraus and R. A. Reidel. Philadelphia: Lea and Febiger.
  1968   The passive role of nasal septal cartilage in midfacial growth. *Plastic and Reconstructive Surgery* 41:536–542.
REHRMANN, A. H., W. R. KOBERG, H. KOCH
  1970   Long-term postoperative results of primary and secondary bone grafting in complete clefts of lip and palate. *Cleft Palate Journal* 7:206–221.
ROBERTSON, N. R. E., A. JOLLEYS
  1968   Effects of early bone grafting in complete clefts of lip and palate. *Plastic and Reconstructive Surgery* 42:414.
ROSENSTEIN, S. W., B. N. JACOBSON
  1967   Early maxillary orthopedics: a sequence of events. *Cleft Palate Journal* 4:197.
ROSENSTEIN, S. W., *et al.*
  1972   A series of cleft lip and palate children five years after undergoing orthopedic and bone grafting procedures. *Angle Orthodontist* 42: 1–8.
ROSS, R. B.
  1970   The clinical implications of facial growth in cleft lip and palate. *Cleft Palate Journal* 7:37–47.
SCOTT, J. H.
  1953   The cartilage of the nasal septum: a contribution to the study of facial growth. *British Dental Journal* 95:37–43.
  1956   Growth at facial sutures. *American Journal of Orthodontics* 42:381–387.
SICHER, H.
  1952   *Oral anatomy*. St. Louis: C. V. Mosby.
VAN LIMBORGH, J.
  1970   A new view of the control of the morphogenesis of the skull. *Acta Morphologica Neerlando-Scandinavica* 8:143–160.
WACHS, R.
  1972   "A comparative cephalometric study of cleft lip and palate patients, with and without bone grafts to the maxilla." Unpublished Master's thesis, Northwestern University Dental School, Chicago.
WOOD, B. G.
  1970   Control of the maxillary arch by primary bone graft in cleft lip and palate cases. *Cleft Palate Journal* 7:194–205.

Variations in the Microstructures of Primate Teeth

STEPHEN MOLNAR

The developing tooth has proven to be a sensitive indicator of the interruptions or variations in mineral metabolism which may occur during various stages of growth (Schour and Massler 1940; Baume and Meyer 1966). These variations in metabolism cause the formation of certain distinctive structures in enamel and dentin. Some of the principal structures are known as striae of Retzius, or incremental lines in the enamel, interglobular dentin, and incremental lines of von Ebner in the dentin. The appearance of these structural features is known to vary in response to the onset and duration of the metabolic insult or "teratogenic" agents (Kraus, Jordan, and Abrams 1969). Because the developmental sequences of the teeth are known it should be possible to estimate, with reasonable accuracy, the time of onset of the metabolic depression and to evaluate certain environmental influences.

Certain of these structures are more pronounced in some primate species than in others as observed by Schuman and Sognnaes (1956). Interglobular dentin (IGD), the failure of dentin to develop properly beyond the predentin stage, occurs more frequently in man than in several cercopithecoid species. Sognnaes' work (1956) suggested an evolutionary ordering of primate families on the basis of the frequency of interglobular dentin. Man has the greatest amount and cercopithecoids have little or none at all. Representative pongids like gorillas and chimps were reported to have had quantities of this structural defect comparable to man.

Because of these species-specific relationships, IGD (interglobular

Microphotographs for Plates 1 through 8 were taken by Russell Potter.
For Plates, see pp. xxi–xxiii, between pp. 330–331.

dentin) is an interesting structure to investigate, particularly because it is considered to be a measure of the dental quality reflective of the level of mineral metabolism. This study makes histological comparisons of thin sections of teeth from several primate species in order to expand our limited knowledge of primate tooth histology and to determine the relative frequency of IGD.

Materials and Methods

Sound teeth were obtained from several representative subhuman primate species (see Table 1); also a number of human teeth, modern and prehistoric, were used for comparative purposes. Prior to sectioning, these teeth were cleaned, then dried in acetone and alcohol, after which they were imbedded in a polyester resin.

Longitudinal sections were made in the buccal-lingual direction. The sections were cut approximately a hundred microns thick with a diamond saw and then were hand-lapped on abrasive paper (number 600) to fifty microns. After cleaning and drying, the sections were mounted under cover slips on microscope slides.

The finished sections were surveyed by an optical microscope under 12x and 50x power. Note was taken of enamel hypoplasia, width and definition of striae of Retzius, dentin incremental lines, and frequency and expression of interglobular dentin. The most significant of these slides were photographed and several prints are offered here (Plates 1 to 8).

Results

The findings, which are summarized in Table 1, indicate that there is a wide variation in the structural quality of primate teeth. Plate 1 shows the well-formed, near-perfect dentin of a gorilla molar which contrasts with Plate 2, a view of chimpanzee molar dentin. The dark spots, though not classifiable as interglobular dentin, may be an imperfection in the calcified dentinal matrix. The chimpanzee molar in Plate 3, in contrast, shows a dense band of IGD which is distributed across the tooth near the dentoenamel junction. Plate 4, a view of a section of human molar dentin, shows a dense cluster of poorly calcified dentin; the black irregular splotches are areas where the calcosphrites failed to calcify (IGD).

Variations in the appearance of incremental lines were seen in all

Table 1. Hypoplasias seen in subhuman primate teeth*

Species	Sex	Tooth	Enamel	Dentin
Macaca mulatta (captive)	M	M^1, M^2	Poorly mineralized, numerous spindles, lamellae, broad striae of Retzius	No IGD, well-defined incremental lines
Macaca nemestrina (A) (captive)	M	2 M^1	Numerous broad hypomineralized areas, few lamellae and tufts	Some IGD, well-defined incremental lines
Macaca nemestrina (B) (captive)	M	2 M^1	Extensive hypomineralized areas, no lamellae and tufts	No IGD, well-defined incremental lines
Macaca speciosa (free-ranging)	F	M_1, M^1	Moderate hypoplasia well-defined striae of Retzius	Some IGD
Macaca arctoides (free-ranging)	F	PM_2, PM^2, M_1, M^1	Moderate hypoplasia, well-defined striae of Retzius	No IGD, well-defined incremental lines, extensive secondary dentin
Papio anubis (A) (captive)	M	C	Well-defined striae of Retzius, some lamellae and tufts	No IGD, exception cervical area, faint incremental lines
Papio anubis (B) (captive)	M	M^1, dm^1, dm^2	Moderate hypoplasia	No IGD, faint incremental lines
Pan (free-ranging)	F	2 M_1	Extensive hypoplasia	Extensive IGD, faint incremental lines
Pan (free-ranging)	M	2 M_1	Broad striae of Retzius	No IGD
Gorilla (captive)	F	2 M^1	"Gnarled" enamel	No IGD, faint incremental lines

* IGD = Interglobular dentin.

sections. Plates 5 and 6 represent extremes seen in a chimpanzee and a gorilla dentinal section. Plate 5 shows well-defined incremental lines which are only faintly seen in Plate 6.

Differences in the quality of enamel as identified by the presence of lamellae, tufts, or irregularly directed rods were seen in every section. However, there was considerable difference in the number of these defects per unit area. The most striking example of interrupted enamel development is seen in Plate 7 which contrasts with the broad striae of Retzius in a section of human enamel (Plate 8).

Discussion

Reference to the photographs and to the table suggests that there is a considerable variation in the expression of what can be called developmental defects in histological structures. However, any description of striae of Retzius or rod direction irregularity as pathological should be made cautiously. There are several studies, however, which do distinguish between pathological and physiological striae (Wilson and Schroff 1970) and there is a probability that striae only become distinct under conditions of pathology (Gustafson 1959). If this is the case, then several teeth show evidence of severe and prolonged metabolic interruption.

Interglobular dentin occurred extensively only in the chimpanzee and human sections, but areas of IGD were also found in two *Macaca* sections and in the baboon canine. The quantity of this defect was small and did not extend across the tooth in a continuous band as seen in Plates 3 and 4. Perhaps the most interesting factor is that two of the three were from animals raised in captivity. The chimpanzee with the most extensive dentin (Plate 3) was raised in captivity while Plate 2 is a photo of a section of tooth from a chimpanzee which had been free-ranging. None of the interglobular areas, however, were as pronounced as that seen in the human molar (Plate 4).

Another microscopic feature of the dentin which seemed to vary between captive and free-ranging animals was the incremental lines of von Ebner (Plate 5). If the distinctiveness of this feature is viewed in the same way as enamel striae, then one could conclude that a difference in mineralization quality had existed.

Conclusions

These results, obtained on a limited but varied sample of subhuman primates, tend to substantiate the Schuman and Sognnaes (1956) original observation that there was a difference in the occurrence of IGD in the teeth of several primate species. Though certain primates may be more prone to develop dentinal defects, some IGD was seen in the reportedly favored cercopithecoids. Added to these results is the fact that differences apparently exist between captive and free-ranging specimens. It seems that dietary quality differed between the two groups and was responsible for developmental variations.

Enamel dysplasias occur in all groups. Irregular hypocalcified enamel was seen in almost every section made, though the degree of occurrence varied widely. No group-specific feature was seen in the enamel which was comparable to IGD variability between species.

This sample was too small to provide evidence for firm conclusions, but these results raised many questions about environmental quality and dental development which are of particular significance if they are taken together with the evidence of variability in dentinal quality found among modern and prehistoric human teeth. Environmental influences acting on the developing primate may be evaluated by careful comparisons of histological tooth sections taken from different populations. But, due to wide individual variation, an adequate sample of each population must be made.

REFERENCES

BAUME, L. J., J. MEYER
  1966 Dental dysplasia related to malnutrition, with special reference to melanodontia and odontoclasia. *Journal of Dental Research* 45: 726–741.
GUSTAFSON, A. G.
  1959 A morphologic investigation of certain variations in the structure and mineralization of human dental enamel. *Odontologisk Tidskrift* 67:361–472.
KRAUS, D. S., R. E. JORDAN, L. ABRAMS
  1969 *Dental anatomy and occlusion.* Baltimore: Williams and Wilkins.
SCHOUR, I., M. MASSLER
  1940 Studies in tooth development: the growth pattern of the human teeth. *Journal of the American Dental Association* 27:1918–1931.
SCHUMAN, E. L., R. F. SOGNNAES
  1956 Developmental microscopic defects in the teeth of subhuman primates. *American Journal of Physical Anthropology* 19:193–209.
SOGNNAES, R. F.
  1956 Histologic evidence of developmental lesions in teeth originating from paleolithic, prehistoric, and ancient man. *American Journal of Pathology* 32:547–567.
WILSON, D. F., F. R. SCHROFF
  1970 The nature of the striae of Retzius as seen with the optical microscope. *Australian Dental Journal* 15:162–171.

The Effect of Heavy Orthopedic Forces on the Sutures of the Facial Bones

HELMUT DROSCHL and THOMAS M. GRABER

A previous paper has discussed the marked retrusive effects of orthopedic force against the maxilla of the growing *Saimiri sciureus* monkey (the squirrel monkey). The retardation over a period of ninety days, with constant heavy traction against the whole maxilla, was in the magnitude of three cusps of the dentition. Gold splints were cemented to the whole maxillary dental arch and forces of 100 gram on each side were attached to horizontal rings in the splint at the canine area. The posterior termini were fixed to a pivoting bar which was mounted behind the monkey's head on a restraining collar brace. The restraining collar plate was used to prevent the hands and arms from manipulating the appliances (Plate 1).

Five growing *Saimiri sciureus* monkeys were used as the experimental animals in this study. All of them were male and approximately twelve to fifteen months of age. Their weight varied from 390 to 420 grams each. At the time of this experiment, all monkeys were in the stage of upper second and third premolar eruption.

All monkeys received metal implants in the significant areas of the maxilla and the mandible. A serial cephalometric roentgenographic study was made (Plate 2). Two monkeys served as controls. Three monkeys were fitted with appliances and restraining braces. The first (M-1) was killed after fourteen days, the second (M-2) after thirty days, and the third (M-3) after ninety days.

Inasmuch as the response of the maxilla to heavy forces was the main objective of this study, the present report is limited to the findings in this area. After two weeks, the first monkey, M-1, showed no macroscopic changes. In both M-2, which was killed after thirty days, and M-3,

For Plates, see pp. xxv–xxxi, between pp. 330–331.

where roentgenographs were made after thirty days, a significant change could already be observed. There was a distinct posterior movement of the maxillary arch with the maxillary first molars moving distally, but not moving vertically at all. The implant in the molar area showed an essentially backward positioning but no vertical change, matching the molar shift. The maxillary incisors moved bodily, distally, and inferiorly into a retrusive or Class III relationship. It could be noted that the implants also moved posteriorly and inferiorly in the anterior portion of the maxilla. The infraorbital ridge implants also followed the same pattern, shifting primarily downward.

In M-3, after ninety days of continuous orthopedic force application, the same general changes were noted, but of far greater magnitude (Plate 3). The whole mid-face was "dished in." A severe maxillary retrusion and relative mandibular prognathism could be seen. When the teeth were brought together in occlusion, there was a discrepancy of three cusps. Not only was there posterior movement, but the molars at the end of the arch moved also posteriorly and superiorly. The upward and backward implant movement, when superimposition was made on sella and anterior cranial base, implies the beginning of the maxillary rotation around a point anterior and superior to the molar area, apparently in the zygomatic arch. Thus, there appeared to be a rotation in the entire nasomaxillary complex in response to orthopedic force (Figure 1). The control monkeys, by contrast, showed a steady downward and forward growth, with the same relationship of the arches at the end as at the beginning.

The purpose of this article is to investigate the histologic aspects of the effects of orthopedic force on the microstructure of facial sutures. As growth sites, they should be the main places to determine the response to change.

Oxytetracycline and Procion Red H-8 BS were used as *in vivo* bone markers in this experiment. The monkeys received one injection of tetracycline (fifty milligrams per kilogram of body weight) intramuscularly at the beginning of the experiment and, at the end, they were given tetracycline and Procion Red (one hundred milligrams per kilogram of body weight) intraperitoneally, two days before death. These markers served for the quantitative and interpretative histologic evaluation.

HISTOLOGIC PREPARATION

The monkeys were killed at the end of the experiment with an overdose of Pentothal Sodium, and the heads were removed. The maxilla and surrounding tissues were cut away with an electric saw and fixed in 10

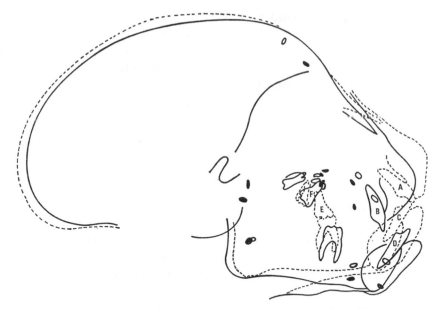

Figure 1.   Cephalometric tracings of Monkey M-3, before application of restraining force on maxilla and after ninety days of continuous force. Tracings are superimposed on anterior cranial base. Note movement of maxillary incisor in a downward and backward direction, from A to B. Mandible is rocked open by rotating maxilla, as shown by vertical movement of lower incisor from C to D. Maxillary rotation is demonstrated by movement of molar upward and backward from E to F

percent buffered formalin. The left half of each maxilla was embedded in bioplastic (methyl methacrylate) for undecalcified sections. These were cut by a microtome to slices between forty and eighty microns. The right half was decalcified, cut to regular histologic slices of eight microns, and stained with Hematoxylin-Eosin. These sutures have been examined

1.   Zygomaticofrontal suture
2.   Zygomaticomaxillary suture
3.   Frontomaxillary suture
4.   Pterygopalatine suture

Normally, in a growing suture, three or four distinct layers can be distinguished. A capsular zone exists right in the middle of this suture (Plates 4A, 5A). It is composed primarily of coarse bundles of mature, thick collagenous fibers. It is generally considered a dense and regular connective tissue with blood vessels. This layer is directly contiguous and continuous with the dense fibrous portion of the periosteum. The adjacent layer (intermediate zone) is much looser in texture and is more cellular. It is composed largely of immature, precollagenous fibrils. As these fibrils approach the suture bone surface, they thicken to become mature, coarse collagenous fibers (the border zone).

Despite the controversy that exists on the primacy of sutural growth, the bulk of evidence seems to indicate that sutural growth is a secondary response, reacting to other expansive growth forces that are responsible for the actual displacement of the bones involved. As the two bones become displaced away from each other, the fibers of the border zone become progressively embedded in the new forming bone that has been added to each sutural bone surface. A new border zone is formed from the old intermediate zone as its fibrils lengthen in a direction away from the bone surfaces. They undergo differentiation into coarse, mature collagenous fibers. Thus, in a physiologic and normal environment, the remodelling of the sutures and the displacement of the bones connected by the sutural tissue are in a state of equilibrium, with the width of the suture remaining almost constant during the growing period.

The intermediate zone is the active part of the sutural growth site. When active growth and remodelling changes stop, the entire suture becomes essentially a single capsular zone.

Since heavy orthopedic forces are well beyond those normally involved, the question is asked, "How will the sutures react to this type of overload?"

HISTOLOGIC FINDINGS WITH HEMATOXYLIN-EOSIN STAIN

M-1, killed after fourteen days, was compared to monkey M-4, a control monkey killed at the same time (Plates 4B, 5B). In both monkeys, the sutures had the characteristics of the above description. It was easy to distinguish the relatively wide and dark fibrous capsular zone with blood vessels, as well as the lighter and looser intermediate zones, that were indicative of regular physiologic function. However, with a careful investigation of the sutures of M-1, who wore an appliance delivering orthopedic force, it was also possible to see a significant number of osteoclasts, which indicates the beginning of cellular activity. In a few places, all three zones began to merge. In the sutures of M-4, very few osteoclasts were discernible.

M-2, killed after one month of orthopedic force, showed tremendous changes with signs of great activity (Plates 4C, 5C). Significantly, the sutures were two to three times as wide as in the control monkeys. The three zones had merged into one loose cellular texture, packed with irregular precollagenous fibrils. Fibers had no organization and seemed to be running in all directions. On the bony periphery of the Howship's lacunae, large numbers of osteoclasts could be observed. They were also seen at the margin of the neighboring bony marrow. The edges of the lacunae were serrated. Many more blood vessels could be observed in M-2 in all areas of the suture when compared to M-4.

M-3, which was killed after three months of experiment, showed a similar appearance to M-2 (Plates 4D, 5D). Nevertheless, the remodelling of the suture seemed to have taken a rather steady course. There was more organization and the three zones had begun to form again. There was less cellular activity and fewer osteoclasts. Although the bony edges were also serrated, as with M-2, this was a bit less obvious and it is possible that there were fewer osteoclasts present. Osteoblasts were attached to the surface of the bony edges in a line, indicating new bone formation.

M-5, a control monkey showed similar characteristics to M-4, which has already been reported (Plates 4E, 5E). There was normal physiologic response. A wide capsular zone could be observed again and the intermediate and border zones seemed normal. The serpentine shape of the sutures, with smooth edges restored again is evident. Relatively few osteoclasts were seen.

An attempt was made to compare the four sutures within the same monkey to determine if there was a different type of activity elicited from one suture to the other. This was not possible since all sutures showed essentially the same pattern of activity. In other words, if there was considerable activity in one suture, there would be the same amount in the remaining ones.

An attempt was also made to compare the periodontal ligament in the different monkeys. Here again, no marked differences could be observed. However, the treated monkeys showed more resorption at the interdental septa. Where there was maximum resorption, the bony tissues appeared isolated and surrounded by wide areas of connective tissue.

Histologic Sections with Ultraviolet Light

When a growing structure is injected with tetracycline, a bright yellow-gold fluorescence may be produced when the undecalcified section is viewed under ultraviolet light. Procion Red H-8 BS can be seen with considerably less brilliance, appearing as a brownish-red color, and this is not confined to the tissues undergoing mineralization. The following observations concern only monkeys M-2, M-3, and M-5.

PTERYGOPALATINE SUTURE   Although the sutures in M-2 and M-3 were very wide and irregular, staining with bone markers did disclose remodelling activity. When compared to the control monkey, M-5, which showed a very regular and small stained area at the bones next to the sutures, M-2 had a much more intensive and wider stained zone but this was irregular and frequently interrupted.

FRONTOMAXILLARY SUTURE   M-2 and M-3 began to show a significantly wider and more intensively stained area on both sides of the sutures than the control monkey, M-5. This would seem to indicate more appositional growth. M-3 had a wider stain zone than M-2, due to the longer treatment time.

ZYGOMATICOMAXILLARY SUTURE   The pattern was very similar to that of the frontomaxillary suture. However, the difference of the width of the stained zones between the treated and untreated monkeys seemed to be smaller.

ZYGOMATICOFRONTAL SUTURE   The stained zone of M-2 and M-3 again was significantly wider when compared to M-5. This coincides with the macroscopic findings in this experiment. Because of the rotational effect on the maxilla, it seems logical that the greatest degree of growth, over and above the normal growth, appears at the frontomaxillary and zygomaticofrontal sutures. Less growth was apparent in the zygomaticomaxillary suture and at the pterygopalatine suture. The remodelling and resorbing activity seemed to be greater.

   The appearance of the staining pattern (intensity, width, distribution) was clear and the growth activity at the different areas could be seen clearly. However, depending on the part of the suture that was cut, and because of the irregular growth and remodelling pattern, it was difficult to get exact measurements of the growth increments beyond what would normally be expected.

DISCUSSION

Heavy orthopedic forces on the maxilla are used in orthodontic therapy, although with some techniques the force is only intermittent. In others, the force is continuous. In this experiment, the heavy orthopedic forces produced significant change through continuous application. Histologically, the sutures of the maxilla were heavily affected. The orthopedic force produced a widening two to three times greater than normal, and there was evidence of intensive remodelling activity in the sutures. The regular pattern changed to a mixture of collagen fibrils and numerous active cells. The amount of growth could be observed with the use of the ultraviolet microscope, along with the use of bone markers. There was significantly more growth to be observed in the treated bones. It was not possible, of course, to determine how much of the additional growth would be permanent. The phenomenon of "catch-up growth" undoubtedly plays a role. But it is certainly apparent that there was a tremendous effect on the sutures — an effect that may not be fully evident to many orthodontists.

SUMMARY

The effect of heavy continuous orthopedic forces was studied in three *Saimiri sciureus* (squirrel) monkeys. Two additional monkeys served as controls. The effect on the maxillary sutures has been investigated microscopically. In addition, the bone markers (tetracycline, Procion Red H-8 BS) served for quantitative evaluation under ultraviolet light.

After two weeks slight remodelling activity could be observed.

After one month tremendous activity was found in the sutures. The width of the sutures was two to three times enlarged, the regular tissue pattern of the sutures had changed to a mixture of precollagen and collagen fibers running in all directions and plenty of active cells. In ultraviolet light there was a take up of markers at the sutural margins.

After three months of treatment, though the sutures showed a similar pattern, the remodelling seemed to take a steady course. The three zones of the sutures began to form again. Osteoblasts were attached to the sutural margins.

REFERENCES

BARGMANN, W.
  1962 *Histologie und mikroskopische Anatomie des Menschen.* Stuttgart: Georg Thieme.
BJÖRK, A.
  1968 The use of metallic implants in the study of facial growth in children: method and application. *American Journal of Physical Anthropology* 29:243–254.

CUTLER, B. S., F. H. HASSIG, D. L. TURPIN
 1972   Dentofacial changes produced during and after use of a modified Milwaukee brace on *Macaca mulatta*. *American Journal of Orthodontics* 61:115–137.

DROSCHL, H.
 1973   The effect of heavy orthopedic forces on the maxilla in the growing *Saimiri sciureus* (squirrel monkey). *American Journal of Orthodontics* 63:449–461.

ENLOW, D. H.
 1968   *The human face*. New York: Harper and Row.

GRABER, T. M.
 1972   *Orthodontics, principles and practice* (third edition). Philadelphia: W. B. Saunders.
 1975   "Extrinsic control factors influencing craniofacial growth," in *Control mechanisms in craniofacial growth*. Edited by J. A. McNamara. Ann Arbor: University of Michigan Center for Human Growth.

MC NAMARA, J. A., *editor*
 1975   *Control mechanisms in craniofacial growth*. Ann Arbor: University of Michigan Center for Human Growth.

MILCH, A., D. P. RALL, J. E. TOBIE
 1958   Fluorescence of tetracycline antibiotics in bone. *Journal of Bone and Joint Surgery* 40:897–909.

PRESCOTT, G. H., D. F. MITCHELL, H. FAHNY
 1968   Procion dyes as matrix markers in growing bone and teeth. *American Journal of Physical Anthropology* 29:219–226.

ROSENBLUM, LEONARD A., ROBERT W. COOPER
 1968   *The squirrel monkey*. New York: Academic Press.

SEITON, E. C., M. B. ENGEL
 1969   Reactive dyes as vital indicators of bone growth. *American Journal of Anatomy* 129(3):373–392.

SICHER, H., E. L. DU BRUL
 1970   *Oral anatomy* (third edition). St. Louis: C. V. Mosby.

WALDEYER, A.
 1965   *Anatomie des Menschen*, volume two. Berlin: Walter de Gruyter.

The Biology of the Human Chin

ROBERT H. BIGGERSTAFF

The chin, that segment of the mandible encompassed between the two canine teeth, is a distinctive anatomical feature of the cephalofacial complex of modern man. Yet the biological processes related to the origin and evolution of the chin remain an enigma in spite of having been studied by innumerable scientists. The concept that the chin of modern man is an indisputable structural entity, which would serve to establish a hierarchy in primates, emerged with the 1866 discovery of the fossil jaw of LaNaulette (Boule 1921). The subsequent discovery and evaluation of other fossils resembling the extraordinary skull cap (discovered in 1856) from the Neander Valley near Düsseldorf furnished many neo-Darwinists with the arguments and presumed proof linking modern man to the ape.

The functional significance of the chin and, indeed, all architectural changes in the skull are of great importance to comparative anatomists, physical anthropologists, paleontologists, human biologists, etc., because the observed changes, no matter how small, are interdependent and reflect the overall evolutionary trends in the skeleton as a whole. Du Brul and Sicher (1954: 22), in a classical treatise, have summarized the direction of thought related to the chin's significance as clustering around four principal theses:

1. THE SHIFTING RELATIONSHIPS OF JAW SEGMENTS. The chin formation was considered to be the result of a peculiar forward and backward shifting of relationships between the basilar and dental elements of the mandible. Having been visualized in the comparative anatomy of primates, it was accommodated to the general *"Fetalisationstheorie"* of man (Bolk 1924).

2. THE EFFECTS OF ARTICULATE SPEECH. The tongue, as an instrument with which man exhibits his superiority by the talent of speech, is fastened to the inner wall of the chin region and is hence adduced as the definitive cause for chin form. Walkhoff (1904) and perhaps Robinson (1914) are to be considered the most loyal retainers of this notion.

3. THE MECHANICAL EFFECTS OF REDUCTION AND RETRUSION OF TEETH. The phylogenetic reduction of the jaws is well documented and the development of the chin as a result has been advocated. It would appear that Weidenreich (1924) states this proposition most carefully.

4. THE EFFECTS OF MUSCLE ACTIVITY. The stresses of the chewing musculature upon the jaw have been suggested as underlying the structuring of the chin. Wegener (1927) and Grunewald (1921) are the major contributors to this premise.

The purpose of this article is to examine the stated hypotheses in an attempt to determine the biological factors which have contributed most to the origin and evolution of the chin. Data will be gathered primarily from the more recent growth and development literature with the goal of synthesizing the pertinent evidence into a hypothetical model that may explain, in some detail, the origin and evolution of the chin. Much of the data will be derived from the orthodontic literature because this subdiscipline of dentistry has contributed much basic information in an attempt to (1) better understand the bony interrelationships of the skull, (2) unravel the complexities of the craniofacial growth, and (3) relate the pertinent growth information to a more profound understanding of occlusion and facial form.

THE MANDIBLE — A COMPLEX OF BONY TISSUES

The mandible is a complex bone with a basal core upon which related, but independent, functioning units are superposed. The BASAL BONE consists of the body of the mandible (exclusive of the alveolar process) and some of the ramus (Moss 1962). The neck and condyle develop from a separate cartilaginous mass. The condylar process seems to exhibit a high degree of independence from the basal core as demonstrated in cases of congenital malformations (Kazanjian 1956; Moss and Rankow 1968), in disease (Engel et al. 1949) and by experimental techniques (Jarabak and Thompson 1951; Sarnat and Engel 1951; Gianelly and Moorrees 1965).

The ontogeny and form of the coronoid process is dependent upon the presence of a functioning temporal muscle (Washburn 1947; Avis 1959). For example, if the temporal muscle is ablated in an experimental animal, the coronoid process fails to continue development (Washburn 1947) and fails to develop if ablation occurs sufficiently early in the development of the organism. The partial removal of the temporal muscle attachment causes not only a slight reduction in size of the coronoid but a marked alteration in its shape (Avis 1959). Thus, the coronoid process represents another relatively independent component of a composite mandible.

The angular process is another component of the composite mandible which is dependent upon muscle function for development (Pratt 1943; Horowitz and Shapiro 1955; Rodgers 1958; Avis 1961; Liebman and Kussick 1965; Nanda et al. 1966), and presumably for its maintenance afterwards. The masseter muscle inserts on the buccal surface while the medial pterygoid muscle and the stylomandibular ligament insert on the lingual surface of the mandibular angle. The function of each muscle and/or ligament influences the shape of the mandibular angle. Experimental evidence (Avis 1961) suggests that (1) "the angular process was greatly reduced when either the superficial masseter muscle or the internal pterygoid muscle was completely removed," and (2) "the angular process was entirely absent when both the superficial masseter and internal pterygoid muscles were completely removed."

On the other hand, Biggerstaff (1971) described an atypical mandible from Żerniki Górne (Poland) that exhibited distinct bony shelves in the middle thirds of the rami for the attachment of the masseter muscles. In this situation, the angular process appeared to be normally shaped although the superficial masseters did not insert at the angle, if, indeed, they were present. It is, therefore, difficult to assess the contribution of each muscle to the development of the mandibular angle.

The alveolar process is a bony process of the mandible which manifests a peculiar behavior. Dental literature is replete with examples attesting to the necessity of teeth (in a healthy state) for the development and maintenance of the alveolar process. The alveolar process never forms in individuals afflicted with anodontia and the associated anhidrotic ectodermal dysplasia (Gorlin and Pindborg 1964: 305). In cases of oligodontia (partial anodontia), e.g. the Ellis-van Creveld (1940) syndrome, the alveolar bone does not develop in areas where tooth units fail to form (Biggerstaff and Mazaheri 1968). These observations strongly suggest that alveolar bone may be a component of the dental complex, and that it develops or resorbs in response to the presence or absence of the teeth. Moreover, the development of the alveolar process also influences the growth of other bones of the face (Baker 1941; Scott 1967) and conversely, the growth patterns of the other bones in the cephalofacial complex may influence the development of alveolar bone as in cases of severe skeletal malocclusions (Björk 1969).

Assuming there is sufficient evidence to support the existence of several independent bony components which collectively form the composite mandible, it is now possible to examine the aforementioned hypotheses from a biological point of view.

THE EFFECTS OF THE TONGUE

There are innumerable literature assertions that the forces generated by the chattering, wagging tongue are responsible for altering the topographical features on the labial and lingual surfaces of the mandibular symphysis (Walkhoff 1904; Robinson 1914). Presumably, these forces cause the stress dissipating bony contours and trabecular patterns of the bony chin. Unfortunately, there is no factual biological evidence proving that a hyperactive, articulating tongue can possibly generate forces capable of modifying the contours of the chin.

Coon (1962) has suggested that the tongue would be severely crowded if mandibular size was reduced, the shape remaining constant. He further hypothesized that "the lower borders of the mandible moved, and the central brace moved from the inside to the outside, producing the chin." This peculiar evolutionary adjustment was said to be necessary because the tongue itself could not be reduced in size along with the teeth and jaws because "we need it for talking, and we talk more than we swallow" (Coon 1962). Such a concept is no longer tenable because it implicitly assumes tongue function, in concert with other balancing forces, to be responsible for the observed morphological changes.

The data presented by Lear (1968) and Brader (1972) have altered the classical concept of "balanced forces" between the opposing labial and lingual musculature. The muscular pressures imposed on the teeth during speech or swallowing are not balanced. Lingual pressures exceed labial pressures (Lear 1968; Lear and Moorrees 1969; Proffit et al. 1969; Proffit and Norton 1970). Yet the teeth remain in equilibrium — in a stable position. Thus, one cannot consider peak lingual pressures generated during swallowing or speaking as dominant forces in the determination of arch form.

Teeth have the capacity to tolerate and withstand intense short-acting forces without moving while they move easily in response to small forces acting over prolonged periods of time (Weinstein et al. 1963). This point becomes even more dramatic when the effects of macroglossia on tooth position (widely spaced teeth) and arch form (excessively large) are considered (Gorlin and Pindborg 1964), as in Hurler's syndrome (gargoylism), or in cases of aglossia with the accompanying gross malocclusions but intelligible speech (Eskew and Shepard 1949; Gorlin and Pindborg 1964).

The size of the dental arches correlates within general limits with other bodily proportions, yet variation is great — large dental arches are observed in small faces and, conversely, small dental arches are found in large, broad faces. While there are no good data on tongue size, there are poor correlations between labial and lingual pressures, arch form, and type of malocclusion (Proffit and Norton 1970). Proffit et al. (1969) found no relationship between the increase in intermolar width and lateral lingual pressure during swallowing. Their data suggested that arch dimensions behave as though they are independent of swallowing pressures. Presumably, then, the evolutionary forces that have influenced jaw size and shape have acted in a similar fashion on tongue size. Therefore, the effects of articulate speech on the evolution of the chin can be dismissed as negligible.

THE EFFECTS OF MUSCULAR ACTIVITY

There is no doubt that the muscles of mastication have been involved in the evolution in the size and shape of the skull, and the influence of muscle function on the evolution of bony contours has long been recognized. Moss' hypothesis (Moss 1960; Moss and Young 1960) of the functional matrix assumes that various functions are primarily responsible for the growth of the components that give form to the mandible. Similarly, some anthropologists believe that changes in the patterns of muscular activity were responsible for the origin and evolution of the chin (Grunewald 1921; Hooton 1946; Howells 1967). Accordingly, their hypothesis suggested that the shortening of the mandible altered the direction of pull of the lateral pterygoid muscles such that the posterior ends of the mandible moved closer to the mid-sagittal plane during function. This action was presumed to cause a buttressing of the symphysis such that the chin developed to reinforce the endangered area. Supposedly, there was absolutely no lateral compensation for the strong inward pull of the lateral pterygoids which were claimed to be active even during lateral excursions.

Osborne (1961) has shown that in wide opening movements, when the lateral pterygoid muscles are most active, the posterior ends of the mandible and, indeed, the posterior segments of the mandibular dental arch are narrowed. This distortion amounts to approximately 0.05–0.10 millimeters in the molar region. Indeed, the distortion of the mandible under physiological forces has been observed by other investigators (Jung 1952, 1959; Picton 1962).

Du Brul and Sicher (1954) applied "Stresscoat" (Evans and Lissner 1948) to mandibles under controlled conditions of temperature and humidity to determine the amount of tension deformation. The material was calibrated to register 0.0006 inch deformation. When the mandibles were deformed by squeezing the condyles together with finger pressure applied to the insertion areas of the lateral pterygoids, transverse lines appeared in the "Stresscoat" on either side of the mental protuberance. Du Brul and Sicher (1954) claimed that the mental protuberance was in essence "a mechanical brace, created to withstand specific bending stress arising from muscular pull."

Additional data related to the effects of the lateral pterygoid muscles on the development of the chin are derived from electromyographic studies (Moyers 1950). The posterior fibers of the masseter muscles tend to counteract the inward pull of the lateral pterygoid muscles, especially when they participate in the forward movement of the mandible. Thus, the presumed compressive tendencies of the pterygoid muscles are well balanced, although the elasticity of the mandibular bony tissues allows deformation to occur.

Attempts to determine the effects of tensile, compressive and shearing forces on the form of the developing bone have led to the evaluation of the controversial split-lines or stress trajectories (Tappen 1953, 1954). But the true biological meaning of split-lines is unclear. Seipel (1948) suggests that split-lines are only the indicators of the main flow of lamellae and the fibrous organization in bone. Usually splits result because the bone has a minute grain analogous to wood (Tappen 1954) which is related to the shape of the bone surface in general (Dempster 1965) and to the Haversian systems where present. The mechanical and functional interpretation of the observed architecture must be done with extreme caution, especially when applying mechanical laws to the problem of bone morphology (Evans 1965).

Bone tissue, composed of collagenous fibers and the apatite crystals, exhibits the properties of all crystalline materials and, when deformed, produces a measurable electrical potential. The biological significance of this generated electrical potential (the piezoelectric phenomenon) is of great importance in the discussion of bone biodynamics (Bassett and Becker 1962; Bassett et al. 1964; Becker et al. 1964; Bassett 1968). When bone bends or is deformed, the concave side is compressed. Conversely, the convex side is subjected to tensile forces which tend to pull the object apart or lengthen it. Presumably, the negative characteristic of the piezoelectric field on the concave side of stressed bone stimulates the activities of osteoblasts to lay down bone matrix, while osteoclastic activity is stimulated on the positively charged convex surface. If this model were applied to the mandible, humans would have "simian shelves" on the lingual surface of the symphysis which is depository in nature (Enlow 1968). Clearly this is not the case, and it is highly unlikely that the muscles of mastication, particularly the lateral pterygoid muscles, have had much influence on the origin and evolution of the chin.

THE EFFECTS OF REDUCED TOOTH SIZE

One need only review the tooth size data in the literature (Brabant and Twiesselman 1964; Moorrees 1957; Robinson 1956) to be convinced that the mesiodistal crown diameters of the postcanine teeth have become progressively smaller through time (probably due to evolutionary processes). Brabant and Twiesselman (1964) argue convincingly that significant reductions in the number and size of the teeth in the human dentition have occurred since the Paleolithic. They suggest that mutations are at least partially responsible for the general manner of dental evolution. On the other hand, Brace and Mahler (1971) argue that the post-Pleistocene reduction in the human dentition proceeded rapidly because of a relaxation of selective forces (probably related to the invention of pottery and changes in the methods of preparing foods).

Even in modern populations, there is much variation in tooth size. The mesiodistal diameters of the postcanine teeth in European whites are clearly smaller than those of American whites. In this regard, there is a hierarchy for increased tooth size for the European white (Brabant and Twiesselman 1964), American white (Moorrees 1957), Australopithecus, and Paranthropus populations (Robinson 1965). One must be mindful, however, that tooth size is a normally distributed variable that does not correlate well with body size. To be sure, one can observe in some modern human populations individuals with tooth sizes that are consistent with the mean values of the protohominid data (Keene 1967).

Associated with the reduction in tooth size is the reduction in the size of the tooth-supporting alveolar bone. Assume that the basal bone of the mandible generally has only slightly changed in size and shape during the last 50,000 years. Assume further that the alveolar bone has regressed posteriorly keeping pace with the reduction in dentition size. On this basis, one can hypothesize a time-related reduction in tooth size and in the amount of supporting alveolar bone required. Unfortunately, there are no data describing the size of alveolar bone or its relative position to the underlying supporting basal bone on which it is superposed.

THE SHIFTING THEORY

There is a growing body of evidence indicating that the two components of the mandibular body grow at differing rates and directions (Lande 1952; Enlow and Harris 1964). These concepts are compatible with Bolk's shifting theory (1924) according to which the basal portion of the mandible can slide forward under the tooth-bearing alveolar process because of differential growth gradients between the two segments. This concept becomes more meaningful when data comparing different species of anthropoids are reviewed.

Enlow's (1968: 182) comparison of the facial growth pattern in man and the rhesus monkey reveals that the basic plan of their facial growth is congruous. "Their respective patterns and directions of growth as well as displacement are comparable in most areas of the different facial bones." However, his data suggest that several distinct differences do exist and that they are associated with gross topographical changes in the regions involved. In the human mandible, the chin region represents an area of marked difference, particularly the labial and lingual symphyseal surfaces. The macaque mandible has a "simian shelf," which is not present in man but is present in other anthropoids. In contrast, the human mandible possesses a mental protuberance, a structure peculiar to *Homo sapiens*. These morphological structures, although unique for the respective species, are the results of differential growth processes.

The chin is not developed in the neonate. Lande (1952) has shown that an increase in mandibular prognathism generally begins after seven years of age. In addition, Lande (1952) showed that alveolar bone growth did not keep pace with the growth of the mandibular base in a horizontal direction. This differential growth process allows the basal component of the mandible to become more prognathic in relation to the brain case while the basal bone of the maxilla shows very little change. In fact, the mandibular base of the male continues to grow well after maturity, 20 to 22 years, while the female mandibular base ceases growth between 16 and 19 years.

The differential growth pattern on the anterior surface of the mandibular symphysis is well documented (Enlow and Harris 1964). The mental protuberance usually grows anteriorly by the periosteal apposition of bone. (It is also displaced anteriorly by growth, in the form of bone deposition on the posterior border of the ramus. Immediately superior to the chin, the alveolar bone grows differentially in a posterior direction because of labial surface resorption and lingual surface apposition). "The differential combination of alveolar regression and a progressive mental protrusion is responsible for the distinctive human chin" (Enlow 1968). The pattern of continued basal bone growth in the mandible (during the late teens and early twenties), in combination with other factors, may be responsible for uprighting the mandibular incisors and/or the incisal crowding that occurs in the young adult (Biggerstaff 1966).

In contrast, the growth pattern of the rhesus monkey occurs by continual periosteal deposition of bone on the entire labial surface of the mandible. Presumably, the alveolar bone of the macaque grows anteriorly and faster over a longer period than does the underlying basal bone. This process accounts for the "snouting" (mandibular prognathism) observed in the macaque mandible.

There is additional evidence that can be utilized in support of the shifting theory. For example, the mandibular canal (and mental foramen) is a component of the basal bone (Moss 1962), representing a channel for the neuro-vascular bundle. In many Neanderthals, the mental foramen opens beneath the mesial root tip of the mandibular first permanent molar. In contrast, the mental foramen of modern man is usually found between the first and second premolars and can be found as far anterior as the space between the canine and the first premolar. In the latter situation, the individual mandible is endowed with a magnificent mental protuberance or chin. Most importantly, these observations can be interpreted as evidence pointing to the posterior regression of the alveolar bone relative to the basal bone.

The proof necessary to show that alveolar bone is ontogenetically distinct from the underlying basal bone is not available. However, in a preliminary report (Biggerstaff 1972), I suggest that alveolar bone arises by a process similar to mesenchymal metaplasia. Initially, a precursor tissue develops which subsequently is transformed into bone. This process is assumed to be the result of an epitheliomesenchymal interaction between the cells of the external dental epithelium and surrounding mesenchymal cells, a process similar to that associated with crown formation.

The data of Kollar and Baird (1969, 1970) suggest that the interaction between the down-growing epithelium and mesenchyme is capable of producing an enamel organ and papilla specific for the region. Thus, an incisor papilla when related to molar epithelium will produce an incisor and vice versa. Through a series of inductive processes the specialized cells of the developing tooth are transformed from more primitive cells, i.e. ameloblasts and odontoblasts.

Apparently, all the hard tissues of the tooth ultimately result from a complex of inductive interactions between the cells of the internal dental epithelium and the mesenchyme of the dental papilla (Billingham and Heldmann 1958; Slavkin et al. 1969; Kollar and Baird 1969, 1970). If alveolar bone arises as suggested, its peculiar behavior in cases of anodontia or oligodontia and tooth loss can be explained. When teeth do not develop, no alveolar bone develops. When teeth are lost, alveolar bone is lost. Alveolar bone, then, may be simply another component of the tooth complex which, in combination with the periodontal ligament and tooth cementum, forms a highly specialized suture system (bone to bone) for supporting the teeth.

The unity of alveolar bone, cementum, and the supporting fibers becomes more obvious when the recent data of Quigley (1970) and Cohn (1970) are examined. These investigators, working independently, utilized special staining and processing techniques to show that the supporting fibers of the periodontal membrane course continuously from root surface to root surface through the interradicular and intraradicular bone. Most importantly, their data show that some of the fibers course from root tip to root tip through the apical alveolar bone. If these data are, in fact, verified by additional experimentation, a mechanism is provided for determining histologically the terminal boundaries of basal bone and alveolar bone. To be sure, these data add to the mounting body of information alluding to the relative independence of alveolar bone, ontogenetically and functionally.

Collectively, these observations indicate that alveolar bone is another component of the composite mandible which develops and matures in concert with the developing tooth roots and the contiguous skull bones. As such, it expresses growth directions which are juxtaposed to that of the underlying basal bone. These observations make Bolk's (1924) shifting theory acceptable, if considered in conjunction with the tooth size reduction hypothesis, and explain the origin and evolution of the chin on a biological basis.

SUMMARY

The chin is formed by the expression of differential growth potentials, in terms of timing and direction, between the basal bone of the mandibular body and the alveolar bone of the tooth complex. Although the details are still sketchy, the chin is "sex-associated" and manifests sexual dimorphism in growth pattern (De Kock et al. 1968; Woodside, personal communication) and size (Horowitz and Thompson 1964) among contemporary human populations. The consequences of the observed sexual dimorphism for chin size and growth pattern have other interesting implications.

Man is a social creature and tends to attach social significance to many anatomical features without apparent reason. The magnificent, prominent, modern-day chin "is a badge of courage, firmness, and decision" (Howells 1967). Therefore, a form of social selection may have been important in the origin and evolution of the chin.

The chin's origin may be due to the same selective forces that have caused the reduction in the size of brow ridges, zygomatic arches, and teeth. In this sense, the chin can be termed "adaptive" (Du Brul and Sicher 1954) or "atavistic" (Berger 1969), as either term is partially, if not fully, descriptive. The chin does not seem to have a special functional significance.

The arguments favoring the effects of speech on the origin and evolution of the chin can be summarily dismissed as untenable and without biological evidence.

The fact that muscles stimulate bones during function is important to the biodynamics of bone physiology. Bones need to be stressed to maintain their form and strength. The effects of muscle function on the evolution and form of the chin are not clear. Indeed, the evidence from split-lines and Stresscoats appears to be in conflict with the significance of the piezoelectric phenomenon especially with regards to the growth patterns of the mental protuberance (Enlow and Harris 1964).

In conclusion, the chin of the adult appears to be a structural consequence of a combination of factors which have exerted their individual influence during the period of growth and development. The differential growth potentials and growth gradients (direction) of the alveolar bone and the basal bone of the mandibular body (Enlow 1968) contribute to the importance of Bolk's (1924) hypothesis. Presumably, the mandibular alveolar bone and basal bone "shift" in such a way that the dentition regresses posteriorly while the mental protuberance progresses anteriorly.

Since there is a time-related reduction in tooth size, one can speculate with some degree of assurance that there was also a reduction in the amount of required alveolar bone.

REFERENCES

AVIS, V.
    1959   The relation of the temporal muscle to the form of the coronoid process. *American Journal of Physical Anthropology* 17:99–103.
    1961   The significance of the angle of the mandible: an experimental and comparative study. *American Journal of Physical Anthropology* 19:55–61.
BAKER, L. W.
    1941   The influence of the formative dental organs on the growth of the bones of the face. *American Journal of Orthodontics* 27:489–506.
BASSETT, C. A. L.
    1968   Biologic significance of piezoelectricity. *Calcified Tissue Research* 1:252–272.
BASSETT, C. A. L., R. O. BECKER
    1962   Generation of electric potential by bone in response to mechanical stress. *Science* 137:1063–1064.
BASSETT, C. A. L., R. J. PAWLUCK, R. O. BECKER
    1964   Effects of electric currents on bone *in vivo. Nature* 204:652–654.
BECKER, R. O., C. A. L. BASSETT, C. H. BACHMAN
    1964   "Bioelectric factors controlling bone structure," in *Bone biodynamics.* Edited by H. M. Frost, 209–232. Boston: Little, Brown.
BERGER, H.
    1969   The chin problem from an orthodontic point of view. *American Journal of Orthodontics* 56:516–521.
BIGGERSTAFF, R. H.
    1966   The anterior migration of dentitions and anterior crowding: a review. *Angle Orthodontist* 37:227–240.
    1971   An atypical mandible from Żerniki Górne, Poland. *American Journal of Physical Anthropology* 35:187–192.
    1973   *In vivo* development of the hamster periodontium and implications for the chin's evolution. *American Journal of Physical Anthropology* 38:59–68.
BIGGERSTAFF, R. H., M. MAZAHERI
    1968   Oral manifestations of the Ellis-van Creveld syndrome. *Journal of*

the American Dental Association 77:1090–1095.

BILLINGHAM, R. E., W. H. HELDMANN
1958   Studies on the immunologic responses of the hamster to skin homografts. *Proceedings of the Royal Society of London,* series B, 148:216–233.

BJÖRK, A.
1969   Prediction of mandibular growth rotation. *American Journal of Orthodontics* 55:585–599.

BOLK, L.
1924   Die Entstehung des Menschenkinnes. Ein Beitrag zur Entwicklungsgeschichte des Unterkiefers. *Verhandelingen der Koninklijke Akademie van Wetenschappen te Amsterdam, Tweede Sectie* 23(5).

BOULE, M.
1921   *Les hommes fossiles.* Paris: Masson.

BRABANT, H., F. TWIESSELMAN
1964   Observations sur l'évolution de la denture permanente humaine en Europe occidentale. *Bulletin du Groupement International pour la Recherche Scientifique en Stomatologie* 7:11–84.

BRACE, C. L., P. E. MAHLER
1971   Post-pleistocene changes in the human dentition. *American Journal of Physical Anthropology* 34:191–204.

BRADER, A. C.
1972   Dental arch form related with intraoral forces: PR=C. *American Journal of Orthodontics* 61:541–561.

COHN, S. A.
1970   A new look at the orientation of cemento-alveolar fibers of the mouse periodontium. *Anatomical Record* 166:292.
1970   A re-examination of Sharpey's fibers in alveolar bone of the mouse. *Archives of Oral Biology* 17:255–260.

COON, S. C.
1962   *The origin of races.* New York: Alfred A. Knopf.

DE KOCK, W. H., V. B. KNOTT, H. V. MEREDITH
1968   Change during childhood and youth in facial form from integumental profile points to a line through bregma and sellion. *American Journal of Orthodontics* 54:111–131.

DEMPSTER, W. T.
1965   The grain of cortical bone in relation to structural features of the adult skull. *Anatomical Record* 151:342–343.

DU BRUL, E. L., H. SICHER
1954   *The adaptive chin.* Springfield: Charles C. Thomas.

ELLIS, R. W. B., S. VAN CREVELD
1940   A syndrome characterized by ectodermal dysplasia, polydactyly, chondro-dysplasia and congenital morbus cordis. *Archives of Diseases of Childhood* 15:65–84.

ENGEL, M. B., J. RICHMOND, A. G. BRODIE
1949   Mandibular growth disturbances in rheumatoid arthritis in childhood. *American Journal of Diseases in Children* 78:728–743.

ENLOW, D. H.
1968   The human face. New York: Harper and Row.

ENLOW, D. H., D. B. HARRIS
1964   A study of the post-natal growth of the human mandible. American Journal of Orthodontics 52:823–830.

ESKEW, H. A., E. E. SHEPARD
1949   Congenital aglossia. American Journal of Orthodontics 35:116–119.

EVANS, F. G.
1965   A commentary on the significance of Stresscoat and split-line patterns on bone. American Journal of Physical Anthropology 23:189–195.

EVANS, F. G., H. R. LISSNER
1948   "Stresscoat" deformation studies of the femur under static vertical loading. Anatomical Record 100:159–190.

GIANELLY, A. S., C. A. F. MOORREES
1965   Condylectomy in the rat. Archives of Oral Biology 10:101–106.

GORLIN, R. J., J. P. PINDBORG
1964   Syndromes of the head and neck. New York: McGraw-Hill.

GRUNEWALD, J.
1921   Über die Beanspruchung und den Aufbau des menschlichen Unterkiefers und die mechanische Bedeutung des Kinnes. Archiv für Anthropologie 46:100.

HOOTON, E. A.
1946   Up from the ape. New York: Macmillan.

HOROWITZ, S. L., H. L. SHAPIRO
1955   Modification of skull and jaw architecture following the removal of the masseter muscle in the rat. American Journal of Physical Anthropology 24:205–214.

HOROWITZ, S. L., R. H. THOMPSON
1964   Variations of the craniofacial skeleton in post-adolescent males and females. Angle Orthodontist 34:97–102.

HOWELLS, W. W.
1967   Mankind in the making. Garden City, New Jersey: Doubleday.

JARABAK, J. R., J. R. THOMPSON
1951   Growth of the mandible following bilateral resection of the mandibular condyles. Journal of Dental Research 30:492.

JUNG, F.
1952   Die Elastizität der Skeletteile des Gebisssystems. Stoma 5:74–93.
1959   Veranderung des Prothesenlagers unter der Teilprothese. Deutsche Zahnaerztliche Zeitschrift 14:105–107.

KAZANJIAN, V. H.
1956   Bilateral absence of the ascending rami of the mandible. British Journal of Plastic Surgery 9:77–82.

KEENE, H. J.
1967   Australopithecine dental dimensions in a contemporary population. American Journal of Physical Anthropology 27:379–384.

KOLLAR, E. J., G. R. BAIRD
1969   The influence of the dental papilla on the development of tooth shape in embryonic mouse tooth germs *in vitro*. *Journal of Embryology and Experimental Morphology* 21:131–148.
1970   Tissue interactions in embryonic mouse tooth germs. *Journal of Embryology and Experimental Morphology* 24:159–171.

LANDE, M. J.
1952   Growth behavior of human bony facial profiles as revealed by serial cephalometric roentgenology. *Angle Orthodontist* 22:78–90.

LEAR, C. S. C.
1968   Symmetry analysis of the palate and maxillary dental arch. *Angle Orthodontist* 38:56–62.

LEAR, C. S. C., C. A. F. MOORREES
1969   Buccolingual muscle force and dental arch form. *American Journal of Orthodontics* 56:379–393.

LIEBMAN, F M., L. KUSSICK
1965   An electromyographic analysis of masticatory muscle imbalance with relation to skeletal growth in dogs. *Journal of Dental Research* 44:768–774.

MOORREES, C. A. F.
1957   *The Aleut dentition. A correlative study of dental characteristics in an eskimoid people.* Cambridge: Harvard University Press.

MOSS, M. L.
1960   Functional matrix analysis of human mandibular growth. *Journal of Prosthetic Dentistry* 10:1149–1154.
1962   "The functional matrix," in *Vistas in orthodontics*. Edited by B. S. Kraus and R. A. Riedel, 85–98. Philadelphia: Lea and Febiger.

MOSS, M. L., R. W. YOUNG
1960   A functional approach to craniology. *American Journal of Physical Anthropology* 18:281–292.

MOSS, M. L., R. M. RANKOW
1968   The role of the functional matrix in mandibular growth. *Angle Orthodontist* 38:95–103.

MOYERS, R. E.
1950   An electromyographic analysis of certain muscles involved in emporomandibular movement. *American Journal of Orthodontics* 30:481–515.

NANDA, S. K., W. W. MEROW, V. SASSOUNI
1966   Repositioning of the masseter and its effect on skeletal form and structure. *International Association for Dental Research Program and Abstracts* (Abstract Number 357):128.

OSBORNE, J. W.
1961   Investigation into the interdental forces occurring between the teeth of the same arch during the clenching of the jaws. *Archives of Oral Biology* 5:202–211.

PICTON, D. C. A.
1962   Distortion of the jaws during biting. *Archives of Oral Biology* 7:573–580.

PRATT, L. W.
    1943   Experimental masseterectomy in the laboratory rat. *Journal of Mammalogy* 24:204–211.
PROFFIT, W. R., B. B. CHASTAIN, L. A. NORTON
    1969   Linguopalatal pressures in children. *American Journal of Orthodontics* 55:566–577.
PROFFIT, W. R., L. A. NORTON
    1970   "The tongue and oral morphology: influences of tongue activity during speech and swallowing." American Speech and Hearing Association Report 5:106–115.
QUIGLEY, M. B.
    1970   Perforating (Sharpey's) fibers of the periodontal ligament and bone. *Alabama Journal of Medical Science* 7:336–343.
ROBINSON, J. T.
    1956   *The dentition of the Australopithecinae*. Transvaal Museum Memoir 9. Pretoria: Transvaal Museum.
ROBINSON, L.
    1914   *The story of the chin*. Annual Report of the Smithsonian Institution, p. 599. Washington, D.C.
RODGERS, W. M.
    1958   The influence of asymmetry of the muscles of mastication upon the bones of the face. *Anatomical Record* 131:617–632.
SARNAT, B. G., M. B. ENGEL
    1951   A serial study of the mandibular growth after removal of the condyle in the *Macaca rhesus* monkey. *Plastic and Reconstructive Surgery* 7:364–380.
SCOTT, J. H.
    1957   Muscle growth and function in relation to skeletal morphology. *American Journal of Physical Anthropology* 15:197–234.
    1967   *Dento-facial development and growth*. New York: Pergamon.
SEIPEL, C. M.
    1948   Trajectories of the jaws. *Acta Odontologica Scandinavica* 8:81–191.
SIMPSON, C. D.
    1962   Response of the gonion to resection of the right internal pterygoid in the rat. *American Journal of Orthodontics* 48:393–394.
SLAVKIN, H. C., P. BRINGAS, L. A. BAVETTA
    1969   Ribonucleic acid within the extracellular matrix during embryonic tooth formation. *Journal of Cellular and Comparative Physiology* 73:179–190.
TAPPEN, N. C.
    1953   A functional analysis of the facial skeleton by split-line technique. *American Journal of Physical Anthropology* 11:503–532.
    1954   A comparative functional analysis of primate skulls by split-line technique. *Human Biology* 26:220–238.
WALKHOFF O.
    1904   Die menschliche Sprache in ihrer Bedeutung für die functionelle Gestalt des Unterkiefers. *Anatomischer Anzeiger* 24:129.

WASHBURN, S. L.
1947 The relation of the temporal muscle to the form of the skull. *Anatomical Record* 99:239–248.

WEGENER, K.
1927 Über Zweck and Ursache der menschlichen Kinnbildung. *Zeitschrift für Morphologie und Anthropologie* 26:165.

WEIDENREICH, F.
1924 Die Sonderform des Menschenschädels als Anpassung an den aufrechten Gang. *Zeitschrift für Morphologie und Anthropologie* 24:157–189.

WEINSTEIN, S., D. C. HACK, L. Y. MORRIS, B. B. SNYDER, H. E. ATTAWAY
1963 On an equilibrium theory of tooth position. *Angle Orthodontist* 33:1–26.

SECTION THREE

Genetics

Dental Genetics

A. LUNDSTRÖM

The teeth are for several reasons very interesting objects for genetic investigations. Each single tooth is a morphological unit, probably influenced by many genes governing appearance, form, and size of the tooth. Also, each tooth presents itself twice in each individual, one on the left and one on the right side. A comparatively large part of this article will cover some of the work that has been done in the form of genetic studies regarding the teeth *per se* but primarily their quantitative variation. I will thereafter present a rather limited perusal of some investigations on variations in the position of the teeth within the jaws as well as in the relationship between the upper and lower jaws. Finally, I will refer to some examples of severe anomalies that have been reported in the literature to be genetically conditioned.

As the X-chromosome is so much larger than the Y-chromosome it is obvious that females have more genetic material than males and the effects which this difference might cause have already been discussed. According to a hypothesis by Lyon the genetic overweight in the female is counteracted through some kind of suppression of one of the X-chromosomes in the so-called Barr's body of the cell nucleus, whereby in each cell only one of the X-chromosomes is active. This hypothesis is partly based on the fact that in abnormal cases with more than two X-chromosomes an increase in the number of Barr's bodies is observed. With three X-chromosomes there are thus two Barr's bodies instead of the normal one.

Genes in the Y-chromosome may obviously cause the special male characteristics, including the overall difference in body size between males and females. These effects may well be secondary to hormonal sex

For Plates, see pp. xxxiii–xxxv, between pp. 330–331.

differences. As the Y-chromosome is small and therefore probably contains comparatively few genes it is not supposed to cause the same kind of "unbalance" as two fully active X-chromosomes would do.

SEX-DIFFERENCES FOR THE TEETH have been studied by several investigators (Bowden and Goose 1969; Garn, Lewis, and Kerewsky 1964, 1965, 1966b, 1967; Garn et al. 1965, 1967; Goose 1967; Lundström 1944; Seipel 1946; Selmer-Olsen 1949). Figure 1 shows some of these findings for the mesiodistal tooth diameter. It is obvious that the sex differences are largest for canines and second molars. It is intriguing to consider what the mechanism could be for such a selective influence of the genes probably responsible, as just mentioned, located on the Y-chromosome. According to Garn, Lewis, and Kerewsky (1966b) the sexual dimorphism is slightly larger for the buccolingual than for the mesiodistal tooth diameter. Oddly enough there seemed to be no close association between the two measures as regards to which individual teeth showed a large or a small sex difference. The lower canines, for instance, had in Garn's material the largest mesiodistal but the smallest buccolingual sex difference of all the teeth.

While sexual dimorphism might well be due to genes on the Y-chromosome there is also evidence available that genes on the X-chromosome play a part in the variation in tooth size. Such evidence was first demonstrated by Garn et al. (1967) through a comparison of correlations between sister-sister, sister-brother, and brother-brother pairs. The means of the correlation-coefficients for these three combinations were 0.64, 0.21, and 0.38. Such a difference can be explained if genes on the X-chromosome affect tooth size. Sisters have at least one X-chromosome in common, inherited from their father, and a 50 percent chance of also having the same second X-chromosome, the one from their mother. Brothers, on the other hand, can only have one similar X-chromosome and this in 50 percent of the sibling relationships. Finally, brother-sister pairs have the same probability as brother-brother pairs for one X-chromosome in common, but as the sisters should have an added chance to deviate through genes on their second X-chromosome, obtained from their father, such pairs should get the smallest correlation-coefficient. Bowden and Goose (1969) and Alvesalo (1970) have performed similar studies and have at least partly substantiated the findings of Garn and his co-workers. In Figure 2 these results are shown together with some calculations of my own on dizygotic twins and family material. The differences obtained fit surprisingly well the theoretical model that tooth-size variation depends on X-chromosome-linked additive genes without any dominant effects (cf. Maynard-Smith, Penrose, and Smith 1961).

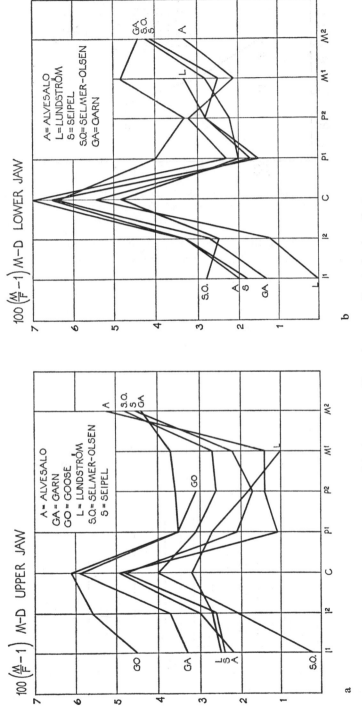

Figure 1a, b.   Sex differences for different teeth in the upper and lower jaws according to five investigators

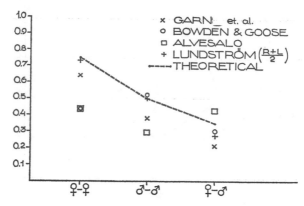

Figure 2.   Correlation-coefficients for mesiodistal tooth widths in sister-sister, brother-brother, and sister-brother pairs compared with the theoretical model that tooth size variation depends on X-chromosome-linked additive genes without any dominant effects

Correlation studies for other combinations of relatives have been published by Lewis and Grainger (1967), Bowden and Goose (1969), and Potter et al. (1968) showing that there is a closer association between father and daughter than between father and son which also points to X-chromosome effects since the father gives an X-chromosome to the daughter but not to the son. Alvesalo (1970) also investigated the different kinds of cousin-pairs with the same general result. As pointed out by Bowden and Goose (1969), there is a definite positive correlation also between fathers and sons. As these have no X-chromosome in common, genes in the Y-chromosome or among the autosomes must also have some influence on tooth size.

Another circumstance indicating that X-chromosome-linked genes can be only partly responsible for the variation in tooth size comes from a comparison of males and females as to the coefficients of variation, as shown in Figure 3 for three upper front teeth (Lundström 1944; Seipel

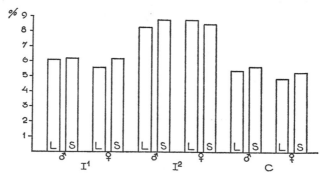

Figure 3.   Coefficients of variation for upper incisors and canines according to Lundström (1944) and Seipel (1946)

1946). The lateral incisor shows the largest variation, which is interesting with regard to other findings of instability for this tooth, i.e. peg-teeth and missing teeth. There is, obviously, no indication that females vary more than males, which might be expected according to the X-chromosome hypothesis. Evidence related to these studies has also been presented by Sofaer, Maclean, and Bailit (1972).

As a general conclusion from the facts available it seems as if we are still lacking necessary evidence for a satisfactory explanation of the mode of inheritance as it is related to tooth size.

In the following — based on earlier investigations (Lundström 1948, 1960, 1967) — I will try to analyze step by step different parts of the population variation; I will start with LEFT-RIGHT DIFFERENCES. Figure 4

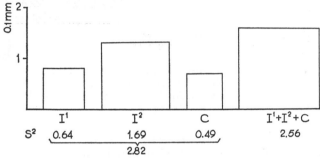

Figure 4. Variances for left-right variability of upper incisors and canines and for the sum of these teeth (Lundström 1960)

demonstrates left-right variability expressed as variances, calculated from means of duplicate measurements on eighty boys and girls. Again, the lateral incisor varies most. If the variances for the three single teeth are added and this sum is compared with the variance for the corresponding tooth-width sum, a rather close agreement is found. This indicates that left-right differences are randomly distributed between the teeth and thus noncorrelated. Therefore such differences are, to some extent, evened out between the teeth. Evidence pointing in the same direction has been published by Vogel and Reiser (1960) while Garn, Lewis, and Kerewsky (1966a) found some tendency for a similar asymmetry for teeth belonging to the same tooth group.

It should be of some interest to see if symmetric differences are better correlated than the asymmetric. The variance for such differences has therefore been determined for single teeth as well as for a corresponding sum of tooth breadths, as shown in Figure 5. The variance for symmetrical differences has then been calculated through a subtraction from the population variance of the variance calculated from left-right differences.

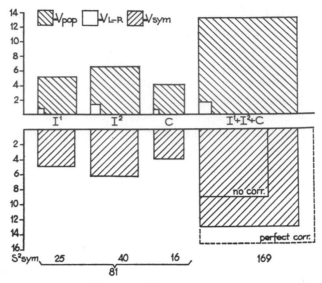

Figure 5. Variances for upper incisors and canines and for the sum of these teeth in the population and for left-right variability; in the lower part of the figure the latter has been subtracted from the population variance, thus presenting the variances for symmetrically acting factors (Lundström 1960)

As this variance is more than twice as large for the sum of the three teeth as for the total of the three teeth taken individually, there is obviously a correlation between the teeth. This is, of course, also to be expected as the main background for symmetrical deviations, since large or small teeth should be genetic factors acting on the whole dental arch. That there is a high correlation in tooth size between the different teeth in the dental arch has also been shown by several authors (Hohl 1934; Martin 1934; Moorrees and Reed 1964; Selmer-Olsen 1949).

The next step in the study of different components in tooth-size variability will be to compare left-right differences with DIFFERENCES BETWEEN MONOZYGOTIC TWINS on their left and right sides respectively. For the same teeth as before Figure 6 shows the variances obtained.

As the variances for monozygotic twins exceed those for left-right asymmetry only to a very moderate degree, environmental factors with a bilateral effect tending to separate monozygotic co-twins from each other as regards tooth size seem to have a rather limited effect. It should be pointed out, however, that Vogel and Reiser (1960) obtained a somewhat larger difference between MZ and left-right variability.

DIZYGOTIC TWINS should most probably have the same possibilities as monozygotic twins to be influenced by nongenetic factors as far as tooth size is concerned. It is therefore reasonable to assume that the variance

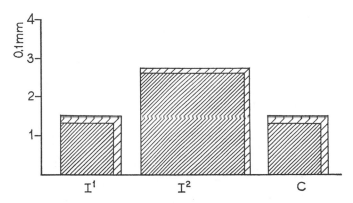

Figure 6. Comparison between left-right and MZ variances for upper incisors and canines (Lundström 1948)

calculated from DIFFERENCES BETWEEN DIZYGOTIC TWINS is composed of two parts: one part due to nongenetic factors and equal to what was found in monozygotic twins and one part due to such genetic differences as characterize siblings.

An important question for twin investigations is the reliability with which mono- and dizygotic twins can be distinguished from each other. It should perhaps also be mentioned that the possibility of a third category of twins has been discussed, where fertilization with two sperms of one egg and its polar body or of a divided egg may have happened. As this latter type should be rare, if it occurs at all, in human beings, it is improbable that twin results are affected to any noticeable degree in such a way.

Present methods for diagnosing twins, based on somatic, blood group, and serological comparisons, give a very high reliability of the classification of twins. It can also be mentioned in this context that twin diagnosis based on comparison of tooth morphology in itself conforms well with such a general classification.

A comparison of the variances for differences between monozygotic and dizygotic twins is shown in Figure 7. In order to facilitate the comparison between the nongenetic and genetic parts of the variances the lower part of the figure shows the latter surface as squares. Osborne, Horowitz, and de George (1958), Hunter (1959), and Vogel and Reiser (1960) have obtained similar results.

So far we have only been dealing with the sibling variance within families. This should obviously be less than between nonrelated individuals. From ENVIRONMENTAL points of view there should be added possibilities for differences BETWEEN families as compared with conditions WITHIN families. GENETICALLY the variability between siblings is also

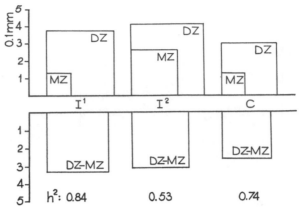

Figure 7.   Comparison between MZ and DZ variances; in the lower part of the figure the MZ variance has been subtracted from the DZ variance thus presenting an expression of the total genetic variance (Lundström 1948)

limited due to the fact that they have the same parents. How much greater the population variance is than the variance for dizygotic twins is shown in Figure 8. The problem then is how much of the between-family variance depends on nongenetic and how much on genetic factors. As regards tooth size it seems likely that the latter are by far the most important.

I would also like to present a few findings regarding TOOTH FORM. It has already been mentioned that individual variations in tooth form are so characteristic that they can be used as an adjunct for the distinction between mono- and dizygotic twins. I myself have studied two series of American twins observed at the dental schools at the University of Michigan in Ann Arbor and at Columbia University in New York (Lundström 1963). The results of these studies are shown in Table 1. Some puzzling observations, however, were made on asymmetry in tooth form as well as corresponding symmetrical differences between monozygotic twins.

Table 1.   Correspondence between general and tooth morphology zygosity diagnoses in 124 twin pairs

		General diagnosis	
		MZ	DZ
Tooth morphology	MZ	66	1
Diagnosis	DZ	6	51

Plate 1a demonstrates how the second lower premolar has quite a different tooth form for one twin on one side in a pair of male monozygotic twins as compared to the other side in this twin and both sides in the

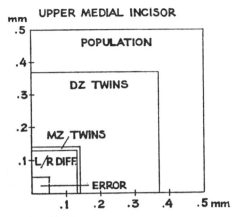

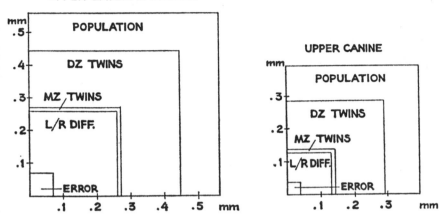

Figure 8. Comparison of variances for different pairs of individuals and double measurements (Lundström 1967).

other. Plate 1b shows a similar bilateral discrepancy between two twins, also diagnosed as monozygotic. The true background for such differences is difficult to assess. Perhaps it is an example of irregular expression for a gene or combination of genes predisposing either for the two- or the three-cusp type of lower premolars (see also Staley and Green 1971).

Another tooth-form variant of interest from a genetical point of view is the peg-tooth as an upper lateral incisor. It has been shown by Grahnén (1956) and Alvesalo and Portin (1969) that this is a kind of expression of the same gene or genes which may also cause missing lateral incisors. Alvesalo and Portin studied the whole population of a comparatively small island, Hilohuoto, in the Baltic in order to determine the inheritance of these two anomalies. They concluded that the different pedigrees best fitted the hypothesis that the same dominant gene or genes caused the

anomalies, but that the penetration was irregular with about 75 percent of the cases having the abnormal gene combination also showing this in the phenotype.

After this rather comprehensive analysis of tooth-size variation I would now like to examine the POSITION OF THE TEETH and OCCLUSION BETWEEN THE UPPER AND LOWER DENTAL ARCHES. I will use the same method, i.e. the twin method, to illustrate the role of genetic factors as I did for the teeth.

Let us start with crowding and spacing of the teeth. Already the fact that crowding is more common in cases with large teeth, and spacing in cases with small teeth, suggests a genetic component in this variation (Lundström 1951, 1959). Such a finding can be explained if some genes with an effect on tooth size are inherited independently of genes that influence arch size. Findings on twins (Lundström 1964a) show, furthermore, that monozygotic twins are more alike in this respect than dizygotic ones (see Figure 9).

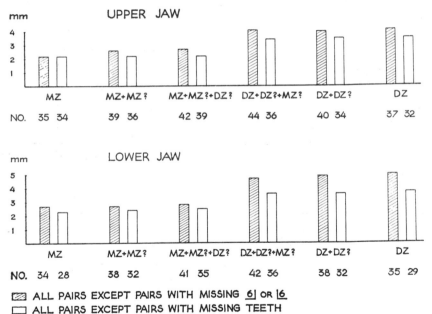

Figure 9.   Comparison of standard deviations for crowding-spacing in different twin pair combinations; MZ? and DZ? means that the zygosity diagnosis was uncertain (Lundström 1964)

As crowding undoubtedly is associated to some extent with environmental factors, it must be discussed whether or not the genes directly, or perhaps indirectly, influence the teeth-arch relationship. If, for instance, the predisposition to extensive caries defects, resulting in early extractions, were genetically determined, this would also lead to closer resemblance between mono- than dizygotic co-twins. A change in the environment, either as a considerable reduction in caries activity or through a systematic early treatment of caries in the deciduous dentition, would then eliminate this kind of secondary genetic influence.

To what extent such secondary influences do play a part is difficult to tell. Available evidence does not indicate that early extraction of deciduous teeth should be of any principal significance in the etiology of crowding. Severe crowding certainly occurs also in cases without early loss of temporary teeth. The association between tooth size and crowding-spacing is, as just mentioned, another finding that is difficult to explain as a consequence of secondary gene effects. My belief is therefore that the greater variation existing between dizygotic, as opposed to monozygotic, co-twins (Lundström 1964a, 1964b) is due primarily to gene differences between the former with a direct bearing on the ontogenetic development of teeth and dental arches.

Regarding the occlusion I will limit my presentation to the antero-posterior relationships. The classic anomaly in this context is, of course, the Hapsburg jaw, the family distribution of which has been demonstrated by several authors. Schulze and Wiese's observations (1965) on the inheritance of the prognathous lower jaw can also be mentioned here.

Humphreys and Leighton (1950) have shown figures indicating a comparatively high incidence of postnormal occlusion among siblings to

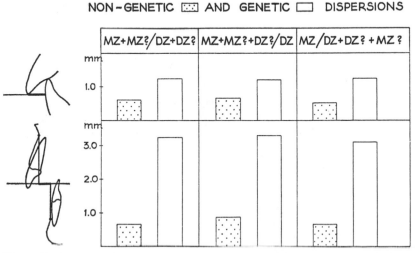

Figure 10. Non-genetic and genetic dispersions for overjet and antero-posterior A-B difference, parallel to occlusal plane

children with the same anomaly. The most probable explanation of this finding would seem to be genetic similarities for genes predisposed to postnormal occlusion, even if family-bound environmental factors theoretically might also be of some significance.

Figure 10 shows twin observations on overjet-overbite and the antero-posterior apical-base relationship. Genetic differences are larger for the horizontal A-B distance than for the overjet which can be regarded as a sign that a small or large A-B distance to some extent tends to be compensated by a suitable incisor inclination.

As with crowding we must ask if genetically conditioned environmental factors may contribute to the results obtained. One factor that can be mentioned in this respect is finger sucking. Figure 11a shows co-twin

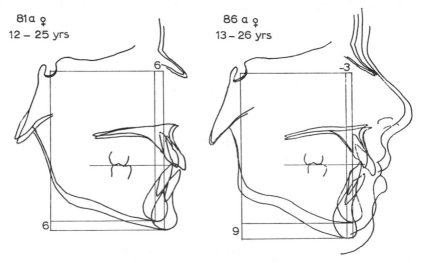

Figure 11a.   Two cases with differences in growth direction for the lowest point of the symphysis in the mandible in relation to the occlusal plane

concordance and discordance for this habit in mono- and dizygotic twins. The differences are larger for the dizygotic than for the monozygotic twins, which is an indication that hereditary factors to some degree are decisive for or against finger sucking.

As finger sucking does not seem to play more than a limited part in the overjet-overbite variation of the young adult it does not seem probable that finger sucking renders any very significant contribution to the difference between the two types of twins. This does not mean, of course, that there are not individual cases with a very prolonged sucking habit that results in severe malocclusion.

Cephalometric measurements are obviously related to antero-posterior

deviations. Twin studies with such a bearing have also been performed
(Hunter 1965; Lundström 1954). An interesting problem in clinical
orthodontics is the growth direction of the maxilla and mandible in
relation to the skull base (Lundström 1969, 1970). As seen in Figure 11a

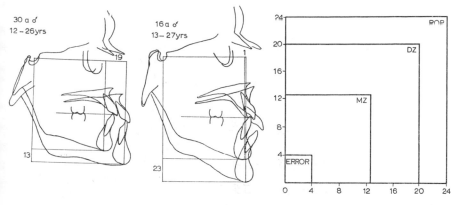

Figure 11b. Variances for the growth direction measured in degrees in different pairs of individuals and double measurements

this direction varies so that some individuals have a more vertical and
others a more horizontal type of growth — horizontal meaning in this
case parallel to the occlusal plane. This type of variable can, of course, be
studied in twins in a corresponding way as was demonstrated for tooth
size. The growth direction was therefore measured from successive profile
radiographs at twelve to fifteen years and at adult age respectively.
Figure 11b shows the result as regards the lowest point of the symphysis of
the mandible. Genetic factors obviously have a noticeable influence in
determining the general growth direction. At the same time nongenetic
factors may modify this direction to a more limited but still significant
extent.

I will now turn to a few more severe congenital anomalies. The first case
I will show is a case of Crouzon's craniofacial dysostosis (Plate 2a, b and
Figure 12). Shiller (1959) observed for this anomaly an autosomal
dominant transmission in four generations with twenty-three affected
members.

I conclude by showing anomalies where the genetic disturbance is
combined with abnormal numbers of chromosomes. The first is Down's
syndrome, in which there is a trisomy or three instead of a pair of
chromosomes for one of the twenty-first or twenty-second chromosomes.
This severe deviation from the normal genetic set-up carries with it many

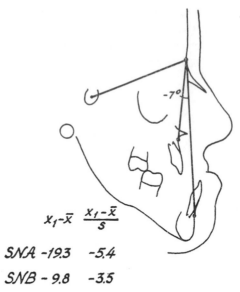

$$x_1 - \bar{x} \qquad \frac{x_1 - \bar{x}}{s}$$

$$SNA \; -19.3 \quad -5.4$$

$$SNB \; - \, 9.8 \quad -3.5$$

Figure 12.   Tracing for a case with craniofacial dysostosis Crouzon

abnormal characteristics, some of which are related to tooth eruption and facial development. Kisling (1966) has studied these deviations on a large scale and Figure 13 is taken from his thesis.

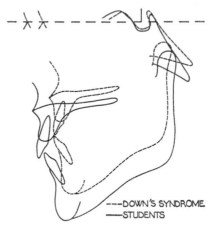

Figure 13.   Comparison of the mean bony facial profile in students and in cases with Down's syndrome (Kisling 1966).

If Down's syndrome is a well-established example of an extra chromosome in relation to the normal number, Turner's syndrome is, of course, characterized by lack of one of the X-chromosomes in the female. Filipsson, Lindsten, and Almquist (1965) have studied the effect of this on skull size and skull form and found significant deviations from the normal as demonstrated in Figure 14 and Plate 3.

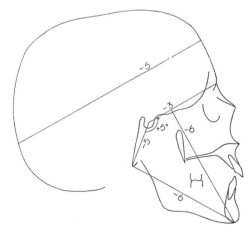

Figure 14. Significant differences between means of measurements on profile roentgenograms (in millimeters and for curvature of skull base in degrees) for normal cases and cases with Turner's syndrome (Filipsson et al. 1965)

REFERENCES

ALVESALO, L.
   1970   "The influence of sex-chromosome genes on tooth size in man." Dissertation, Turku.

ALVESALO, L., P. PORTIN
   1969   The inheritance pattern of missing, peg-shaped, and strongly mesio-distally reduced upper lateral incisors. *Acta Odontologica Scandinavica* 27:6–563.

BOWDEN, D. E. J., D. H. GOOSE
   1969   Inheritance of tooth size in Liverpool families. *Journal of Medical Genetics* 6:55–58.

FILIPSSON, R., J. LINDSTEN, S. ALMQUIST
   1965   Time of eruption of the permanent teeth, cephalometric and tooth measurement and sulphation factor activity in 45 patients with Turner's syndrome with different types of X-chromosome aberrations. *Acta Endocrinologica* 48:91–113.

GARN, S. M., A. B. LEWIS, R. S. KEREWSKY
   1964   Sex difference in tooth size. *Journal of Dental Research* 43:306.
   1965   X-linked inheritance of tooth size. *Journal of Dental Research* 44:439–441.
   1966a The meaning of bilateral asymmetry in the permanent dentition. *Angle Orthodontist* 36:55–62.

1966b Sexual dimorphism in the buccolingual tooth diameter. *Journal of Dental Research* 45:1819.
1967 Sex difference in tooth shape. *Journal of Dental Research* 46:1470.

GARN, S. M., A. B. LEWIS, R. S. KEREWSKY, K. JEGART
1965 Sex differences in intraindividual tooth-size communalities. *Journal of Dental Research* 44:476–479.

GARN, S. M., A. B. LEWIS, D. R. SWINDLER, R. S. KEREWSKY
1967 Genetic control of sexual dimorphism in tooth size. *Journal of Dental Research* 46:963–972.

GOOSE, D. H.
1967 Preliminary study of tooth size in families. *Journal of Dental Research* 46:959–962.

GRAHNÉN, H.
1956 *Hypodontia in the permanent dentition.* Lund: CWK Gleerup.

HOHL, F.
1934 *Die Vererbung der Eckzahngrösse.* Göttingen: A. F. Pieper.

HUMPHREYS, H. F., B. C. LEIGHTON
1950 A survey of anteroposterior abnormalities of the jaws in children between the ages of 2 and $5\frac{1}{2}$ years of age. *British Dental Journal* 88: 3–15.

HUNTER, W. S.
1959 "The inheritance of mesiodistal tooth diameter in twins." Unpublished doctoral dissertation, University of Michigan, Ann Arbor.
1965 A study of the inheritance of craniofacial characteristics as seen in lateral cephalograms of 72 like-sexed twins. *European Orthodontic Society*, pages 59–70.

KISLING, E.
1966 *Cranial morphology in Down's syndrome.* Copenhagen: Munksgaard.

LEWIS, D. W., R. M. GRAINGER
1967 Sex-linked inheritance of tooth size. *Archives of Oral Biology* 12: 539–544.

LUNDSTRÖM, A.
1944 Förtidiga mjölktandsförluster och tandställningen. *Svensk Tandläkare-Tidskrift* 37:698–727.
1948 *Tooth size and occlusion in twins* (second edition). Basel and New York: S. Karger.
1951 The aetiology of crowding of the teeth (based on studies of twins and on morphological investigations) and its bearing on orthodontic treatment (expansion or extraction). *European Orthodontic Society*, pages 176–191.
1959 The importance of genetic and non-genetic factors in the facial skeleton studied in 100 pairs of twins. *European Orthodontic Society*, pages 92–107.
1960 Asymmetries in the number and size of the teeth and their aetiological significance. *European Orthodontic Society*, pages 167–185.
1963 Tooth morphology as a basis for distinguishing monozygotic and dizygotic twins. *American Journal of Human Genetics* 15: 34–43.
1964a Size of teeth and jaws in twins. *British Dental Journal* 117: 321–326.

1964b Crowding of the teeth in twins. *European Orthodontic Society*, pages 470–480.
1967 Genetic aspects of variation in tooth width based on asymmetry and twins studies. *Hereditas* 57:403–410.
1969 Horizontal and vertical growth of the incision superior, incision inferior and menton. *European Orthodontic Society*, pages 125–136.
1970 Method errors in an analysis of the forward and vertical growth of the lower incisors from serial profile radiographs of the head. *Schweizerische Monatsschrift für Zahnheilkunde* 80:527–534.

MARTIN, W.
1934 *Über die Vererbung der Schneidezahngrösse*. Göttingen.

MAYNARD-SMITH, S., L. S. PENROSE, C. A. B. SMITH
1961 *Mathematical tables for research workers in human genetics*. London: J. and A. Churchill.

MOORREES, C. F. A., R. B. REED
1954 Biometrics of crowding and spacing of the teeth in the mandible. *American Journal of Physical Anthropology* 12: 77–88.
1964 Correlations among crown diameters of human teeth. *Archives of Oral Biology* 9: 685–697.

OSBORNE, R. H., S. L. HOROWITZ, F. V. DE GEORGE
1958 Genetic variation in tooth dimensions: a twin study of the permanent anterior teeth. *American Journal of Human Genetics* 10:350–356.

POTTER, R. H. Y., P.-L. YU, A. A. DAHLBERG, A. D. MERRITT, P. M. CONNEALLY
1968 Genetic studies of tooth size factors in Pima Indian families. *American Journal of Human Genetics* 20:89–100.

SCHULZE, C., W. WIESE
1965 Zur Vererbung der Progenie. *Fortschritte der Kieferorthopädie* 26: 213–229.

SEIPEL, C. M.
1946 *Variation of tooth position*. Lund: H. Ohlssons.

SELMER-OLSEN, R.
1949 *An odontometrical study on the Norwegian Lapps*. Oslo: A. W. Brøggers.

SHILLER, J. G.
1959 Craniofacial dysostosis of Crouzon. *Pediatrics* 23: 107–112.

SOFAER, J. A., C. J. MAC LEAN, H. L. BAILIT
1972 Heredity and morphological variation in early and late developing human teeth of the same morphological class. *Archives of Oral Biology* 17:811–816.

STALEY. R. N., L. GREEN
1971 Bilateral asymmetry in tooth cusp occurrence in human monozygotic twins, dizygotic twins, and non-twins. *Journal of Dental Research* 50: 83–89.

VOGEL, F., H.-E. REISER
1960 Zwillingsuntersuchung über die Erblichkeit einiger Zahnbreiten. *Anthropologischer Anzeiger* 24:231–241.

The 47,XYY-Male, Y-Chromosome and Tooth Size: A Preliminary Communication

LASSI ALVESALO, RICHARD H. OSBORNE and
MARKKU KARI

INTRODUCTION

The quantitative differences between male and female phenotypes in humans thus far have been mainly attributed to the differentially balanced hormone production during pre- and postnatal growth. It is therefore presumed that the first step in quantitative differentiation takes place after the qualitative differentiation of gonadal tissues in the male or female direction during the sixth and seventh week of embryogenesis, and after this time, because of the automatic continuation of sex dimorphism in hormonal production, there is no special need for X- or Y-chromosomes to affect the quantitative differentiation of the two sexes. There is, however, some evidence which suggests that the X- and Y-chromosomes do have a further role in quantitative growth and development of bony structures.

In a study of human tooth sizes (Alvesalo 1971), it was concluded on the basis of analysis of male and female cousin groups that the X- and Y-chromosomes carry genes which affect the genetic determination of tooth sizes and that the influence that these chromosomes exert differs in this respect. It was also suggested that the observed metric difference between male and female tooth sizes was related to this different quantitative action of X- and Y-chromosomes. The results of the studies on relatives (Garn and Rohmann 1962) and patients with

We thank Drs. Pertti Aula, Albert de la Chapelle, Jaakko Leisti and Lauri Pelliniemi of Finland and Drs. Richard Daley (Madison, Wisconsin), Herbert Lubs (Denver, Colorado) and Michael Cohen, Jr. and David Smith (Seattle, Washington) for making the patients available.

different sex-chromosome aberrations (Filipsson et al. 1965; Gorlin et al. 1965; Shapiro 1966; Tanner et al. 1959) are strongly suggestive of the possible role of X- and Y-chromosomes on dental and bony maturation and growth. These observations, together with the propitious characteristics of human teeth from the point of view of developmental and quantitative studies, led to the present study of 47,XYY-males.

MATERIAL AND METHODS

For the present study eight individuals with 47,XYY chromosome constitution were examined. Five of them were from Finland and three from different parts of the United States. Each subject was verified as having an extra Y-chromosome. The age range of XYY-individuals was from seven to thirty-one years. The average height of adults was 187 centimeters (based on three observations); one nine-year-old boy was 140 centimeters tall and one seven-year old was 131 centimeters.

The dental study was performed by taking impressions from upper and lower dentitions of each study subject. The dental casts made from the impressions were then used to measure tooth sizes. The measurements were maximum mesiodistal (m–d) and labiolingual (l–l) dimensions, and were made as previously described (Alvesalo 1971) on each available permanent tooth. All measurements of the teeth of the XYY-individuals as well as measurements of the teeth of the Finnish control population were performed by the same investigator. The measurements of the Finnish XYY-males and the Finnish control population of normal males were compared by the t-test. The 47,XYY-males from the United States were not included in the statistical comparison because of the lack of a relevant United States control group, but the means and other statistical indexes were calculated combining the observations with Finnish 47,XYY-males. Generally these XYY-individuals had poor dental hygiene and had suffered a high rate of tooth loss, but there were no signs of any gross morphological abnormalities or defects.

RESULTS

Tables 1–4 give the calculated mean tooth dimensions of the Finnish 47,XYY-males and the control population. The numbers in parentheses are the values of all XYY-males. The number of possible observations of 47,XYY-males was the decisive factor in choosing the side of the jaw for the comparisons.

It is clear from the tables that tooth sizes of 47,XYY-males generally appear to be larger than those of normal control males. From the

Table 1.   Upper jaw – left side (mesiodistal diameter) [a]

47,XYY-males   Control group

Tooth	M	S.D.	n	Total range		M	n	M	n
						Males		Females	
I1	9.5	0.5	5 (5)	8.9– 9.9	**	8.8	148	8.6	118
I2	7.0	0.5	4 (4)	6.3– 7.4		6.8	116	6.6	99
C	8.3	0.5	5 (5)	7.8– 9.0		8.1	103	7.7	91
P1	7.5 (7.5)	0.5 (0.4)	3 (4)	7.0– 8.0	°	7.1	111	7.1	78
P2	7.4 (7.1)	0.2 (0.6)	3 (4)	6.3– 7.6	°	6.8	92	6.7	67
M1	11.7 (11.5)	0.7 (0.6)	2 (3)	11.0–12.2	**	10.2	110	10.1	87
M2	10.6 (10.8)	0.2 (0.5)	2 (3)	10.4–11.3		10.0	66	9.7	39

[a]   Mean tooth sizes of Finnish 47,XYY-males and control group (population of Hailuoto, Finland). The numbers in parentheses indicate the values of all observed 47,XYY-males. The statistically significant or indicative differences between Finnish 47,XYY-males and control males have been noted in the table, if existing. M is mean tooth size in millimeters; S.D. is standard deviation; and n is number of observations. This applies to Tables 1–4.

** $= p < 0.01$
° $= p < 0.1$

Table 2.   Upper jaw – left side (labiolingual diameter)

47,XYY-males   Control group

Tooth	M	S.D.	n	Total range		M	n	M	n
						Males		Females	
I1	8.0	0.4	5 (5)	7.6– 8.5	*	7.5	64	7.3	64
I2	7.0	0.4	4 (4)	6.5– 7.3		6.7	44	6.5	41
C	8.5	0.5	5 (5)	7.9– 9.1		8.7	75	8.2	81
P1	9.8 (9.9)	0.5 (0.6)	4 (5)	9.2–10.6	°	9.4	122	9.2	97
P2	9.6 (9.6)	0.3 (0.3)	4 (5)	9.2– 9.9		9.4	106	9.2	81
M1	12.0	0.2	3 (3)	11.8–12.1	°	11.4	112	11.3	101
M2	11.9 (12.1)	0.3 (0.5)	3 (4)	11.5–12.7		11.6	64	11.2	52

° $= p < 0.1$
* $= p < 0.05$

twenty-six possible comparisons, the means of the 47,XYY's exceed those of the control males twenty-four times. In only two cases is this trend reversed, and both of these involve the labiolingual dimensions

Table 3.   Lower jaw – right side (mesiodistal diameter)

47,XYY-males   Control group

Tooth	$\overline{M}$	S.D.	n	Total range	Males $\overline{M}$	n	Females $\overline{M}$	n
I1	5.7 (5.7)	0.4 (0.4)	5 (6)	5.2– 6.0	5.5	116	5.4	108
I2	6.6 (6.6)	0.4 (0.4)	5 (4)	6.2– 7.2	* 6.1	135	5.9	123
C	7.2	0.3	4 (4)	7.1– 7.7	7.1	131	6.7	121
P1	7.5	0.4	3 (3)	7.1– 7.8	7.2	143	7.1	120
P2	7.9 (8.0)	— (0.1)	1 (2)	7.9– 8.1	7.3	103	7.0	81
M1	12.3	0.2	2 (2)	12.1–12.4	*11.2	91	11.0	66
M2	11.8	0.6	2 (2)	11.4–12.3	*10.7	59	10.4	46

* = p < 0.05

Table 4.   Lower jaw – right side (labiolingual dimension)

47,XYY-males   Control group

Tooth	$\overline{M}$	S.D.	n	Total range	Males $\overline{M}$	n	Females $\overline{M}$	n
I1	6.7	0.5	4 (4)	6.2– 7.2	° 6.2	36	6.0	48
I2	7.3 (7.0)	0.5 (0.5)	4 (5)	6.5– 7.6	* 6.5	38	6.4	54
C	7.7 (7.9)	0.5 (0.6)	5 (6)	7.2– 8.6	8.1	78	7.5	87
P1	8.4 (8.4)	0.5 (0.5)	3 (4)	8.0– 9.0	8.0	138	7.8	122
P2	8.7 (9.1)	— (0.5)	1 (2)	8.7– 9.4	8.6	115	8.3	99
M1	11.5 (11.6)	0.2 (0.3)	3 (4)	11.3–12.0	*10.8	94	10.6	77
M2	11.4	0.4	4 (4)	11.2–12.0	*10.5	58	10.3	46

° = p < 0.1
* = p < 0.05

of the canines. The differences between tooth sizes of the controls and XYY's reach statistical significance (p<0.01 or p<0.05) in nine comparisons and are indicative (p<0.1) in five cases. In all of these the teeth of the 47,XYY-males are larger than the teeth of control males. When the tooth sizes of normal control females are compared to normal control males and to XYY-males, the general impression is that the control female values and the control male values are closer to each other than are the 47,XYY-male and control male values.

DISCUSSION

The possible reasons for the larger tooth sizes of XYY-males will be discussed later in detail, however it seems apparent that in regard to tooth size these 47,XYY-males form an atypical group of individuals.

The crowns of the permanent teeth reach their final size early in postnatal life (Moorrees et al. 1963). Therefore it is possible by the aid of the present results to approach the problem of the timing of excess growth of 47,XYY-individuals in early stages of development. Unfortunately there is no adequate data available concerning the dental maturation in XYY-individuals, and therefore the following timing appraisals are approximations.

The Timing of Excess Growth

The first permanent teeth to achieve their final, mineralized form and size are the first molars (Moorrees et al. 1963). According to different authors, the time of the completion of the crown varies from two to three years of postnatal life. This suggests that no later than three years after birth the excess of growth in this part of the hard tissues of the 47,XYY-males has become apparent and final. The time needed for this excess growth would then be the period between the initiation of tooth crown formation and the completion of the crown, which in the case of first molars would mean the period between the final five to six months of prenatal growth (Scott and Symons 1964; Kraus and Jordan 1965) and the first two to three years of childhood. In fact, from the point of view of dimensional growth being due to the mitotic activity (Kraus and Jordan 1965), the total time needed for the achievement of excess growth could be much shorter. As pointed out previously, however, the application of normal developmental standards to XYY growth may be misleading.

Therefore, it is important to note that two of the present 47,XYY-males (the boys seven and nine years old) showed delayed eruption of their first permanent molars and anteriors, which may also reflect a delayed maturation in other aspects of their dental development.

Disregarding third molars, the last permanent teeth to achieve completed crown size are the second molars. According to population standards this occurs at about the age of six or seven years. Beginning with incisors, all other permanent teeth achieve final crown development during the time the first and second molars complete their crowns. The present results, therefore, strongly suggest that the process of excess growth is not limited in time to a certain critical period in pre- or postnatal life, but is apparently the result of a continuous influence in dental growth and that this influence is not selective as to the different teeth and dimensions. Based on the present results the exception are the canines, which are moderate in size. It is possible that this reflects developmental and genetical independence of these teeth in relation to the other teeth as previously suggested (Osborne et al. 1958).

On the basis of the present results it can be concluded that a factor or factors influencing excess growth of 47,XYY-males are without doubt in effect very early in postnatal life, and are probably in effect during prenatal life. The time period needed for the achievement of final excess growth is relatively short. That the birth heights and weights of XYY-individuals do not seem to differ significantly from normal males (Barlow 1973; Owen 1972) has led to a general view that the growth excess occurs postnatally. The present results, on the other hand, indicate that growth excess in some parts of the body may well have occurred in prenatal life.

The reasons why the teeth of 47,XYY-males are larger than the teeth of normal subjects and the factors that may influence this deviation require further discussion.

The Nature of Excess Growth of 47,XYY-Individuals

There are three likely explanations for 47,XYY-individuals having larger tooth sizes than the average: (1) the teeth of the parents of the 47,XYY-individuals are larger than the average in the population, and also, although the correlation between body height and tooth size is relatively low (Garn et al. 1968), the parents of XYY-individuals would be expected to be tall individuals on the average; (2) the endocrinic function of the 47,XYY-individuals is different from that of normal males and favors growth increase; and (3) there is a specific growth factor in the Y-chromosome, and two Y-chromosomes in the same genome have an additive effect on growth.

The Parental Inheritance

Unfortunately, there were no data available for tooth dimensions or for the heights of the parents or other relatives of the present 47,XYY-males. For the sake of further discussion, it is thus necessary to make an assumption that the tooth sizes of the parents of XYY-males do not differ significantly from the average values in the population they represent. In order to evaluate the correctness of this assumption the following should be taken into consideration.

To explain the fact that on the average the discovered XYY-males are tall men, it has been pointed out that the parents of the 47,XYY-males studied are possibly also relatively tall. However, when the heights of the parents or siblings of 47,XYY-males are compared it has been found that almost invariably the 47,XYY-males were taller than parents and/or siblings (Owen 1972). Also the data that are available indicate that 47,XYY-men do exceed control groups in height and that the differences reach the level of statistical significance (Jacobs et al. 1965; Bartlett et al. 1968; Hook and Kim 1971).

The Endocrine Function

It was evident from Table 1 that tooth size difference between XYY-males and normal males is generally greater than the difference between normal males and normal females. If a difference in hormonal function between males and females is the only causative factor producing sexual dimorphism in tooth size, then the difference in hormonal production and its influence on growth should be greater, in quality and/or quantity, between normal males and XYY-males. Unfortunately there is no information available concerning hormone production of the 47,XYY-males in the very early stages of development which might throw light on the matter. However, reports on hormonal production in XYY-males in later stages of development show that, in spite of exceptionally high or low values, the hormone levels of XYY-males usually are within the normal limits (Owen 1972). The hormones investigated include testosterone, pituitary gonadotropins, follicle stimulating hormones, luteinizing hormone, and growth hormone, and have been studied mainly in adult 47,XYY-males.

The Genetic Influence of the Y-Chromosome

The finding that the Y-chromosome could carry genes affecting tooth size in normal males (Alvesalo 1971) suggests that the extra Y-chromosome in 47,XYY-males could cause the observed size differences between normal and 47,XYY-males. The two Y-chromosomes in the genome may thus act in an additive manner on growth. If there is a specific growth factor on the Y-chromosome, what would be the nature of its effect on growth?

Size increase in the crowns of developing teeth is at first a function of mitotic activity (Kraus and Jordan 1965). As the maturation proceeds, mitosis becomes gradually a less important factor in the growth of the crown (Kraus and Jordan 1965). At a certain stage, increase in size becomes purely a function of enamel apposition over the surface of the crown (Kraus and Jordan 1965). The resemblance of tooth sizes between relatives, as shown in many studies (Alvesalo 1971), may therefore arise from the similarity in the number of mitotic divisions, i.e. the number of cells affecting size of the crown of the tooth. In a study of human tooth sizes (Alvesalo 1971), two male cousin groups were compared. One group consisted of male cousin pairs where members of the pairs had identical Y-chromosomes by descent, but the X-chromosomes were derived randomly from the population. The pairs of the other cousin group had greater than random possibility of having identical X-chromosomes, but the Y-chromosomes came randomly from the population. The results showed that the tooth sizes within the pairs of the former group were more similar than tooth sizes of the latter group. This difference in similarity of tooth sizes may be explained by the effect of similar or dissimilar Y-chromosomes on the cell cycle within the developing tooth.

Although the finding presented here that the eruption of the teeth of 47,XYY-males is delayed is based on two observations, there seems to be an interesting association between final tooth size, the timing of the achievement of final size, i.e. the timing of the formation and maturation of enamel, and the number of Y-chromosomes in the genome: it would appear that the teeth of XYY-males are not only larger but achieve their maturation later than teeth of normal XY-males. Although the mitotic rate of XYY-cell lines may be slower than that of XY's, as suggested by Barlow (1973), it is also possible that the larger tooth sizes of XYY-males over XY-males result from a relatively longer active mitotic period.

Because of the observation presented in this article that excess growth of the teeth of XYY-males may well begin at an early stage of development, i.e. when the mitotic divisions apparently still are contributing to the tooth size increase, we would like to present a tentative hypothesis for the influence of one versus two Y-chromosomes on tooth growth. That is that the effect of the Y-chromosome primarily is on the timing of cell differentiation within the internal enamel epithelium of the developing tooth germ. The role of the Y-chromosome might then be to inhibit differentiation for a time, and the two Y-chromosomes might have an additive inhibitory effect. This would mean that

the cells of the developing XYY-tooth germ begin to differentiate ameloblasts later than the cells of the XY-tooth germ. As a consequence,
it is possible that XYY-cells exercise relatively more mitotic divisions
than XY-cells before they differentiate ameloblasts. This may lead to
the size increase of the XYY-tooth germ over the XY-tooth germ at an
early stage of development, although the tooth germs may not be at an
equivalent maturational stage at the same chronological age.

SUMMARY

For the present study permanent teeth of eight individuals with
47,XYY-chromosome constitution have been examined. The results
showed that the tooth sizes of XYY-males were larger than those of
normal control males or females. In many instances the differences
were statistically significant. With the aid of these results it was possible
to conclude that a factor or factors which influence excess growth of
XYY-males probably are in effect during prenatal life, but without
doubt must have been in effect very early in postnatal life. The time
period needed for the achievement of final excess growth is relatively
short, in the case of first permanent molars probably only from two
and a half to four years. On the basis of the finding that Y-chromosomes could carry genes affecting tooth sizes in normal males (Alvesalo
1971), it was suggested that the extra Y-chromosome could cause the
observed size difference between normal and 47,XYY-males. The nature of the influence of one Y-chromosome versus two Y-chromosomes on growth was discussed in terms of the possible influence of
the Y-chromosome on the cell cycle within the developing tooth germ.

REFERENCES

ALVESALO, L.
    1971   The influence of sex-chromosome genes on tooth size in man.
           Proceedings of the Finnish Dental Society 67:3–54.
BARLOW, P.
    1973   The influence of inactive chromosomes on human development.
           Humangenetik 17:105–136.
BARTLETT, D. J., W. P. HURLEY, C. R. BRAND, E. W. POOLE
    1968   Chromosomes of male patients in a security prison. *Nature* 219:
           351–354.
FILIPSSON, R., J. LINDSTEN, S. ALMQUIST
    1965   Time of eruption of the permanent teeth, cephalometric and
           tooth measurement and sulphation factor activity in 45 patients

with Turner's syndrome with different types of X-chromosome aberration. *Acta Endocrinologica* 48:91–113.

GARN, S. M., A. B. LEWIS, R. S. KEREWSKY
1968   The magnitude and implications of the relationship between tooth size and body size. *Archives of Oral Biology* 13:129–131.

GARN, S. M., C. G. ROHMANN
1962   X-linked inheritance of developmental timing in man. *Nature* 196:695.

GORLIN, R. J., R. S. REDMAN, B. L. SHAPIRO
1965   Effect of X-chromosome aneuploidy on jaw growth. *Journal of Dental Research* 44:269–282.

HOOK, E. G., D. S. KIM
1971   Heights and antisocial behavior in XY and XYY boys. *Science* 172:284–286.

JACOBS, P. A., M. BRUNTON, M. M. MELVILLE, R. P. BRITTAIN, W. E. MCCLEMONT
1965   Aggressive behavior, mental subnormality and the XYY male. *Nature* 208:1351–1352.

KRAUS, B. S., R. J. JORDAN
1965   *The human dentition before birth.* Philadelphia: Lea and Fabiger.

MOORREES, C. F. A., E. A. FANNING, E. E. HUNT, JR.
1963   Age variation of formation stages for ten permanent teeth. *Journal of Dental Research* 42:1490–1502.

OSBORNE, R. H., S. L. HOROWITZ, F. V. DE GEORGE
1958   Genetic variation in tooth dimensions. A twin study of the permanent anterior teeth. *American Journal of Human Genetics* 10: 350–356.

OWEN, D. R.
1972   The 47, XYY male: a review. *Psychological Bulletin* 78:209–233.

SCOTT, J. H., N. B. SYMONS
1964   *Introduction to dental anatomy.* Edinburgh: E. S. Livingstone.

SHAPIRO, B. L.
1966   "Metric studies of normal and reportedly malformed human palates." Unpublished doctoral dissertation, University of Minnesota, Minneapolis.

TANNER, J. M., A. PRADER, H. HABICH, M. A. FERGUSON-SMITH
1959   Genes on the Y-chromosome influencing rate of maturation in man. *Lancet* 2:141–144.

Crown-Size Reduction in Congenital Defects

M. MICHAEL COHEN, BRUCE J. BAUM, STANLEY M. GARN,
CARLOS H. OSORIO, and HERROLD M. NAGY

Crown-size reduction has been shown to be a characteristic of several conditions of prenatal origin. No comparison has been made, however, of the magnitude of tooth-size reduction in congenital disorders nor has it been possible to study these entities according to such data. With the development of simple methods of crown-size profile pattern analysis, it has been possible to compare various culturally and geographically distinct groups according to odontometric data. The application of these methods to the study of developmental anomalies is merely simple extension. Thus, defects of genetic, infectious, and multiple etiology can be examined from a new vantage point.

Several investigators such as Kraus, Clark, and Oka (1968), McMillan and Kashgarian (1961), and Cohen et al. (1970) have studied the occurrence of morphological variants in dental traits within birth-defect groups and the literature abounds with case histories of dental abnormalities associated with congenital malformations. However, Spitzer commented in 1963 that these dental abnormalities must be more than coincidence, and it is to this question that this investigation is directed.

Materials and Methods

Odontometric data was collected on 255 subjects representing five different congenital defects: (1) Down's syndrome, (2) hypodontia, (3) cleft palate, (4) prenatal rubella, and (5) congenital syphilis. All individuals included in this study were of European ancestry. The Down's syndrome sample consisted of 29 males and 45 females from ages 16 to 36 years.

Each individual had a karyotype typical of Trisomy 21 by cytogenitic analysis. The hypodontia group included 32 males and 69 females, 6 to 24 years old. Each individual was mentally and physically normal and had radiographically proven agenesis of one or more permanent teeth. The cleft palate group (38 males and 25 females) ranged in age from 7 to 10 years. Various cleft types (unilateral, bilateral, cleft lip) were pooled together for this study. Medical records revealed the cleft as the major defect in each individual with no other syndromes associated. The prenatal rubella sample consisted of 4 males and 2 females, ages 6 to 26. All were institutionalized, and medical histories indicated a maternal rubella infection during the first trimester of pregnancy. These individuals presented several congenital anomalies, including various levels of mental retardation, cataract formation, deafness, and severe muscle spasticity. The congenital syphilis group included 2 males and 9 females, ages 31 to 69, all institutionalized. Medical records revealed maternal luetic history with a positive serology for each case. All had some degree of mental retardation, however cytogenetic examination revealed normal karyotypes.

Mesiodistal crown dimensions were made on plaster casts of alginate dental impressions following the method of Moorrees et al. (1957). Every raw measurement was converted into a comparable Z-score or standard score, against a reference population consisting of more than 600 individuals (Garn, Lewis, and Walenga 1968a). The magnitude of size reduction observed was expressed as a percentage and ranked in a hierarchical order. Male and female crown-size profile patterns were plotted and compared using the statistic r_T as described in Garn, Lewis, and Walenga (1968b). Intersyndrome comparisons were also made using r_T. This approach, using standard scores, corrected for morphological class and for sex, made possible the pooling of data for all individuals within a syndrome group.

In addition to the simple measures of size and size reduction, the crown-size profile pattern of the mesiodistal tooth-size dimensions was calculated, using Z-scores or standard deviation units in comparison with the reference population (cf. Garn, Lewis, and Walenga 1968b). The crown-size profile patterns for each of the congenital disorders studied were compared to each other, using the pattern profile similar index (r_T), which is effectively the product moment correlation of the paired Z-scored measurements. As with the simple product moment correlation, the magnitude of r_T indicated the degree of similarity, while negative values of r_T indicated that crown-size profile patterns tended to be the reverse of each other.

Results

Taking all the data into consideration, there was good agreement between the amount of size reduction in both sexes. For all five conditions of prenatal origin, the crown-size profile patterns of males and females exhibited various degrees of similarity (Table 1). Correspondence between sexes was highest in Down's syndrome ($r_T = 0.926$) and lowest in hypodontia ($r_T = 0.307$). Clearly, crown-size reduction in the permanent teeth affects both sexes, though an apparent gradient of sex specificity has been indicated; this, given generally smaller crown-size dimensions in the female both in normal individuals and those with various congenital defects.

Table 1. Male-female crown-size pattern similarity

Syndrome	Sex similarity (r_T)
Down's	0.926
Cleft palate	0.767
Prenatal rubella	0.457
Syphilis	0.446
Hypodontia	0.307

The magnitude of size reduction (given as a mean Z-score) and corresponding percentage reduction, for each prenatal defect, are found in Table 2. Greatest dimensional reduction was observed in Down's syndrome and least in the cleft palate syndromes. It is interesting that size

Table 2. Crown-size reduction in defects of prenatal origin

Syndrome	Number	Sex	Crown-size reduction	
			Z-Score	Percent
Down's syndrome	29	Males	−1.25	7.9
	45	Females	−1.45	9.6
	74	Combined	−1.35	8.8
Congenital syphilis	2	Males	−0.97	6.5
	9	Females	−0.81	5.3
	11	Combined	−0.89	5.9
Hypodontia	32	Males	−0.99	6.2
	69	Females	−0.65	4.3
	101	Combined	−0.82	5.3
Prenatal rubella	4	Males	−0.81	4.9
	2	Females	−0.63	4.0
	6	Combined	−0.72	4.5
Cleft palate	38	Males	−0.46	2.7
	25	Females	−0.42	2.7
	63	Combined	−0.44	2.7

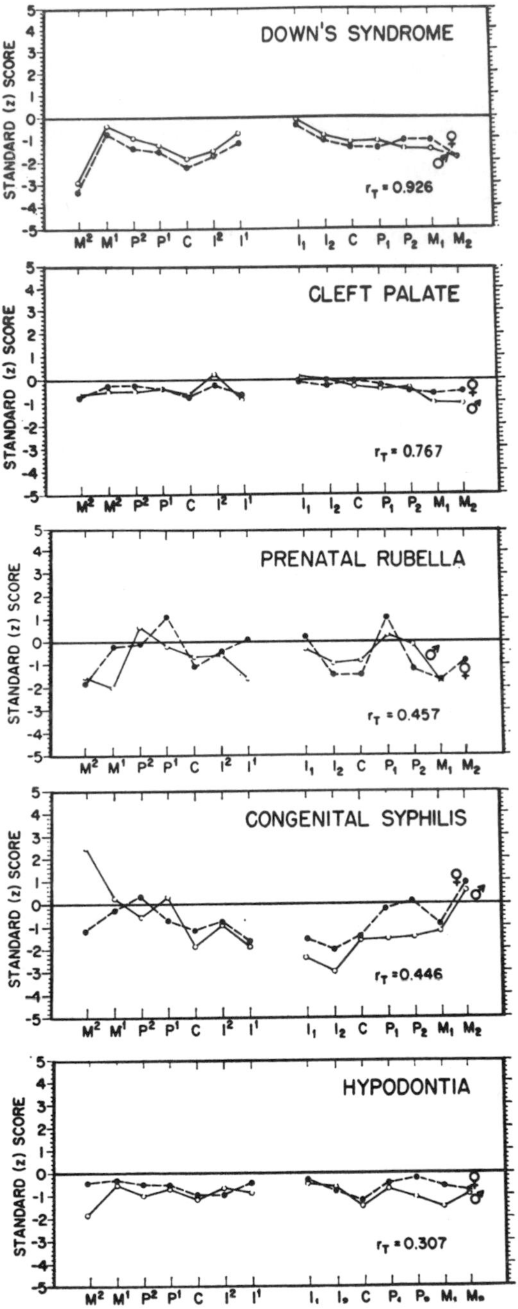

Figure 1. Plots of the crown-size profile patterns for the five syndromes here studied. Male-female pattern similarity is indicated by using the statistic r_T

reduction in both congenital syphilis and prenatal rubella, each on intrauterine infection, is approximately the same. In addition, the crown-size reduction in simple hypodontia is of comparable magnitude.

Analyzing the crown-size reductions by conditions, there were important differences observed in the extent to which individual teeth were affected (Figure 1). In the Down's syndrome group, for example, second molars presented the greatest percent-size reduction in both jaws. Also, mandibular teeth were characterized by an anterior to posterior gradient of increasing size reduction. Individuals with congenital syphilis were observed to have a disproportionate reduction of anterior teeth in both sexes and arches. The prenatal rubella group presented greatest size reduction in the canine and molar areas in both the maxilla and mandible. In the sample with simple or multiple hypodontia the canine was the tooth relatively the most affected in both jaws: a possible artifact deriving from the observation that the most size-reduced teeth of other classes are often those congenitally absent. Cleft palate cases showed as much tendency toward reduction of posterior teeth as of those nearer the area of the cleft. Similarly mandibular teeth were as much size reduced as maxillary teeth involving the jaw characterized by the defect.

The results of crown-size profile pattern comparisons are found in Table 3. In all interactions, excepting those involving congenital syphilis, there was some degree of pattern similarity. Congenital syphilis, rather,

Table 3. Crown-size pattern similarity (r_T) between syndromes

	Down's	Clefts	Rubella	Syphilis
Clefts	0.435	—	—	—
Rubella	0.228	0.343	—	—
Syphilis	–0.345	–0.210	–0.027	—
Hypodontia	0.578	0.217	0.335	–0.052

differed moderately from both Down's syndrome cases ($r_T = -0.345$) and cleft palate cases ($r_T = -0.210$), while correlations with prenatal rubella and hypodontia were effectively 0.0 (Figure 2).

The greatest observed pattern similarity was between Down's syndrome and hypodontia ($r_T = 0.578$) (Figure 3). This, we believe, is most unusual in view of the markedly different nature of these two conditions. While hypodontia, heretofore, has been construed as a relatively simple and innocuous developmental anomaly, Down's syndrome represents a gross chromosomal aberration.

Cleft palate and rubella cases exhibited a moderate degree of pattern similarity ($r_T = 0.343$) as did rubella and agenesis ($r_T = 0.335$) and cleft palate and Down's syndrome ($r_T = 0.435$). Overall, these profile com-

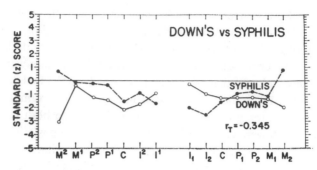

Figure 2.   Plot of crown-size profile pattern of Down's syndrome and congenital syphilis. Similarity index (r_T) indicates moderate difference between these two prenatal defects

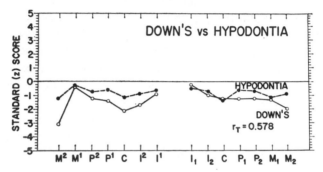

Figure 3.   Plot of crown-size profile pattern of Down's syndrome and hypodontia. A moderately high degree of pattern similarity ($r_T = 0.578$) is observed here

parisons indicated that none of these five conditions were closely related in magnitude and pattern of crown-size reduction, except possibly Down's syndrome and hypodontia.

Summary

Dental traits have long been employed by physical anthropologists and others as an aid to measure genetic distances between population groups, and significant contributions have been made to our knowledge of racial differences through these studies. Using applications of pattern analysis (Garn 1955), it has recently been possible to routinely compare genetic similarities in certain dental characteristics, notably mesiodistal crown-size (Garn, Lewis, and Walenga 1968b). In this investigation, we have attempted to apply these techniques and analytical methods to reexamine five often studied congenital syndromes.

Our findings indicate that a gradient of sex similarity in crown-size profile pattern exists for the five conditions examined here. In addition, a hierarchical order of crown-size reduction in these groups has been noted, as well as several individual syndrome pattern differences.

Of special interest is the independence of congenital syphilis from the other syndromes in crown size pattern. This may offer some clue as to the unique nature of this particular prenatal disease. The same may be mentioned of the pattern similarity between Down's syndrome and hypodontia.

As these studies have demonstrated, the crown-size profile patterns are not only characteristic of particular taxonomic populations, contemporary or fossil, but are also specific for prenatal disorders involving the dentition.

REFERENCES

BAUM, B. J., M. M. COHEN
1971 Agenesis and tooth size in the permanent dentition. *Angle Orthodontist* 41:100–102.

COHEN, M. M., F. J. BLITZER, M. G. ARVYSTAS, R. H. BONNEAU
1970 Abnormalities of the permanent dentition in trisomy G. *Journal of Dental Research* 49:1386–1393.

GARN, S. M.
1955 Applications of pattern analysis to anthropometric data. *Annals of the New York Academy of Science* 63:537–552.

GARN, S. M., A. B. LEWIS
1970 The gradient and the pattern of crown size reduction in simple hypodontia. *Angle Orthodontist* 40:51–57.

GARN, S. M., A. B. LEWIS, A. J. WALENGA
1968a Maximum confidence values for permanent tooth size. *Archives of Oral Biology* 13:841–844.
1968b Crown-size profile pattern comparisons of 14 populations. *Archives of Oral Biology* 13:1235–1242.

GECIAUSKAS, M. A., M. M. COHEN
1970 Mesiodistal crown diameters of permanent teeth in Down's syndrome (mongolism). *American Journal of Mental Deficiency* 74:563–567.

KRAUS, B. S., G. R. CLARK, S. W. OKA
1968 Mental retardation and abnormalities of the dentition. *American Journal of Mental Deficiency* 72:905–917.

MC MILLAN, R. S., M. KASHGARIAN
1961 Relation of human abnormalities of structure and function to abnormalities of the dentition, part one: relation of hypoplasia of enamel to cerebral and ocular disorders. *Journal of American Dental Association* 63:38–48.

MOORREES, C. F. A., S. Ø. THOMSEN, E. JENSEN, P. K. YEN
  1957 Mesiodistal crown diameters of the deciduous and permanent teeth in individuals. *Journal of Dental Research* 36:39–47.
OSORIO, C. H.
  1970 "Variations in the mesiodistal coronal diameter of permanent teeth in individuals with oral clefts." Unpublished Master's thesis, University of Michigan.
SPITZER, R.
  1963 Developmental anomalies in teeth and skulls in mental defectives. *International Dental Journal* 13:678–683.

SECTION FOUR

*Dental Anthropology
and Population Studies*

The Adaptive Significance of Eskimo Craniofacial Morphology

WILLIAM L. HYLANDER

INTRODUCTION

For physical anthropologists, comparative anatomists, and paleontologists, studies of craniofacial form have always been an important source of adaptive and phylogenetic data. Physical anthropologists have also attempted to utilize the skull, particularly the jaws and teeth, as a source of information in determining genetic distances between living and fossil hominid populations. Unfortunately, there has been little interest in investigating the adaptive significance of hominid craniofacial form, particularly among modern human populations. Notable exceptions are Coon et al. (1950), Coon (1962), Wolpoff (1968), Steegman (1970, 1972), Koertvelyessy (1972).

This article is a review of a more detailed study on the adaptive significance of the Eskimo craniofacial region (Hylander 1972), in which the Eskimo skull was compared with the skulls of other human populations, particularly those of American Indians. In addition to traditional craniometric procedures, this analysis also utilizes a roentgenographic craniometric technique. This technique has the advantage of allowing

I wish to thank Dr. Charles F. Merbs, Dr. T. M. Graber, and especially Dr. Albert A. Dahlberg for their help in directing the research on which this article is based. I am also indebted to the Anthropology Department at the University of Kentucky and to the Museo Nacional de Antropología in Mexico City for allowing me to examine, radiograph, and photograph skeletal material in their collections. I would also like to thank my colleague, Dr. Matt Cartmill, for both his invaluable contributions during our many discussions on biomechanics and for his helpful comments on the manuscript. The study from which most of the conclusions presented here are taken (Hylander 1972) was supported by the Hines Fund at the University of Chicago and also by USPHS DE173 Training Grant in physical anthropology.

For Plates, see pp. xxxvii–xxxix, between pp. 330–331.

one to relate important features of the face to endocranial structures and therefore allows one to clarify more easily certain morphological relationships. This analysis also relies heavily on morphological observations of various human populations, in addition to published morphological observations and craniometric data.

Eskimo populations, as pointed out in some of the earlier works on Eskimo cranial morphology (Hrdlička 1910; Furst and Hansen 1915; Hawkes 1916), are often characterized by the following: large spacious orbits, a narrow nasal aperture, reduced nasal bones, increased facial flatness (i.e. large nasomalar and zygomaxillary angles), an enlarged zygomaxillary region, high temporal lines, a robust mandible with a wide, low, and oblique ascending ramus, a shallow mandibular notch, large bicondylar dimensions of the mandible, palatal and mandibular tori, a thick tympanic plate, sagittal keeling, a weakly developed brow, pronounced gonial eversion, and a high incidence of third molar agenesis. In addition, many Eskimo populations are also characterized by a dolichocephalic head form.

Various hypotheses have been advanced to explain the functional significance of both the peculiarities of the Eskimo skull and the soft tissues that are importantly related to it. In general, these theories fall into the following two classes: (1) those theories which suggest that many of the peculiarities of the Eskimo craniofacial region are adaptations to cold, i.e. the Eskimo face (and the face of certain northern Asiatic populations) is especially adapted to withstand the harsh arctic and subarctic climate; and (2) those theories which suggest that many of the peculiarities of the Eskimo craniofacial region are related to their chewing activities. According to this latter notion, some of the characteristic features of the Eskimo skull are adaptations to produce large biting forces while others are tissue responses to these forces. For example, Hrdlička (1910, 1930, 1944) views mandibular and palatal tori as adaptations designed to strengthen the jaws. Furthermore, the dolichocephalic head form of various Eskimo populations, according to Hrdlička, is due to the influence of the hyperactive temporalis muscles on the growth of the expanding brain and neurocranium. In the following section, these two main theories will be briefly reviewed and discussed.

COLD ADAPTATION HYPOTHESIS

In Hrdlikča's first major publication on the craniology of the Eskimo (1910), he suggested that the narrow nasal aperture of the Eskimo was importantly related to the effects of the arctic cold; however, he did not discuss the functional significance of this narrowing. Other workers have noted the apparent correlation between the nasal index (nasal breadth/nasal height × 100) of various human populations and climate. It has been shown that populations from hot moist climates generally have a larger nasal index than populations from cold dry climates (Thomson and Buxton 1923; Davies 1932). The Eskimos fit into this pattern with their rather low nasal index, i.e. their narrow and high nasal skeletal aperture.

The use of the nasal index to characterize nose form has undergone some criticism. Hoyme (1965) and Wolpoff (1968) criticized the use of the index on the grounds that skeletal nasal height, a measurement used in the calculation of the nasal index, is functionally unrelated to nose form. Although nasal breadth is a reasonable approximation of the width of the nasal aperture, the measurement designated as skeletal nasal height is a poor approximation of the height of the nasal aperture. This is because nasion, a point that has little to do with the skeletal nasal aperture, is utilized as one of the landmarks for determining this dimension.

Wolpoff (1968), after suggesting that the nasal breadth dimension is an indicator as to how effectively (or efficiently) inspired air can be warmed and moistened, analyzed nasal breadth measurements in two modern human populations: an Eskimo skeletal population from Alaska and an Australian aboriginal skeletal population from New South Wales. Both of these populations are distributed over a large, climatically variable area. He noted that within the area occupied by the Australians, the climate becomes cooler and dryer as one proceeds from north to south while among the Eskimos the same is true as one proceeds from south to north. In both of these populations, Wolpoff found that the nasal aperture decreased in breadth along this climatic continuum (from the warmer and moister regions toward the colder and dryer regions). He considered this to be good evidence that the nasal skeletal aperture width was responding to climatic conditions (see Hrdlička 1930 for similar comments regarding Alaskan Eskimos).

Other authors (e.g. Coon 1962; Brose and Wolpoff 1971; Steegman 1972) have suggested that some of the characteristic craniofacial features of the Western European Neanderthals are also cold adaptations. Brose and Wolpoff (1971) state that the GREAT nasal breadth of the Neanderthals is one of these cold-adapted features. Thus, BOTH narrow and wide nasal apertures are viewed as cold adaptation.

In a discussion of nose morphology, Coon correctly points out that modern human populations living in cold and/or dry climates generally have a narrow nasal aperture. The Neanderthals, however, have large broad noses. According to Coon, they could not reduce the breadth of the nasal aperture in response to the cold because of the large size of the anterior dentition, i.e. they have large intercanine dimensions. This statement was based on a study that demonstrated a positive correlation between nasal breadth and intercanine breadth (Schwalbe 1887, cited by Coon 1962). Because of this apparent correlation, Coon assumes that nasal breadth dimensional changes can only be accomplished in conjunction with intercanine dimensional changes. Therefore, if there are intense selective forces favoring a large anterior dentition (a large intercanine dimension), a reduction in the width of the nasal aperture cannot be realized. An increase in nasal aperture breadth, without an accompanying increase in intercanine dimensions, could conceivably be limited, i.e. unlimited expansion of the nasal aperture breadth might encroach upon the supporting bone for the roots of the maxillary canines. However, a reduction of the nasal breadth, accomplished simply by bone deposition along the lateral walls of the nasal aperture need not be correlated with any change in intercanine dimensions. Thus, it is difficult to accept Coon's explanation as to why the "cold-adapted" Neanderthals are not characterized by a narrow nasal aperture.

The most famous cold adaptation hypothesis is one advanced by Coon et al. (1950). It deals primarily with the craniofacial region, and suggests that the "Mongoloid" face (not just the Eskimo face) is especially adapted to harsh arctic and subarctic climatic conditions. According to these authors, the principal concern of the occupants of these harsh environments "is to keep from freezing their faces when out of doors" (1950:66). They suggest that the important adaptive changes that have occurred in the face in response to cold stress are the following:

The bony orbit of the mongoloid has been extended vertically, to make room for a heavy fat padding surrounding the eyeball. Brow ridges, with their vulnerable sinuses, are reduced. The nasal skeleton is flush with the corneas, and in extreme cases the eyeballs protrude more than the nasal bridge. The mechanism by which this has been produced is simple. In order to reduce the protrusion of the external nose, the malars had to be extended forward and enlarged. The nose could be moved backward a little way, but not far. Although a wide face permitted a lateral compensation in the size of the nasal resonance chamber, needed for speech, the nasal passage system had to remain deep to heat the air taken in. The only other shift possible was for the malars to move forward; this had the selectively advantageous effect of reducing the effective salient of the nose (1950:69).

Again, in regard to the malars, they note that:

The malars, thus distended, provide a flat surface to the cold; over them are paired fatty pads. The maxillary sinuses are protected likewise. Although the nasal skeleton has been flattened, the nasal passages have not been endangered; in fact, the channels through which the air passes to the lungs are just as long as before, and entirely inside. If an engineer were to sit down with pencil and paper and try to figure out how to make over the face of an undifferentiated human being to meet the world's greatest cold, he could only end up with a blue-print of existing Mongoloid features (1950:71).

Several problems are apparent with this particular hypothesis. Steegman (1970, 1972) has recently demonstrated that the "Mongoloid" face appears to have no special cold adaptation attributes in regard to surface temperatures. In addition, Steegman (1967) rejects the notion that frostbite is a powerful selective force in the arctic, following a survey of arctic frostbite cases.

The notion that fat-padded malars are an adaptation to cold is unconvincing. If one assumes that these facial fat deposits have an insulative function, then the skin overlying the malars (an area supposedly vulnerable to frostbite), would be insulated FROM the warm deeper portions of the face. The significance of malar positioning is also unconvincing. In passing, one might note that if facial flatness, i.e. flaring malars, is an indication of cold adaptation, then Olduvai hominid #5 ("Zinjanthropus") is one of the most cold-adapted hominids known.

Coon (1962), as noted above, has suggested that many of the facial features that characterize Western Neanderthals are also the result of cold adaptation. These hominids have wide protruding noses, weakly developed malars, and are the least flat-faced of all hominid fossils. This combination of facial features is quite unlike the condition found among Eskimos; nevertheless, these facial features are also said to be adaptations to cold.

Large bony orbits are another "Mongoloid" characteristic thought to be related to cold adaptation. Large orbits, lined with thick deposits of fat, are said to insulate the vulnerable eye from the cold (Coon et al. 1950). Unfortunately these authors did not elaborate on this point, so it is not known what structure(s) these fat deposits insulate the eye from. Surely the eye need not be insulated from the brain or from the temporalis muscle. Depending on one's view of the functional significance of facial sinuses, it might be argued that the eye is being insulated from the maxillary sinus, but this is not persuasive.

According to certain authors, facial sinus size is related to cold adaptation (Coon et al. 1950; Coon 1962; Brose and Wolpoff 1971; Steegman 1972; Koertvelyessy 1972); but these authors have presented conflicting interpretations of these structures. Coon et al. (1950) have suggested that the Eskimo's small frontal sinus is an adaptation to cold. On the other hand, because Neanderthals are thought to be cold-adapted, their large frontal sinuses are also thought to be adaptations to cold (Brose and Wolpoff 1971). Among the Neanderthals, the frontal sinus supposedly takes on an insulative function (insulates the brain), while among the Eskimo, the vulnerable frontal sinus must be reduced because of cold stress (Coon et al. 1950). A radiographic biometric analysis of the frontal sinus among various Alaskan Eskimo skeletal populations suggests that the more northerly populations are characterized by a smaller frontal sinus (Koertvelyessy 1972). Because of this clinal distribution, Koert-velyessy suggested that sinus size was responding to climatic factors, although exactly how the frontal sinus functions in response to temperature is clearly not known. Further comments regarding frontal sinus size will be deferred until later.

It should also be noted that it has been hypothesized that during facial cold stress, blood flow to the Eskimo face increases (Coon 1962), but this has not been experimentally verified.

In summary, the craniofacial region of the Eskimo is obviously protected from cold injury by cultural protective adaptations (e.g. clothing and housing). However, physiological and morphological mechanisms are not well established. Nose size and skeletal nasal aperture dimensions in the Eskimo are probably in part related to cold adaptation, as originally suggested by Hrdlička (1910). However, the notion that the Eskimo malars (facial flatness) are a special adaptation for protecting facial parts from frostbite is doubtful. Clearly climate has been an important selective force in shaping the cultural attributes of Eskimo populations. However, the extent to which their biological attributes have been modified by climate are at present unknown.

HARD CHEWING HYPOTHESIS

Hrdlička (1910), Furst and Hansen (1915), and Hawkes (1916) were among the earliest workers to make significant contributions to the craniology of the Eskimo. These workers tended to view many of the morphological features of the Eskimo skull as being related to Eskimo chewing behavior. This hypothesis has been termed the "hard-chewing hypothesis" (Collins 1951). Proponents of this notion have suggested that features of the Eskimo skull, such as robust muscle attachment areas, mandibular and palatal tori, sagittal keeling, a robust mandible, and a thickened tympanic plate are importantly related to the vigorous chewing activities of the Eskimo.

These workers have not, however, adequately explained the functional significance of some of the above morphological features (e.g. the thickened tympanic plate and tori), nor have they recognized the functional significance of such Eskimo features as increased facial flatness or the large gonial angle.

NEW DATA ON THE ESKIMO SKULL

A more detailed account of the results of the biometric analysis employed in this study has been reported elsewhere (Hylander 1972). In addition to confirming many of the morphological characteristics of the Eskimo skull that have already been noted by other investigators, it was found that the Eskimo skull is characterized by a low and robust coronoid process. In addition, certain aspects of facial flatness were clarified. The increased amount of facial flatness in the Eskimo skull is apparently due to a more anteriorly positioned postorbital bar and anterior root of the zygoma, as opposed to a depressed midsagittal region. Therefore, the large nasomalar (upper facial) and zygomaxillary (lower facial) angles in the Eskimo (Woo and Mourant 1934; Oschinsky 1962, 1964) are primarily the result of two factors: the wide face and the anterior positioning of the zygomaxillary complex. A recent study by Howells (1972) furnishes additional evidence of the more anteriorly positioned zygomaxillary complex in the Eskimo skull, substantiating the impressionistic views of earlier workers (e.g. Le Gros Clark 1920).

In the Eskimo skull, the origins of the muscles that elevate the mandible are positioned more anteriorly, relative to both the dentition and to the temporo-mandibular joint (Hylander 1972). This muscular arrangement, which has important biomechanical effects on the masticatory apparatus, will be discussed shortly.

Following the biometric analysis and an extensive review of the cranial morphology, dentition and ethnographic literature of the Eskimo and other human populations, it became apparent that a more parsimonious theory, incorporating portions of the "hard-chewing" hypothesis, might be advanced that would explain many of the characteristic morphological features of the Eskimo craniofacial region. This theory states that the Eskimo craniofacial region is especially adapted for the GENERATION and DISSIPATION of heavy vertical occlusal forces. Before the morphological attributes and the functional significance of the Eskimo skull are discussed, the evidence for the presence of unusually large occlusal forces among the Eskimos will be documented. This evidence comes from three sources: dentition studies, maximum bite-force data, and observations in the field.

DENTITION EVIDENCE

The dental evidence for the presence of unusually large occlusal forces among the Eskimos is supported by the occurrence of the following morphological features of the teeth and jaws: (1) root resorption, (2) fractures and chipping of the dental crowns, and (3) the high occurrence of bony exostoses of the jaws (torus palatinus and torus mandibularis).

It is generally accepted among members of the dental profession that root resorption is caused by both local and systemic factors; however, local factors are considered to be most common. One of the most important of these local factors relates to abnormally large forces acting upon the dentition (Thoma and Goldman 1960; Gorlen and Goldman 1970). Abnormal in this sense refers to (1) unusually large forces, (2) forces that are unfavorably delivered to the teeth, or (3) teeth that cannot withstand normal forces due to a weakened support system.

Orthodontists, in attempting to reposition teeth and influence the growth of the jaws, apply forces to the teeth and jaws with various types of appliances. Frequently, if not always, the application of forces to the teeth causes damage to the apical portion of the roots, resulting in varying amounts of root resorption (Reitan 1969). In carefully managed cases, this damage is usually minimal, and upon removal of the forces, the resorbed region usually spontaneously heals. Root resorption has also been observed in teeth serving as bridge abutments (Glickman 1968). In these instances, essentially normal teeth are carrying a greater proportion of the occlusal load than they ordinarily would. Periodontists have also noted that root resorption frequently results from traumatic occlusion (Orban 1928), i.e. normal occlusal biting forces directed along malpositioned teeth. Ramfjord and Ash (1971) note the frequent occurrence of root resorption among patients suffering from bruxism. These individuals forcibly clench and habitually grind their teeth together, often chipping and fracturing the coronal portion of the tooth, while simultaneously damaging the root and periodontal ligament.

According to Thoma and Goldman (1960), the roots of teeth respond in one of two ways following an increase in the amount of force being applied to them. Many times, the root responds by building up additional layers of cementum (hypercementosis), but once the biting forces have gone beyond certain physiological limits (undefined and probably individually variable), osteoclasts invade the traumatized region and begin to resorb cementum. Eventually, if the offending forces continue, the underlying dentin in this region is also resorbed. The removal of the abnormal forces usually results in a cessation of the above disease process, although a shortened root does not regain its original dimensions (Reitan 1969). In addition to abnormal forces, other local factors can cause root resorption, e.g. chronic infection in the periapical region, eruptive forces from neighboring teeth, cysts, or tumors, etc.

Pedersen (1949), in his excellent monograph on the dentition of the East Greenland Eskimo, noted the frequent occurrence of what he termed secondarily shortened roots, i.e. roots which had undergone root resorption. In addition to describing this condition, he also published photographs and X rays to substantiate the presence of widespread root resorption in this population. This condition was encountered only among nonmolar teeth, and Pedersen noted that the maxillary incisors were the most frequently involved in the resorptive process. In discussing the morphology of the Eskimo roots, Pedersen states, "Such changes (resorption and hypercementosis) are of a nature generally considered pathological, but in the Eskimo they are so widespread that they should rather be considered normal. The apical resorption leads to a decrease in height which is quite often considerable" (1949:199). Pedersen implicated the heavy forces from strenuous mastication as the cause of this resorptive process.

While examining the skeletal remains of a Canadian Thule Eskimo population, it became apparent that many of these individuals had unusually short incisor, canine, and premolar roots. A large number of these teeth obviously had undergone extensive root resorption during life. However, many of the teeth with unusually short roots did not exhibit the surface irregularities and scalloping that is said to be characteristic of teeth undergoing resorption (Thoma and Goldman 1960). These teeth appeared to be normal, except for the diminutive size of their roots.

These short but otherwise seemingly normal roots are possibly roots that have previously been shortened by extensive resorption and have subsequently healed; a new layer of cementum has been deposited over the resorptive lesion, giving the tooth an essentially normal surface appearance. Another possibility for the presence of unusually short but apparently unresorbed roots relates to the developing tooth. Following eruption, the root of the tooth is still incompletely developed, even though the crown is in functional occlusion. Thoma (1950) states that stunting of the developing root can occur if excessive intrusive forces are applied to the tooth. This condition has been produced experimentally by Gottlieb and Orban (1931). Whether these shortened roots are the result of root resorption, a stunting effect from occlusal forces, or are genetically programed as such, there is nevertheless good evidence for the presence of root resorption in this Eskimo population.

Among the East Greenland and Canadian Thule Eskimos, those individuals with pronounced root resorption did not have generalized resorption of all roots, but instead had only a few teeth whose roots were clearly affected, suggesting that the resorption was induced by local factors. According to Pedersen's observations and radiographs, cysts, tumors, or infections do not seem to be associated with the resorbed roots, and the same is true of the Canadian Thule Eskimo population. There is always the remote possibility that systemic factors are the causative agent, although I know of no good evidence to implicate them as initiating the observed processes.

The second major category of morphological evidence for the presence of unusually large occlusal forces among the Eskimo relates to the chipping and fracturing of the coronal portion of the dentition. Leigh (1925a), following an examination of prehistoric Eskimo skeletons from Alaska, Greenland, and Siberia noted the virtual absence of caries, but the frequent occurrence of alveolar abscesses. Out of 324 crania, there were 114 alveolar abscesses in 61 crania. These lesions were usually caused by extensive tooth wear (50.9 percent), or by periodontal disease (39.4 percent). However, 9.7 percent of these lesions were associated with dental crowns that had been fractured. Leigh interpreted the coronal damage as resulting primarily from blows to the face and large biting forces in the jaws of these Alaskan Eskimos. Among Greenland Eskimos, Pedersen (1949) noted the presence of extensive fractures of the dental crowns, and in addition, the presence of "multiple small traumatic lesions of the enamel and dentin" (1949:70). He interpreted these lesions in the same way as he interpreted the presence of root resorption, i.e. as being caused by excessive occlusal forces. Turner and Cadien (1969) report the occurrence of dental chipping among Aleuts, Eskimos, and American Indians. The dental chipping reported by these investigators is probably the same phenomenon as Pedersen's "multiple small traumatic lesions of the enamel and dentin." According to Turner and Cadien, the Eskimos have a much higher frequency of dental chipping (71.9 percent), than do the Aleuts (22.8 percent) or Indians (18.4 percent). Dental chipping is considered by the above authors to be the result of vigorous tooth use.

Pronounced dental attrition among various human populations (including Eskimos) has often been cited as evidence for vigorous masticatory activity. The amount of dental attrition is in part a function of the texture and abrasive content of the food. Pronounced dental attrition, although probably indicating vigorous masticatory activity, is not necessarily correlated with unusually powerful occlusal forces. However, root resorption, dental chipping, and fractured crowns are associated with such forces.

The final category of morphological evidence for documenting the presence of powerful occlusal forces relates to the bony exostoses of the jaws that are so frequently encountered among Eskimo populations. Ramfjord and Ash (1971) have noted that the frequency of occurrence of mandibular and maxillary bony exostoses (tori) is higher among individuals suffering from bruxism. They also note that these exostoses will reappear following their surgical removal if the bruxism condition is not eliminated. This suggests that there is an important relationship between abnormally large occlusal forces and the development of the bony exostoses. Eskimos, as has been noted by many workers, have a rather high occurrence of tori compared to most other human populations (Hrdlička 1910, 1940a; Furst and Hansen 1915; Oschinsky 1964). In addition to the Eskimos, northern European populations living under arctic conditions have high frequencies of tori. The medieval Norse of the Greenland (Fischer-Moller 1942; Broste et al. 1944) and Icelandic settlements (Hooton 1918) were found to have an unusually high occurrence of mandibular and palatal tori. Furthermore, these frequencies were much higher than those of their parent population in Europe (see Hrdlička 1940a). It is also of interest to note a number of Eskimo-like features of the skull of the Europeans of Iceland, i.e. the frequent occurrence of sagittal keeling, thickened tympanic plates, and increased gonial eversion. However, the skulls in general were very similar to Norwegian skulls and were not at all like Eskimo skulls (Hooton 1918). They did not have the flat face, pinched nasal bones, large gonial angle or flaring zygomas, etc., that are characteristic of Eskimo skulls.

Various theories have been advanced to explain the presence of mandibular and palatal tori, but the two notions cited most often are: (1) tori are genetically determined (Furst and Hansen 1915), and (2) they are functionally determined (Hrdlička 1910). Tori have also been considered to be pathological (Mellquist and Sandberg 1939) or caused by chemical irritation (van den Broek 1945). Regarding the two hypotheses which we will consider in this article, an advocate of the "functional" hypothesis would contend that mandibular tori (or palatal tori) arise solely in response to heavy chewing (nongenetic change), while an advocate of the genetic hypothesis would hold that the presence or absence of tori is solely a function of genetic factors.

The genetics of mandibular and palatal tori have been investigated by Moorrees et al. (1957) and Suzuki and Sakai (1960) and although the exact mode of inheritance has not been determined, the familial studies suggest the presence of a genetic component. In addition to the already cited evidence, studies on an Alaskan Eskimo population (Waugh 1930), a Canadian Eskimo population (Mayhall 1970), and a South African Bushman population (Drennan 1937) also point to a functional component in the development of tori. In these studies, it was found that those populations living a more aboriginal way of life had higher frequencies of mandibular tori than those populations living under settlement conditions. These authors have concluded that the aboriginal conditions required more vigorous masticatory action, and that the shift to European foods and settlement conditions resulted in a decrease in the frequency and degree of development of mandibular tori.

In summary, although there appears to be a genetic component in the development of mandibular and palatal tori, these traits appear to be strongly affected by masticatory stress. The common occurrence of fractured and chipped crowns and extensive root resorption among various Eskimo populations is primary evidence for the presence of unusually large occlusal forces being generated in the jaws of these populations, while the high frequencies of mandibular and palatal tori tend to support this interpretation.

BITE FORCE EVIDENCE

In addition to the morphological evidence for the presence of unusually large occlusal forces among the Eskimos, actual biting forces have been measured in some Alaskan Eskimos (Waugh 1937). Maximum biting forces were measured on the first molars of males and females (over 14 years old) and the following results were obtained: for the males, there were 19 between 200 and 250 pounds; 34 were between 250 and 300; 14 were between 300 and 330; 14 were over 330; and the highest was 348 (mean about 287 pounds). For the females, there were 12 between 200 and 250 pounds; 9 were between 250 and 300; 3 were over 300; and the highest was 326 (mean about 267 pounds).

In a modern Scandanavian population, the mean maximum biting force among adult males and females (18 to 31 years old) was 49 kilograms (about 108 pounds) and 43 kilograms (about 95 pounds), respectively (Linderholm and Wennstrom 1970). In a United States university

male population, 108 football players had a mean maximum biting force
of 126 pounds while 108 dental students had an average maximum biting
force of 125 pounds (Brekhaus et al. 1937). Klatsky (1942) reported that
among 100 adult males from the United States, the mean maximum
bite force was about 120 pounds, with the maximum value being about
210 pounds. Among women, the mean value was about 86 pounds, with
a maximum value of 165 pounds.

Maximum bite force data are also available for several Central and
South American Indian populations that presumably are still living to a
large extent on aboriginal diets (Neuman and DiSalvio 1958). Among the
eight populations reported on, the Shipido adults of Peru (males and
females?) had the lowest mean values (135 pounds), while the Aymara
of Peru (Army draftees) had the largest mean values (186 pounds).
The sample sizes were 24 and 51 respectively. Unfortunately individual
maximum values were not reported. To my knowledge, maximum bite
force data are not available for any African, Asian, or North American
Indian populations; therefore, it is premature to conclude that the
largest maximum biting force values are found among the Eskimos.
However, assuming that the results from the various studies are reasonably comparable, the magnitude of the Eskimo values is indeed impressive.
These values are even more impressive in view of the fact that some of the
Eskimos tested were adolescents and therefore their masticatory apparatus
was not completely developed.

ETHNOGRAPHIC EVIDENCE

The ethnographic literature also tends to reinforce the morphological
evidence for the existence of large occlusal forces being generated in the
jaws of the Eskimos. Eskimos have been observed to use their teeth and
jaws vigorously during mastication, skin preparation, and as an all-
purpose plier, vise, or as a "third hand" (de Poncins 1941).

As to mastication, many foods eaten by the Eskimos require powerful
chewing (dried meat, bones, frozen food, etc.). For example, among the
Caribou Eskimos, Rasmussen (1927) notes that during the winter these
people are in such short supply of fuel that they do not ordinarily cook
their food. Consequently, they are forced to eat large quantities of frozen
caribou and fish. Again, in regard to mastication, a vivid description by
de Poncins (1941) of three Eskimo men eating a fifty-pound seal is
worthy of quoting:

They ground their teeth and their jaws cracked as they ate, and they belched ... and still like beasts, they picked up chunks and flung them down in order to put their teeth into other and perhaps more succulent bits. They had long since stopped cutting the meat with their circular knives; their teeth sufficed, and the bones of the seal cracked and splintered in their faces. What those teeth could do, I already know. When the cover of a gasoline drum could not be pried off with the fingers, an Eskimo would take it between his teeth and it would come easily away. When a strap of sealskin freezes hard — and I know of nothing tougher than sealskin — an Eskimo will put it in his mouth and chew it soft again. And those teeth were hardly to be called teeth. Worn down to the gums, they were sunken and unbreakable stumps of bone. If I were to fight with an Eskimo, my greatest fear would be lest he crack my skull with his teeth (1974:71–72).

As de Poncins points out, frozen sealskin becomes extremely hard. Ordinarily, certain articles of clothing, such as the Eskimo male's hunting boots, are made of sealskin, and prior to a day of hunting, the Eskimo wife must resoften these sealskin boots by laboriously chewing them. Dried skins of the walrus and seal must also be softened by chewing, in order to fabricate various types of clothing, dog lines and harnesses, and other important domestic products (Boas 1907; Thalbitzer 1914; Hawkes 1916).

Figure 1 and Plate 1 illustrate the use of the teeth in male hunting activities. Figure 1 demonstrates how a Caribou Eskimo uses his jaws as a vise in shaping a wooden rib for his kayak. Plate 1 is a photograph

Figure 1.   Drawing of a photograph of a Caribou Eskimo shaping a wooden rib for his kayak. (From *The epic of man*, Time-Life 1961; drawing by Dr. Matt Cartmill)

of an Eskimo soapstone carving from the Canadian Arctic, showing an Eskimo hunter using his "third hand" in order to remove a harpooned seal from the water. (To my knowledge, this behavior has not been reported in the ethnographic literature.) De Poncins' mention of the gasoline drum cover (1941), the tightening, untying and holding of lines with the teeth and jaws, and the holding of the bow drill bit between the teeth are but a few of the many functions undertaken by the Eskimo masticatory apparatus (Merbs 1968).

Although tooth-using behavior has generally been ignored by most ethnographers and explorers of the Arctic, enough information has been recorded to establish that powerful jaws and large occlusal forces are an important factor in the Eskimo's successful adaptation to the harsh conditions of the Arctic. What morphological features of the Eskimo masticatory apparatus contribute to this adaptation?

MUSCLES OF MASTICATION

The generation of vertical biting force is brought about primarily by three paired muscles: the masseters, the internal pterygoids, and the temporales. Observations of living Eskimos and the morphology of the muscle attachment areas of the Eskimo skull both demonstrate that these muscles are enormous in Eskimo populations.

The Eskimo skull is characterized by a robust appearance of the lateral pterygoid plates and of the angle of the mandible, in addition to pronounced gonial eversion. It also has an extensive roughened area along the inferior border of the zygomatic arch, terminating anteriorly in an unusually prominent zygomaxillary tuberosity. These features indicate that the masseter and internal pterygoid muscles are well developed in the Eskimo. Hypertrophied masseter muscles are also apparent in photographs of living Eskimos (Birket-Smith 1940; Coon 1965). The large size of the temporalis muscle among Eskimos is evident from its attachment areas on the mandible and cranium. High temporal lines, indicating robust temporalis muscles, are a common occurrence on Eskimo skulls; Hrdlička (1910) reported on a Central Eskimo skull with only seven millimeters separating the left and right superior temporal lines. The high temporal lines of Eskimos become all the more impressive when one considers that many Eskimos are characterized by a neurocranium that is long, narrow and HIGH (Hrdlička 1910; Furst and Hansen 1915). Both the anterior border of the ascending ramus and the coronoid process are robust and well developed, also indicating a large temporalis muscle. The space enclosed by the zygomatic arch along the lateral aspect of the Eskimo skull also reflects temporalis hypertrophy. This space, which is bounded laterally by the medial border of the zygomatic arch and medially by the lateral wall of the neurocranium, is a rough approximation of the cross-sectional area of the temporalis muscle; as Plate 2 shows, it is comparatively very large in Eskimos.

In summary, the Eskimo, because of extremely large muscles of mastication, is capable of generating exceptionally large occlusal forces. Moreover, there are important structural modifications of the Eskimo skull that make this system mechanically more efficient for generating VERTICAL occlusal forces.

TOOTH SIZE AND NUMBER

Although the Eskimos have very large jaws, large masticatory muscles, and robust muscle attachment areas along the skull, their dentition is comparatively small. This is evident in both the modest dental dimensions and the common occurrence of congenitally missing teeth. Hawkes (1916) was impressed by both of these factors, especially the high occurrence of third molar agenesis.

Other workers have also reported on the rather high incidence of third molar agenesis among Eskimo populations. Pedersen (1949) found that 36.6 percent of a modern East Greenland Eskimo population (n = 257) had one or more congenitally missing third molars (20.6 percent of the maxillae and 31.1 percent of the mandibles), while among a modern southwest Greenland Eskimo population (n = 210), 19 percent of the maxillae and 22.9 percent of the mandibles were so affected. Hellman (1928) reported an incidence of 28 percent for third molar agenesis in the Eskimo mandible. Mayhall (1969) examined 121 Eskimo mandibles from the Silimiut site and found an incidence of 20.5 percent for congenitally missing mandibular third molars. Published studies on the incidence of third molar agenesis among other human populations demonstrate that Eskimos have a very high incidence of third molar agenesis. This is particularly evident when Eskimos are compared to other New World populations. At Indian Knoll (a Middle Archaic site in west-central Kentucky), only 12.3 percent of 105 individuals had one or more congenitally missing third molars (8.6 percent of the maxillae and 5.7 percent of the mandibles). Goldstein (1948) reported that the incidence for one or more congenitally missing third molars among prehistoric and protohistoric Texas Indians (n = 173) was 19.5 percent (7.5 percent of the maxillae and 14 percent of the mandibles). Brothwell et al. (1963) utilizing unpublished data and also data from Hellman (1928), reported an incidence of 12.6 percent for third molar agenesis among American Indians (n = 119).

In summary, congenitally missing third molars are rather common among Eskimo populations. In fact, the frequency of congenitally missing teeth in Eskimo populations exceeds the figures for most other human populations analyzed (Brothwell et al. 1963). Furthermore, those teeth which Eskimos do have are similar in size to those of most American Indian and Asiatic populations (Pedersen 1949; Dahlberg, Hylander, and Mayhall, unpublished data), even though other elements of the Eskimo masticatory apparatus are clearly much larger. In brief, an estimate of the amount of tooth material in various human populations, based on size and agenesis data, demonstrates that Eskimos have a rather small dentition relative to the other elements of their masticatory apparatus.

The evolution of tooth size is importantly related to tooth wear. Among populations adapting to an extremely high attrition environment, there would be selection for a large amount of tooth material, while in a low attrition environment, these forces would tend to be relaxed. Although most discussions of Eskimo cranial and dental morphology direct attention to the presence of unusually large amounts of dental attrition, many of the investigators use European or European-derived modern populations as their frame of reference. Since these populations generally exhibit abnormally low attrition rates, it is misleading to compare them with Eskimo populations. Comparison of attrition rates in various non-Eskimo New World populations shows that the amount of dental attrition among some American Indian populations is far greater than that seen among the Eskimos.

The observed amount of dental attrition in a given population is a function of several factors (age at death, diet, etc.). Although the Eskimos examined here (a Canadian Thule population) did exhibit a considerable amount of dental attrition, the rate of attrition was markedly less than in many American Indian populations. Exposure of the dental pulp by attrition occurred only occasionally among the Eskimos, whereas this occurrence was extremely common among several Mesoamerican and North American extinct populations. Goldstein (1948), comparing attrition rates of Texas Indians and Eskimos, noted the same differences between his samples.

These lower rates of attrition among the Eskimos probably relate to several factors, one of which is the nature of their diet. The Eskimo diet is composed of high-energy food. Therefore it is unnecessary to process excessively large amounts of food per day. Although eating frozen meat and crunching bones might necessitate a powerful bite, attrition rates associated with this diet would be less than with a diet consisting of low energy food items with relatively large amounts of abrasives.

In summary, it is evident that certain American Indian populations have higher rates of attrition than Eskimo populations. Unlike the Eskimos, American Indian populations were adapting to a greater variety of environments, some of which were associated with conditions causing high attrition. Under such conditions, dental reduction (tooth size and agenesis) would be selected against. By contrast, the lower rates of attrition and high frequencies of third molar agenesis among Eskimo populations suggest that selective pressures favoring large tooth size have been relaxed.

JAW MECHANICS

Several models have been used in analyzing the mechanics of the mammalian jaw. The mammalian jaw apparatus has generally been viewed as operating as a lever system (Cuvier 1805; Ryder 1878; Gysi 1921; Carlsoo 1952; Smith and Savage 1959; Moss 1960; Crompton and Hiiemae 1969; Turnbull 1970; Barbenel 1972; and many others). Others, however, have considered this view erroneous (Wilson 1920, 1921; Robinson 1946; Moyers 1950; Gingerich 1971; and Tattersall 1973). This latter group, i.e. those workers who deny that the mandible ordinarily acts as a lever, are in error in certain fundamental respects. These errors are discussed elsewhere (Hylander 1975). The position taken here is that the mandible functions as a lever during biting.

When the masticatory apparatus is viewed in the lateral projection, it is evident that its mechanical efficiency can be improved by moving the masticatory muscles' resultant line of action away from the mandibular condyle (increasing the power or moment arm of the mandibular lever), or by moving the teeth backward toward the mandibular condyle (decreasing the load arm), or both. The masticatory apparatus should also be analyzed in the frontal projection, in addition to the lateral projection. This is particularly important during powerful unilateral molar biting because the bite point is located quite far from the midsagittal plane. The electromyographic data (Moller 1966) suggest that during powerful unilateral biting, the combined muscle force in the frontal projection is shifted slightly to the working (biting) side of the jaw. Therefore, when viewed in the frontal projection (Figure 2), the combined muscle force is seen to be between the bite point and the balancing (nonbiting side) mandibular condyle. In this projection, in order for this system to be in equilibrium during unilateral molar biting, a reaction force must be acting on the balancing mandibular condyle. This model explains why during unilateral molar biting, individuals with a pathological (painful) temporomandibular joint bite on the side of the diseased joint (Ramfjord and Ash 1971). When the diseased joint is on the balancing side during unilateral molar and premolar biting, pain is experienced on that side because the reaction forces are larger on the balancing side than on the working (biting) side.

Looking at the skull in the frontal projection suggests several ways that the masticatory system can be made mechanically more efficient during unilateral biting. One way would be to simply narrow the dental arch. This has the effect of bringing the bite point closer to the muscle force resultant. Another way would be to increase the bicondylar breadth. This, like the narrow arch, has the effect of shifting the load arm/power arm ratio towards a mechanically more advantageous value. Hrdlička (1910) noted that the Eskimo mandible is characterized by an enormous bicondylar dimension. During hard unilateral molar biting with bilateral masticatory muscle activity (see Figure 2), the enlarged bicondylar dimension in the Eskimo results in a shift in the ratio of the power to the load arm and thus a mechanically more advantageous condition.

Increased facial flatness is one of the most distinctive characteristics of the Eskimo face. Woo and Mourant (1934) have reported that Eskimos have the flattest faces among all modern human populations, as measured by the nasomalar and zygomaxillary angles. Facial flattening, as previously mentioned, is thought by some to be related to cold adaptation; however, Coon (1962) has also suggested that increased facial flatness

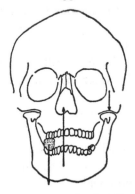

Figure 2.   Jaw mechanics in the frontal projection. During powerful unilateral molar biting, the combined muscle force is located between the bite point and the balancing mandibular condyle. In order for this system to be in equilibrium, a reaction force must be acting on the balancing condyle (in addition to a bite force acting on the active or working side of the mandible)

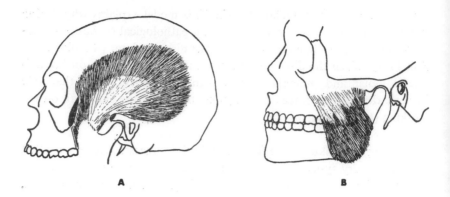

Figure 3.   Relationship between the temporalis muscle and the postorbital bar (A), and the masseter muscle and the anterior root of the zygomatic arch (B)

among "Mongoloids" (when compared to "Caucasoids") is also related to a more anterior positioning of the temporalis and masseter muscles. In addition, Washburn (1963) has noted that the flat facial appearance of certain Asiatic populations is possibly related to the nature of the masseter muscle. These workers did not offer a biomechanical interpretation of these traits. As previously discussed, the increased upper facial flatness (an increased nasomalar angle) among Eskimo populations is primarily related to a more anteriorly positioned postorbital bar. As seen in Figure 3(A), repositioning the postorbital bar anteriorly also positions the temporalis more anteriorly. Coupled with this morphological alteration is the very wide mandibular ramus of the Eskimo. Hrdlička (1940b, 1940c) found that the Eskimos have the widest ascending mandibular ramus of any human population examined. Since the temporalis muscle attaches to the coronoid process and the anterior border of the ascending mandibular ramus, the farther the temporalis muscle is positioned anteriorly along the cranium, and the wider the ramus, the larger the moment arm of the temporalis muscle.

Various workers have noted that the Eskimo mandible is characterized by having a rather shallow mandibular notch. Actually, the appearance of a shallow notch is due to a low, strongly developed, coronoid process (Plate 3). The strong development of the coronoid process is related to a very stout temporalis tendon, while its low position in effect reorients the temporalis muscle and tendon more vertically. The more vertical reorientation of the Eskimo's temporalis muscle probably reduces the strength of forceful retrusive mandibular movements, unless there is a compensatory enlargement of the digastric muscles. However, the more vertically positioned muscle fibers would yield a temporalis resultant with a greater vertical component.

Increased lower facial flatness (increased zygomaxillary angle) among the Eskimos is primarily due to a wider face, a more anterior positioning of the anterior root of the zygoma and an anterior shift of the zygomaxillary tuberosity. The last two morphological features, in addition to the wide mandibular ramus, point to a powerful, more anteriorly positioned masseter muscle (see Figure 3B). This masseteric repositioning, like that of the positioning of the temporalis muscle, increases the mechanical efficiency of the Eskimo masticatory system by increasing the moment arm of the masseter muscle.

In Plate 2, a line has been fitted to the anterior termination of the superficial masseter attachment area. In the non-Eskimo specimen the line passes through the distal portion of M^1, while in the Eskimo it passes through the mesial portion of M^1 and also through the alveolus of P^4. This was a consistent finding, suggesting that relative to the dentition the anterior portion of the superficial masseter muscle is more anteriorly positioned among the Eskimos.

The relative position of the internal pterygoid was not recorded; however, among Eskimos, the temporomandibular joint is shifted posteriorly relative to the pituitary fossa (Hylander 1972). In terms of jaw mechanics, a more posteriorly positioned temporomandibular joint causes the ratio of the load arm to the power arm to be shifted to a mechanically more advantageous condition.

In summary, compared to other human populations, the Eskimo masticatory apparatus is mechanically more efficient in generating vertical occlusal forces. In addition, extremely large masticatory muscles are associated with this masticatory system. The amount of force generated in the Eskimo face is importantly related to these two factors. In order for the face to maintain a state of equilibrium during powerful biting, it must be structurally adapted to withstand and dissipate these forces effectively.

DISSIPATION OF VERTICAL OCCLUSAL FORCES

Dentition

This study and other, unpublished, investigations (Hylander 1972; Dahlberg, unpublished data) indicate that relative to the size of the dentition, the incisors of the Eskimo appear to be unusually vertical in orientation. If Eskimo incisors are more vertically positioned, this has important functional significance. In general, maxillary incisors in human populations are unfavorably inclined relative to vertically directed biting forces. Maxillary incisor root morphology and the nature of the distribution of the periodontal ligament along this root are adaptations to combat this unfavorable inclination. In order to counter a vertically directed biting force, the lingual surface area of the maxillary incisor root is larger than the labial surface, allowing the great majority of the fibers of the periodontal ligament to be concentrated along this larger lingual surface.

Biting forces are more efficiently transferred from tooth to alveolar bone when the forces are transmitted along the long axis of the tooth (Kronfeld 1931). A force directed along the long axis of the tooth engages more of the periodontal ligament and thus brings more of the fibers of the periodontal ligament under tensile stress. Therefore, the more vertically positioned Eskimo incisors can be viewed as an adaptation to distribute a vertical bite force along the maximum number of periodontal ligament fibers. Despite this adaptation, many of the Eskimos examined still exhibited root resorption, presumably because the tensile strength of the suspensory apparatus of the tooth was exceeded.

Eskimos also have extremely high frequencies of three-rooted mandibular molars (Turner 1971). Possibly this is also an adaptation to excessive biting forces, since the extra root allows an increase in the number of periodontal ligament fibers that attach the tooth to the alveolar process.

Mandibular and Palatal Tori

The functional significance of mandibular and palatal tori is a much debated topic. Many investigators have suggested that in some human populations, the high incidence of tori is significantly related to arctic environmental conditions. Although these workers are not always explicit, they have usually implicated skin-chewing activities or the nature of the Eskimo diet as causative factors (Hrdlička 1910, 1940a; Furst and Hansen 1915; Hawkes 1916; Hooton 1918; Cameron 1923; Ritchie 1923; Jorgensen 1953; Mayhall 1970).

Most of these workers have suggested that the tori act as buttresses in order to strengthen the jaw. In addition, they view the excessive biting forces in the Eskimo as being responsible (at least in part) for the formation of mandibular and palatal tori. Hrdlička (1910:211) states the following in regard to mandibular tori:

This physiological hyperostosis presents a more or less irregular surface and is undoubtedly of functional origin, the result of extraordinary pressure along the line of teeth most concerned in chewing, yet its occurrence in infant skulls indicates that at least to some extent the feature is already hereditary in these Eskimos.

Hooton (1918 : 55) has a similar interpretation. While discussing masticatory pressure, he states that:

The pressure toward the median line necessitates the lingual reinforcement of the mandibular torus in cases where the natural strength of the alveolar processes and of the mandibular arch is not sufficient to withstand the strain directed medially in mastication. In many primitive races with massive masticatory apparatus which is subjected to hard usage, the mandibular torus is entirely lacking or very rare. This, I take, is because the natural strength of the mandible is adequate without reinforcement.

The Eskimo, as has frequently been observed, makes an altogether abnormal demand upon his masticatory apparatus, not only by his diet, but also, in the case of the women, by chewing leather, and, in the case of the men, by using the teeth in tying knots, etc. Therefore, although the Eskimo jaw is naturally strong and massive, the additional reinforcement of the mandibular torus is required. This torus is doubly necessary in the case of the Icelander, who belonging to the Nordic race, has the reduced jaws characteristic of civilized European peoples, and yet makes the demands on his masticatory apparatus that a fish and flesh diet in a sub-arctic climate entails.

The position taken by Hrdlička and Hooton has been extensively criticized, especially by Ritchie (1923:65c). Ritchie criticized Hrdlička on the grounds that he "advances no facts in support of his statement and consequently one may consider it as merely a plausible guess."

Moreover, Ritchie questioned why, if tori were responding to excessive chewing pressure, they were more developed in the premolar region, instead of the molar region where the greater biting forces occur. As an alternative hypothesis, Ritchie suggested that

... when the jaws are forcibly closed, the horizontal rami are under a "torsional stress" which tends to evert the lower and invert the upper margin of the bone. This effect is greatest in the premolar region and since the alveolar ridge is weakened by the sockets of the teeth, a compensatory growth of bone is provided on the lingual alveolar wall in an effort to counteract the action of the powerful muscles involved.

In general, the various hypotheses which suggest that mandibular tori are a bony response to buttress the jaws can be divided into basically two positions. The first (Hrdlička 1910) states that tori are reinforcing the alveolar process against excessive biting forces from the adjacent teeth. The second (Ritchie 1923) states that tori are countering torsion in the mandible. Hrdlička would contend that a mandibular torus in the P_3 region is responding to masticatory forces being transferred from P_3 (with lesser contributions from C and P_4) to the alveolar bone. Ritchie would see the same torus as reinforcing the mandibular body when under torsion from biting and muscle forces.

During forceful unilateral biting and simultaneous movement of the mandible toward the midline, the mandibular cheek teeth are tilted buccally, placing the periodontal fibers along the gingival half of the lingual root surface under tension (see Figure 4). Muhleman (1954) has experimentally demonstrated that when force is applied to a tooth, the tension side of the alveolus distorts. Mandibular tori might then be viewed as bars of bone adapted to resist bending moments along the lingual plate of the alveolar bone during forceful unilateral grinding movements.

Ritchie's notion that mandibular tori are adaptations to counter a hypothetical torsion in the body of the mandible is unconvincing. Since the supposed "torsional stress" hypothesized by Ritchie would tend to separate the left and right sides of the mandible at the symphysis, buttressing of the mandibular symphysis would be highly advantageous in countering this force. However, the bony torus does not extend into the symphyseal region.

During forceful biting, particularly in the anterior region, large vertical bending moments are acting on the mandibular body (Figure 5). Possibly tori function is assisting the mandibular body in countering these large

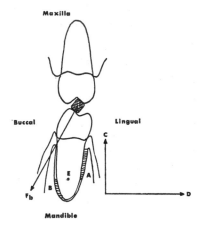

Figure 4.   The active or working side of the mandible during unilateral biting. The mandible is moving in the direction of C and D. Fb represents the bite force acting on a postcanine tooth. Fibers A and B of the periodontal ligament are under tension. The fibers in A probably distort the thin lingual plate of alveolar bone (Muhleman 1954). E represents the axis of rotation of the tooth

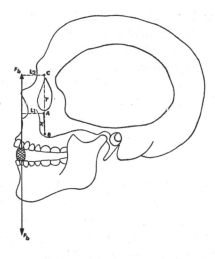

Figure 5.   Dissipating bending moments in the face. Bending moments acting on the face are more efficiently countered by increasing the length of x or y. Decreasing the length of L_1 and L_2 reduces the magnitude of the bending moment. F_b equals the bite force

bending moments by increasing its second moment of area of the cross section. However, a much more efficient way to counter such bending moments would be to deposit compact bone along the inferior border of the mandible in order to increase the vertical height of the mandibular body. This would be a more economical way to increase the second moment of area of the cross section (see Alexander 1968).

As previously discussed, population studies have indicated that an increase or decrease in masticatory activity can modify the expression of tori, indicating that the functional activity of the masticatory apparatus is an important factor in determining their final form. However, once tori have been formed, it is not known if increased function is required to maintain their presence. A photograph of a female Eskimo mandible from Kodiak Island (USNM, #374611) published by Hrdlička (1940a) is worthy of comment here. This female lost all her posterior teeth during life and the alveolar ridge appears to be well healed. However, in spite of the tooth loss, the large well-developed bilateral mandibular tori in the molar and premolar region persist. This photo might be used to support the position that mandibular tori are responding to large bending moments generated in the face, and thus are not dependent on the presence of direct biting forces from the posterior teeth for their continuing presence.

The suggestions advanced here regarding the functional significance of mandibular tori remain speculative. There is always the distinct possibility that tori do not function in reinforcing the jaws against excessive biting forces. However, the association of tori and arctic life (and also with bruxism) is indeed impressive, and it is evident that tori, at least in part, are a bony response to large occlusal forces, although the resulting bony exostoses might be of no functional significance to the jaws.

Mandibular Height

Hrdlička (1940b) biometrically analyzed the human mandible in various European, African, Asiatic, American Indian, Eskimo, and Aleut populations. Two of his measurements are of particular interest: the height of the mandible at the symphysis and the height of the mandible in the molar region. Of the many populations analyzed, the Eskimos have the largest mean values for symphyseal height, except for one American Indian population from the Yukon which has slightly larger values. For the vertical height of the mandible in the M_2 region, an Eskimo population from Kodiak Island has particularly large dimensions. Only one non-Eskimo population (an American Indian population from Florida) has larger values for this dimension. In general, Eskimo mean values for these two dimensions exceed those of most other human populations.

The strength of the body of the mandible is importantly related to its cross-sectional area and its second moment of area of the cross section. These can be increased by either increasing its vertical or medio-lateral dimensions. In order to withstand large vertical bending moments during forceful biting (Figure 5), a unit increase in the vertical dimension is mechanically more advantageous than the same unit increase in the medio-lateral dimension. Although medio-lateral dimensions were not determined, it is clear that the vertical dimensions of the Eskimo mandible are enlarged, indicating that the Eskimo mandible is adapted to withstand large vertical bending moments.

During unilateral biting or clenching, the mandibular symphysis transmits muscle force from the balancing to the working (biting) side of the jaw. This type of biting results in a tendency for the two halves of the mandible to shear against one another. An enlarged symphysis, as found in the Eskimo jaw, is obviously better adapted to withstand these shearing forces that are acting on it.

According to Hrdlička (1940b), although the Eskimos are characterized by large vertical dimensions in the M_2 and symphyseal regions, the distinguishing feature of the Eskimo mandible is that the symphyseal height is greater than the height at M_2. Because of this differential increase in the symphyseal height, the mean gonial angle of the Eskimo is unusually large (Plate 3).

Prognathism

According to Hrdlička (1930), the Eskimos have the largest faces among all modern human populations. Although the Eskimo face is exceptionally high and broad, prognathism is slight, particularly in the maxilla. The relative lack of prognathism among Eskimos has been noted by Furst and Hansen (1915) and Birket-Smith (1940). A comparison of published prognathic values from Australian aborigines (Craven 1958; Brown 1965), Swedes (Björk 1947; Björk and Palling 1954), Japanese (Kayukawa 1957), Bantu (Björk 1950), Aztecs and the skeletal population at Indian Knoll (Hylander 1972), and Chinese (Wei 1968) demonstrates that Eskimos are characterized by low prognathic values. In human populations, large faces tend to be more prognathic than small faces. Although the Eskimos have enormous faces, they have prognathic values that are similar to those of the Swedes, a population that is characterized by a considerable amount of tooth and jaw reduction.

Due to the presumed direction of the biting force, unfavorable bending moments are acting on the face. A reduction in the amount of prognathism would reduce the distance between the bite force and points A, B, and C in Figure 5. Reducing this distance in effect reduces the bending moment acting on these points. Therefore, the low prognathism typical of Eskimos is viewed here as an adaptation to reduce the bending moments acting on the facial skeleton, in order to more effectively dissipate the excessively large biting forces in the anterior region of the Eskimo skull.

It was previously noted that Eskimo populations are characterized by high frequencies of congenitally missing third molars. Possibly this reduction in the number of teeth is related to reducing the amount of prognathism.

Nasal Bones and Nasal Aperture

The Eskimo skull is characterized by having a narrow nasal aperture and reduced nasal bones (Plate 5). Woo and Mourant (1934), in a biometric study of eighty-three human populations from Europe, Africa, Asia,

Oceania, and the New World, found that the Eskimos have the SMALLEST mean values for minimum breadth of the nasal bones. Hrdlička (1910), in his earliest major publication on Eskimo osteology, found that, although the nasal bones of the Eskimo were markedly reduced, there did not appear to be a corresponding reduction in the interorbital breadth. This finding is confirmed by published interorbital breadth dimensions. The interorbital breadth among Eskimos is virtually identical to that which we find in other human populations. It follows, therefore, that the nasal processes of the maxillae in the Eskimo must be enlarged. Hrdlička (1910) suggested that the reduction of the Eskimo nasal bones is a climatic adaptation to extreme cold. However, he felt that the enlarged nasal processes of the maxillae were in no small part due to the extraordinary use of the Eskimo's jaws, and should be viewed as strengthening the jaws. This observation and interpretation regarding the nasal bones and the nasal processes of the maxillae have largely been ignored.

Recent experimental work on the human skull (Endo 1970) has demonstrated that during biting, particularly anterior biting, the nasal processes of the maxillae are carrying large compressive forces to the nasal process of the frontal bone, while the nasal bones are carrying negligible amounts of bite force. This supports Hrdlička's (1910) proposal that nasal bone reduction and enlargement of the nasal processes of the maxillae is an adaptation to transfer biting forces from the jaws to the neurocranium. The medial enlargement of the nasal processes of the maxilla increases the cross-sectional area of this buttress, enabling it to carry larger compressive forces and to counter larger bending moments in the face.

Modifications in the morphology of the interorbital region, presumably due to biting forces, also characterize certain leaf-eating primates. In *Alouatta, Propithecus*, and colobines, the interorbital region is enlarged. This enlargement is presumably an adaptive response to heavy masticatory stress, due to their relatively tough fibrous diet. This enlargement does not, however, imply that large biting forces are being generated primarily in the anterior dentition (as they probably are in Eskimos); Endo (1966) has shown that the nasal processes are also stressed considerably during premolar biting.

The narrow nasal aperture of the Eskimo has traditionally been viewed as an adaptation to extreme cold. However, reducing the width of the nasal aperture, i.e. depositing bone along the lateral borders of the nasal aperture, has the effect of increasing the cross-sectional area of this stress-bearing portion of the maxilla (assuming that the maxillary sinus is not undergoing compensatory enlargement). Therefore, even if the reduced nasal aperture of the Eskimo is an adaptation to extreme cold, a secondary effect of this width reduction is the strengthening of that part of the maxilla which, during anterior biting, transmits considerable amounts of bite force.

Although not directly related to the problem at hand, comments by Hunt (1960) regarding the size of nasal apertures in human populations need a brief reexamination here. Hunt suggested that the Australian aborigines have a wide nasal aperture because vigorous chewing has retarded vertical growth of the face while lateral growth has been encouraged, whereas different chewing habits in modern European or European-derived populations have retarded lateral growth while encouraging vertical growth of the face. If Hunt had substituted Eskimo populations for Australian populations, he would have come to precisely the opposite conclusion; the vigorous chewing among the Eskimos correlates with a narrow nasal aperture and accentuated vertical growth of the face. Population differences in facial morphology clearly reflect more than ontogenetic changes due to altered chewing habits.

Vertical Facial Dimensions

As noted by various investigators, Eskimos are characterized by rather large vertical facial dimensions (Hylander 1972), including the height of the anterior root of the zygoma (see Plates 4 and 5). The functional significance of the enlarged anterior root of the zygoma among Eskimos probably relates to bending moments in the face. Cartmill (1974) has suggested that the role of the enlarged vertical dimensions of the anterior root of the zygoma in *Daubentonia* is to counter bending moments in the face during incisal gnawing. In addition to the enlarged anterior root of the Eskimo zygoma, this notion would also apply to the overall enlarged vertical facial height dimensions of the Eskimo. During anterior biting, bending moments will be acting on the entire face, including the anterior root of the zygoma. In Figure 5, let A, B, and C represent different portions of the face that are being bent. The moment arm of the bite force around A or B is L_1, while the moment arm around C is L_2. If the face is viewed as a bony beam that is being bent, there are several ways to more efficiently dissipate biting forces in the above system. One way is to reduce the amount of prognathism (as previously discussed). The other way is to reposition the anterior root of the zygoma more anteriorly. Both of these structural modifications reduce bending moments in the face, i.e. they reduce the length of L_1 or L_2. Increasing the vertical dimensions of the face assists in countering the bending moments by increasing the length of x or y, which in effect increases the second moment of area of the cross section. The above structural alternatives, which characterize the Eskimo craniofacial region, are conceivably adaptations to more effectively dissipate excessive biting forces.

Brow Ridge and Frontal Sinus

It has been noted by various workers that the Eskimos have rather small frontal sinuses, a weakly developed brow region, and a high vertical forehead. Although the functional significance of brow ridges is a much debated subject (Thomson 1903; Weidenreich 1945; Tappen 1953; Moss and Young 1960; Biegert 1963), their development is, at least in part, related to the size of the brain relative to the size and position of the face.

Relative to sella and nasion, the Eskimo glabella is more anteriorly positioned than in various American Indian populations. In addition, the thickness of the bone between the endocranial and ectocranial surface in this region, which is a rough approximation of the anteroposterior dimension of the frontal sinus, is reduced in Eskimos while the distance between sella and nasion is increased by comparison with various American Indian populations (Hylander 1972).

The above analysis suggests that high vertical forehead and weakly developed brow region in the Eskimo are related to a long anterior cranial fossa. The large anteroposterior dimensions of the anterior portion of the Eskimo brain apparently displace the frontal bone anteriorly.

The functional significance (if any) of the high vertical forehead and weakly developed brow region in the Eskimo skull is unclear. Endo (1966) has stated that the high vertical forehead is more efficient to withstand bending moments during biting. His experimental work suggests that stress from bending moments in a low forehead is concentrated in the glabella region, while in a more vertical forehead the bending moment is resisted by the whole forehead. Regardless of its functional significance, the high vertical forehead in the Eskimo is structurally related to the large endocranial dimensions of the anterior part of the skull.

As previously mentioned, Koertvelyessy (1972) has noted that the frontal sinus among Alaskan Eskimo populations increases in size from north to south. This change in sinus size has been considered to be an adaptation to climate. Hrdlička (1930) has shown that there are also clinal differences in regard to head form among Alaskan Eskimos. As

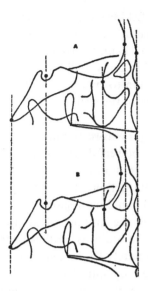

Figure 6. Brow ridge morphology and frontal sinus size. In A the anterior cranial base length is larger than in B. In response to the larger anterior cranial base dimensions, the frontal sinus is reduced in size and the brow region is weakly developed, as compared to the condition found in B

one proceeds south from northern Alaska, the Eskimo skull becomes more brachycephalic (see Gessain 1960; Laughlin 1966). A structural relationship possibly exists between frontal sinus size and head form. Among modern human populations the longer head with its longer anterior cranial fossa appears to have a smaller frontal sinus size while the broader shortened head has a larger frontal sinus (Figure 6). Such a relationship exists between the dolichocephalic Canadian Thule Eskimo, the brachycephalic Aztec and intermediate Indian Knoll skulls (Hylander 1972). This relationship should be investigated among Alaskan Eskimos. If confirmed, it would support the notion that the larger frontal sinuses of the southwestern Alaskan Eskimos are simply structural modifications due to changes in head form. One could, of course, suggest that head form (i.e. brain shape) is responding to climatic conditions; however, the process of brachycephalization, a worldwide phenomenon, is probably not due to climatic changes (Weidenreich 1945; Hulse 1963).

Sagittal Keeling

This feature occurs rather frequently among Eskimo populations. Several frontal radiographs of Eskimo skulls and examination of fragmentary crania confirm that sagittal keeling in part reflects a bony buildup in the midline region of the Eskimo frontal and parietal bones. Hrdlička (1910) suggested that this bony buildup strengthens the cranial vault. He attributed its formation to two factors. The most important was the upward forced expansion of the cranium along the line of least resistance during growth of the brain. Hrdlička stated that this forced expansion upwards was due to the growth-restricting lateral pressure exerted on the developing brain by the powerful temporalis muscle. Hrdlička's second factor was the increased tension along the midline during skull growth. This tension, due to contraction of the temporalis muscles, stimulates bone deposition along the midline region.

It is debatable whether the muscles of mastication have a significant effect on the growth of the brain as Hrdlička suggests. In *Homo sapiens* brain growth is approximately 95 percent complete by six years of age. At this time, the masticatory muscles are still diminutive and will not approach adult size for another ten years. Therefore, Hrdlička's notion that the powerful temporalis markedly modifies brain growth appears dubious.

Hrdlička's second notion — that the sagittal sutural area of the cranium is under tension during temporalis contraction — seems reasonable. Actually, this area would be under tension from both the temporalis and masseter muscles, due to the nature of the attachment of the masseter muscles and the fact that the temporalis fascia is acting as suspensory bracing for the zygomatic arch (Sicher 1950). Therefore, the bony buildup along the midsagittal region of the parietal and frontal bones probably represents an adaptation to resist powerful tensile stresses, generated from the temporalis and masseter muscles. Whether this buildup is simply a bony response to increased stress during ontogeny (a non-genetic change) is unclear.

SUMMARY

Various workers have noted that the Eskimo skull is strikingly different from the skulls of other human populations (extant and extinct). The Eskimo skull is characterized by large spacious orbits, a narrow nasal aperture, reduced nasal bones, increased facial flatness (i.e. large naso-malar and zygomaxillary angles), an enlarged zygomaxillary region, high temporal lines, a shallow glenoid and canine fossa, a robust mandible with a wide, low, oblique ascending ramus, a high incidence of palatal and mandibular tori, increased thickness of the tympanic plate, sagittal keeling, a weakly developed brow, pronounced gonial eversion and a high incidence of third molar agenesis.

Two theories have been advanced to explain some of the above listed features of the Eskimo skull. The more recent of these suggests that the reduced brow ridges, the widely flaring zygomas, the spacious orbits, and the increased facial flatness of the Eskimo skull are adaptations to reduce heat loss in the arctic environment (Coon et al. 1950). The other (older) theory (Hrdlička 1910) associates some of the above morphological features of the Eskimo skull with powerful chewing. The large attachment fields of the muscles of mastication (e.g. high temporal lines), the robust mandible, palatal and mandibular tori and sagittal keeling are features commonly cited as being importantly related to a powerful masticatory apparatus.

A reconsideration of the above "cold adaptation" hypothesis and a review of the experimental studies on cold response in various human populations (including Eskimos) suggest that evidence for cold adaptation in the Eskimo craniofacial region is scanty.

Based on a biometrical and morphological analysis of the craniofacial region of several human populations, coupled with published craniometrical and morphological data, a more parsimonious theory, similar to the Hrdlička theory was advanced. This theory, which explains most of the unusual bony features of the Eskimo craniofacial region, states that the Eskimo skull is especially adapted to GENERATE and DISSIPATE large vertical biting forces.

The existence of large biting forces among Eskimos is well documented. The evidence for the existence of these forces is based primarily on morphological and ethnographic data. Dentition studies have established that the Eskimo dentition is characterized by frequent occurrences of root resorption, dental chipping, and fractured crowns. Mandibular and palatal tori are also a frequent occurrence in the Eskimo jaws. All of the above features are often associated with an increase in occlusal or biting force. In addition, maximum bite force data in various human populations reveal impressively high values among the Eskimos. The chewing of seal skins, frozen food and bones, and the use of the jaws as a "third hand" or as an all-purpose vise is well documented among various Eskimo populations. These activities require the generation of considerable amounts of occlusal force.

As mentioned above, the Eskimo masticatory apparatus is especially adapted to generating excessively large occlusal forces. This adaptation relates to the following: (1) the large size of the muscles of mastication, and (2) the positioning of these muscles. The enlarged muscles, inferred from the muscle attachment areas of the skull and observations in the field, contribute importantly to the increased power of the Eskimo masticatory apparatus. Repositioning the Eskimo's muscles of mastication improves the mechanical efficiency of the masticatory apparatus. The increased facial flatness and flaring zygomas, rather than being related to cold adaptation, are associated with a more anterior positioning of the temporalis and masseter muscles.

The amount of force generated is limited by the ability of the face to effectively dissipate these forces. As expected, the Eskimo's capability to generate large biting forces is correlated with morphological features that are capable of dissipating large biting and muscle forces. Although the Eskimos have the largest faces of any modern human population, they display a reduction in prognathism which reduces unfavorable bending moments in the face during forceful anterior biting. Nasal bone reduction is another important structural modification that is related to dissipating biting forces. Eskimos have the most reduced nasal bones of all modern human populations; however, their interorbital dimensions are apparently unaffected. This suggests that they have enlarged nasal processes of the maxillae. This enlargement is an adaptation to effectively dissipate the large biting forces in the anterior part of the Eskimo face.

Other morphological features of the skull were discussed and hypotheses regarding their functional significance were advanced.

REFERENCES

ALEXANDER, R. MC NEILL
  1968   *Animal mechanics.* Seattle: University of Washington Press.
BARBENEL, J. C.
  1972   The biomechanics of the temporomandibular joint: a theoretical study. *Journal of Biomechanics* 5: 251–256.
BIEGERT, J.
  1963   "The evaluation of characteristics of the skull, hands and feet for primate taxonomy," in *Classification and human evolution.* Edited by S. L. Washburn. Chicago: Aldine.
BIRKET-SMITH, K.
  1935   *The Eskimos.* New York: E. P. Dutton.
  1940   Anthropological observations on the Central Eskimos. *Report of the Fifth Thule Expedition, 1921–1924,* 2.
BJÖRK, A.
  1947   The face in profile. *Svensk Tandkälare-Tidskrift* 40 (supplement 5B). Lund: Berlingska.

1950 Some biological aspects of prognathism and occlusion of the teeth. *Acta Odontologica Scandinavica* 9:1–40.

BJÖRK, A., M. PALLING
1954 Adolescent age changes in sagittal jaw relation, alveolar prognathy, and incisal inclination. *Acta Odontologica Scandinavica* 2:201–232.

BOAS, F.
1907 *The Eskimo of Baffin Land and Hudson Bay*. Bulletin of the American Museum of Natural History 15.

BREKHAUS, P., W. D. ARMSTRONG, W. J. SIMON
1937 Strength of bite and condition of teeth in men and supermen. *Journal of Dental Research* 16: 309.

BROSE, D. S., M. H. WOLPOFF
1971 Early Upper Paleolithic Man and Late Middle Paleolithic tools. *American Anthropologist* 73: 1156–1194.

BROSTE, K., K. FISCHER-MOLLER; P. PEDERSON
1944 The Mediaeval Norsemen at Gardar. *Meddelelser om Grønland* 89: 48–51.

BROTHWELL, D. R., V. M. CARBONELL, D. H. GOOSE
1963 "Congenital absence of teeth in human populations," in *Dental anthropology*. Edited by D. R. Brothwell. New York: Pergamon.

BROWN, T.
1965 *Craniofacial variations in a Central Australian tribe*. Adelaide: Libraries' Board of South Australia.

CAMERON, J.
1923 Osteology of the Western and Central Eskimo. *Report of the Canadian Arctic Expedition, 1913–1918* 12: 1–58.

CARLSOO, S.
1952 Nervous coordination and mechanical function of the mandibular elevators: an electromyographic study of the activity and an anatomic analysis of the mechanics of the muscles. *Acta Odontologica Scandinavica* 10 (supplement 11): 1–132.

CARTMILL, M.
1974 "Daubentonia, Dactylopsila, woodpeckers and klinorhynchy," in *Prosimian biology*. Edited by G. A. Doyle, R. D. Martin, and A. Walker. London: Duckworth.

COLLINS, H. B.
1950 *The origin and antiquity of the Eskimo*. Annual Report of the Smithsonian Institution. Washington, D.C.

COON, C. S.
1962 *The origin of races*. New York: Alfred A. Knopf.
1965 *The living races of man*. New York: Alfred A. Knopf.

COON, C. S., S. M. GARN, J. B. BIRDSELL
1950 *Races: a study of the problems of race formation in man*. Springfield, Illinois: Charles C. Thomas.

CRAVEN, A. H.
1958 A radiographic cephalometric study of the Central Australian aboriginal. *Angle Orthodontist* 28: 12–35.

164   WILLIAM L. HYLANDER

CROMPTON, A. W., K. HIIEMAE
1969   How mammalian molar teeth work. *Discovery* 5: 23–34. Yale Peabody Museum.

CUVIER, G.
1805   *Leçons d'anatomie comparée*, volume three. Paris: C. L. Duvernoy.

DAVIES, A.
1932   A re-survey of the morphology of the nose in relation to climate. *Journal of the Royal Anthropological Institute* 62: 337–359.

DE PONCINS, G.
1941   *Kablooma*. New York: Reynal.

DRENNAN, M. R.
1937   The torus mandibularis in the Bushman. *Journal of Anatomy* 72: 66–70.

ENDO, B.
1966   Experimental studies on the mechanical significance of the form of the human facial skeleton. *Journal of the Faculty of Science* 3: 1–106.
1970   Analysis of stresses around the orbit due to masseter and temporalis muscles, respectively. *Journal of the Anthropological Society of Nippon* 78: 251–266.

FISCHER-MOLLER, K.
1942   The Mediaeval Norse settlements in Greenland. *Meddelelser om Grønland* 89: 61–63.

FURST, C. M., F. HANSEN
1915   *Crania Groenlandica*. Copenhagen: Reitzel.

GARDNER, E., D. GRAY, R. O'RADHILLY
1966   *Anatomy*. Philadelphia: W. B. Saunders.

GESSAIN, R.
1960   Contribution à l'anthropologie des Eskimo d'Angmagssalik. *Meddelelser om Grønland* 161:128–134.

GINGERICH, P. D.
1971   Functional significance of mandibular translation in vertebrate jaw mechanics. *Postilla* 152: 3–10.

GLICKMAN, IRVING
1968   *Clinical periodontology*. Philadelphia: W. B. Saunders.

GOLDSTEIN, M. S.
1932   Congenital absence and impaction of the third molar in the Eskimo mandible. *American Journal of Physical Anthropology* 16: 381–388.
1948   Dentition of Indian crania from Texas. *American Journal of Physical Anthropology* 6: 63–84.

GORLEN, R. J., H. M. GOLDMAN
1970   *Thoma's oral pathology*. St. Louis: C. V. Mosby.

GOSS, C. M.
1966   *Gray's anatomy* (twenty-eighth edition). Philadelphia: Lea and Febiger.

GOTTLIEB, B., B. ORBAN
1931   Tissue changes in experimental traumatic occlusion, with special reference to age and constitution. *Journal of Dental Research* 11: 505–510.

GYSI, A.
1921   Studies on the leverage problem of the mandible. *Dental Digest* 27:

74–84, 184–190, 203–208.

HAWKES, E. W.
1916 Skeletal measurements and observations on the Point Barrow Eskimos with comparisons from other Eskimo groups. *American Anthropologist* 18: 203–234.

HELLMAN, M.
1928 Racial characters in human dentition. *Proceedings of the American Philosophical Society* 67: 157–174.

HIIEMAE, K.
1971 The structure and function of the jaw muscles in the rat, *Rattus norvegicus L.* III: the mechanics of the muscles. *Zoological Journal of the Linnean Society* 50: 111–132.

HOOTON, E. A.
1918 On certain Eskimoid characters in Icelandic skulls. *American Journal of Physical Anthropology* 1: 53–76.

HOWELLS, W. W.
1972 "Analysis of patterns of variation in crania of recent man," in *The functional and evolutionary biology of primates.* Edited by R. Tuttle, 123–151. Chicago: Aldine-Atherton.

HOYME, L. E.
1965 The nasal index and climate: a spurious case of natural selection in man (abstract). *American Journal of Anthropology* 23: 336–337.

HRDLIČKA, A.
1910 *Contribution to the anthropology of Central and Smith Sound Eskimos.* Anthropological Papers of the American Museum of Natural History 5, part two.
1930 *Anthropological Survey in Alaska.* Forty-Sixth Annual Report of the American Bureau of American Ethnology, 1928–1929.
1940a Mandibular and maxillary hyperostoses. *American Journal of Physical Anthropology* 27: 1–68.
1940b Lower jaw. The gonial angle, I. The bigonial breadth, II. *American Journal of Physical Anthropology* 27: 281–308.
1940c Lower jaw: further studies. *American Journal of Physical Anthropology* 27: 383–467.
1942 Catalog of human crania in the United States National Museum Collections: Eskimos in general. *Proceedings of the United States National Museum* 91: 169–429.
1944 *The anthropology of Kodiak Island.* Philadelphia: Wistar Institute.

HULSE, F.
1963 *The human species.* New York: Random House.

HUNT, E.
1960 The continuing evolution of modern man. *Cold Spring Harbor Symposium on Quantitative Biology* 24: 245–254.

HYLANDER, W. L.
1972 "The adaptive significance of Eskimo craniofacial morphology." Unpublished doctoral dissertation, University of Chicago.
1975 The human mandible: lever or link? *American Journal of Physical Anthropology* 43: 227–242.

JORGENSEN, J. B.
   1953   The Eskimo skeleton. *Meddelelser om Grønland* 146.
KAYUKAWA, H.
   1957   Studies on morphology of mandibular overjet, part three: radiographic cephalometric analysis. *Journal of Japanese Orthodontic Society* 16: 1–25.
KLATSKY, M.
   1942   Masticatory stresses and their relation to dental caries. *Journal of Dental Research* 21: 387–390.
KOERTVELYESSY, T.
   1972   Relationships between the frontal sinus and climatic conditions: a skeletal approach to cold adaptation. *American Journal of Physical Anthropology* 37: 161–172.
KRONFELD, R.
   1931   Histologic study of the influence of function on the human periodontal membrane. *Journal of the American Dental Association* 18: 1242, 1274.
LAUGHLIN, W. S.
   1966   "Genetical and anthropological characteristics of Arctic populations," in *The biology of human adaptability*. Edited by P. T. Baker and J. S. Weiner. Oxford: Clarendon Press.
LE GROS CLARK, W. E.
   1920   On a series of ancient Eskimo skulls from Greenland. *Journal of the Royal Anthropological Institute* 50: 281–298.
LEIGH, R. W.
   1925a Dental pathology of the Eskimo. *Dental Cosmos* 67: 884–898.
   1925b Dental pathology of Indian tribes of varied environmental and food conditions. *American Journal of Physical Anthropology* 8: 179–199.
   n.d.   Dental pathology of aboriginal California. *American Archeology and Ethnology* 23: 399–440.
LINDERHOLM, H., A. WENNSTROM
   1970   Isometric bite force and its relation to general muscle force and body build. *Acta Odontologica Scandinavica* 28: 679–689.
LOCKHART, R. D., G. F. HAMILTON, F. W. FYFE
   1959   *Anatomy of the human body*. Philadelphia: J. B. Lippincott.
MAYHALL, J.
   1969   Thule culture Eskimo mandibles: a radiographic study. *American Journal of Physical Anthropology* 31: 264.
   1970   The effects of culture change upon the Eskimo dentition. *Arctic Anthropology* 7: 117–121.
MELLQUIST, C., T. SANDBERG
   1939   Odontological studies of about 1,000 medieval skulls from Hallan and Scania in Sweden and from the Norse colony in Greenland, and a contribution to the knowledge of their anthropology. *Odontologica Tidskrift* 3B: 1–83.
MERBS, C.
   1968   Anterior tooth loss in arctic populations. *Southwestern Journal of Anthropology* 24: 20–32.

MOLLER, E.
1966   The chewing apparatus. An electromyographic study of the action of the muscles of mastication and its correlation to facial morphology. *Acta Physiologica Scandinavica* 69 (supplement 280).

MOORREES, C. F. A., R. H. OSBORNE, E. WILDE
1957   Torus mandibularis: its occurrence in Aleut children and its genetic determinants. *American Journal of Physical Anthropology* 10: 319–329.

MOSS, M.
1960   "Functional anatomy of the temporomandibular joint," in *Disorders of the temporomandibular joint.* Edited by L. Schwartz. Philadelphia: W. B. Saunders.

MOSS, M., R. YOUNG
1960   A functional approach to craniology. *American Journal of Physical Anthropology* 18:281–292.

MOYERS, R. E.
1950   An electromyographic analysis of certain muscles involved in temporomandibular movement. *American Journal of Orthodontics* 36: 481–515.

MUHLEMAN, H. R.
1954   The mechanism of tooth mobility. *Journal of Periodontology* 25: 128–135.

NEUMAN, H. H., N. A. DI SALVIO
1958   Caries in Indians of the Mexican Cordillera, the Peruvian Andes and at the Amazon headwaters. *British Dental Journal*, pages 13–17.

ORBAN, B.
1928   Tissue changes in traumatic occlusion. *Journal of the American Dental Association* 15: 2090–2106.

OSCHINSKY, L.
1962   Facial flatness and cheekbone morphology in arctic mongoloids: a case for morphological taxonomy. *Anthropologica* 4: 349–377.
1964   *The most ancient Eskimos.* Ottawa: University of Ottawa Press.

PEDERSEN, P. O.
1949   The East Greenland Eskimo dentition. *Meddelelser om Grønland* 142: 1–244.

POSSELT, U.
1969   *Physiology of occlusion and rehabilitation.* Oxford: Blackwell.

RAMFJORD, S. P., M. ASH
1971   *Occlusion.* Philadelphia: W. B. Saunders.

RASMUSSEN, K.
1927   *Across Arctic ice.* New York: G. P. Putnam's.

REES, L.
1954   Structure and function of the mandibular joint. *British Dental Journal* 96: 125–233.

REITAN, K.
1969   "Biomechanical principles and reactions," in *Current orthodontic concepts and techniques.* Edited by T. M. Graber. Philadelphia: W. B. Saunders.

RITCHIE, S. G.
    1923   The dentition of the Western and Central Eskimos. *Report of the Canadian Arctic Expedition, 1913–1918* 12: 59–66.
ROBINSON, M.
    1946   The temporomandibular joint: theory of reflex-controlled nonlever action of the mandible. *Journal of the American Dental Association* 33: 1260–1271.
RYDER, S. A.
    1878   On the mechanical genesis of tooth forms. *Proceedings of the Academy of Natural Science* 79: 45–80.
SCHWALBE, G.
    1887   *Lehrbuch der Anatomie der Sinnesorgane*. Erlangen: Besold.
SICHER, H.
    1950   *Oral anatomy*. St. Louis: C. V. Mosby.
SMITH, J. M., R. J. G. SAVAGE
    1959   The mechanics of mammalian jaws. *School Science Review* 40: 389–401.
STEEGMAN, A. T.
    1967   Frostbite of the human face as a selective force. *Human Biology* 39: 131–144.
    1970   Cold adaptation and the human face. *American Journal of Physical Anthropology* 32: 243–250.
    1972   Cold response, body form, and craniofacial shape in two racial groups of Hawaii. *American Journal of Physical Anthropology* 37: 193–221.
STEWART, T. D.
    1933   The tympanic plate and external auditory meatus in the Eskimos. *American Journal of Physical Anthropology* 17: 481–496.
    1939   *Anthropometric observations on the Eskimos and Indians of Labrador*. Field Museum of Natural History, Anthropology Series 31 (1).
SUZUKI, M., T. SAKAI
    1960   A familial study of torus palatinus and torus mandibularis. *American Journal of Physical Anthropology* 18: 263–372.
TAPPAN, N. C.
    1953   A functional analysis of the facial skeleton with split-line technique. *American Journal of Physical Anthropology* 11:503–532.
TATTERSALL, I.
    1973   *Cranial anatomy of the Archeolemurinae (Lemuroidea, Primates)*. Anthropological Papers of the American Museum of Natural History 52, part one.
THALBITZER, W.
    1914   The Ammassalik Eskimo. *Meddelelser om Grønland* 39 (part one).
THOMA, K.
    1950   *Oral pathology*. St. Louis: C. V. Mosby.
THOMA, K. H., H. M. GOLDMAN
    1960   *Oral pathology*. St. Louis: C. V. Mosby.
THOMSON, A.
    1903   A consideration of some of the more important factors concerned

in the production of man's cranial form. *Journal of the Anthropological Institute* 33: 135–166.

THOMSON, A., L. H. D. BUXTON
1923   Man's nasal index in relation to certain climatic conditions. *Journal of the Royal Anthropological Institute* 53: 92–122.

TURNBULL, W. D.
1970   Mammalian masticatory apparatus. *Fieldiana*: Geology 18 (2).

TURNER, CHRISTY G., II
1971   Three-rooted mandibular first permanent molars and the question of American Indian origins. *American Journal of Physical Anthropology* 34: 229–241.

TURNER, C., J. CADIEN
1969   Dental chipping in Aleuts, Eskimos and Indians. *American Journal of Physical Anthropology* 31: 303–310.

VAN DEN BROEK, A. J. P.
1945   On exostoses in the human skull. *Acta Neerlandica Morphologica* 5: 95–118.

WASHBURN, S. L.
1963   "The study of race," in *The concept of race*. Edited by M. F. Ashley Montagu. New York: Free Press.

WAUGH, L. M.
1930   A study of the nutrition and teeth of the Eskimos of North Bering Sea and arctic Alaska. *Journal of Dental Research* 10: 387–393.
1937   Dental observations among Eskimos. *Journal of Dental Research* 16: 355–356.

WEI, S. H. Y.
1968   A roentgenographic cephalometric study of prognathism in Chinese males and females. *Angle Orthodontist* 38: 305–321.

WEIDENREICH, F.
1945   The brachycephalization of recent mankind. *Southwestern Journal of Anthropology* 1: 1–54.

WILSON, G. H.
1920   The anatomy and physics of the temporomandibular joint. *Journal of the National Dental Association* 7: 414–420.
1921   The anatomy and physics of the temporomandibular joint. *Journal of the National Dental Association* 8: 236–241.

WOLPOFF, M.
1968   Climatic influence on skeletal nasal aperture. *American Journal of Physical Anthropology* 29: 405–423.

WOO, T. L., G. MOURANT
1934   A biometric study of the flatness of the facial skeleton in man. *Biometrika* 26: 196–250.

WOODBURNE, R. T.
1969   *Essentials of human anatomy*. London: Oxford University Press.

Variations in Dental Traits Within Populations

PATRICIA SMITH

The minor differences in tooth size and morphology present between even closely related populations (Dahlberg 1963; Garn et al. 1968; Rosenzweig 1970; Sofaer et al. 1972) are usually attributed to genetic drift rather than selective pressures, a proposition that is, however, normally difficult to test in human population studies.

Recent findings by Bonné (1971) on the genetic and anthropometric characteristics of the patrilineages composing the Habbanite[1] isolate indicated that these lineages would provide an excellent model for carrying out such an examination.

She found that each of the four lineages composing the isolate was endogomous. No significant interlineage differences were present in standard anthropometric measurements of the head, face, total height, weight, and skinfold thickness, or in the major blood groups, including Rh, Ro, and V systems. Significant differences were, however, present in other blood group and serum systems[2] as well as in dermatoglyphic patterns, and these differences were maintained when successive generations were compared.

Bonné considered that these findings substantiated the claim of the community that marriages took place within rather than between the lineages, and suggested that each lineage could be considered a "sub-isolate" within the main isolate.

[1] The Habbanites, now living in Israel, dwelt for many hundreds of years in Habban, Southern Arabia. They form an isolate that differs from the populations, both Jewish and non-Jewish, who were their immediate neighbors, in many features (Bonné et al. 1970; Rosenzweig 1970).
[2] Interlineage differences were significant (P<.001) for frequencies of ABO, MNS, Duffy, P, Haptoglobins and Sutter systems.

For Plates, see p. xli, between pp. 330–331.

Following these conclusions, tooth size and morphological traits were selected for study and compared by lineage and sex. Hydrocal casts were used for measurement of mesiodistal and buccolingual dimensions of the teeth and scoring of morphological traits. Of the 180 individuals studied, 83 belonged to lineage 1; 48 to lineage 2; 34 to lineage 3; and 15 to lineage 4.

Initial calculations showed no significant right/left asymmetry in either metric or morphologic traits, so that all further calculations were based on teeth from the right side, antimeres being used to compensate for missing data. Because of the small number of individuals in lineage 4, this lineage was omitted from further calculations.

Means and standard deviations were calculated for both dimensions of all permanent teeth and Student's "t" test used to test for interlineage and between-sex differences. Morphological traits were compared for the lower permanent teeth and second deciduous $molar_1$ using X^2.

Figures 1 and 2 show the relationship of tooth diameters in males of the three lineages numbering most individuals (Groups 1, 2 and 3) compared with females of the first lineage.

Interlineage differences were small, but significant at the 5 percent level between lineages 1 and 3 in the incisors, and between 1 and 3 and 1 and 2 in the second premolars, for mesiodistal measurements.

Male/female differences were most marked in the lower canine, and upper and lower first molars ($P < .025$) but also present in the incisors ($P < .05$). Examination of trait frequencies showed that interlineage differences in traits examined were consistent throughout each tooth group (Figures 3 and 4).

Only one tooth from each series was therefore selected for further comparison — the canine, second premolar and first molar.

Male/female differences were less pronounced in trait frequencies than in metric parameters: they were significant in the canine ($P < .025$) for one trait only, whereas significant interlineage differences in trait frequencies were present in all teeth (Tables 1 to 3).

The anterior teeth of lineage 2 were characterized by a high frequency of trace or semishovelling. In lineage 1 the labial surface was flat, and in lineage 3 there was a high frequency of reduction of both mesial and distal canine lobes.

Male/female differences were significant ($P < .025$) in the degree of reduction of mesial and distal canine lobes — in the female the incisal edge was flat, all three lobes being fused, or occasionally the distal lobe was reduced. Using this feature only, 78 percent of all individuals were accurately sexed (Plate 1).

Lineages 2 and 3 showed a high degree of individuality in both pre-molars. Differences in the frequency of individual traits such as presence of a central prominence on the buccal aspect, occlusal tubercles, occlusal-lingual grooves and transverse ridges crossing the mesiodistal groove, accounted for 8–10 percent of differences found. Females had a slightly higher incidence of 3-cusped forms, but the differences were not statistically significant.

Molars showed a high frequency of wrinkling and occlusal tubercles (Plate 2). These tubercles were localized in the occlusal region of the cusps, and were scored as absent, 1 present, or multiple. Deflecting wrinkles were present in 48 percent of lineage 1 and 14 percent of lineage 3 in M_1 (P<.05). More unexpectedly, significant interlineage differences were also found in frequencies of 6 cusps (all gradations from double grooves included) and 4 cusps in the first permanent molar. Lineage 3 had more 4-cusped first molars, and lineage 2 fewer 4-cusped molars than lineage 1. Lineage 2 also had a higher frequency of 6 cusps than the other two lineages (P<.025 between lineages 1 and 2).

Since lineage 1 contained the largest number of individuals it was assumed that this lineage was the most "stable" and thus more representative of the parent population. If differences in trait frequencies in lineages 2 and 3 are considered to reflect random drift, they should differ more from each other than from lineage 1. Using Sanghi's X^2 as modified by Sofaer et al. (1972), various combinations of traits were compared to estimate the "distance" between the three lineages (Figure 5). Using several combinations of trait frequencies, from different tooth groups, the relative distances between lineages 2 and 3 were consistently greater than those separating either from lineage 1.

All lineages were living in close proximity and exposed to identical environmental pressures. Differences present would seem therefore to reflect random drift, although its role was probably "weakened" by interlineage marriages that did take place (now accounting for 40 percent of all unions, according to Bonné) [1971].

It is interesting to note that interlineage differences in metric parameters were found in teeth with a high component of variability — second premolar and incisor — and absent in those with a low component of variability, but which display marked sexual dimorphism, namely the canine and first molar. These findings agree with those of other workers such as Lunt (1969), who compared three neighboring Danish medieval villages: they appear to be sufficiently generalized to permit

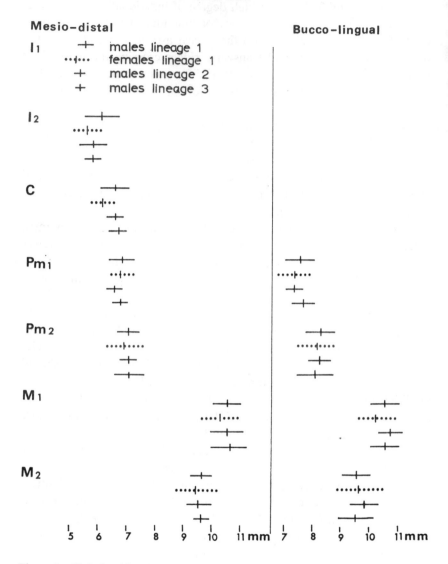

Figure 1.   Relationship of tooth diameters in males of lineages 1, 2, 3 and females of lineage 1 plotted for mean value ± 1 standard deviation

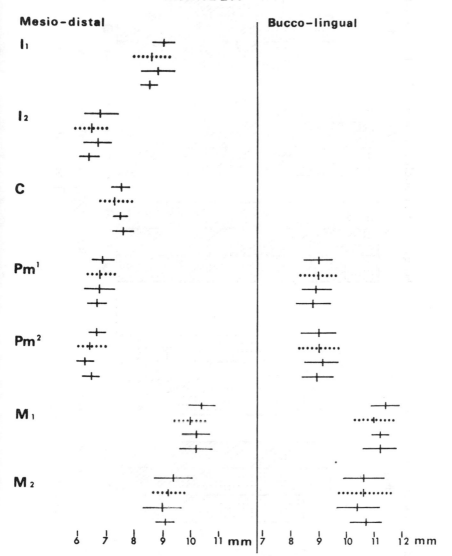

Figure 2. Relationship of tooth diameters in males of lineages 1, 2, 3 and females of lineage 1 plotted for mean value ± 1 standard deviation

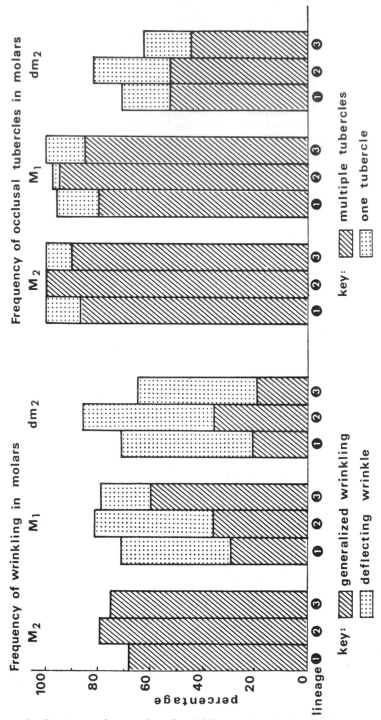

Figure 3. Percentage frequencies of wrinkling and occlusal tubercles

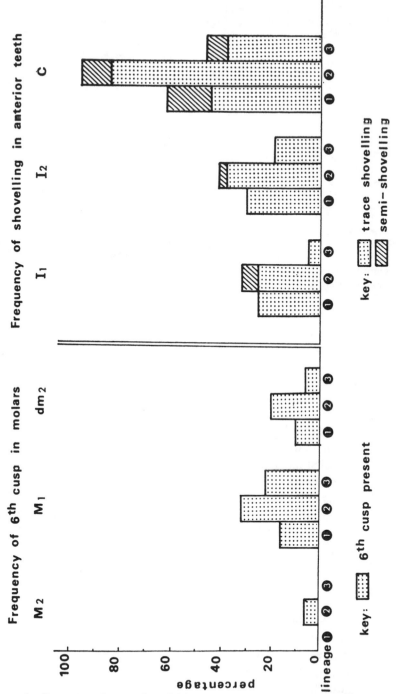

Figure 4. Percentage frequencies of 6th cusp in molars and shovelling in anterior teeth

Table 1.   Frequency distribution of traits in the mandibular canine

	Lineage 1	Lineage 2	Lineage 3	All lineages Males	All lineages Females
Number of individuals	27	24	14	31	34
Vertical outline[1]					
flat	.3	.03	0	.17	.12
convex	.7	.97	1.0	.83	.88
Incisal edge[2]					
flat	.36	.48	.4	.16	.61
mesial lobe reduced	.07	.0	.06	.08	—
distal lobe reduced	.39	.45	.27	.46	.32
both reduced	.18	.07	.27	.30	.07
Shovelling[3]					
absent	.38	.04	.54	.3	.26
trace	.44	.84	.38	.57	.58
semishovel	.18	.12	.08	.13	.16
Lingual tubercle					
absent	.85	.8	.67	.61	.82
bulge	0	.2	.11	.11	.14
ridge to incisal edge	.15	—	.22	.27	.04

Using X^2
[1]   Lineage 1 differs from 2 and 3 ($P < .05$).
[2]   Lineage 2 differs from 1 and 3 ($P < .05$); males differ from females ($P < .025$).
[3]   Lineage 3 differs from 1 and 2 ($P < .05$).

their utilization in the interpreting of data in comparing teeth of individuals of unknown sex. Differences in diameters of teeth other than canines and first molars would then reflect interpopulation differences, whereas differences primarily present in the canine and first molar should be suspected as reflecting differences in male/female sex ratios.

Morphological traits are generally considered to be free from sex bias. Garn et al. (1966) found none in Carabelli's cusp in Ohio whites, but Goose and Lee (1971) found significant male/female differences in this trait in Liverpool families. The study by Snyder et al. (1969) indicates that dimorphism in traits may vary for different populations in the same way as dimorphism in tooth size.

In the Habbanite trait dimorphism was present to a minor degree in each of two teeth, and relatively insignificant compared with interlineage differences. As demonstrated here, trait frequencies may be highly group specific even between populations that are closely related. This suggests that the number of factors responsible for specific morphologic traits may be fewer than those governing tooth size.

Table 2.   Trait frequencies in the second premolar

	Lineage 1	Lineage 2	Lineage 3	Male	Female
Number of individuals	32	21	13	38	28
Occlusal outline[1]					
narrow mesiodistal	.12	.2	.27	.18	.14
square	.70	.52	.64	.64	.66
trapezoid	.18	.28	.09	.18	.20
Cusp number					
2	.46	.48	.64	.47	.33
3	.54	.52	.36	.53	.67
Occlusal tubercle[1]					
absent	.64	.45	.36	.47	.56
on buccal	.07	.05	.27	.20	.06
on lingual	.25	.45	.36	.30	.35
on both	.04	.05	—	.03	.08
Buccal aspect[1]					
smooth	.89	.91	73	84	85
central prominence	.11	9	27	16	15
Marginal ridges					
continuous	35	42	44	47	36
mesial crossed by groove	35	35	12	21	36
distal crossed by groove	—	06	44	16	07
both crossed by groove	.3	17	0	16	21
Occluso-lingual groove[1]					
absent	.67	.50	.6	.52	.6
located centrally	.07	.05	.2	.11	.08
located distally	.29	45	.1	37	.28
two present	—	—	.1	—	.06
Mesiodistal groove[1]					
continuous	11	28	30	15	30
interrupted by transverse ridge	89	72	70	85	70
Occlusal fossa[1]					
mesial larger	.16	.05	.29	22	37
both equal	.36	.21	.29	48	30
distal larger	.48	.74	.42	30	33

[1]   Interlineage differences present (P<.05).

The combination of group specificity and low or absent sexual dimorphism in trait frequencies provides further confirmation of their usefulness, and the level of discrimination that may be achieved by their use in population and family studies.

Table 3.   Frequency of traits in lower first permanent molar

	Lineage 1	Lineage 2	Lineage 3	Males	Females
Number of individuals	76	41	32	71	70
Cusp number[1]					
5 cusps	.75	.83	.67	.81	.76
4 cusps	.25	.17	.33	.19	.24
6th cusp					
absent	.85	.67	.79	.81	.16
2 grooves	—	—	.07	—	.02
cusp	.15	.33	.14	.19	.82
7th cusp					
absent	.91	.88	.84	.88	.87
2 grooves	.04	.02	.09	.05	.04
cusp	.05	.1	.07	.07	.09
Wrinkling[2]					
absent	.23	.19	.21	.23	.2
general	.29	.44	.60	.37	.38
deflecting	.48	.37	.19	.4	.42
Occlusal tubercles					
absent	.04	.02	—	.05	.03
1 present	.16	.02	.06	.07	.03
multiple	.8	.96	.94	.88	.94

[1]   Lineage 3 differs from lineage 2 (P<.025).
[2]   Lineage 3 differs from both lineages 1 and 2 (P<.05).

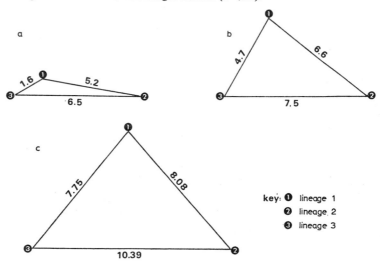

Figure 5.   Interlineage distances calculated from trait frequencies:
(a)   1 trait — canine — shovelling
(b)   4 traits — as in (a) plus first molar — 4 cusps, 6th cusp and occlusal tubercles
(c)   7 traits — as in (b) plus second premolar — smooth buccal aspect, occlusal lingual groove, and occlusal tubercles

REFERENCES

BONNÉ, B.

1971 Lineages as sub-isolates within inbred communities. *Excerpta Medica International Congress Series* 233:30.

BONNÉ, B., S. ASHBEL, M. MODAL, M. J. GODBER, A. E. MOURANT, D. TILLS, B. G. WOODHEAD

1970 The Habbanite isolate 1: genetic markers in the blood. *Human Heredity* 20:609–622.

DAHLBERG, A. A.

1963 "Analysis of the American Indian dentition," in *Dental Anthropology*. Edited by D. Brothwell, 149–177. Oxford: Pergamon.

GARN, S. M., R. S. KEREWSKY, A. B. LEWIS

1966 Extent of sex influence on Carabelli's polymorphism. *Journal of Dental Research* 45:18–23.

GARN, S. M., A. B. LEWIS, A. J. WALENGA

1968 Crown-size profile pattern comparisons of fourteen human populations. *Archives of Oral Biology* 13:1235–1242.

GOOSE, D. H., G. T. R. LEE

1971 The mode of inheritance of Carabelli's trait. *Human Biology* 43: 64–69.

LUNT, D. A.

1969 An odontometric study of mediaeval Danes. *Acta Odontologica Scandinavica* (Supplement 55) 27:1–173.

ROSENZWEIG, K. A.

1970 Tooth form as a distinguishing trait between sexes and human populations. *Journal of Dental Research* 49:1423–1426.

SNYDER, R. G., A. A. DAHLBERG, C. C. SNOW, T. DAHLBERG

1969 Trait analysis of the dentition of the Tarahumara Indians and Mestizos of the Sierra Madre Occidental, Mexico. *American Journal of Physical Anthropology* 31.65–76.

SOFAER, J. A., J. D. NISWANDER, C. J. MAC LEAN, P. L. WORKMAN

1972 Population studies on southwestern Indian tribes 5. Tooth morphology as an indicator of biological distance. *American Journal of Physical Anthropology* 37:357–366.

The Dental Condition of Chinese Living in Liverpool

DENYS H. GOOSE

Although many articles have been published on the dental morphology of Mongoloid populations (Dahlberg 1951; Moorrees 1957; Nelson 1938; Pedersen 1949), very little attention has been paid to the Chinese themselves. In Liverpool, there is one of the largest groups of Chinese in the United Kingdom. It seemed worthwhile to find out how much their dental characteristics were related to other Mongoloid groups and how much they contrasted with the local Caucasoid population.

As one of the principal objects of the investigation was to study the pattern of inheritance of dental traits, it was important to find as many families as possible. Eventually one hundred of these families living in Liverpool and the surrounding districts, who were either known personally or through contacts, were visited. The average age of the parents was thirty-eight with a range of twenty-nine to fifty-five years, while the average age of the children was twelve with a range of seven to twenty-two years. Nearly all the parents were immigrants, most having been born in the Canton area of South China or in Hong Kong. However, in the case of the children, over 70 percent were born in the United Kingdom.

First of all, the adult Chinese with respect to their dental morphological characteristics and arch size will be described and, secondly, the condition of their children with respect to dental caries and gingivitis will be contrasted with their Caucasoid neighbors.

I would like to express my thanks to the Medical Research Council for their grant toward the work, and to Professor A. B. Semple, Medical Officer of Health, Liverpool, for his help in organizing part of the study. Also my thanks are due to Mr. G. T. R. Lee and Mr. T. F. Varley for their diligence in collecting the data.

ADULTS

Material and Methods

There were eighty-one males and eighty females available for measurement; they were visited in their own homes and impressions were taken in packaged alginate for standardization. The impressions were then cast in Kaffir D stone as soon as possible and the casts so produced were measured by means of dial callipers calibrated to 0.05 millimeters.

Three measurements of arch width were taken (the first two having been used by a number of investigators [Lundström 1948]):

1. Between the first molars between the deepest points in the central fossae,

2. Between the first premolars from the midpoint of the fissure,

3. Between the canines, the minimum breadth opposite the internal ridge of enamel descending from the point of the cusp (Dockrell, Clinch, and Scott 1954).

If bilateral tooth loss had occurred in front of the teeth to be measured, no measurement was recorded. If there was unilateral tooth loss, then the distances of the two teeth from the incisive papilla were separately measured, and, if these measurements were the same, the arch width was recorded.

It was felt that the measurement of arch length has little meaning since it is largely dependent on tooth size and position when measured in the living and has in the past caused some unwarranted conclusions (Goose 1962).

Errors of measurement were tested by measuring five randomly chosen models four times each and calculating an analysis of variance. The probability was less than 0.01 in the three measurements, showing that measurement errors were insignificant compared with the difference between individuals.

The following observations were made on the teeth:

1. Mesiodistal and buccolingual diameters of the incisors, canines, premolars, and molars;

2. Shoveling in the maxillary incisors;

3. Presence or absence of hypocone in maxillary molars;

4. Carabelli's trait on maxillary molars; and

5. Mandibular cusp number and fissure pattern.

The measurements were made on teeth on the right side only. However, where a tooth was missing or could not be accurately measured owing to the loss of measuring points through caries, restoration, or attrition, then the corresponding contralateral tooth was used. The measurements were made using dial callipers with modified beaks to allow measuring of the interproximal surfaces, the mesiodistal diameter being measured between the contact points and the greatest buccolingual diameter taken at right angles to it (Goose 1963).

The term shoveling is used to describe a combination of a concave lingual surface and elevated marginal ridges enclosing a central fossa in incisor teeth. Hrdlička (1920) classified shoveling into four categories:
1.   Shovel: enamel rim distinct with the enclosed fossa well developed;
2.   Semi-shovel: enamel rim dstinct but enclosed fossa is shallow;
3.   Trace-shovel: distinct traces of enamel rim but which could not be classed as semi-shovel; and
4.   No shovel: no perceptible trace of rim or fossa.
Using this system of grading and with the aid of models prepared by Dahlberg (1956), each tooth was examined and classified accordingly.

In modern man maxillary molars may have three or four cusps. Generally, the first molar exhibits four cusps, but the second and third molars have probably undergone evolutionary reduction by elimination of the hypocone or distolingual cusp. Two intermediate forms have been described, one where the hypocone is reduced to a cuspule, 3+ pattern, or where it is only slightly reduced in size, 4– pattern (Dahlberg 1951). In the present study only three categories have been used, 4, 3+ and 3, the 4– being included in 4 (Turner 1969).

Carabelli's trait is found on the lingual aspect of the mesiolingual cusp of the maxillary first and, to a lesser extent, second and third molars. It may take the form of a pit, fissure, or cusp, and is usually represented to the same degree on either side. As the form of Carabelli's trait is so variable, classification is difficult; Dahlberg (1963) divided it into seven categories ranging from a pit to a full accessory cusp. In the present study, following Kraus (1951) four categories have been used: (a) no evidence of Carabelli's trait — smooth surface with the absence of pits or fissures; (b) pits or fissures; (c_1) cusp without free tip; and (c_2) cusp with free tip.

The occlusal form of mandibular molars in man may vary from the primitive five-cusp *Dryopithecus* pattern bearing the Y fissure configuration to extreme modification of four main cusps with an X-shaped configuration. The Y fissure pattern shows contact of the mesiolingual cusp with the middle buccal cusp. The + pattern shows a cruciform fissure configuration where there is a point contact between the four main cusps, and an X pattern is also described (Jørgensen 1955). In the present study, the mandibular first and second molars were classified into four- or five-cusped teeth and into Y or + fissure configurations.

Results

Table 1 gives the findings for male and female Chinese separately for palate widths. There was a significant sex difference in each case ($P<0.05$ for C–C and <0.01 for P^1–P^1 and M^1–M^1).

Table 1.   Chinese population in Liverpool

	Male			Female		
	n	$\bar{x}$	S.D.	n	$\bar{x}$	S.D.
C–C	49	26.08	1.71	56	25.36	1.91
P^1–P^1	48	37.63	2.22	50	36.41	1.94
M^1–M^1	14	49.96	2.65	26	47.18	2.60

A search through the literature produced very little accurate information on the size of Chinese arches, and here only one is referred to for comparison. Hong (1965) examined fifty-eight boys and fifty-five girls and gave the distances between the tips of the buccal cusps of the maxillary first premolars as 43.45 and 42.69 millimeters respectively. In order to compare Hong's results with those of the present study, it is necessary to subtract a correction equal to twice the distance between the tip of the buccal cusp and the fissure. On measuring this in the present series, it was found to be 3.5 millimeters, and, therefore, on subtracting twice this measurement from Hong's measurements, the following figures are obtained: 36.45 and 35.69 millimeters. Bearing in mind that Hong's subjects were eleven-year-old children, the results accord well with the present ones, making allowance for growth.

It was clear by inspection that many of the Chinese palates were very wide compared with British ones, and this was tested against the figures in Table 2 from a parallel Caucasoid family study in Liverpool (Bowden and Goose 1968) giving $P<0.01$ for all comparisons except M^1–M^1 males (only <0.05).

Although most of the Chinese jaws were broad, there were several which were grossly narrowed. The process which started to occur in Britain in the seventeenth century appears to have started also in the Chinese group examined in the present study. It is interesting, therefore, to observe the closeness of these measurements to those of some medieval skeletal material examined by Goose (1962): male P^1–P^1 37.84

Table 2. Caucasoid population in Liverpool *

	Male			Female		
	n	x̄	S.E.x̄	n	x̄	S.E.x̄
C–C	71	24.11 ± 0.22		85	23.14 ± 0.17	
P^1–P^1	41	35.89 ± 0.48		42	33.69 ± 0.28	
M^1–M^1	14	47.61 ± 0.84		9	44.18 ± 1.15	

* Bowden (1967).

and M^1–M^1 50.27, and female P^1–P^1 35.39 and M^1–M^1 47.62.

In the case of the Chinese, it is difficult to say what is the most likely cause because environmental differences are obviously considerable and miscegenation quite likely, although there was no apparent Caucasoid element in the sample.

Table 3 below shows the mesiodistal and buccolingual diameters, for the maxillary and mandibular teeth separately. The lower numbers presented for first molars were a result of frequent loss of these teeth, and the labiolingual diameters of many lower incisors could not be used because of calculus. Measurements were recorded to within 0.1 millimeters, and the method of double determination (Lundström 1943) was employed to test the accuracy of the measuring technique. It was found that in all the mesiodistal and buccolingual measurements, the standard error ranged from a minimum of 0.068 millimeters for the mesiodistal diameter of the maxillary first premolar to a maximum of 0.130 millimeters for the mesiodistal diameter of the mandibular first molar, giving a range of error of 0.93 to 1.18 percent respectively.

It can be seen from Table 3 that in all cases the male results were larger, being most noticeable in the canines. This has also been found by other workers on various races (Garn et al. 1966; Mijsberg 1931; Moorrees 1957).

There is a scarcity of other Chinese data, but those of both Hong (1965) and Hosaka (1936) were compared with the present data and found to be more or less identical.

Owing to lack of data, it was not possible to compare the present results with those from the white population in Liverpool. However, comparison with Caucasoid samples of Garn et al. (1966) and Seipel (1946) corroborates others' findings that the lateral maxillary incisor is a larger tooth in Mongoloids than in Caucasoids (Dahlberg 1951).

Where possible, X^2 test was applied to the aspects of morphology investigated to determine whether there was a sex difference. It was found that there was no significant difference in any of the character-

Table 3.   Dimensions of permanent teeth (in mm)

Tooth		Mesiodistal			Buccolingual		
		Number	Mean	Standard deviation	Number	Mean	Standard deviation
Maxillary							
I1	M	74	8.55	0.49	71	7.45	0.51
	F	74	8.29	0.45	73	7.19	0.42
I2	M	74	7.02	0.60	71	6.83	0.57
	F	68	6.91	0.53	69	6.52	0.48
C	M	77	7.96	0.45	76	8.51	0.60
	F	77	7.65	0.36	79	8.01	0.51
PM1	M	78	7.25	0.41	76	9.51	0.58
	F	73	7.19	0.45	74	9.21	0.52
PM2	M	77	6.86	0.43	74	9.41	0.52
	F	71	6.79	0.41	75	9.10	0.54
M1	M	62	10.43	0.53	61	11.40	0.57
	F	67	10.19	0.48	69	10.94	0.47
M2	M	64	9.79	0.65	63	11.44	0.65
	F	55	9.47	0.63	57	10.95	0.66
Mandibular							
I1	M	73	5.47	0.47	44	6.24	0.48
	F	73	5.37	0.39	59	6.03	0.46
I2	M	76	6.03	0.44	46	6.61	0.53
	F	78	5.96	0.35	62	6.45	0.43
C	M	74	7.04	0.45	42	7.95	0.53
	F	78	6.64	0.34	67	7.47	0.56
PM1	M	74	7.11	0.45	75	8.00	0.55
	F	73	7.05	0.44	74	7.72	0.48
PM2	M	75	7.18	0.46	74	8.25	0.50
	F	62	7.06	0.48	64	8.11	0.21
M1	M	50	11.23	0.54	51	10.78	0.54
	F	49	10.94	0.51	50	10.40	0.46
M2	M	58	10.41	0.77	58	10.61	0.53
	F	60	10.12	0.59	59	10.24	0.53

istics, and Tables 4 to 7 show percentages of male and female taken together and other Mongoloid and Caucasoid data.

Marked shoveling is primarily a Mongoloid trait. For example, Hrdlička (1920) found that shoveling occurred almost universally and to a pronounced degree in all Mongoloid groups that he examined. Conversely, the trait has a very low frequency in other races. For example, he found the trait almost nonexistent in the Caucasoids. Table 4 gives a comparison of the present study with other data from the literature and shows similarity with the Mongoloid figures but obvious differences from those of the Caucasoids.

Table 4. Percentage frequency of shovel-shaped incisors (male and female combined)

	Central					Lateral				
	n	a	b	c	d	n	a	b	c	d
Present study	138	77.5	21.7	0.8	0	127	70.1	29.1	0.8	0
Aleut										
(Moorrees 1957)	75	62.6	34.7	2.7	0	70	65.7	31.4	2.9	0
East Greenland										
Eskimos										
(Pedersen 1949)				116*	83.6	14.7	0.		0.	
Finns (Koski and										
Hantala 1952)	423	3.8	10.9	76.4	9.0	408	2.9	16.7	73.3	7.1
Caucasoids										
(Hrdlička 1920)	2,000	2.0	6.4	23.2	68.4	2,000	1.2	8.1	33.2	54.8

a = shovel, b = semi-shovel, c = trace shovel, d = no shovel.
* Central and lateral incisors combined.

Dahlberg (1963) found that the hypocone was most prominent in the deciduous second molar and that there was a progressive reduction in the permanent first, and more so in the second molar, with complete absence in the third molar. In Table 5, simplification of the occlusal form of maxillary molars by the reduction or elimination of the hypocone does not vary a great deal between the various groups, although in Keene's (1968) data there seems to be rather too high a proportion of three-cusped first molars.

Table 5. Percentage frequency of maxillary molar cusps (male and female combined unless stated otherwise)

	First molar				Second molar			
	n	3	3+	4	n	3	3+	4
Present study	133	2.2	0	97.8	135	31.1	12.6	56.3
Aleut (Moorrees 1957)	60	0*		100.0	55	30.9*		69.2
East Greenland Eskimos								
(Pedersen 1949)	186	0*		100.0	181	34.3*		65.7
American whites								
(Dahlberg 1945)	106	2.0	3.0	95.0	92	42.0	20.0	38.0
American white males								
(Keene 1968)	778	39.3*		60.7	773	39.2*		60.8

* 3 and 3+ combined.

Carabelli's trait has not normally been found to be well marked in Mongoloid groups and the present findings support this, Table 6 giving some comparisons with other groups, including Caucasoids from Liverpool; the latter show a very different pattern, the trait being much more common.

Table 6.   Percentage frequency of Carabelli's trait (male and female combined)

	First molar					Second molar				
	n	a	b	c_1	c_2	n	a	b	c_1	c_2
Present study	134	70.9	21.7	5.2	5.2	133	99.2	0.8	0	0
Aleut (Moorrees 1957)	60	86.7		13.3*						
East Greenland Eskimos (Pedersen 1949)	106	100.0		0*		162	99.4		0.6*	
British (Goose and Lee 1971)	602	21.1	58.4	9.7	9.1					
American whites (Keene 1968)	773	40.0	38.2	14.2	7.6	778	97.3	1.8	0.5	0.4

a = no evidence, b = pits or grooves, c_1 = cusp without free tip, c_2 = cusp with free tip.
* b, c_1, and c_2 combined.

It can be seen from Table 7 that in all groups the mandibular first molar tends to follow the primitive *Dryopithecus* pattern of five cusps and Y configuration, although in the Aleuts there is a higher proportion of the + configuration. In the second molar, however, there are varying degrees of departure from the Y5 to the more "advanced" +4 pattern with +5 and Y4 as intermediates. The Caucasoid second molar has a greater tendency for extreme modification, although cusp number of the present study is similar to that of the Caucasoid groups.

Table 7.   Percentage frequency of mandibular molar cusps and fissure configuration

		n	5 cusps	4 cusps	n	Y	+
Present study	M_1	94	92.6	7.4	48	91.6	8.4
	M_2	116	11.2	88.8	81	0	100.0
Aleut (Moorrees 1957)	M_1	29	100.0	0	29	41.4	58.6
	M_2	36	55.5	44.5	36	0	100.0
East Greenland Eskimos	M_1	143	98.5	1.5	143	95.7	4.3
(Pedersen 1949)	M_2	115	61.0	39.0	115	23.0	77.0
British (Lavelle et al.	M_1	135	94.6	5.4	135	76.3	23.7
1970)	M_2	135	7.6	92.4	135	5.8	94.2
Modern Dutchmen	M_1	756	89.8	10.2	627	76.5	23.5
(Jørgensen 1955)	M_2	691	14.0	86.0	658	21.0	79.0

The results of the present study show a similarity with other Mongoloid data in tooth size and morphology, and contrast partially with Caucasoid data. Maxillary lateral incisor size, frequencies of Carabelli's cusp, and shoveling show a fairly distinct difference between the Mongoloid and Caucasoid groups. Maxillary and mandibular molar cusp frequency and fissure configuration are not as revealing in this respect. Dahlberg (1951) and Hanihara (1967) referred to the term "Mongoloid dental complex" to denote a series of characteristics, including shoveling, with a relatively high frequency in the Mongoloid. On the other hand, high frequencies of Carabelli's trait contribute to the "Caucasoid dental complex."

Unfortunately, these morphological characters may not be so useful in indicating the underlying genetic makeup since recent results by Lee and Goose (1972) have shown that inheritance patterns are far from simple, and that probably a multifactorial system is more applicable.

CHILDREN

The examination of the Chinese children was merely part of a more general investigation of immigrants, and only the age group seven to eleven years was studied. There were thirty-six boys and twenty-nine girls in the schools chosen, and they were inspected under standardized conditions using a headlamp and replaceable probe points (Varley and Goose 1971). The mean ages of the groups were very close: for boys the Chinese were 114.4 months and the Caucasoid 114.0, and similarly for girls, 113.4 and 114.3 respectively.

Their dental condition was expressed for caries as a mean DMF and for gingivitis as a periodontal index (PI). These are shown along with the data for native British children from the same schools in Table 8.

Table 8. Mean DMF and periodontal indices for children

	DMF		PI	
	Boys	Girls	Boys	Girls
Chinese	1.83	2.24	0.54	0.52
Caucasoid	1.55	1.69	0.43	0.39

There had been an impression that the Chinese adults in this area had preserved their dentitions considerably better than the native British, and so it came as a surprise to see that for both dental caries and gingivitis the Chinese children appeared worse. On testing, the DMF significance was not reached, but for the periodontal index, boys showed $P < 0.01$ and girls were on the borderline of < 0.05 (using a nonparametric method, the Kolmogorov-Smirnov two-sample test [Goose and Varley 1971]).

It is interesting to speculate why this phenomenon is found, but presumably it is an environmental factor affecting the children who were born mainly in the United Kingdom, as opposed to their parents who were born in China or Hong Kong. This factor is being investigated further and seems, in the case of caries, to be likely to be related to the increased sugar consumption consequent on living in the United Kingdom.

REFERENCES

BOWDEN, D. E. J.
  1967   "Some observations of the role of inheritance in tooth and jaw size, examined by a family study." Master's thesis, University of Liverpool.
BOWDEN, D. E. J., D. H. GOOSE
  1968   The inheritance of palatal arch width in human families. *Archives of Oral Biology* 13:1293–1295.
DAHLBERG, A. A.
  1945   The changing dentition of man. *Journal of the American Dental Association* 32:676–690.
  1951   "The dentition of the American Indian," in *The physical anthropology of the American Indian*. Edited by W. S. Laughlin, 138–176. New York: Viking Fund.
  1956   "Materials for the establishment of standards for classification of tooth characters, attributes and techniques in morphological studies of the dentition." Mimeograph. Chicago: University of Chicago, Zoller Laboratory of Dental Anthropology.
  1963   "Analysis of the American Indian dentition," in *Dental anthropology*. Edited by D. R. Brothwell, 149–177. New York: Pergamon Press.
DOCKRELL, R. B., L. M. CLINCH, J. H. SCOTT
  1954   The faces, jaws and teeth of Aran Island children. *Transactions of the European Orthodontical Society*, 159–220.
GARN, S. M., A. B. LEWIS, R. S. KEREWSKY
  1966   Sexual dimorphism in the buccolingual tooth diameter. *Journal of Dental Research* 45(6):1819.
GARN, S. M.
  1968   The magnitude and implications of the relationship between tooth size and body size. *Archives of Oral Biology* 13:129–131.
GOOSE, D. H.
  1962   Reduction of palate size in modern populations. *Archives of Oral Biology* 7:343–350.
  1963   "Dental measurement: an assessment of its value in anthropological studies," in *Dental anthropology*. Edited by D. R. Brothwell, 125–148. New York: Pergamon Press.

GOOSE, D. H., G. T. R. LEE
1971 The mode of inheritance of Carabelli's trait. *Human Biology* 32: 64–69.

GOOSE, D. H., T. F. VARLEY
1971 Periodontal conditions of children of immigrants in Liverpool. *Journal of Dental Research* 50:77.

HANIHARA, K.
1967 Racial characteristics in the dentition. *Journal of Dental Research* 46:923–926.

HONG, Y. C.
1965 A study on the relationship of tooth material to coronal and basal arches in Chinese children of accepted normal occlusion. *Journal of the Formosan Medical Association* 64:14–22.

HOSAKA, T.
1936 Statistische Untersuchungen über die Zähne bei Chinesen mit besonderer Berücksichtigung der Rassenunterschiede. *Journal of Oriental Medicine* 24:1065–1090, 1230–1251; 25:41, 348–368.

HRDLIČKA, A.
1920 Shovel-shaped teeth. *American Journal of Physical Anthropology* 3:429–465.

JØRGENSEN, K. D.
1955 The Dryopithecus pattern in recent Danes and Dutchmen. *Journal of Dental Research* 34:195–208.

KEENE, H. J.
1968 The relationship between Carabelli's trait and the size, number and morphology of the maxillary molars. *Archives of Oral Biology* 13:1023–1025.

KOSKI, K., E. HANTALA
1952 On the frequency of shovel-shaped incisors in Finns. *American Journal of Physical Anthropology* 10:127–132.

KRAUS, B. S.
1951 Carabelli's anomaly of the maxillary molar teeth. *American Journal of Human Genetics* 3:348–355.

LAVELLE, C. L. B., E. H. ASHTON, R. M. FLINN
1970 Cusp pattern, tooth size and third molar agenesis in the human mandibular dentition. *Archives of Oral Biology* 15:227–237.

LUNDSTRÖM, A.
1943 Intermaxillara tandbreddsförhållanden och tandställningen. *Svenska Tandläkare Tidskrift* 36:574–624.
1948 *Tooth size and occlusion in twins.* Basel: S. Karger.

LEE, G. T. R., D. H. GOOSE
1972 The inheritance of dental traits in a Chinese population in the U.K. *Journal of Medical Genetics* 9:336–339.

MIJSBERG, W. A.
1931 On sexual differences in the teeth of the Javanese. *Proceedings of the Koninklijke Nederlandse Akademie van Wetenschappen, Series C: Biological and Medical Sciences* 34:1111–1115.

MOORREES, C. F. A.
1957 *The Aleut dentition. A correlative study of dental characteristics*

in an Eskimoid people. Cambridge: Harvard University Press.

NELSON, C. T.
1938   The teeth of the Indians of Pecos Pueblo. American Journal of Physical Anthropology 23:261–293.

PEDERSEN, P. O.
1949   The East Greenland Eskimo dentition: numerical variations and anatomy. Meddelelser om Grønland 142(3):1–256.

SEIPEL, C. M.
1946   Variation of tooth position. Svenska Tandläkare Tidskrift 39, supplement.

TURNER, C. G.
1969   Microevolutionary interpretations from the dentition. American Journal of Physical Anthropology 30:421–426.

VARLEY, T. F., D. H. GOOSE
1971   Dental caries in children of immigrants in Liverpool. British Dental Journal 130:27–29.

Dentition of the Ainu and the Australian Aborigines

KAZURO HANIHARA

The Ainu are a unique population living in Hokkaido and Sakhalin. The racial origin of this population is still a subject of argument, and several different theories have so far been proposed. Among the most popular theories are: (1) Caucasoid origin, and (2) Australoid origin of the Ainu population.

At the International Congress of Anthropological and Ethnological Sciences held in Tokyo in 1968, I expressed the opinion that the Ainu were very similar to the Mongoloids in their dental characteristics, and largely differed from the Caucasoids. Later, in 1969, I had an opportunity to examine the large collection of dental casts of the Australian Aborigines at the University of Adelaide, Australia. Although the data obtained in Australia are now under detailed analysis, it is quite clear that the dentition of the Aborigines shows several unique characteristics and differs from that of the Ainu.

This paper is a preliminary report on a comparison of the crown characteristics in the Ainu and the Australian Aborigines. At the same time, racial affinities will be discussed on the basis of data from some other populations that I investigated.

MATERIALS AND METHODS

Plaster casts of the Ainu dentition were collected from some 600 Ainu individuals living in Hidaka district, the southern part of Hokkaido, under the auspices of the Human Adaptability Section of the International Biological Programme. Most of the subjects were junior high

I am deeply indebted to Dr. Albert A. Dahlberg of the University of Chicago, and to Professor A. M. Horsnell and Dr. M. J. Barrett of the University of Adelaide for inviting me to their laboratories and giving me permission to investigate valuable dental material in their collections.

school pupils of twelve to fourteen years of age and were hybrids between the Ainu and the ordinary Japanese. Of these, 105 individuals were selected and used for investigation because their rate of admixture had been estimated to be one-half or less on the basis of pedigree analysis. The average rate of admixture of this group was estimated to be 0.23.

The materials from the Australian Aborigines were plaster casts from inhabitants of the Yuendumu settlement in central Australia and were collected by the research group of the Department of Oral Biology, University of Adelaide. In addition, the control groups used in this study were composed of Japanese, Pima Indians, Eskimos, and Caucasians living in the United States. The materials from these populations were in the collections of the Department of Anthropology, University of Tokyo, and the Department of Anthropology, University of Chicago.

The crown characters investigated were as follows:

a.   Shovel-shape in the upper central incisor — the depth of the lingual fossa was measured using a specially designed dial gauge (see Hanihara, Tanaka, and Tamada 1970), and incisors with the depth of 0.51 millimeters or over were referred to as shovel-shaped;

b.   Sixth cusp, seventh cusp, and deflecting wrinkle in the lower first molar — the teeth carrying the traits were simply counted;

c.   Protostylid in the lower first molar — the so-called pit type of the protostylid was excluded from calculation of frequencies;

d.   Carabelli's cusp in the upper first molar — only the cusp type of this trait was counted for calculation.

These crown characters were selected because they showed relatively distinct differences between racial populations in their frequency distributions (Hanihara 1969). The investigation was made on the right-side teeth, the left-side teeth having been observed only when the antimeres were badly damaged. As no significant differences between sexes were observed, the combined-sex series were used in this study.

COMPARISONS OF CROWN CHARACTERS

i.   Shovel-shape: The frequencies of the shovel-shaped upper central incisors are quite similar for the Ainu and the Australian Aborigines, both of whom show slightly lower values compared to the Mongoloids such as the Japanese, Pima Indians, and Eskimos. The same trend is also recognized in the average values of depth of the lingual fossa: the

Ainu (0.88 millimeters) are very close to the Aborigines (0.82 millimeters), but relatively lower than the Japanese (0.99 millimeters), Pimas (1.20 millimeters), and Eskimos (1.13 millimeters). See Table 1.

Table 1. Frequency distributions of the crown characteristics (in percents)

Population	Shovel-shape	Sixth cusp	Seventh cusp	Deflecting wrinkle	Protostylid	Carabelli's cusp
Ainu	81.4 (97)	26.6 (79)	4.8 (83)	25.6 (78)	12.2 (82)	9.5 (105)
Japanese	95.6 (432)	25.3 (1046)	6.7 (60)	29.6 (395)	6.6 (425)	6.5 (444)
Australian Aborigines	89.8 (166)	52.5 (162)	6.5 (155)	41.1 (163)	6.1 (165)	15.7 (159)
Pima Indian	99.1 (222)	26.6 (207)	8.2 (208)	39.5 (205)	19.4 (217)	6.9 (216)
Eskimo	100.0 (21)	50.0 (30)	20.0 (30)	44.4 (27)	28.6 (14)	13.0 (23)
Caucasian	27.7 (83)	5.2 (58)	5.1 (59)	3.6 (56)	0.0 (81)	39.0 (59)

Figures in parentheses indicate the number of individuals observed.

ii.   Sixth cusp: The frequency of this cusp in the Ainu is almost the same as that in the Japanese and Pimas, but significantly lower than in the Aborigines and Eskimos.

iii.   Seventh cusp: The frequencies of this trait show relatively few differences among the populations investigated with the exception of the Eskimos who show higher incidence of the seventh cusp.

iv.   Deflecting wrinkle: This trait shows relatively low frequencies in the Ainu and Japanese compared with the Aborigines, Pimas, and Eskimos.

v.   Protostylid: The protostylid is relatively frequent in the Pimas and Eskimos, less frequent in the Japanese and Aborigines, and intermediate in the Ainu. No individual carrying this trait was found among the Caucasoids.

vi.   Carabelli's cusp: In contrast to the crown characters mentioned above, the Carabelli's cusp is frequently found in the Caucasoids, but relatively infrequently in the other populations. Also, it is noteworthy that the Caucasoids tend to carry the well-developed cusp, or the so-called cusp type of the Carabelli's tubercle. In this regard, the teeth carrying the cusp with a more or less free apex separated from the lingual surface with a groove were counted in this investigation. The frequency of teeth with such a trait is highest in the Caucasoids, intermediate in the Aborigines and Eskimos, and lower in the Ainu, Japanese, and Pimas.

Table 2. The mean measure of divergence (biological distance) between populations (computed by C. A. B. Smith's method)

	Ainu	Japanese	Pima Indian	Eskimo	Australian Aborigine	Caucasian
Ainu	–	3.13	9.14	2.12	7.24	50.43
Japanese	3.13	–	3.34	13.84	7.59	73.13
Pima Indian	9.14	3.34	–	3.33	11.53	102.21
Eskimo	2.12	13.84	3.33	–	11.71	134.01
Australian Aborigine	7.24	7.59	11.53	11.71	–	78.08
Caucasian	50.43	73.13	102.21	134.01	78.08	–

The figures are indicated by a hundredfold of the original values.

As a whole, the Ainu are very similar to the Japanese but greatly different from the Caucasoids in frequency distribution of the crown characters. On the other hand, differences between the Ainu and the Aborigines are more difficult to summarize because the two populations are similar to each other in some characters but not in others.

To make this point clearer, multivariate analysis was employed. The method used in this study was that devised by C. A. B. Smith (see Berry and Berry 1967), and a "mean measure of divergence," or biological distance, was calculated between every pair of the populations presented here (Table 2).

As shown in Table 2, the biological distance is quite large between the Caucasoids and all other populations, but considerably smaller between any pair of the latter populations. The distance is extremely small between the Ainu and Japanese, Ainu and Eskimos, Japanese and Pimas, and Pimas and Eskimos. This trend seems to be important because the Japanese, Pimas, and Eskimos belong to the Mongoloid stock, and they share common characteristics in dental morphology (Hanihara 1969). In contrast to this, the Aborigines are somewhat distant from the Ainu compared to the three Mongoloid populations, although the distance is much smaller than between the Aborigines and Caucasoids.

On the other hand, one of the most remarkable characteristics in the Aboriginal dentition is an evident trace of the fovea anterior which is especially marked in the lower second molar. This trait seems to have derived from the generalized type of molars found in fossil hominoids and hominids such as Dryopithecus, Australopithecus, Homo erectus, and Neanderthal man. In this connection, this is probably an archaic characteristic in the dentition, and relatively infrequent and only weakly developed in recent man.

In the second lower molar of the Aborigines, this characteristic was found in 95 individuals out of 154 (61.7 percent), and among the Japanese in 14 out of 60 (23.3 percent). Further, the degree of development is considerably higher in the Aborigines than in the Japanese. Although detailed observations have not yet been made on the other populations, it is quite likely that the trend is almost the same as in the Japanese. In this regard, the Aboriginal dentition seems to show a unique characteristic which separates the Aborigines from the other populations.

CONCLUSION

As a result of investigation of dental characters, it is revealed that the Ainu are very similar to the Japanese and the Eskimos, but far different from the Caucasoids. The biological distance between the Ainu and the Australian Aborigines is not as large, but they are quite different from each other in the frequency and expression of the fovea anterior in the lower second molar. In addition, the Ainu differ somewhat from the Pima Indians, but we can find little evidence of difference between the two populations in frequency distribution of the crown characters.

In view of these facts, it seems quite likely that the Ainu might have derived from the Mongoloid stock and have a common ancestor with the neighboring populations such as the Japanese, Eskimos, and American Indians. It is worth noting that almost the same results were obtained from investigations of the finger and palm print patterns (Kimura 1962), the red-cell enzyme systems and serum protein groups (Omoto 1972), and the blood groups (Misawa 1975).

In contrast to this, difference between the Ainu and the Aborigines, although not so large as between the Ainu and Caucasoids, is supported by osteological studies (Yamaguchi 1967) and polymorphic characters (Omoto 1972), so that the theory that attributes the origin of the Ainu to the Australoid stock can hardly be adopted.

Studies on the dentition of the Ainu and the Aborigines are now in progress, and the conclusion presented here is still provisional. However, many additional data are being accumulated so that a more extensive view on this problem is expected to be advanced in the near future.

REFERENCES

BERRY, A. C., R. J. BERRY
1967 Epigenetic variation in the human cranium. *Journal of Anatomy* 101:361–379.

HANIHARA, K.
1969 Mongoloid dental complex in the permanent dentition. *Proceedings of the Eighth International Congress of Anthropological and Ethnological Sciences, Tokyo and Kyoto, 1968*, 298–300. Tokyo: Science Council of Japan.

HANIHARA, K., T. TANAKA, M. TAMADA
1970 Quantitative analysis of the shovel-shaped character in the incisors. *Journal of the Anthropological Society of Nippon* 78:90–98.

KIMURA, K.
1962 The Ainus, viewed from their finger and palm prints. *Zeitschrift für Morphologie und Anthropologie* 52:176–198.

MISAWA, S.
1975 "Genetic composition of the Ainu: blood groups," in *Human adaptability*, volume two: *Anthropological and genetic studies on the Japanese*. Edited by S. Watanabe, S. Kondo, and E. Matsunaga, 265–273. Tokyo: University of Tokyo Press.

OMOTO, K.
1972 Polymorphisms and genetic affinities of the Ainu of Hokkaido. *Human Biology in Oceania* 1:278–288.

YAMAGUCHI, B.
1967 *A comparative study of the Ainu and the Australian Aborigines.* Australian Institute of Aboriginal Studies Occasional Papers 10.

A Comparative Study of the Dental, Cranial, and Facial Phenotypes of Subjects Having Congenital Defects of the Superior Lateral Incisors

PIERRE LE BOT

The relationship between the absence of certain teeth and the modification of the rest of the denture has been demonstrated in numerous studies. But these studies have mainly dealt with the third molars. Garn and his associates (Garn and Lewis 1962, 1969; Garn, Lewis, and Bonné 1961; Garn, Lewis, and Vicinus 1962; Garn, Lewis, and Kerewsky 1963, 1964) and Keene (1964) have researched this question. With regard to the superior lateral incisors (SLIs), although some fairly complete studies have been carried out by Grahnćn (1956), it seems to us that a project similar to that of Garn on the third molars might be of interest. In fact, lateral incisors are absent less than third molars, and such an absence appears to us to be related to more severe defects of the other teeth.

MATERIAL AND METHODS

The first stage of this research consisted of determining the individuals within a certain population who have congenitally missing or reduction forms of the superior lateral incisors. An approximately equal number of control subjects were then compared with regard to a number of characteristics and to facial and cranial dental measurements.

The Population

The population was composed of young men gathered together at the

Centre de Sélection Militaire de Vincennes for a stay prior to their induction into military service. All young Frenchmen must attend such a convocation. In our case, out of 5,738 subjects, only fifteen were not present. Thus we can conclude that there was no preliminary selection process involved here. The only factor the subjects had in common was that they were all born in Paris.

The disadvantages we faced had to do with the extremely heterogeneous and fluctuating character of the Parisian population and with the fact that all the participants were male. Our goal was to study the mechanisms of congenital absence of teeth which was not affected by the foregoing.

The teeth of Parisians are generally in better condition than those of rural populations. The advantages of this for our work are indeed important.

The mean age of our subjects was twenty years. The wisdom teeth were calcified and were visible by X ray. Memory and factual data were indispensable for a differential diagnosis between agenesis and extraction. The subject had to be fairly young so that he had not forgotten about extractions.

General Screening Examinations

The subjects were selected according to a simple examination of their SLIs, whether absent or reduced. The criterion of reduction is that used by Grahnén (1956) which is the conoid tooth. The cases that were doubtful were eliminated. The author worked alone in this research.

Approximately 150 men were examined each day; less than ten were of interest as experimental subjects, and about the same number were chosen as control subjects.

Dental Examinations

The following examinations were then carried out:
1.   Direct study of the entire denture, with notation of all missing teeth.
2.   Questioning for differential diagnosis to distinguish between extraction and agenesis.
3.   Verification of findings by X ray: 1,500 X rays were taken, one hundred of which were panoramic.

4.   Dental models of the teeth provided twenty tooth measurements and four measurements of the arcade. They included mesiodistal and vestibulolingual diameters of I^1, C, Pm^1, Pm^2, M^1, and transverse diameters of the arcade, viz: between grooves of Pm's and M's, the vestibular faces of the second molars, and between the distal surfaces of the second molars and the central incisors.

The dental measurements were obtained to the tenth of a millimeter on plaster of Paris molds, by the same experimenter, according to the Moorrees method (Moorrees et al. 1957).

Morphological Examinations

Morphological examinations included maximum length glabella-opisthocranion and width, head measurements and height (gnathion-nasion), and bizygomatic width facial measurements. We therefore had twenty-eight parameters per subject. After having ascertained that there was no significant difference between the measurements of the teeth on the right and the left side of the mouth, we decided to use only those of the right.

RESULTS

Defects of the Superior Lateral Incisors

Of 5,738 subjects examined, 200 could be included in our studies. We did not find any crowded SLIs. The different combinations between right and left sides led us to posit eight different groups. Table 1 shows our results.

We can group these subjects according to whether they have absence or reduction of the SLIs, which gives us the results in Table 2. These results show no marked asymmetry. There is a slight superiority of the left side that is not significant.

Agenesis of the Other Teeth as a Function of the Defects of the SLIs

Can the agenesis or reduction of the SLIs be related to the agenesis of the other teeth? The answer to this question is affirmative, as results will show. Tooth by tooth comparisons were made.

Table 1.   Number of subjects in the eight experimental groups

Form of the defect of the SLIs	Number
Right normal — left missing	16
Right missing — left normal	14
Right normal — left reduced	28
Right reduced— left normal	26
Right missing — left missing	49
Right reduced— left reduced	37
Right reduced— left missing	18
Right missing — left reduced	12
Total	200

Table 2.   Frequency of subjects having an absence or a reduction of SLIs

Subjects	Number	Percentage
With absence of one or two SLIs (the other being normal or reduced)	109	1.9
With reduction of one or two SLIs	91	1.6
Total	200	3.5

The results of the groups of men studied follow.

The results relating to third molars are shown in Table 3. There is an increase of the percentage of missing third molars from 12.4 percent of the control subjects to 39.6 percent of the experimental subjects having two missing SLIs.

It has also been ascertained that the location of the affected SLI, right or left, has no influence upon the third molar. The symmetry is perfect between right and left sides.

Table 3.   Ageneses of the third molar in the experimental and control subjects

Groups	Total number of teeth examined	Absences	
		Number of teeth missing	Percentage of teeth missing
Control group	1,000	124	12.4
Candidates with one or two SLIs reduced	296	71	24.0
Candidates with one SLI missing;	208	43	20.7
two SLIs missing	192	76	39.6
	$X^2 = 87.8$	$P < 0.001$	

Table 4. Ageneses of the lower incisors ,of the canines, and of the upper and lower premolars in experimental and control group members

Groups	Total number of teeth examined	Number of teeth missing	Percentage of teeth missing
Control group	4,000	15	0.4
Candidates with one or two SLIs reduced	1,376	18	1.3
Candidates with one SLI missing; two SLIs missing	896 784	13 39	1.4 5.0
	$X^2 = 117.0$	$P < 0.001$	

The inferior third molars are a bit more crowded than the upper ones.

In Table 4 we have regrouped the ageneses of all the teeth except the molars. The first and second molars were excluded from these results because of the unreliability of the information. In this table the agenesis with regard to certain teeth, in both experimental and control group members, is compared. The results appear to be even more striking when we note the change from 0.4 to 5.0 percent within the same category (control group, experimental group with some reduction, and experimental group with some absence). We must, however, take into account subjects with multiple agencis (one of the subjects had fourteen missing teeth). For that data, we counted the number of subjects with defects and not the number of missing teeth. The differences between the groups remain highly significant.

Measurements of the Teeth

For this study, we separated our control group into two subclasses: one class in the complete control group who had all thirty-two teeth, and one class of those control members who had at least one agenesis.

In Figure 1 can be seen the averages of the mesiodistal diameters as they pertain to the control group members, the ones with one missing SLI, and the others with reduction of SLIs.

The reduction of the measurements is evident in the order as follows: "complete" control groups members, experimental subjects with some SLI missing, and experimental subjects with some reduction in SLI size. This difference is highly significant. All the teeth are not equally affected.

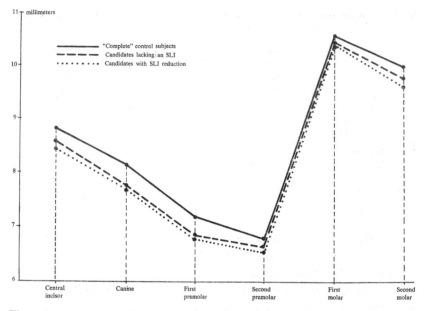

Figure 1

Taking the absolute value of the reduction from the tooth which is the most affected to the one which is least affected, we find the following order: C, P^1, I^1, M^2, P^2, M^1.

If we analyze the variance between the three groups of subjects mentioned above, the following order is apparent: C, P^1, P^2, I^1, M^2, M^1.

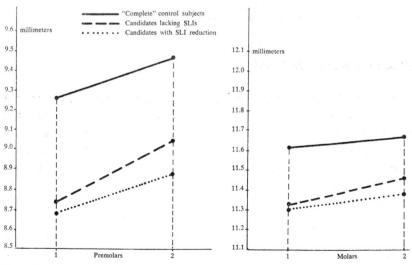

Figure 2

Figure 2 shows the buccolingual diameters of the molars and the premolars. It can be seen here that premolars are much more reduced than are the molars, and that buccolingual diameters are more affected than are the mesiodistals.

If we now place the control subjects with those having agenesis (Figure 3) on a chart, they will be seen to fall exactly between the "complete" control subjects and the experimental subjects.

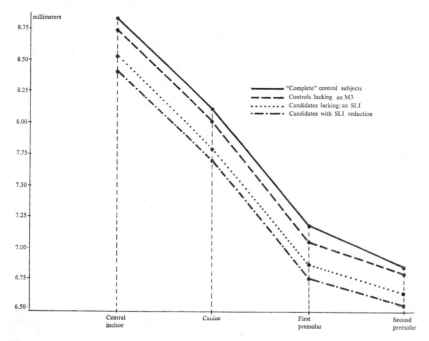

Figure 3

Measurements of the Arcades

The differences between the control subjects and the candidates are all highly significant for the length of the arcade. Between control subjects and candidates missing some SLIs, the differences are still significant for the transverse diameters of the arcade, this difference diminishing, however, from the most anterior to the most posterior diameter.

Between control subjects and experimental subjects with some reduction in the SLIs, there is no significant difference in the transverse diameters.

Measurements of the Head and Face

The results are much less significant with regard to these measurements. Although the subjects exhibit smaller numbers on these parameters, the differences are rarely significant.

Only the height of the face shows a significant difference between control subjects and experimental subjects with reduction of the superior lateral incisors. The averages are not extremely different among the various groups. The extent of the distribution is less important in the experimental subjects than in the control subjects.

In the analyses by principal components, we have seen fit to divide the measurements two by two: (1) width of the head and width of the face, and (2) length of the head and height of the face.

The widths appear to be particularly related. There also appears, in the control subjects, an almost complete independence between these two groups of two measurements.

Let us examine for example the relationships of our four measurements with the three primary axes F_1—F_2—F_3 of our analysis by principal components. For F_1, we are too close to the origin to obtain a clear interpretation, but in F_2 and F_3 the opposition between these two groups of measurements can be clearly distinguished (see Table 5).

Table 5. Head and face measurements in control subjects

	F_1	F_2	F_3
Length of head	0.1543	−0.0690	−0.5685
Width of head	−0.0056	−0.8421	−0.2579
Width of face	0.2123	−0.8093	−0.2925
Height of face	0.3128	0.1623	−0.6675

In contrast, if we take the experimental subjects missing some SLIs, for example, this independence becomes much less obvious. It is necessary to examine the same parameters in the analysis by principal components (see Table 6). One can see immediately the clear connection between these data. We find the same result in our subjects with reduction of the SLIs.

Table 6. Head and face measurements in experimental subjects

	F_1	F_2	F_3
Length of head	0.1662	−0.5873	−0.2452
Width of head	−0.0494	−0.8303	−0.2047
Width of face	−0.0407	−0.8499	−0.1177
Height of face	0.4157	−0.2909	−0.3228

I should like to insist once more upon the extreme importance of finding the same phenomena in our various categories of experimental subjects in comparison with those of our control subjects. It is in this way that we become convinced of the importance of a fact which sometimes seems too weak to be borne out by any statistical testing, but which through repetition proves its importance.

DISCUSSION

With regard to the results on agenesis or reduction of the superior lateral incisors, the research which is most similar to ours is that of Meskin and Gorlin (1963) which was carried out at the University of Minnesota using 5,165 male students as subjects. The differences are very perceptible in all categories of candidates examined; our figures are always much higher.

The percentages found by Rose (1966) with Europeans appear to be much closer to ours. Can it then be deduced that what is at issue is a racial difference? It seems difficult to draw such a conclusion if the various studies on this subject are considered. Because there is no standardization of this sort of research, it is impossible to really compare them. However, the work done by Meskin and Gorlin (1963) seems to have followed the same rules as we have, and we think that the differences in our results merit some attention.

Our goal was mainly to compare our experimental subjects with our control group subjects. We have found a definite influence of the defects of the superior lateral incisors upon the agenesis of other teeth.

Garn, Lewis, and Vicinus (1962) carried out the same sort of study with regard to third molars. They have in fact compared a group of one hundred subjects who were lacking at least one third molar with a group of 398 control subjects who had all four molars. They ascertained, as we did, that the agenesis of the third molars is more frequent in the mandible than in the superior maxillary. The symmetry of defects between right and left sides was also noted.

Increase in the incidence of agenesis for the other teeth is also quite striking in their subjects. They found thirteen times more teeth missing in these subjects than in the control group subjects. In our experiment, the experimental subjects had thirty-two times more teeth missing than the control group subjects, if we do not include the third molars in these figures.

Garn et al. (1961) remark upon a slow process of evolution of other teeth in their subjects. We could verify this only with regard to the third molars because of the age of our subjects. Our results do not permit us to ascertain any slow evolution in our candidates. Nearly 50 percent of the third molars were cut in our different groups, without differences between the groups.

It is thus obvious that the agenesis of a single tooth is not an isolated fact. It represents a defect in the entire denture by a process which has a tendency to reduce the number of its elements. This process acts selectively in certain especially vulnerable points of the denture. The reduction of one tooth thus would appear here to be the intermediate phenotype between presence and absence.

With regard to the measurements of the other teeth, our results do not confirm the classical notion that the most distal teeth are the least stable ones. In fact, P^1 is clearly more reduced than P^2.

Another important point, concerning the reduction of the diameters in our candidates, is that the subjects with reduction of the SLIs have a phenotype which is much more extreme than the subjects with missing teeth. Therefore one can no longer maintain that reduction is an intermediary phenomenon between presence and absence of teeth.

Table 7 summarizes the situation. For each group of subjects, it gives the results concerning the ageneses of the other teeth on the one hand and the reduction of the sum of their diameters on the other.

Table 7.   Ageneses of other teeth and the reduction of the sum of their diameters

	Percentage of reduction of the sum of the mesiodistal diameters in controls	Percentage of reduction of the sum of the vestibulolin-gual diameters in controls	Percentage of agenesis of wisdom teeth	Percentage of agenesis of the I-C-P_1-P_2
Candidates lacking SLI	2.4	3.3	30.0	3.0
Candidates with reduction of SLI	3.4	4.1	24.0	1.3

In this area as well, we shall compare our results with those of Garn, Lewis, and Kerewsky (1963, 1964). They have measured the mesio-distal diameters of the teeth of 658 subjects, of whom eighty-two exhibited agenesis of one or several wisdom teeth, and nineteen had multiple ageneses most often of the incisors or the premolars.

They have found, as have we, that there is reduction of the mesiodistal diameters in the following order: "complete" control subjects, subjects with missing wisdom teeth, and subjects with multiple ageneses.

It is notable in these two studies that it is the molars that are the least affected. Garn has even found that, in his group of subjects with multiple agenesis, the molars are bigger, just as we have reported in our group of control subjects with agenesis of the third molar. The particular nature of the molars in relationship with the other teeth has thus been confirmed.

The order found by Garn and Lewis (Table 8) has led them to conclude that there is some gradient in the defects of the teeth, regularly decreasing from the central incisor to the molars. While the gradient appears to us to be quite obvious, its regularity from front to back is less noticeable in our data than in theirs. In fact, for us, it is the canines and the premolars which are the most reduced.

Table 8. Order of proportional reduction of the mesiodistal diameters of the superior maxillary teeth

	1	2	3	4	5	6
Garn	I_1	C	P_1	P_2	M_1	M_2
Le Bot	C	P_1	P_2	I_1	M_2	M_1

However, it remains true that reduction of the teeth is not influenced by any missing adjacent teeth. The schema would stay nearly the same, whether the missing tooth is a third molar or an SLI.

To conclude this discussion, we can say that the differences found in the diameters of the arcade might have a purely mechanical explanation. Also teeth are more reduced and less numerous in the experimental subjects examined. Muscular action can then explain the reduction of the diameters.

SUMMARY

Extensive research on the agenesis of the SLIs was carried out on 5,738 male subjects from age eighteen to twenty-five. The incidence of agenesis was 1.91 percent and that of reductions was 1.58 percent.

The following data was gathered on 268 control subjects and several groups of experimental subjects:

1.   Enumeration of all the teeth with radiographic verification of possible absences.

2.   Molds of the two arcades, permitting measurement of all the teeth, as well as of the transverse diameters and of the length of the upper arcade.

3.   Measurements of the head and face.

The following results were obtained:

1.   Highly significant increase of agenesis of all teeth in the subjects.

2.   Highly significant reduction of the diameters of the other teeth in these subjects. This reduction is differential, and its gradient approaches that of dental reduction in the course of phylogenesis.

3.   Modification of head and face measurements in the subjects according to the increase in the correlation of the measurements. Such a phenomenon was earlier established with regard to tooth measurements.

The teeth are reduced in number and in volume in the subjects examined. The measurements of the teeth, of the head, and of the face are not independent in that all seem to be controlled by a general constraint.

REFERENCES

GARN, S. M., A. B. LEWIS
   1962   The relationship between third molar agenesis and reduction in tooth number. *Angle Orthodontist* 32:14–18.
   1969   The effect of agenesis on the crown size profile pattern. *Journal of Dental Research* 48:1314.
GARN, S. M., A. B. LEWIS, B. BONNÉ
   1961   Third molar polymorphism and the timing of tooth formation. *Nature* 192:989.
GARN, S. M., A. B. LEWIS, R. S. KEREWSKY
   1963   Third molar agenesis and size reduction of the remaining teeth. *Nature* 200:488–489.
   1964   Third molar agenesis and variation in size of the remaining teeth. *Nature* 201:839.
GARN, S. M., A. B. LEWIS, J. H. VICINUS
   1962   Third molar agenesis and reduction in the number of other teeth. *Journal of Dental Research* 41:717.
GRAHNÉN, H.
   1956   Hypodontia in the permanent dentition: a clinical and genetical investigation. *Odontoloegisk Rev* 7 (Supplement 3).
HANIHARA, K.
   1970   Upper lateral incisor variability and the size of the remaining teeth. *Journal of the Anthropological Society of Nippon* 78: 316–323.
KEENE, H. J.
   1964   Third molar agenesis, spacing and crowding of teeth, and tooth

size in caries-resistant naval recruits. *American Journal of Orthodontics* 50:445–451.

1965　The relationship between third molar agenesis and the morphologic variability of the molar teeth. *Angle Orthodontist* 35:289–298.

1966　The relationship between maternal age and parity, birth weight and hypodontia in naval recruits. *Journal of Dentistry for Children* 33:135–147.

LE DOT, P.

1972　"Biométrie dento-faciale des sujets présentant une atteinte congénitale des incisives latérales supérieures." Unpublished thesis, Paris.

MESKIN, L. H., R. J. GORLIN

1963　Agenesis and peg-shaped permanent maxillary lateral incisors. *Journal of Dental Research* 42:1476–1479.

MOORREES, C. F. A., S. THOMSENS, E. JENSEN, P. K. YEN

1957　Mesiodistal crown diameters of the deciduous and permanent teeth in individuals. *Journal of Dental Research* 36:39–47.

ROSE, J. S.

1966　A survey of congenitally missing teeth, excluding third molars, in 6000 orthodontic patients. *Dental Practice* (Bristol) 17:107.

Cultural and Environmental Influences on the Eskimo Dentition

JOHN T. MAYHALL

If one were to survey the popular literature written in the last few years or to watch the television documentaries concerning the Eskimo culture, it would be easy to reach the opinion that this is a static culture. In fact, even some scientific books and papers appear to illustrate a culture that is still dependent upon snow houses, dog teams, harpoons, etc. Many people around the world still think of the Eskimo as he must have lived shortly after the initial contact with explorers and traders. These oral and written traditions die hard, but they certainly do not apply to the vast majority of Eskimos in North America today. Arctic communities are buzzing with the noise of snowmobiles; the airplane and the helicopter have become more common to Eskimo children than dog teams in some areas, and women now do a large amount of shopping at well-stocked stores.

The same time lag appears to apply to the Eskimo dentition from an anthropological viewpoint. While the heavy dependence on a specialized dentition may have been necessary only a few years ago, today the majority of young Eskimos are utilizing their teeth as would any other North American. Dahlberg (1963: 149) discussed in detail the attributes he found in the American Indian dentition. In that important paper he

This study was supported by the International Biological Programme, Human Adaptability Section, with funds from the National Research Council of Canada.

The author wishes to thank Dr. D. R. Hughes, director IBP-HA, University of Toronto, and Dr. J. A. Hildes, University of Manitoba, for their encouragement and helpfulness. Also, I would like to thank Melinda F. Mayhall for her statistical and clerical assistance. Finally, I would be remiss if I did not express my sincere appreciation to the residents of Igloolik and Hall Beach, N.W.T., for their co-operation. Special appreciation must go to Mr. Simon Iyerak for his assistance.

stated, "Many elements of form and size in the American Indian dentition suggest the existence of some evolutionary advantage." The same
statement applies to almost any aboriginal group that has been studied,
including Eskimos. I hope to show here that traits which to our present
knowledge were advantageous, or at least neutral, may have recently
shifted to a position of being a detriment to the individual. This does
not necessarily imply that in an evolutionary sense they have changed,
although this might be the case in some of the examples utilized in this
article.

NORTHERN FOXE BASIN ESKIMO CULTURE CHANGE

A multidisciplinary study of the Eskimos of Igloolik, Northwest Terri-
tories, Canada was initiated in 1968 under the auspices of the Canadian
International Biological Programme, Human Adaptability Section. Involved in the study were physical anthropologists, physiologists, epi-
demiologists, social scientists, and other investigators. From the vast
amount of data collected it has been possible to assess accurately some
of the effects of a changing culture on the Eskimos.

Igloolik and Hall Beach are two isolated communities in the Foxe
Basin area (69° north latitude, 82° west longitude). The settlement of
Igloolik is located on a small island of the same name just off the Melville Peninsula, while Hall Beach is located south of Igloolik on the
mainland. Igloolik did not see permanent establishment of a trading
post until 1947 (Damas 1963: 27). Hall Beach was not in evidence as a
community until the establishment of a DEW-line site in 1955–1956
(Damas 1963: 29). Until this time, in fact until the 1960's most of the
residents of the Foxe Basin area lived in hunting and fishing camps and
only periodically visited the two centers for trading purposes. Most of
the trading took place at Igloolik because Hall Beach had no trading
post until the sixties. As Damas (1963: 28) notes, ". . . until the late
'30's (when a small ship made an annual visit) one resident priest and
a half-dozen explorers were the only Europeans that the Igluligmiut
were regularly in contact with. . . ." Damas also points out that until the
DEW-line site was established, the yearly Hudson's Bay Company ship
was the only white contact that these Eskimos had. In 1961 only 25.8
percent of the population lived in Igloolik or Hall Beach, but by 1968
it had reached 81.3 percent (Foote 1969: 14–17). It has never reached
100 percent for a sustained period because many people live in the
communities for a period of time and then return to the land. But there

are numerous people who appear to be permanently settled now and have a rather long history of a wage-earning subsistence.

The changes in these two communities have been rapid. When the study was initiated in 1968, Igloolik had no regular air service. To reach the island in the summer meant flying to the DEW-line site and taking a freight canoe on a six-hour, cold, damp journey. Five years later, the two communities had generated enough demand for twice-weekly scheduled air service to Frobisher Bay, from which one can board a jet to Montreal.

A further indication of the rapid rate of culture change can be derived from figures quoted in an economic study of the area (Crowe 1969: 77). In 1964 wages amounted to approximately $22,000, but by 1966 this figure was about $47,000. In the same time interval the funds received from trapping had plummeted from $70,000 per annum to about $25,000. During this period the total income for the Foxe Basin area had dropped about $10,000 to $150,000 per annum. Thus, the emphasis in a short period had shifted more toward wages and away from a land-based economy.

These brief examples give some broad indication of the rapid change under way during the period of the IBP-HA study in this area. In general, we arrived at a time when the residents were land-oriented and completed our study in a time of rapid change to a wage-oriented economy.

What effect does this change have on the dentition? In an earlier paper (Mayhall 1970) I pointed out the dichotomy in pathological rates between individuals living off the land and those residing in the community. This difference was assumed at that time to be due to a dietary change. Individuals who were subsisting almost totally on a diet of sea mammals, caribou, and fish exhibited one-quarter the caries rate of those on a European-type diet (Table 1). This was further confirmation of the work of Russell et al. (1961) and Price (1934) who demonstrated the relationship between diet and caries in Eskimos. When we view the caries rates in historical perspective we note the same trends (Table 2).

Table 1.   Caries experience[+]: Igloolik, N.W.T. Eskimos

| | Percentage of native food | | | | | |
	0–25	26–50	51–75	76–100	0–40	60–100
Males	5.98	5.61	2.96	1.40	6.09	1.94
Females	8.11	4.12	4.25	2.02	6.90	2.82

[+]   Decayed, missing, and filled permanent teeth per individual.

Table 2.   Caries experience for selected Eskimo groups (males and females)

Population		N	DMFT +
Precontact (Thule culture)	approximately	300	0.00
Pangnirtung, N.W.T. (1937)*		82	1.07
Igloolik, N.W.T. (1969)		423	3.81
Hall Beach, N.W.T. (1969)		160	5.50
Wainwright, Alaska (1968)**		244	13.93

+   Decayed, missing, and filled teeth per individual.
*   McEuen   (1938: 374–377).
** Mayhall, Dahlberg, and Owen (1970: 886).

Morphological Traits

With this background let us explore some of the dental traits that have a higher than normal incidence in Eskimos. Discrete or quasi-continuous traits such as shovel-shaped incisors, enamelless buccal pits on mandibular molars, occlusal tubercles or premolars (evaginated odontomes), and complex occlusal groove patterns are all found in high incidences in Eskimos.

SHOVEL-SHAPED INCISORS   Shovel-shaped incisors are one of the principal components of the "Mongoloid dental complex" proposed by Hanihara (1966). This implies, of course, that they are widespread throughout the Mongoloid race. It appears that the greatest expression is to be found in North American Indians, but many Eskimos have a strong development of the lingual marginal ridges of the incisors. It has been postulated that this strong development contributed extra strength to the teeth, and they were thus able to withstand excessive force when necessary. To my knowledge, no one has actually tested this hypothesized strengthening, but it certainly is a plausible explanation. Very few broken or chipped teeth were noted among the people at Igloolik.

Explorers have noted almost superhuman uses of the teeth in the Eskimo. Everything from holding the traces of their active dog teams to opening oil drums has been attributed to the dentition of the Eskimo. While some of the feats noted may be difficult to confirm, there is no doubt that their teeth are subjected to extreme forces during the movements required for hunting on the land and at sea.

This large development of the marginal ridges is certainly an advantage, but a concomitant development is not. Often at the juncture of the two marginal ridges in the cingulum area a small pit is present. This pit was of no consequence in the era of a caries-free environment, but with the change to a caries-prone diet this lingual pit has become a definite liability. With the marginal ridges acting more or less as a funnel it is easy to entrap food in this pit. If oral hygiene were optimal it would still be a hard area to keep clean, but with an almost complete lack of any type of oral hygiene this area becomes carious very quickly. Also, because of its location, the subject does not detect this lesion until it is well advanced. The progress of the lesion is enhanced by the sporadic dental care which is the rule in arctic North America, and the dentist may not see the lesion until the pulp is involved. This may lead ultimately to the loss of the tooth, thus putting the person who may still rely heavily upon this tooth at a decided disadvantage.

PREMOLAR OCCLUSAL TUBERCLES   A curious occurrence found on the occlusal surfaces of premolars also deserves attention. The premolar occlusal tubercle, or evaginated odontome, is prevalent in Eskimos. The incidence of this trait has been reported as between 3 percent (Curzon et al. 1970: 327) and 15 percent (Alexandersen 1970: 590) in Eskimos, which is higher than that found in Caucasians or in other Mongoloids.

This tubercle consists of an enamel covering, dentin and usually a pulp horn. It is found in the mesiodistal midline on the occlusal slope of the buccal cusps. This is a trait which was disadvantageous even before a dietary change. Curzon et al. (1970) describe the complications as the possibility of pulpal exposure through attrition or trauma to the tubercle and interference with occlusion with the resulting sequelae of displacement and loosening during traumatic occlusion. While these complications alone were enough, the position of the tubercle has considerably complicated any treatment of caries in the occlusal surface of these teeth. With the advent of a carious diet the occlusal pits and fissures are frequent areas of attack. With the recommended treatment of caries removal and "extension for prevention," i.e. the extension of the cavity preparation along the fissures into a self-cleansing area, the area of the tubercle may be directly or indirectly involved. Curzon et al. (1970: 326) show a ground section of such a premolar in which a restoration was placed in a preparation where the tubercle had been removed. This section clearly demonstrates the danger of pulpal exposure when instrumentation involves the tubercle. Indirectly, the tubercle may be involved because of the weakening of the area around the cavity preparation. This amalgam is not as strong as the tooth structure, resulting in an increased risk of fracture of the tubercle.

Here, then, we have a trait which was probably a disadvantage before a change in diet, but now is even more dangerous because of the treatment necessary for the eradication and prevention of caries.

THREE-ROOTED MANDIBULAR MOLARS   The molar series presents four morphological variations which have seen a change in their role due to the dietary change.

Several authors have noted the high incidence of a third root on mandibular first molars in Indians and Eskimos (Pedersen 1949: 115; Turner 1967: 133–144, 1971; Curzon and Curzon 1971; Somogyi-Csizmazia and Simons 1971; Mayhall 1969). It can be hypothesized that this supernumerary root (usually distolingual) adds to the stability of the molars. This stabilizing effect would have been necessary in a traditional culture due to the heavy demands placed upon the dentition. This is not to imply that the third root was absolutely necessary, but rather that it was a welcome aid to stability which increased the surface area available for attachment of the teeth to the alveolus. This root has become a detriment in today's culture only in that it increases the difficulty in alleviating oral pain. Because of this root and the resultant increased number of furcations and increased caries and periodontal disease, more teeth are extracted. Further, because of the remoteness and lack of facilities of many of the dental clinics it is not always possible to avail oneself of radiographs; thus, these roots are often undetected. In fact, Curzon and Curzon (1971: 72) agree with Pedersen when they state, "Periapical radiographs will not show the presence of such a supernumerary root because it is masked by the larger distobuccal root." It can be seen then that these roots are difficult to detect when the root is still in the alveolus.

With this difficulty in detection and the increasing numbers of molars requiring extraction, we can assume that more dental personnel will experience difficulty with extractions and/or broken roots which, under field conditions, may be difficult to handle.

ENAMEL EXTENSIONS   Pedersen and Thyssen (1942) studied thousands of molars of Eskimos and classified the extension of the cemento-enamel junction (CEJ). They found that these extensions of the enamel were found to be "very common on Eskimo molars which carried either bifurcations or longitudinal grooves on the root surfaces involved" (Pedersen 1949: 138). The same results are evident for Thule culture skeletal material and living individuals in the Foxe Basin area. Again, these extensions were probably an innocuous trait given an aboriginal diet, but with the switch to a mushy, nonrigid diet a change is evident.

A study of the Keewatin Eskimos by McPhail et al. (1972) demonstrates clearly the advance of periodontal disease. They showed that 6.07 percent of the coastal Eskimo children and 14.20 percent of the inland Eskimo children in the seven-to-seventeen-year age group had severe periodontal disease. Even at these young ages some pocket formation was evident. The same trends apply to the Foxe Basin area, but the disease is not yet as far advanced. Sperber (1972) pointed out that because of the lack of any attachment apparatus to this enamel extension area, natural pockets are formed where debris can accumulate. In fact, Masters and Hoskins (1964) showed that 90 percent of all teeth with isolated bifurcational periodontal problems had enamel extension into the disease site.

BUCCAL PITS   Pedersen (1949: 17–19) has demonstrated that there is a large percentage of buccal pits among Greenland Eskimo mandibular molars, many of which have no enamel lining. I also have been able to demonstrate this high incidence of pits on Canadian Eskimos and on Thule culture skeletal material from the west coast of Hudson Bay. This trait obviously was of little consequence when caries was nonexistent, but with an increase in the disease a completely different picture emerges. Pedersen noted that the buccal pits are usually the first site of caries in the Eskimo. Without preventive measures caries can spread rapidly with rapid pulpal involvement. Here it is easy to demonstrate the change from a neutral trait to one that is a definite disadvantage because of a concomitant change in the culture and diet.

CUSP AND GROOVE PATTERNS   A significant area of caries attack at present is on the fissures and grooves of maxillary and mandibular molars. Before the advent of a caries-prone diet the complicated groove patterns seen in Eskimos were not of major consequence. In fact, the usual *Dryopithecus* pattern of mandibular molars and the development of the hypocone provided the maximal number of cusps and ridges for efficient mastication. Many authors have commented on tooth size and its efficiency in mastication, but they have paid little heed to the morphology of the occlusal surface in this regard. It seems probable that a complex occlusal pattern and the number of transverse and oblique ridges would contribute greatly to the efficiency of mastication. While the traditional concept of the function of the posterior teeth has been one of grinding and crushing, Every (1970) has suggested that these same teeth are useful for shearing. While it is not the intent of this paper to deliberate at length on Every's hypothesis, it is of interest to note that many of the oblique and transverse ridges of posterior teeth do, indeed, become "sharpened" through attrition and can conceivably contribute to this shearing. If this is the case, then a complex series of ridges and cusps could be extremely advantageous in the comminution of food.

Dahlberg (1963: 168) showed that the mandibular first molar of the Eskimo is more frequently five-cusped when compared to his Chicago white sample. The mandibular second and third molars showed the same trend with the majority of all three teeth having five cusps. The large number of major cusps carries the possibility of a complex set of grooves and fissures, and each of these grooves and fissures is a potential nidus for dental caries. Although analysis is still under way, it would appear that in the Foxe Basin Eskimos one of the principal areas of caries attack is the occlusal area, with much less interproximal caries.

Once again, we can observe the hypothesized change of an advantageous trait to one which is a disadvantage.

It would be speculative to suggest that these traits are changing in their adaptive significance. This would imply that in some way they were necessary for survival and/or reproductive fitness. Obviously, this is not true. There are many Eskimos today who are edentulous and still subsisting on a diet of raw seal, caribou, and other aboriginal foods. These individuals claim that they can manage any foods relatively easily without dentures. But the traits that I discussed earlier do take on a new role, albeit a detrimental one, when the culture changes with a resultant change in diet and habits.

Tooth Loss

Until now I have been discussing dental morphological traits of Eskimo teeth and their changing roles. I would like to shift here to another aspect of the effect of culture change on the Eskimo dentition, namely, its effect on the loss of teeth. Many people, including myself, have hypothesized that the patterns and amount of tooth loss reflect, primarily in the Eskimos, the activity patterns of the individuals concerned.

Eskimos have always been one of the prime examples of a group who used their teeth as a "third hand." Ethnographers and explorers have marveled at the demands the Eskimo placed on the dentition. Women were described as softening skins and holding sewing implements with their teeth, while men placed even greater immediate demands on their dentitions by pulling seals from water with their teeth and by using their teeth as a vise when bending wood for kayak ribs. These were cultural activities which were necessary only a short time ago. Now, however, European technology is replacing many of the tasks and implements held to be part of the traditional culture. Today, women may use electric sewing machines and purchase tanned skins at the local store. Men are forsaking the dog team for a snowmobile; holes are more commonly drilled with a quarter-inch drill rather than a bow drill; and many of their boats are purchased at local retail outlets.

Skeletal material from two Thule culture sites on Hudson Bay was compared with the Foxe Basin data to analyze whether there was, in fact, any significant change in tooth loss between a traditional culture and a modern one. This supposes that the Thule culture population was the biological predecessor of the modern Eskimo. While analysis is still under way, it appears that this is the case, which would support the current archaeological theories. While the exact methods of analysis were presented earlier (Mayhall 1972: 445) it should be noted that the analysis was closely calibrated for the Thule and modern groups. The status of a tooth was recorded as unerupted, partially erupted, fully erupted and present, lost postmortem, lost antemortem, or congenitally missing. Obviously, the postmortem loss category was deleted in the modern Eskimo. Additionally, the residents of Igloolik and Hall Beach were questioned about the reason for a missing tooth. The percentage of loss for each tooth was determined by dividing the antemortem loss by the sum of the fully erupted teeth plus the teeth lost both before and after death. Eliminated from this determination were congenitally missing teeth, partially erupted teeth and unerupted teeth. While the age profiles for the two groups (Thule and modern) would demonstrate a much larger proportion of young individuals in the recent population, this was partially compensated for by not including in the percentage either unerupted or partially erupted teeth, as well as by eliminating deciduous teeth.

Looking first at the males (Table 3) one can note the larger percentage of incisors lost in the mandible of the Thule culture group, while there appears to be a much larger loss of third molars in the recent group. This latter difference may simply be due to the inability to ascertain which of these molars were congenitally missing and eliminate these from the sample. However, another equally plausible explanation is the higher rate of caries in the modern group. In this regard, the Thule group showed no evidence of caries, while the DMFT (decayed, missing, and filled [permanent] teeth) rates for Hall Beach were 5.50 teeth affected and 3.81 affected teeth for Igloolik.

Table 3.   Tooth loss in Eskimos

	Males Modern		Thule		Females Modern		Thule	
Tooth	N+	Percent loss	N	Percent loss	N	Percent loss	N	Percent loss
M³	134	15.7	53	11.3	112	22.3	61	11.5
M²	182	8.8	64	10.9	173	10.4	74	12.2
M¹	238	9.2	71	11.3	219	11.4	75	12.0
Pm²	184	4.9	71	9.9	184	8.7	73	13.7
Pm¹	190	5.3	72	6.9	186	7.5	77	9.1
C	180	3.3	72	0.0	175	5.1	79	5.1
I²	201	7.0	70	4.3	193	5.7	72	8.3
I¹	216	5.6	68	8.8	205	3.4**	70	15.7**
M₃	109	30.3**	64	10.9**	105	22.9	72	19.4
M₂	178	16.3	77	13.0	176	13.1*	92	22.8*
M₁	235	8.5	78	12.8	216	12.5	94	16.0
Pm₂	183	6.0	79	10.1	180	5.6	93	11.8
Pm₁	188	3.2	79	2.5	187	1.1**	93	11.8**
C	187	1.6	78	1.2	191	0.5**	91	7.7**
I₂	218	1.8	75	5.3	204	0.5**	89	14.6**
I₁	222	3.6**	71	14.1**	209	7.6**	83	26.5**

+   Number of teeth examined (right side only).
*   Significant difference between modern and Thule culture groups at 95 percent level of confidence.
**   Significant difference between modern and Thule culture groups at 99 percent level of confidence.

The comparison of the females (Table 3) showed the same general findings for the anteriors, but the posterior teeth of the Thule females demonstrated a much higher loss than did their male counterparts. As expected, the canines were the most infrequently lost teeth in all groups.

While more specific comparisons were made in an earlier study, the major conclusions demonstrated a diminished overall loss of teeth in the recent males and females. The major reductions in males were in the anterior loss and in the females the anteriors and premolars showed significant reductions in loss.

Obviously, several causes could be hypothesized for these differences other than trauma. Caries would be a likely candidate except that the larger losses were in the Thule group where no evidence of caries was found in the remaining teeth. Since no incipient lesions were noted this can be ruled out. Periodontal disease is another possibility. While it is difficult, if not impossible, to diagnose periodontal disease accurately in skeletal material, there is still this possibility. However, when the modern group was divided according to their dietary intake, the group consuming European-type food was the group with the higher rate of periodontal disease. Those Eskimos subsisting on primarily a traditional diet showed low rates.

The other principal causes of tooth loss are sudden trauma and sustained low levels of trauma. It seems entirely possible that many teeth were lost in the Thule males by sudden trauma. However, this may have been overemphasized in the literature as it is easier to determine this type of loss by inquiry. People are more likely to recall the reasons for loss when the teeth are lost by sudden trauma.

The more difficult causation to elicit is that of prolonged low levels of trauma. Upon questioning older informants, they only recollect that their teeth grew loose and either were extracted or exfoliated on their own. This might indicate periodontal disease, widespread periapical infections, tumors, or sustained trauma.

If we compare the crown heights of older males with the crown heights for the older females of Igloolik we see that the molars are approximately the same height, indicating about the same amount of wear of the molars for each sex. But large differences are noticeable in the anteriors. Keep in mind that the females showed tooth loss principally in their mandibular premolars and anteriors. The older males from Igloolik display relatively unworn anteriors, while the females have heavily worn anteriors and premolars.

The females assumed this pattern of wear because of the necessity of drawing a skin over the lower teeth to soften it, this producing wear predominantly on the anteriors and particularly on the mandibular anteriors. On the other hand, the males' teeth are used mainly for gripping objects which tends to produce less wear and little sustained trauma.

With a reduction in the female's role of producing boots there is a concomitant reduction in the amount of sustained trauma. This is particularly true among the younger women who have not had to produce as many pairs of boots for the family because spring and summer footwear now consists of rubber boots rather than sealskin. Thus, with the continuing rapid culture change in the northern Foxe Basin the disparity between Thule women's tooth loss and that of modern women will increase.

As for the males, there will probably not be the dramatic differences, because they have lost relatively few teeth from trauma when compared with the females. However, there is the possibility that this pattern will change with increasing use of the snowmobile and increased alcohol consumption which either alone, or in tandem, have the distinct possibility of raising the incidence of loss by sudden trauma.

SUMMARY

This article has demonstrated the effect of a changing culture and environment on facets of Eskimo dentition which are commonly used in odontology to illustrate the relationships between these features. All of the morphological traits discussed appear to have taken on new and, in most cases, detrimental roles in the mastication of food and other cultural usages. The ultimate insult on a tooth is its loss, which results in diminished efficiency in comminution of food, speech, and esthetics. These changes may invite a future reevaluation of their adaptive significance.

REFERENCES

ALEXANDERSEN, V.
   1970   Tandmorfologisk variation hos Eskimoer og andre Mongoloide populationer. *Tandlaegebladet* 74:587–602.
CROWE, KEITH J.
   1969   *A cutural geography of northern Foxe Basin, N.W.T.* Northern Science Research Group 69–2. Ottawa: Department of Indian Affairs and Northern Development.
CURZON, M. E. J., JENNIFER A. CURZON
   1971   Three-rooted mandibular molars in the Keewatin Eskimos. *Journal of the Canadian Dental Association* 37:71–72.
CURZON, M. E. J., JENNIFER A. CURZON, H. G. POYTON
   1970   Evaginated odontomes in the Keewatin Eskimo. *British Dental Journal* 29:324–328.
DAHLBERG, A. A.
   1963   "Analysis of the American Indian dentition," in *Dental anthropology*. Edited by D. R. Brothwell, 149–177. Oxford: Pergamon.
DAMAS, DAVID
   1963   *Igluligmiut kinship and local groupings: a structural approach.* National Museum of Canada Bulletin 196. Ottawa: Department of Northern Affairs and National Resources.
EVERY, R. G.
   1970   Sharpness of teeth in man and other primates. *Postilla* 143:1–30. Peabody Museum, Yale University.
FOOTE, DON C.
   1969   *Human ecological studies at Igloolik, N.W.T.* University of Toronto Anthropological Series 1, pages 1–43.
HANIHARA, KAZURO
   1966   Mongoloid dental complex in the deciduous dentition. *Journal of the Anthropological Society of Nippon* 74:61–71.
MASTERS, D. H., S. W. HOSKINS
   1964   Projection of cervical enamel into molar furcations. *Journal of Periodontology* 35:49–53.

MAYHALL, J. T.
1969 Thule culture Eskimo mandibles: a radiographic study. *American Journal of Physical Anthropology,* n.s. 31:264.
1970 The effect of culture change upon the Eskimo dentition. *Arctic Anthropology* 7:117–121.
1972 Tooth loss in prehistoric and recent Eskimos. *American Journal of Physical Anthropology* 37:445.

MAYHALL, J. T., A. A. DAHLBERG, D. G. OWEN
1970 Dental caries in the Eskimos of Wainwright, Alaska. *Journal of Dental Research* 49:886.

MC EUEN, C. S.
1938 An examination of the mouths of Eskimos in the Canadian eastern Arctic. *Canadian Medical Association Journal* 38:374–377.

MC PHAIL, C. W. B., T. M. CURRY, R. D. HAZELTON, K. J. PAYNTER,
R. G. WILLIAMSON
1972 The geographic pathology of dental disease in Canadian central Arctic populations. *Journal of the Canadian Dental Association* 38:288–296.

PEDERSEN, P. O.
1949 The East Greenland Eskimo dentition: numerical variations and anatomy. *Meddelelser om Grønland* 142(3):1–256.

PEDERSEN, P. O., H. THYSSEN
1942 Den cervicale em aljerands forløb hos Eskimoer. *Odontologisk Tidskrift* 50:444–492.

PRICE, W. A.
1934 Relation of nutrition to dental caries among Eskimos and Indians in Alaska and northern Canada. *Journal of Dental Research* 14:227–229.

RUSSELL, A. L., C. F. CONSOLAZIO, C. L. WHITE
1961 Dental caries and nutrition in Eskimo scouts of the Alaska National Guard. *Journal of Dental Research* 40:594–603.

SOMOGYI-CSIZMAZIA, W., A. J. SIMONS
1971 Three-rooted mandibular first permanent molars in Alberta Indian children. *Journal of the Canadian Dental Association* 37: 105–106.

SPERBER, G. H.
1972 Dental morphology of American Indians and Eskimos (letter to the editor). *Journal of the Canadian Dental Association* 38:231–232.

TURNER, CHRISTY G., II
1967 "The dentition of Arctic peoples." Unpublished doctoral dissertation, University of Wisconsin.
1971 Three-rooted mandibular first permanent molars and the question of North American Indian origins. *American Journal of Physical Anthropology* 34:229–241.

Dentition of Easter Islanders

C. G. TURNER, II and G. R. SCOTT

It is the purpose here to describe the dentition of living Easter Islanders and see to what extent dental anthropology can help solve the problem of the origin of Polynesians.

ANTHROPOLOGICAL BACKGROUND

Easter Island, a small volcanic island 2,300 miles west of Peru and 1,200 miles east of Pitcairn Island, was discovered by the Dutchman Jacob Roggeveen on Easter Sunday, 1722. Prominent subsequent visitors included, among others, Gonzalez, 1770; Cook, 1774; and La Pérouse, 1786 (Shapiro 1935). These voyagers' population estimates for Easter ranged from 600 to 3,000 inhabitants, but the latter may be more accurate because rarely, if ever, was the entire population encountered, as many of the islanders, especially women, hid during their visits (Métraux 1940). Population size was reduced to less than 200 individuals during the 1860's but has since increased to about 1,000 (Skoryna 1965). Correspondingly, the native culture of Easter was essentially destroyed by 1862 through the cumulative effects of Peruvian slavers, famine, disease, internecine strife, and European influence (Métraux 1940).

The authors express their appreciation to Major Alexander G. Taylor, odontologist in the 1964–1965 Canadian Medical Expedition to Easter Island who made the casts studied here, and also to Dr. Stanley C. Skoryna, director of that expedition. We thank Dr. Robert J. Meier for providing the stimulus for the loan of Dr. Taylor's casts to the senior author. The Department of Anthropology at Arizona State University has generously provided space and funds for this study. The junior author has received support from an NIH genetics training grant (5 T01 GM01433-03), directed by Dr. Charles M. Woolf, and a Dissertation Year Fellowship from Arizona State University. Portions of this paper were done while the senior author held a fellowship at the Center for Advanced Studies in the Behavioral Sciences, Stanford, California.

Ethnographic reconstruction and archaeology have shown that the precontact Easter Island culture was Polynesian in character, although the presence of well-fitted masonry construction, certain statuary types, and the sweet potato, among other items, during the Early Period (A.D. 400–1100), suggest possible South American origins (Heyerdahl 1961; Ferdon 1961). R. Green (1967) accepts the cultural and botanical influence from South America but does not find the evidence for contact satisfactory much before A.D. 800.

Early chroniclers believed Polynesians were originally from Asia or Indonesia but many remarked on their Caucasian physical features (for a review see Heyerdahl 1953; Linton 1955; Howard 1967). Recent carbon 14 dates indicate that the western Polynesian islands of Samoa and Tonga were initially settled between 2,500 and 2,000 years ago whereas eastern Polynesia appears to have been settled a few centuries later. The Norwegian Archaeological Expedition to Easter Island reports two basal radiocarbon dates of A.D. 318 ± 250 and A.D. 380 ± 100 (Smith 1961) so this outlier was possibly one of the first eastern Polynesian islands to be settled; the population is thought to have been derived from the Marquesas prior to the settlement of New Zealand and Hawaii (Sinoto 1968; Emory 1968).

The language of Easter Island is a dialect of Polynesian and belongs to an Asian affiliated family according to I. Dyen (in Murdock 1964):

Austronesian phylum
  Malayo-Polynesian family
    Heonesian subfamily
      Polynesian branch
        East Polynesian cluster
          "Easter"

One well-received hypothesis on the immediate origins of Polynesians has been that of Buck (1938 and elsewhere) and Weckler (1943) who propose that ancestral Polynesians migrated from Indonesia via the Micronesian islands. In contrast, Emory (1959) and Green (1967) suggest that Polynesians can be traced back to eastern Melanesia, a position supported by linguistic and archaeologic evidence. Still, it has been difficult for many writers to reconcile the physical differences between Melanesians and Polynesians; the former have frizzly hair, dark brown to black skin, and are generally dolichocephalic while the latter have straight to wavy hair, variable brown skin, and are prevailingly brachycephalic (Hooton 1935). Regarding blood groups, Melanesians have moderate A_1, low B, M, and R_2 whereas Polynesians differ slightly in having high A₁, generally no B, and moderately high M and R₂ (Simmons 1962).

The possibility that Polynesians originated in the New World was suggested by a few early authors (reviewed in Howard 1967), but the strongest case for this view was assembled in 1953 by Heyerdahl. He opposes settlement by Melanesian and Micronesian routes largely because of the nature of prevailing ocean currents and the distribution of several cultural and botanical traits which are common to Polynesians and American Indians but not to other Pacific groups (Heyerdahl 1968). All other Polynesian origin theories are too improbable for consideration at this time.

Easter Islanders are assigned to the Polynesian geographical race because of their blood group frequencies and variability of hair form, skin color, body build, and nose form (Garn 1971). This assignment is not without qualification because European and Chilean admixture is plainly evident (Meier 1970) and complicates all considerations of population origins based solely on the living. This problem was circumvented in part by Murrill's study (1968) of precontact skeletons obtained by the Norwegian Archaeological Expedition. He showed them to be wholly within the known morphologic and metric range of other Polynesian skeletons and dismissed the possibility of New World migrants settling Easter Island. On this question Turner (1968) pointed out that, had the sample been subdivided by time period rather than studied as a single unit, an initial American Indian origin could be proposed indirectly for the earliest Easter population.

Polynesian Dental Anthropology

In our search for comparative studies dealing with Polynesian dentition, we have found only about a dozen publications. Possibly the first work on Polynesian dentition *per se* is by Violet George (1926) who found New Zealand Maori teeth to be larger, more regular, and in better condition than those of British-born New Zealand whites. Her views were later corroborated by R. Taylor (1963) who worked with osteological material. Equally sound were the teeth of skeletal Hawaiians studied by Chappel (1927), who also noted that shoveling was infrequent, enamel extensions were common on the molars, and mandibular second molar cusp reduction was frequent. More restricted trait studies such as Hartweg's review (1947) of mandibular molar cusp number include Polynesian material, as does an earlier study by Wissler (1931) employing the data on cusp number collected on Hawaiians by Sullivan. The most recent study of molar variation is by Suzuki and Sakai (1960 and elsewhere). Incisor shoveling in Polynesians was considered by A. Hrdlička (1920), Chappel (1927), Riesenfeld (1956), and Suzuki and Sakai (1964). In all, Polynesian between-group dental variation seems considerable but just how much is attributable to differential historic admixture is unknown. The dental morphology of Easter Islanders does not seem to have been studied previously, despite the long-time interest in Easter by anthropologists and laymen alike.

EASTER MATERIALS

The basis of this study is a series of 175 plaster dental impressions (97 males, 78 females) obtained in 1964–1965 by Major A. G. Taylor of the Canadian Medical Expedition to Easter Island, under the directorship of Dr. S. C. Skoryna. Dr. Taylor took the impressions from all nonedentulous Easter Islanders, aged 18–79. He also studied their dental pathology and found tooth morbidity and loss to be absolutely and relatively high for all age groups (A. Taylor 1966).

Crown Trait Definitions

With the exception of four traits, the definitions of crown variation used here are those that have long been employed by anthropologists and paleontologists. These have proven valuable for comparative studies because they partition trait variation about as finely as possible for accurate and easy identification by observers. The exceptions are incisor medial lingual ridge number (Table 3); incisor marginal interruptions (Table 4), and cusps 6 and 7 on the mandibuar molars (Tables 12 and 13).

The rationale for adhering to these definitions is that their use has generated a valuable, although small, body of comparable literature on all human geographical races, many local races, all tooth-bearing fossil men, and many nonhuman primates. These ranked classifications can be criticized as being arbitrary (Sofaer 1970), but our experience has shown that it is preferable to employ "arbitrary," but well-defined, classifications of trait variation which minimize the loss of information on expression, than it is to rely on discrete (+ or –) groupings.

We offer that the use of present or absent classifications serves no analytical or higher purpose and may, indeed, do genetic, functional, developmental, and anthropological studies a disservice. Such classifications (1) telescope variation and fail to describe accurately the nature of the variation, (2) facilitate misidentification of weak trait expression as absent when no comparative "weak" standard is established, (3) hide PATTERNS of trait variation such as bimodality of expression range (Turner 1970) or correlations between total incidence and expressivity (Scott 1971, 1972), (4) inhibit measuring the degree of bilateral symmetry for tests of penetrance or fitness (Bailit et al. 1970; Turner 1970), and (5) mask within- and between-group variation regarding the degree of expression as in estimating sex dimorphism (Moorrees 1957) or racial differences. For example, Aleut-Eskimos and Pima Indians both show nearly 100 percent shoveling, but the Pima exhibit almost no intermediate expressions (Dahlberg 1963) whereas the frequency of such forms is about 35 percent in Aleut-Eskimos (Turner 1967a). Easter Islanders also have a high frequency of shoveling (Table 1) but more than 60 percent of the expression is at the trace end of the occurrence spectrum. To assert that Easter Islanders, American Indians, and Aleut-Eskimos all have high frequencies of shovel-shaped incisors ignores the highly informative differences in their respective degrees of shoveling expression.

Counting Procedure

Because of antimeric relationships between teeth in the two sides of the jaw, fluctuating asymmetry is possible and this introduces a problem in deriving the total trait incidence for a population. As the many methods for counting dental morphologic traits do not always provide strictly comparable results, it is considered necessary to outline the procedure followed here:

1. All traits were counted per individual rather than per side or per tooth.

2. When a trait exhibited presence-absence asymmetry, it was scored as present. When multiple categories were used and asymmetry was present, the highest category was counted.

3. When an individual had only one side present (the other side broken or worn off), we counted the available side and assumed symmetry.

4. When an individual was symmetrical we counted the trait once.

This procedure emphasizes the genetic basis of any trait being studied because it takes into account the occurrence of that trait on an individual basis (points 1 and 2; Turner 1967b, 1969a). In addition, counting whichever side is present (point 3) allows sample size to be maximized. Traits whose frequencies are very low will be biased in the direction of decreasing their frequency but this is preferred to the bias introduced by reduced sample size when incomplete individuals are not considered.

The data are reported with the sexes pooled except for upper third molar and lower first molar cusp pattern and the palatine torus; chi-square tests for sex dimorphism showed no significant difference at the 0.05 level for any other trait.

EASTER ISLAND DENTAL CHARACTERISTICS

Starting with traits on the maxillary teeth (Tables 1–7), we find that marked shoveling, which characterizes Asian and Asian-derived peoples, including the Sakhalin Ainu, Japanese, Chinese, Aleut-Eskimos, and American Indians, is as uncommon in Easter teeth (see Table 1) as it is among Melanesian Nasioi (Bailit et al. 1968), Australians (Campbell 1925), and Micronesians from Guam (Leigh 1929), and, of course, modern Europeans and Africans (Hrdlička 1920; Carbonell 1963) and prehistoric whites (Brabant 1969; Greene 1967). Central incisor rotation or winging is present (ca. 11 percent; Table 2) but in much lower frequency than in many American Indian and Asian groups. The status of winging in other Oceanic populations is unknown, although it is likely to be more than the 3 percent found in American whites (Dahlberg 1963). The frequency of multiple medial lingual ridges on Easter maxillary central incisors approaches 50 percent (Table 3). As with winging, we do not know how often these ridges occur in other Pacific groups. Maxillary lateral incisor marginal interruptions occur in only 10 percent of the Easter sample (Table 4). This condition, a true interruption in the formation of the marginal border, is common in American Indians.

Simplification (Dahlberg 1951; Moorrees 1957) seems to characterize the molars as well as the incisors. The first maxillary molar has cusp 5 present about 20 percent of the time and the frequency of cusp 6 on the same tooth is only 5 percent (Table 5). Total loss of the hypocone, an important component of dental simplification, is relatively common (ca. 22 percent) on the maxillary second molars (Table 6). The first molar has no expression of Carabelli's trait in 70 percent of the sample (Table 7). This is not only in contrast to

Europeans, who have a very high frequency of this trait, but also to Africans, Asiatic Indians, and American Indians (Kraus 1959; Scott 1972), when all grades of occurrence are considered. For this feature, Easter is aligned with Oceanic (Bailit et al. 1968; Scott 1972) and Asiatic groups (Suzuki and Sakai 1957; Tsuji 1958), including Aleuts and Eskimos (Turner 1967a; Zubov 1969).

Table 1. Maxillary shovel-shaped incisors (individual count, sexes pooled)

Tooth	n	None	Grades* Trace	Semi-	Shovel	Sex dimorphism tests X_1^2	P
I^1	118	15 (12.7)	70 (59.3)	29 (24.6)	4 (3.4)	1.40	.2–.3
I^2	124	8 (6.5)	81 (65.3)	30 (24.2)	5 (4.0)	0.27	>.5
I_1	147	106 (72.1)	41 (27.9)	0 (0.0)	0 (0.0)	1.22	.2–.3
I_2	148	92 (62.2)	56 (37.8)	0 (0.0)	0 (0.0)	0.09	>.5

* After Hrdlička (1920). Numbers in parentheses are percentages.

Table 2. Maxillary central incisor winging* (individual count, sexes pooled)

n	Bilateral	Unilateral	Straight	Unilateral counterwing	Bilateral counterwing	Sex dimorphism tests X_1^2	P
118	13 (11.0)	1 (0.9)	99 (83.9)	0 (0.0)	5 (4.2)	1.46	.2–.3

* After Enoki and Dahlberg (1958). Numbers in parentheses are percentages.

Table 3. Incisor medial lingual ridges (individual count, sexes pooled)

Tooth	n	Ridge number* 0	1	2	3	Sex dimorphism tests X_1^2	P
I^1	106	15 (14.2)	35 (33.0)	54 (50.9)	2 (1.9)	1.17	.2–.3
I^2	111	70 (63.1)	29 (26.1)	11 (9.9)	1 (0.9)	0.00	>.5
I_1	128	118 (92.2)	10 (7.8)	0 (0.0)	0 (0.0)	0.99	.3–.5
I_2	134	111 (82.8)	23 (17.2)	0 (0.0)	0 (0.0)	0.61	.3–.5

* After Turner (1967a). Numbers in parentheses are percentages.

Table 4. Maxillary incisor marginal interruptions, lingual surface* (individual count, sexes pooled)

Tooth	Position	n	Absent	Present	Sex dimorphism tests X_1^2	P
I^1	Mesial	107	107 (100.0)	0 (0.0)	0.00	–
	Distal	110	109 (99.1)	1 (0.9)	0.67	.3–.5
I_2	Mesial	114	109 (95.6)	5 (4.4)	0.00	>.5
	Distal	117	106 (90.6)	11 (9.4)	0.71	.3–.5

*   After Turner (1967a). Numbers in parentheses are percentages.

Table 5. Supernumerary cusps of the maxillary molars (individual count, sexes pooled)

Tooth	n	Distal cusp 5* Present	Absent	Sex dimorphism x_1^2	P	Mesial cusp 6* Present	Absent	Sex dimorphism tests X_1^2	P
M^1	95	19 (20.0)	76 (80.0)	0.04	>.5	6 (6.3)	89 (93.7)	1.22	.2–.3
M^2	124	10 (8.1)	114 (91.9)	0.11	>.5	8 (6.5)	116 (93.6)	0.09	>.5
M^3	53	1 (1.9)	52 (98.1)	1.02	.3–.5	1 (1.9)	52 (98.1)	1.02	.3–.5

*   After Turner (1967a). Numbers in parentheses are percentages.

Table 6. Maxillary molar cusp pattern* (individual count, sexes pooled)

Tooth	Sex	n	4	4–	3+	3	2+	H	Sex dimorphism tests X_1^2	P
M^1	M, F	107	87 (81.3)	19 (17.8)	1 (0.9)	0 (0.0)	0 (0.0)	0 (0.0)	0.00	–
M^2	M, F	141	16 (11.4)	56 (39.7)	38 (27.0)	31 (22.0)	0 (0.0)	0 (0.0)	2.18	.1–.2
M^3	M	32	2 (6.3)	2 (6.3)	6 (18.8)	18 (56.3)	1 (3.1)	3 (9.4)	4.42	.01–.05
	F	31	0 (0.0)	3 (9.7)	15 (48.4)	10 (32.3)	1 (3.2)	2 (6.5)		

*   After Dahlberg (1951). Hypoplastic (H) molars not included in computation of X^2 values. Numbers in parentheses are percentages.

Table 7.   Carabelli's trait (individual count, sexes pooled)

Tooth	n	Grades*								Sex dimorphism tests	
		0	1	2	3	4	5	6	7	X_1^2	P
M¹	105	70	8	6	9	1	6	5	0	2.41	.1–.2
		(66.7)	(7.6)	(5.7)	(8.6)	(1.0)	(5.7)	(4.8)	(0.0)		
M²	143	129	2	3	3	3	2	1	0	0.32	>.5
		(90.2)	(1.4)	(2.1)	(2.1)	(2.1)	(1.4)	(0.7)	(0.0)		
M³	44	39	0	1	1	1	1	1	0	0.14	>.5
		(88.6)	(0.0)	(2.3)	(2.3)	(2.3)	(2.3)	(2.3)	(0.0)		

*   0 = no cusp (smooth)
   1 = line or furrow
   2 = pit
   3 = double line or furrow
   4 = Y-form
   5 = no contact with lining groove
   6 = small contact with lining groove
   7 = high cone
After Dahlberg (1963) and elsewhere. Numbers in parentheses are percentages.

In the lower jaw, the premolars do not reflect the overall simplification found in the other teeth (Tables 8 and 9) as there is a high frequency of three-cusped first (ca. 40 percent) and second premolars (ca. 60 percent). Asian and Asian-derived groups apparently have three-cusped second premolars more often than Europeans and Africans (Ludwig 1957).

Cusp 6 on the first and second mandibular molars is in low to moderate frequency (ca. 25 percent and 8 percent respectively; Table 12), much lower than that found in Samoans (Suzuki and Sakai 1960), Solomon Islanders, and Hopi Indians (Turner 1970). Both cusps 5 and 6 are missing on the second lower molar more than 50 percent of the time (Table 11), intermediate to populations showing pronounced hypoconulid (i.e. cusp 5) reduction (e.g. Europeans, Asiatic Indians, Melanesians) and those which have generally retained this cusp (e.g. American Indians, Eskimos, Micronesians). The protostylid is as rare in Easter Islanders as in American whites and Africans; only 7 percent of first lower molars express any degree of the actual cusp (Table 14), while Asians and American Indians have a considerably higher frequency of this variant (Dahlberg 1950; Hanihara 1969). Lower molar buccal pits are not infrequent (ca. 30 percent) but are small and shallow when present. Cusp 7 occurs in moderate frequency (ca. 23 percent) on the first lower molar but is almost entirely limited in its expression (grade 1A) in which the feature is still incorporated in the metaconid, similar to the situation which characterizes this cusp when expressed on the deciduous second lower molar (Table 13).

Athough there is probably some error in size estimation because of the soft tissue covering the body of the mandible, the occurrence of mandibular torus was studied and found to be uncommon (ca. 10 percent) and generally small (Table 15). Palatine torus is also infrequent (ca. 14 percent) but, interestingly, is significantly more common in females than in males (Table 16).

Table 8.   Mandibular first premolars (individual count, sexes pooled)

Features of PM_1*	Number	Percent	Sex dimorphism tests X_1^2	P
0. No external lingual groove	94	(63.1)		
1. One external lingual groove	49	(32.9)	0.37	>.5 (2 d.f.)
2. Two external lingual grooves	6	(4.0)		
	n = 149	(100.0)		
3. Interrupted sagittal sulcus	129	(91.5)		
4. Uninterrupted sagittal sulcus	12	(8.5)	1.66	.1–.2
	n = 141	(100.0)		
5. Lingual cusp is mesial	93	(66.9)		
6. Lingual cusp is distal	9	(6.5)	0.87	>.5 (2 d.f.)
7. Lingual cusp is medial	37	(26.6)		
	n = 139	(100.0)		
8. One lingual cusp	83	(57.2)		
9. Two lingual cusps	61	(42.1)		
10. Three lingual cusps	1	(0.7)	2.15	.1–.2
11. Four lingual cusps	0	(0.0)		
	n = 145	(100.0)		
12. Single medial occlusal ridge (buccal cusp)	17	(35.4)		
13. Divergent medial occlusal ridge (buccal cusp)	31	(64.6)	0.19	>.5
	n = 48	(100.0)		
14. One occlusal pit	45	(32.8)		
15. Two occlusal pits	92	(67.2)	0.60	.3–.5
	n = 137	(100.0)		
16. Fused lingual and buccal cusp	104	(75.4)		
17. Independent lingual and buccal cusp	34	(24.6)	0.47	.3–.5
	n = 138	(100.0)		

*   After Kraus and Furr (1953).

Table 9. Mandibular second premolars (individual count, sexes pooled)

Features of PM₂*	Number	Percent	Sex dimorphism tests X²ᵢ	P
0. One distal accessory ridge (buccal cusp)	10	(31.3)		
1. One mesial accessory ridge	2	(6.3)	1.42	.3–.5 (2 d.f.)
2. Mesial and distal accessory ridge	20	(62.5)		
	n = 32	(100.0)		
3. Single occlusal ridge (buccal cusp)	22	(51.2)		
4. Divergent	21	(48.8)	0.19	>.5
	n = 43	(100.0)		
5. Lingual cusp is medial	41	(29.7)		
6. Lingual cusp is mesial	96	(69.6)	0.81	>.5 (2 d.f.)
7. Lingual cusp is distal	1	(0.7)		
	n = 138	(100.0)		
8. One lingual cusp	48	(35.3)		
9. Two lingual cusps	85	(62.5)		
10. Three lingual cusps	2	(1.5)	0.82	.3–.5
10a. Four lingual cusps	1	(0.7)		
	n = 136	(100.0)		
11. Lingual cusp is independent	129	(97.7)		
12. Lingual cusp is fused	3	(2.3)	0.09	>.5
	n = 132	(100.0)		
13. Multiple lingual cusp is medial	0	(0.0)		
14. Multiple lingual cusp is distal	86	(94.5)	0.08	>.5
15. Multiple lingual cusp is mesial	5	(5.5)		
	n = 91	(100.0)		
16. Sagittal sulcus is interrupted	41	(32.5)		
17. Sagittal sulcus is not interrupted	85	(67.5)	0.86	.3–.5
	n = 126	(100.0)		

* After Ludwig (1957).

Table 10. Mandibular molar cusp pattern (individual count)

Tooth	Sex	n	Classes* Y	X	+	Sex dimorphism tests X²ᵢ	P
M₁	M	31	27 (87.1)	2 (6.5)	2 (6.5)		
	F	11	5 (45.5)	1 (9.1)	5 (45.5)	9.59	.01–.001
M₂	M, F	45	5 (11.1)	23 (51.1)	17 (37.8)	3.43	.1–.2
M₃	M, F	26	0 (0.0)	22 (84.6)	4 (15.4)	0.76	.3–.5 (1 d.f.)

* After Gregory (1916), Hellman (1928), and Jørgensen (1955). Numbers in parentheses are percentages.

Table 11.   Mandibular molar cusp number* (individual count, sexes pooled)

Tooth	n		Cusp number			Sex dimorphism tests	
		6	5	4	H	X_1^2	P
M_1	51	13	36	2	0	0.44	>.5
		(25.5)	(70.6)	(3.9)	(0.0)		
M_2	91	8	32	48	3	0.85	>.5
		(8.8)	(35.2)	(52.7)	(3.3)		
M_3	77	9	34	15	19	3.47	.1–.2
		(11.7)	(44.2)	(19.5)	(24.7)		

* Modified after Gregory (1916), see Turner (1967a). Numbers in parentheses are percentages.

Table 12.   Mandibular molar "entoconulid" (cusp 6) variation (individual count, sexes pooled)

Tooth	n			Grades*				Sex dimorphism tests	
		0	1	2	3	4	5	X_1^2	P
M_1	46	37	1	7	1	0	0	1.11	.2–.3
		(80.4)	(2.2)	(15.2)	(2.2)	(0.0)	(0.0)		
M_2	84	76	0	2	2	1	3	0.20	>.5
		(90.5)	(0.0)	(2.4)	(2.4)	(1.2)	(3.6)		
M_3	63	54	1	2	3	1	2	2.99	.05–.1
		(85.7)	(1.6)	(3.2)	(4.8)	(1.6)	(3.2)		

* After Turner (1970). Numbers in parentheses are percentages.

Table 13.   Mandibular molar cusp 7 variation (individual count, sexes pooled)

Tooth	n			Grades*				Sex dimorphism tests	
		0	1	1A	2	3	4	X_1^2	P
M_1	60	46	1	12	1	0	0	0.72	.3–.5
		(76.7)	(1.7)	(20.0)	(1.7)	(0.0)	(0.0)		
M_2	86	74	0	12	0	0	0	0.62	.3–.5
		(86.0)	(0.0)	(14.0)	(0.0)	(0.0)	(0.0)		
M_3	30	25	0	1	1	1	2	0.74	.3–.5
		(83.3)	(0.0)	(3.3)	(3.3)	(3.3)	(6.7)		

* After Turner (1970). Numbers in parentheses are percentages.

DISCUSSION OF RELATIONS AND SIMPLIFICATION

Dental morphologic traits reflect the genetic constitution of a population since trait expressions are notably affected by the environment only in some diseases such as congenital syphilis, when wear or

Table 14.   Mandibular molar protostylid variation (individual count, sexes pooled)

Tooth	n	Grades* 0	1	2	3	4	5	6	Sex dimor-phism tests X_1^2	P
M_1	57	34 (59.7)	17 (29.8)	2 (3.5)	2 (3.5)	2 (3.5)	0 (0.0)	0 (0.0)	1.78	.1–.2
M_2	101	84 (83.2)	9 (8.9)	5 (5.0)	2 (2.0)	0 (0.0)	0 (0.0)	1 (1.0)	0.50	.3–.5
M_3	72	54 (75.0)	1 (1.4)	4 (5.6)	3 (4.2)	0 (0.0)	4 (5.6)	6 (8.3)	0.17	>.5

*   0 = no cusp, straight buccal groove
    1 = no cusp, pit in buccal groove
    2 = no cusp, curved or slanting buccal groove
    3 = small cusp, buccal groove just beginning
    4 = slight cusp
    5 = moderate cusp
    6 = large cusp
    After Dahlberg (1963) and elsewhere. Numbers in parentheses are percentages.

Table 15.   Mandibular torus (maximum individual expression, sexes pooled)

n	Grades* 0	1	2	3	4	Sex dimor-phism test X_1^2	P
160	142 (88.8)	14 (8.8)	3 (1.9)	1 (0.6)	0 (0.0)	0.36	>.5

*   0 = absent
    1 = trace
    2 = medium
    3 = large
    4 = very large (as in some Eskimo).
    Numbers in parentheses are percentages.

Table 16.   Palatine torus (maximum individual expression)

Sex	n	Grades* 0	1	2	3	4	Sex dimorphism test X_1^2	P
M	95	92 (96.8)	3 (3.2)	0 (0.0)	0 (0.0)	0 (0.0)	21.28	<0.001
F	75	54 (72.0)	15 (20.0)	5 (6.7)	1 (1.3)	0 (0.0)		

*   0 = absent
    1 = trace
    2 = medium
    3 = large
    4 = very large (as in some Eskimo).
    Numbers in parentheses are percentages.

erosive decay removes surficial features, or in the presence of bizarre dietary regimens (Turner 1967a). Genetics-based phylogenies and description are our primary objectives, but we recognize that the characterizations of dental morphology only approximate genetic characterizations. It is also evident that an unknown amount of microevolution has occurred in the gene pool leading to present-day Easter Islanders (see Meier 1970). Still, there is sufficient evidence to argue that genetic changes have not been so great as to obliterate the ancestral origin of these people because of the inherent conservatism generally exhibited by dental morphology in the fossil and subfossil record, and because some normal dental characters, such as root number (Turner 1971), are so distinctive of particular populations that even considerable evolution, by whatever process, does not completely mask past relationships between groups.

Pending the further development and broader use of standards of trait variation, some suggestions on origins and relationships are nevertheless possible: (1) It is our impression that Easter Islanders' teeth show more similarity with those of "Asians" than those of any other geographic race. It appears, for the present at least, that Easter Islanders, as a known sample of the Polynesian gene pool, are no more like Australians, Melanesians, and possibly Micronesians, than samples drawn from Asia and, in particular, Southeast Asia. (2) The greatest dissimilarity is between Easter Islanders and American Indians — a finding which contradicts theories on the peopling of Polynesia from the New World. (3) Easter Island teeth appear to represent a simplified Asian dentition. This evolutionary simplification (see Figure 1) is not due solely to white admixture because the frequency of Carabelli's trait has not increased as would be expected, congenitally missing teeth are uncommon, and the V-shaped maxillary dental arcade, more common to Europeans than all other groups, is rare in Easter jaws. There is no MARKED resemblance to Europeans as would be the case if white admixture alone was responsible for the Easter toothcrown simplification. (4) We suspect that further biological studies on the Easter population, like that of Meier (1970), will show that founder's effect, genetic bottlenecking, and white admixture are the principal factors that have determined the dental variability of extant Easter Islanders. It is also possible that the highly cariogenic Polynesian diet may have played some selective role in the formation of the simplified tooth crowns. (5) Given the character of other Oceanic and Australian dentitions, as well as those of American Indians, Europeans, and Africans, we conclude, by a process of elimination, that the ancestors of contemporary Easter Islanders, ignoring historic white ones, originated somewhere in the southern, less Mongoloid region of eastern Asia. At present, there seems to be no evidence to directly link Easter with the more Mongoloid Ainu, Japanese, Chinese, Mongols, Aleut-Eskimos, or other paleo-Asiatics.

There is nothing novel about the last suggestion. Anthropologists have long held that Polynesians are a complex polymorphic and polytypic group showing physical resemblances with peoples of Indonesia and Southeast Asia. What is important, however, is that dental characteristics, because they seemingly support other lines of physical evidence, are now in a position to be used for answering more concise questions regarding Polynesian origins when prehistoric Oceanian dental collections are obtained by archaeological means. Thus, the stage

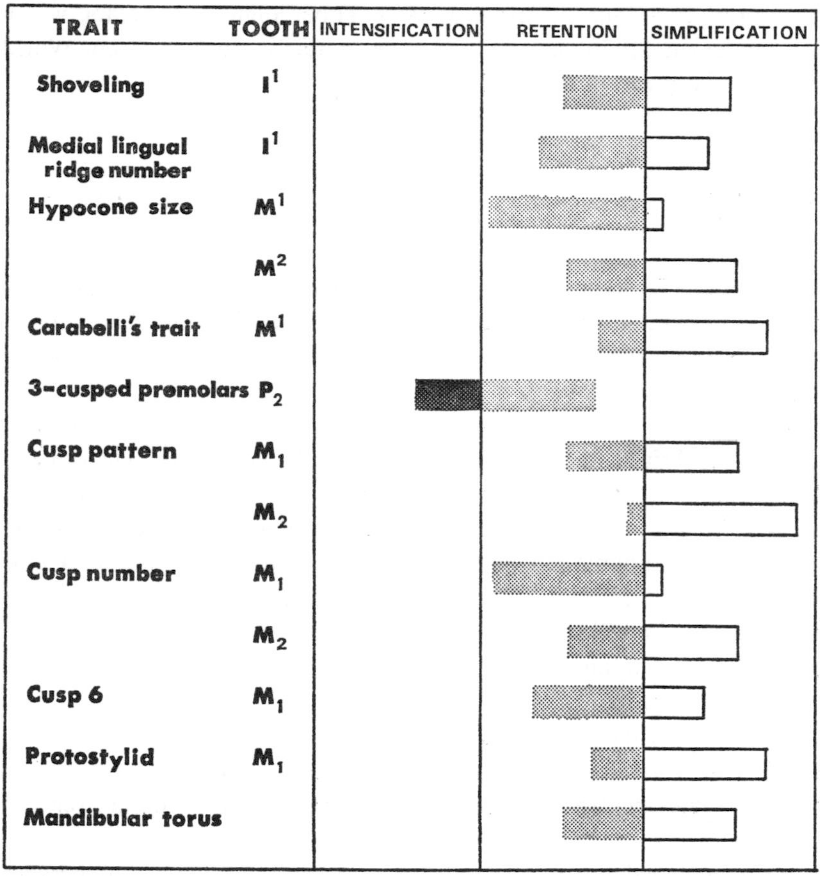

TRAIT	TOOTH	INTENSIFICATION	RETENTION	SIMPLIFICATION
Shoveling	I^1			
Medial lingual ridge number	I^1			
Hypocone size	M^1			
	M^2			
Carabelli's trait	M^1			
3-cusped premolars	P_2			
Cusp pattern	M_1			
	M_2			
Cusp number	M_1			
	M_2			
Cusp 6	M_1			
Protostylid	M_1			
Mandibular torus				

Figure 1. Easter Island dental plan; after Dahlberg (1951) and Moorrees (1957).

is set for a cooperative study of dental anthropology and archaeology concerning the peopling of Polynesia.

Additional Observations

Not presented in Tables 1–16 are the following observations on the character of Easter Island teeth. There are no examples of cosmetic incising or ablating of teeth. Crown chipping, so characteristic of Eskimos, is almost totally absent. Supernumerary teeth appear to be very rare. Hypoplastic disturbance lines are frequent and suggest considerable child-development problems. As Taylor (1966) demonstrated, the number of decayed, missing, and filled teeth is quite high (DMF = 17.57 per person). Markedly incisiform mandibular canines are present in rare individuals (Turner 1969b). Tuberculated premolars, which Alexandersen (1970) has shown to be a fairly common New World trait, are very rare in Easter Islanders.

SUMMARY

Casts from 175 living Easter Islanders have been studied for 26 morphologic dental characteristics plus incisor winging, mandibular torus, and palatine torus. Ranked standards were used for data collection on individuals where possible.

It appears that the Easter Island dentition exhibits more similarity to Southeast Asians than to Melanesians, Micronesians, Australians, Europeans, and Africans, and is most unlike that of the American Indian. White admixture has influenced the present genetic makeup of the Easter population but certain tooth characters, such as Carabelli's trait, indicate that this miscegenation alone cannot account for the overall simplification of the Easter Island dental pattern. This pattern's outstanding characteristics are:

a. A low frequency of marked shoveling (ca. 5 percent).
b. Winging in moderate frequency (ca. 10 percent).
c. Carabelli's trait in low frequency (ca. 33 percent).
d. Moderate incidence of three-cusped upper second molars (ca. 22 percent).
e. Three-cusped lower premolars in high frequency (ca. 40 percent in P_1 and 60 percent in P_2).

f. Four-cusped lower second molars of intermediate frequency (ca. 50 percent).

g. Cusps 6 and 7 and the protostylid relatively infrequent ($<$ 25 percent), especially the more pronounced expressions of these features.

h. Mandibular and palatine torus uncommon (10–15 percent) but soft-tissue masking may, of course, bias this frequency downward.

REFERENCES

ALEXANDERSEN, V.
  1970   Tandmorfologisk variation hos Eskimoer og andre Mongoloide populationer. *Tandlaegebladet* 74:587–602.
BAILIT, H. L., S. J. DEWITT, R. A. LEIGH
  1968   The size and morphology of the Nasioi dentition. *American Journal of Physical Anthropology* 28:271–288.
BAILIT, H. L., P. L. WORKMAN, J. D. NISWANDER, C. J. MAC LEAN
  1970   Dental asymmetry as an indicator of genetic and environmental conditions in human populations. *Human Biology* 42:626–638.
BRABANT, H.
  1969   Observations sur les dents des populations mégalithiques d'Europe occidentale. *Bulletin du Groupement International pour la Recherche Scientifique en Stomatologie* 12:429–460.
BUCK, P. H.
  1938   *Vikings of the sunrise.* New York: F. A. Stokes.
CAMPBELL, T. D.
  1925   *Dentition and palate of the Australian aboriginal.* University of Adelaide Publications 1. Adelaide: The Hassell Press.
CARBONELL, V. M.
  1963   "Variations in the frequency of shovel-shaped incisors in different populations," in *Dental anthropology.* Edited by D. R. Brothwell, 211–234. New York: Pergamon.
CHAPPEL, H. G.
  1927   Jaws and teeth of ancient Hawaiians. *Memoirs of the Bernice P. Bishop Museum* 9:249–268.
DAHLBERG, A. A.
  1950   The evolutionary significance of the protostylid. *American Journal of Physical Anthropology* 8:15–25.
  1951   "The dentition of the American Indian," in *Papers on the physical anthropology of the American Indian.* Edited by W. S. Laughlin, 138–176. New York: The Viking Fund.
  1963   "Analysis of the American Indian dentition," in *Dental anthropology.* Edited by D. R. Brothwell, 149–177. New York: Pergamon.
EMORY, K. P.
  1959   Origin of the Hawaiians. *Journal of the Polynesian Society* 68: 29–35.
  1968   "East Polynesian relationships as revealed through adzes," in *Pre-*

historic culture in Oceania. Edited by I. Yawata and Y. H. Sinoto, 151–169. Honolulu: Bishop Museum Press.

ENOKI, K., A. A. DAHLBERG
1958   Rotated maxillary central incisors. *Orthodontic Journal of Japan* 17:157–169.

FERDON, E. N., JR.
1961   "A summary of the excavated record of Easter Island prehistory," in *Reports of the Norwegian Archaeological Expedition to Easter Island and the east Pacific,* volume one: *Archaeology of Easter Island.* Edited by T. Heyerdahl and E. N. Ferdon, Jr., 527–535. Stockholm: Victor Pettersons Bokindustri Aktiebolag.

GARN, S. M.
1971   *Human races.* Springfield: C. C. Thomas.

GEORGE, V.
1926   A comparative study of the jaws and occlusion of Maori and of British-born in New Zealand. *International Journal of Orthodontics* 12:20–24.

GREEN, R. C.
1967   "The immediate origins of the Polynesians," in *Polynesian culture history.* Edited by G. A. Highland, R. W. Force, A. Howard, M. Kelly, and Y. H. Sinoto, 215–240. Honolulu: Bishop Museum Press.

GREENE, D. L.
1967   *Dentition of Meroitic, X-group, and Christian populations from Wadi Halfa, Sudan.* University of Utah Anthropological Papers 85.

GREGORY, W. K.
1916   Studies on the evolution of the primates; part one: the Cope-Osborn "theory of trituberculy" and the ancestral molar patterns of the primates; part two: phylogeny of recent and extinct anthropoids, with special reference to the origin of man. *Bulletin of the American Museum of Natural History* 35:239–355.

HANIHARA, K.
1969   Mongoloid dental complex in the permanent dentition. *Proceedings of the Eighth International Congress of Anthropological and Ethnological Sciences, Tokyo and Kyoto, 1968,* 298–300. Tokyo: Science Council of Japan.

HARTWEG, R.
1947   Les variations cuspidaires de la première molaire inférieure et leur signification évolutive chez les populations americaines. *Congrès International des Americanistes* 28:3–18.

HELLMAN, M.
1928   Racial characters in human dentition. *Proceedings of the American Philosophical Society* 67:157–174.

HEYERDAHL, T.
1953   *American Indians in the Pacific.* Chicago: Rand McNally.
1961   "General discussion," in *Reports of the Norwegian Archaeological Expedition to Easter Island and the east Pacific,* volume one: *Archaeology of Easter Island.* Edited by T. Heyerdahl and E. M.

Ferdon, Jr., 493–526. Stockholm: Victor Pettersons Bokindustri Aktiebolag.
1968   *Sea routes to Polynesia.* Chicago: Rand McNally.
HOOTON, E. A.
1935   *Up from the ape.* New York: Macmillan.
HOWARD, A.
1967   "Polynesian origins and migrations: a review of two centuries of speculation and theory," in *Polynesian culture history.* Edited by G. A. Highland, R. W. Force, A. Howard, M. Kelly, and Y. H. Sinoto, 45-101. Honolulu: Bishop Museum Press.
HRDLIČKA, A.
1920   Shovel-shaped teeth. *American Journal of Physical Anthropology* 3:429–465.
JØRGENSEN, K. D.
1955   The Dryopithecus pattern in recent Danes and Dutchmen. *Journal of Dental Research* 34:195–208.
KRAUS, B. S.
1959   Occurrence of the Carabelli trait in Southwest ethnic groups. *American Journal of Physical Anthropology* 17:117–123.
KRAUS, B. S., M. L. FURR
1953   Lower first premolars; part one: a definition and classification of discrete morphologic traits. *Journal of Dental Research* 32:554–564.
LEIGH, R. W.
1929   Dental morphology and pathology of prehistoric Guam. *Memoirs of the Bernice P. Bishop Museum* 11:255–273.
LINTON, R.
1955   *The tree of culture.* New York: Alfred A. Knopf.
LUDWIG, F. J.
1957   The mandibular second premolars: morphologic variation and inheritance. *Journal of Dental Research* 36:263–273.
MEIER, R. J.
1970   "The Easter Islander: a study in human biology." Unpublished Ph.D. dissertation, University of Wisconsin, Madison.
MÉTRAUX, A.
1940   *Ethnology of Easter Island.* Bulletin 160 of the Bernice P. Bishop Museum.
MOORREES, C. F. A.
1957   *The Aleut dentition.* Cambridge: Harvard University Press.
MURDOCK, G. P.
1964   Genetic classification of the Austronesian languages: a key to Oceanian culture history. *Ethnology* 3:117–126.
MURRILL, R. I.
1968   *Cranial and postcranial skeletal remains from Easter Island.* Minneapolis: University of Minnesota Press.
RIESENFELD, A.
1956   Shovel-shaped incisors and a few other dental features among the native peoples of the Pacific. *American Journal of Psysical Anthropology* 14:505–521.

SCOTT, G. R.
1971   "Canine *tuberculum dentale*." Paper presented at the Fortieth Annual Meeting of the American Association of Physical Anthropologists, Boston, Massachusetts.
1972   "An analysis of family and population data on Carabelli's trait and shovel-shaped incisors." Paper presented at the Forty-first Annual Meeting of the American Association of Physical Anthropologists, Lawrence, Kansas.

SHAPIRO, H. L.
1935   Mystery island of the Pacific. *Natural History* 35:365–377.

SIMMONS, R. T.
1962   Blood-group genes in Polynesians and comparisons with other Pacific peoples. *Oceania* 32:198–210.

SINOTO, Y. H.
1968   "Position of the Marquesas Islands in east Polynesian prehistory," in *Prehistoric culture in Oceania*. Edited by I. Yawata and Y. H. Sinoto, 111–118. Honolulu: Bishop Museum Press.

SKORYNA, S. C.
1965   "Medical expedition to Easter Island: preliminary report." Unpublished manuscript.

SMITH, C. S.
1961   "Radio carbon dates from Easter Island," in *Reports of the Norwegian Archaeological Expedition to Easter Island and the east Pacific*, volume one: *Archaeology of Easter Island*. Edited by T. Heyerdahl and E. N. Ferdon, Jr., 393–396. Stockholm: Victor Pettersons Bokindustri Aktiebolag.

SOFAER, J. A.
1970   Dental morphological variation and the Hardy-Weinberg law. *Journal of Dental Research* 49:1505–1508.

SUZUKI, M., T. SAKAI
1957   The living Sakhalin Ainu dentition. *Anthropological Reports* 18:303–346. (Department of Anatomy, School of Medicine, Shinshu University.)
1960   Number of cusps of the lower molars in the recent Polynesians. *Acta Anatomica Nipponica* 35:445.
1964   Shovel-shaped incisors among the living Polynesians. *American Journal of Physical Anthropology* 22:65–72.

TAYLOR, A. G.
1966   Dental conditions among the inhabitants of Easter Island. *Journal of the Canadian Dental Association* 32:286–290.

TAYLOR, R. M. S.
1963   Cause and effect of wear of teeth: further nonmetrical studies of the teeth and palate in Moriori and Maori skulls. *Acta Anatomica* 53:97–157.

TSUJI, T.
1958   Incidence and inheritance of the Carabelli's cusp in a Japanese population. *Japanese Journal of Human Genetics* 3:21–31.

TURNER, CHRISTY G., II
1967a "The dentition of Arctic peoples." Unpublished Ph.D. dissertation, University of Wisconsin.
1967b Dental genetics and microevolution in prehistoric and living Koniag Eskimo. *Journal of Dental Research* 46:911–917.
1968 Review of *Cranial and postcranial skeletal remains from Easter Island*, by R. I. Murrill. *Science* 162:555–556.
1969a Microevolutionary interpretations from the dentition. *American Journal of Physical Anthropology* 30:421–426.
1969b Directionality in the canine field model. *Journal of Dental Research* 48:1310.
1970 "New classifications of non-metrical dental variation: cusps 6 and 7." Paper presented at the Thirty-ninth Annual Meeting of the American Association of Physical Anthropologists, Washington D.C.
1971 Three-rooted mandibular first permanent molars and the question of American Indian origins. *American Journal of Physical Anthropology* 34:229–242.
WECKLER, J. E.
1943 *Polynesians: explorers of the Pacific*. Smithsonian Institution War Background Studies 6, Washington D.C.
WISSLER, C.
1931 Observations on the face and teeth of the North American Indian. *Anthropological Papers of the American Museum of Natural History* 33:1–33.
ZUBOV, A. A.
1969 "Odontological analysis of cranial series from Ekven and Uelen cemeteries," in *Ancient cultures of Asiatic Eskimos*. Edited by G. F. Debets, 185–194. Moscow: Science Publishers.

Uncommon Dental Traits in Population Studies

PENTTI KIRVESKARI

Dental traits clearly have great value in comparative racial, population, and genetic studies owing to the considerable variability of most traits in different populations. However, difficulties of measuring or recording the differences are numerous. The continuous variability of most traits forces us to use arbitrary classes for the degree of phenotypic expression, and to rely on more or less subjective criteria in classifying them. The frequency of occurrence and degree of expression of a single trait seldom, if ever, has the potential of placing a population into a certain larger population, subrace, or race. On the other hand, isolated and inbred populations are known to achieve individuality in form and range of variability (Dahlberg 1965). The value of population comparisons is thus dependent on the number of variable traits used, as well as on the accuracy and comparability of the frequencies of different degrees of their expressions.

This study is made in order to demonstrate the potential of certain dental traits less commonly used in comparative population studies.

My sincere thanks are first of all due to Dr. A. A. Dahlberg, at whose suggestion this study was made. His encouragement and guidance have been the all-important impetus in carrying through the work. Docent B. Ingervall, Odontologiska Kliniken, Gothenburg, is sincerely thanked for letting me examine the serial casts of the Swedish subjects. For the same reason I wish to express my gratitude to Professor K. Koski, Institute of Dentistry, University of Turku, Finland.

Financial help has been granted by Odontologiska Fakulteten, Gothenburg ("Främjande av ograduerade forskares vetenskapliga verksamhet") on two occasions.

For plates, see pp. xliii–xliv, between pp. 330–331.

MATERIAL

The Skolt Lapps are the main subject of this study. In 1965 a total of 515 pure Skolts lived in the north of Finland. The Human Adaptability group of the International Biological Programme undertook extensive field studies in 1967–1970, during which time odontological fieldwork was carried out. Over 90 percent of the Skolts living in Finland were examined, and dental casts were prepared of all the examined, aged five years or more. In spite of the apparently high number of subjects, repeated field studies were badly needed before a sufficient number of intact teeth could be secured for the purpose of morphological studies. This circumstance was due to the overwhelmingly high incidence of dental caries.

From a genetic viewpoint the Skolt Lapps may be considered to be a relatively pure and inbred isolate, the geographical distances and their Greek Orthodox faith being the main isolating factors. An introduction to the biological characteristics of the Skolt Lapps with comprehensive data on their history, demography, genealogy, and other subjects, was published in *Suomen Hammaslääkäriseuran Toimituksia* 67, supplement 1 (1971).

For the sake of comparison, serial casts of about 150 Swedish and 250 Finnish children and adolescents were examined. Individuals in question were orthodontic patients in the Odontologiska Kliniken, Gothenburg, Sweden, and the Institute of Dentistry, Turku, Finland, respectively. Serial casts to be examined were chosen randomly from the relatively large number of casts available. Cases with gross anomalies, such as cleft palate, were excluded from this study.

METHOD

All observations are indirect, made after a careful examination of casts under laboratory circumstances. The casts were made by taking alginate impressions and pouring them in hard dental stone according to standard methods.

Only one observation per trait and individual was registered for the statistics. It was normally taken from the right side, but if the trait in question was observable only on the left side, it was accepted. The decision to do this was based on negative results in lateral dominance studies of the traits in Skolts.

All casts in this study were examined and the traits registered by the author. The three morphological traits used were chosen after an over-all screening of the casts of the Skolt population. As no generally accepted standards for the classification of the expressions of these traits seemed to be available, it was necessary to establish some standards that could be adhered to in all three populations. After a series of random duplicate determinations, the following classification criteria were found to give the best (about 90 percent) reproducibility:

1. "Bulging" of the Lingual Aspect of the Buccal Cusp of Maxillary Premolars.

a.   Normal contour, corresponding to the standard descriptions of dental anatomy textbooks.

b.   Bulging, whenever the main lingual crest shows conspicious extra convexity with buildup of enamel just lingual to the cusp tip. An impression of a bucco-lingually dividing cusp is readily at hand (Plate 1). Slight wear at the tip of the cusp results in a contour that is rather close to the one described above. Furthermore, pit-like enamel defects at the top of the cusp are not uncommon in premolars of the Skolts. Such a defect often "divides" the cusp tip without the buildup of enamel occurring at all. Thus it proved imperative to restrict the observations to erupting or newly erupted teeth, and reject a relatively large number of slightly worn teeth.

2. Reduction of the Mesial Lobe of Maxillary Permanent Canines.

a.   Fully developed or hypertrophied.

b.   Reduced, whenever the incisal crests form an exceptionally acute angle indicating reduction of both mesial and distal lobes; or whenever only the mesial lobe is reduced in comparison with the distal lobe, closely resembling the anatomy of a corresponding deciduous tooth. A handy indicator is the location of contact points: normally the distal one is more apical. If the mesial contact point was more cervical the mesial lobe was labeled as reduced (Plate 2).

3. Lingual Tubercles of Maxillary Permanent Central Incisors.

a.   Number and size of the lingual tubercles appear to be the simplest criteria for the division of the expressions of this trait into different classes. With only two categories of size, small and large, a minimum of seven rating classes becomes available. They are (1) no tubercles, (2) single small, (3) double small, (4) single large, (5) large plus small, (6) double large, and (7) multiple—three or more tubercles of any size.

Very fine and shallow furrows over the basal tubercle were not taken as indicative of the presence of the trait (although this may, in reality, very well be the case) for practical reasons. Only when discernible enamel elevation could be observed was the presence of a tubercle registered. The size categories were distinguished by an arbitrary limit which is quite impossible to define accurately in words or with the help of photographs. Only a three-dimensional master model can serve as a reasonably good reference.

Such a master model was selected for this study. A small tubercle could be described as a finger-like projection: a narrow enamel ridge extending from the basal tubercle to the lingual fossa. Also, tubercles that were of more cusplet-like form were counted as small if they did not stand out from the surrounding enamel very clearly and well defined. In Plate 3 multiple tubercles can be seen on the right central incisor. The size of all three would be classified as small, representing the upper limit of the class, whereas the tubercle on the left central incisor clearly belongs to the large category.

RESULTS

The frequencies of occurrence of bulging of the lingual aspect of buccal cusps of maxillary permanent premolars are shown in Table 1 and Figure 1. The trait appears to be more common in Swedish and Skolt

Table 1.   Occurrence of bulging of the lingual aspect of buccal cusps of maxillary permanent premolars in Swedes, Finns, and Skolt Lapps.

		P1			P2		
		Number	"Normal"	"Bulging"	Number	"Normal"	"Bulging"
Swedes	Male	52	43	9	44	38	6
	Female	62	56	6	48	44	4
	Total	114	99	15	92	82	10
Finns	Male	84	80	4	85	75	9
	Female	132	119	13	135	117	18
	Total	216	199	17	220	192	27
Skolts	Male	47	33	14	53	35	18
	Female	54	41	13	55	47	8
	Total	101	74	27	108	82	26

boys than girls, while the Finns showed the opposite trend. However, the sexual dimorphism reaches statistical significance only for P^2 in Skolts ($\chi^2 = 4.555$, 1 df; p<.05). For combined sexes, Swedes and Finns show rather similar frequencies while those of Skolts are higher

percent

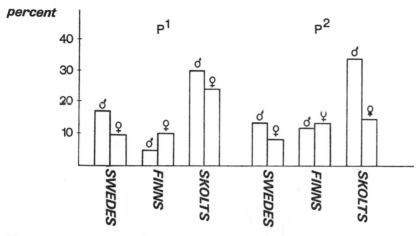

Figure 1. Percentage occurrence of bulging of the lingual aspect of buccal cusps of maxillary permanent premolars

for both premolars, the difference being statistically significant for both Swedes ($\chi^2 = 5.444$, 1 df, p<.05 in P¹; $\chi^2 = 5.008$, 1 df, p<.05 in P²), and Finns ($\chi^2 = 18.936$, 1 df, p<.001 in P¹; $\chi^2 = 6.508$, 1 df, p<.05 in P²).

Maxillary permanent canines with reduced mesial lobe are more common in boys than in girls in all three populations (Table 2 and Figure 2). The sexual dimorphism is statistically significant in Skolts ($\chi^2 = 10.401$; 1 df, p<.01) and in Finns ($\chi^2 = 6.491$, 1 df, p<.05). When the sexes are treated separately, significant differences are found between Swedish and Skolt boys ($\chi^2 = 15.717$, 1 df, p<.001) and girls

Table 2. Occurrence of maxillary permanent canines with reduced mesial lobe in Swedes, Finns, and Skolt Lapps

		Number	Mesial lobe fully developed	Mesial lobe reduced
Swedes	Male	39	32	7
	Female	58	51	7
	Total	97	83	14
Finns	Male	78	60	18
	Female	138	125	13
	Total	216	185	31
Skolts	Male	69	28	41
	Female	66	46	20
	Total	135	74	61

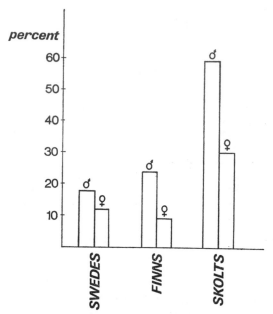

Figure 2.   Percentage occurrence of maxillary permanent canines with reduced mesial lobe

($\chi^2 = 5.003$, 1 df, p<.05) as well as Finnish and Skolt boys ($\chi^2 = 18.643$, 1 df, p<.001) and girls ($\chi^2 = 12.860$, 1 df, p<.001).

The frequency of occurrence of lingual tubercles on maxillary permanent central incisors divided in seven different classes of expression is given in Table 3. For statistical purposes, the results are regrouped

Table 3.   Occurrence of lingual tubercles on maxillary central permanent incisors in Swedes, Finns, and Skolt Lapps

		Number	No tubercles	Single small	Double small	Single large	Large and small	Double large	Multiple
Swedes	Male	73	25	16	16	4	2	2	8
	Female	75	39	18	14	0	2	0	2
	Total	148	64	34	30	4	4	2	10
Finns	Male	81	35	18	17	1	3	2	5
	Female	138	60	32	35	1	3	1	6
	Total	219	95	50	52	2	6	3	11
Skolts	Male	103	41	24	24	2	4	3	5
	Female	95	46	18	21	3	4	0	3
	Total	198	87	42	45	5	8	3	8

into three morphological classes (Figure 3). No significant sex or interpopulation differences are found.

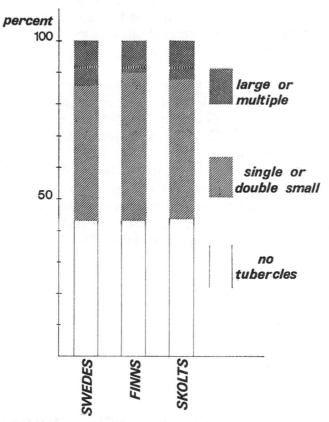

Figure 3. Percentage occurrence of lingual tubercles on maxillary permanent
central incisors

DISCUSSION

Orthodontic patients representing Swedes and Finns in this study are
clearly not unbiased samples, and the results may not be applicable to
whole populations of Sweden and Finland. However, as the demonstra-
tion of variation is the main objective of this study, such samples can
be said to serve the purpose satisfactorily. Naturally, the availability of
materials plays a part, too.

Only a preliminary description of the "bulging" trait of the Skolts
has been published so far (Kirveskari, Hedegård, and Dahlberg 1972).
It is obvious that the trait can occur on different cusps: the metacone
occasionally shows prominent bulging, and in mandibular teeth, the

protoconid of premolars can possess a bulge similar to that of the maxillary teeth, although the frequency of occurrence appears to be much lower. On permanent lower molars, the protoconid and hypoconid do not seem to express the trait, at least not the more prominent forms of it. However, the metaconid often shows cuspal morphology that closely resembles that of the bulging trait. This type of cuspal morphology is perhaps a result of a phenomenon referred to as isolation of the cusp from its "Randleiste," the marginal crest (Remane 1960). A related structure is maybe the "small knob-like and rather circumscribed swelling" (Weidenreich 1937), or the "inciso-lingual enamel pearl" (Pedersen 1949) sometimes seen just lingual to the cusp tip of maxillary canines.

The appearance of the bulging trait is largely determined by two factors: the extra buildup of enamel, and the development of associated accessory grooves. Deeply incising accessory grooves alone can give a cusp the characteristic bulging appearance, especially on maxillary second deciduous and first permanent molars. Therefore it was decided to restrict this particular study to maxillary premolars, and pay no attention to the development of the accessory grooves. By doing this it was ensured that the same feature was registered in all three populations.

Not much can be said about the significance of this peculiar phenomenon in cusp morphology, and its phylogenetic and genetic background. The significantly higher frequency of occurrence in Skolts as compared to Swedes and Finns shows, at any rate, that an isolated and inbred human population can achieve some individuality in tooth morphology. The true difference between these populations may very well be larger than the above figures indicate. The essentially continuous (or quasi-continuous) trait was treated as a qualitative one, without an attempt to evaluate the size of the structure. If such an evaluation could be made without introducing more bias, the Skolts also would be likely to show the larger structures in addition to the higher frequency.

It is typical of human canines that the crown base is large in comparison to the cusp. This is due to well-developed mesial and distal lobes. Consequently, the mesial and distal incisal crests form an obtuse angle (Remane 1960). Very well developed mesial and distal lobes give the canine an incisor-like appearance. This incisivization probably culminated in the mandibular canines of *Sinanthropus*, and secondary reduction of the lobes has taken place in the canines of modern man (Weidenreich 1937). Although a slightly obtuse angle between the incisal crests seems to be the rule in dental anatomy textbooks, variation is reported in the degree of development of both mesial and distal lobes (Kraus, Jordan, and Abrams 1969: 38). In addition to the detailed descriptions of *Sinanthropus* (Weidenreich 1937) and australopithecine canines (Robinson 1956), recent and modern human canine morphology is also described in some reports, for instance the American Indian (Dahlberg 1949), East Greenland Eskimo (Pedersen 1949), the Jarmo population (Dahlberg 1960), and the Teso (Barnes 1969)

Measuring the angle between the incisal crests would seem to be the method of choice for comparisons of the development of the lobes, especially if results of different authors are to be used. However, while the determination of the direction of the mesial crest is relatively easy, the distal crest often proves difficult in this respect. Besides being generally more convex, it quite often makes a sharp bend at the site of the distal accessory ridge. That is why only subjective evaluation of the degree of development of the mesial lobe was considered adequate for the purpose of this study.

Both the sexual dimorphism and the interpopulation differences were unexpected findings. Little sexual dimorphism has been found in population studies on morphological reduction of human teeth, and whenever it is found to occur, females usually show more reduction than males. Odontometrically the canines are known to show considerable sexual dimorphism. According to preliminary computations the Skolts seem to follow the rule. Thus the higher frequency of reduced mesial lobes in the male sex does not appear to have any impact on the essentially opposite sexual dimorphism of the mesiodistal diameter of the tooth on a population basis. Also the fact that the mesial lobe seemed to be more affected by reduction than the distal lobe is in sharp contrast to reduction phenomena in other tooth groups, where the distal part of the tooth is regularly first affected.

The lingual tubercles of upper canines and incisors have long drawn odontographers' attention. Occurrence of the tubercles does not seem to be a racial characteristic (Weidenreich 1937; Hanihara 1965). Yet, differences between populations have been demonstrated at least for the lateral incisor (Carbonell 1963). At first sight, Skolts also displayed a wide variation of expressions on the central incisor. That is why the central incisor was selected for this study. In contrast to the previous traits, the expressions of the lingual tubercles showed almost striking similarity of distribution in all three populations. No sexual dimorphism was found, either. Meaningful comparisons cannot be made with the few frequency reports available in the literature because of methodological differences. Sexual dimorphism has been reported in the occurrence of finger-like projections, but the classification used was entirely different from the present one (Barnes 1969).

The present results are in line with the thought that these features are of secondary nature, taking the form of convenience rather than that of definite plan (Dahlberg 1960). On the other hand, the classification of the expressions used may not reflect the true variability of the trait. Certain facts were overlooked in this study, such as the heterogenous origin of the lingual tubercles. It has been pointed out that the tubercles can originate in the basal cingulum only, or that remnants of the central lingual ridge can contribute to these formations. Distinguishing between these two types may be difficult in individual cases, however (Remane 1960). Also, the size of the tubercles was placed into two arbitrary categories, a fact which is clearly not compatible with the real situation.

CONCLUSIONS

1.   Morphological characteristics other than those commonly used and/or recognized in population studies may prove to be valuable contributions to the comparative odontography of populations.

2.   The Skolt Lapps, an isolated and inbred population in the north of Finland, are clearly different from samples of their neighbor Swedes and Finns in respect to the distribution of two morphological characteristics: the bulging of the lingual aspect of buccal cusps of maxillary permanent premolars, and the reduction of the mesial lobe of the maxillary canine. The occurrence of lingual tubercles on maxillary central permanent incisors showed similarity of distribution in all three populations studied.

3.   More refined methods than the rather crude subjective evaluation of morphological characteristics would be likely to yield more accurate results as well as make comparisons between different workers possible. If measurements cannot be used, three-dimensional standard models are to be preferred for reference, such as the P-series of plaques prepared by Dr. Dahlberg and issued by the Zoller Clinic in 1956. Expansion of the series is indicated.

REFERENCES

BARNES, D. S.
   1969   Tooth morphology and other aspects of the Teso dentition. *American Journal of Physical Anthropology* 30:183–194.
CARBONELL, VIRGINIA M.
   1963   "Variations in the frequency of shovel-shaped incisors in different populations," in *Dental anthropology*. Edited by D. R. Brothwell, 211–234. Oxford: Pergamon Press.
DAHLBERG, ALBERT A.
   1949   "The dentition of the American Indian," in *Papers on the physical anthropology of the American Indian*. Edited by W. S. Laughlin, 138–176. New York: Viking Fund.
   1960   The dentition of the first agriculturalists (Jarmo, Iraq). *American Journal of Physical Anthropology* 18:243–256.
   1965   Evolutionary background of dental and facial growth. *Journal of Dental Research* 44:151–160.
HANIHARA, KAZURO
   1965   Some crown characters of the deciduous incisors and canines in Japanese-American hybrids. *Zinruigaku Zassi* 72:135–145.
KIRVESKARI, P., B. HEDEGÅRD, A. A. DAHLBERG
   1972   Bulging of the lingual aspects of buccal cusps in posterior teeth of Skolt Lapps from northern Finland. *Journal of Dental Research* 51:1513.
KRAUS, B. S., R. E. JORDAN, L. ABRAMS
   1969   *Dental anatomy and occlusion* (first edition). Baltimore: Williams and Wilkins.
PEDERSEN, P. O.
   1949   *The East Greenland Eskimo dentition*. Copenhagen: C. A. Reitzels.
REMANE, ADOLF
   1960   "Zähne und Gebiss," in *Primatologia III*. Edited by H. Hofer, A. H. Schulz, and D. Starck, 637–846. Basel: Karger.
ROBINSON, J. T.
   1956   *The dentition of the Australopithecinae*. Transvaal Museum Memoir 9:1–179.
WEIDENREICH, F.
   1937   The dentition of *Sinanthropus Pekinensis*: a comparative odontography of the hominids. *Palaeontologia Sinica* 101:1–180.

Craniofacial Description of Wainwright Alaskan Eskimos

ROBERT CEDERQUIST and ALBERT A. DAHLBERG

Beginning in the summer of 1968 and for five consecutive years lateral roentgenographic cephalograms, together with dental casts and other records, have been taken of the Eskimo population at Wainwright, Alaska. This project ("the Wainwright Project") is a part of the International Biological Programme and has been sponsored by the University of Alaska, the University of Wisconsin, and the University of Chicago.

Wainwright is located on latitude 70° 38'N and longitude 160°01'W on the northwestern coast of Alaska, approximately midway between Point Hope and Point Barrow. This part of Alaska is populated by Taremuit, although considerable admixture exists. In 1969 the Eskimo population at Wainwright was estimated at 285 individuals by the Federal Field Committee for Development Planning in Alaska.

PURPOSE OF INVESTIGATION

The aim of the investigation is to describe the craniofacial skeletal morphology as seen on lateral roentgenographic cephalograms of the Wainwright population and to study differences between age groups, detectable on a two-dimensional radiograph in norma lateralis, of the various cranial and facial skeletal components that can be seen.

MATERIAL AND METHODS

Of the 340 individuals who were registered in the project file in 1968, which also included 55 relatives from the area surrounding Wainwright, 255 participated and have been radiographed one to five times. For those who were radiographed more than once, the intervals between examination dates were 11 and/or 13 months (11 months between 1968 and 1969 and between 1970 and 1971, 13 months between 1969 and 1970 and between 1971 and 1972). The roentgenograms were taken with a Universal X-ray apparatus at a constant anode-midsagittal plane distance of 60 inches. The midsagittal plane-film distance varied for each individual. A total of 566 lateral roentgenographic cephalograms of the 255 individuals were taken. The cephalograms were later rated and grouped into two main categories:

1.   Acceptable films; and
2.   those films which are unacceptable due to:
     a.   poor film quality or anatomical parts cut off,
     b.   mandible positioned somewhere on the path of closure but not in central occlusion,
     c.   mandible pushed anteriorly from central occlusion, or
     d.   incomplete data.

After this procedure the first category, "Acceptable films," consisted of 361 roentgenograms from 188 individuals. This sample has been used for further processing in this investigation. Table 1 illustrates the

Table 1.   Distribution of roentgenographic cephalograms for sample according to sex and age at the time of first examination

Number of cephalograms	1		2		3		4		5		1, 2, 3, 4, or 5		
Age class	F	M	F	M	F	M	F	M	F	M	F	M	F+M
5/0 – 9/11	5	13	8	9	6	8	7	1	1	–	27	31	58
10/0 – 14/11	11	4	12	10	6	5	3	1	2	–	34	20	54
15/0 – 19/11	6	5	4	5	3	3	1	–	–	–	14	13	27
20/0 – 24/11	3	4	1	–	–	–	–	–	–	–	4	4	8
25/0 – 29/11	–	2	2	2	–	–	–	–	–	–	2	4	6
30/0 – 34/11	5	4	–	–	–	–	–	–	–	–	5	5	9
35/0 – 39/11	1	6	–	–	–	–	–	–	–	–	1	6	7
40/0 – 44/11	–	3	1	1	–	–	–	–	–	–	1	4	5
45/0 – 49/11	–	1	–	1	–	–	–	–	–	–	–	2	2
50/0 – 54/11	–	2	–	–	–	–	–	–	–	–	–	2	2
55/0 – 59/11	1	–	1	1	–	–	–	–	–	–	2	1	3
60/0 – 64/11	1	1	–	2	–	–	–	–	–	–	1	3	4
65/0 – 69/11	–	1	–	–	–	–	–	–	–	–	–	1	1
70/0 – 74/11	1	1	–	–	–	–	–	–	–	–	1	1	2
Total number of individuals	34	47	29	31	15	16	11	2	3	–	92	96	188
Total number of roentgenographic cephalograms	34	47	58	62	45	48	44	8	15	–	196	165	361

age and sex distribution of the sample and distribution of roentgeno-grams. The age and sex distribution for the sample is the same as for the population.

Thirty-one anatomical reference points, as defined by Björk (1947, 1960) and Hylander (1972), were recorded for each roentgenogram with a SAC Graf/Pen Model GP-2 digitizing system, and the following reference lines have been used:

1. Axis of mandibular incisor (Björk 1960).
2. Axis of maxillary incisor (Björk 1960).
3. Balance axis of the head (Björk 1960).
4. Chin line (Björk 1960).
5. Facial line (Margolis 1947).
6. Functional occlusal line (Moyers 1973).
7. Inferior occlusal line (Björk 1960).
8. Mandibular line (Björk 1960).
9. Maxillo-zygomatic line (Hylander 1972).
10. Nasal line (Björk 1960).
11. Nasion-sella line (Björk 1960).
12. Nasion-sella perpendicular (Lindegard 1953).
13. Occipital foramen line (Björk 1960).
14. Superior occlusal line (Björk 1960).

The reference points are situated in the midsagittal plane or are projected on this plane. Midpoints were used in cases of left and right projections. The recordings were made on the roentgenograms, i.e. no tracings were made. The recorded coordinates were transferred to computer cards and a computer program has been written for the calculation of the different linear and angular measurements, which are according to definitions by Björk (1960), Hylander (1972) and Lindegard (1953). Sixty-two measurements were calculated and divided into five categories:

1. Cranial base measurements.
2. Measurements for facial vertical dimensions.
3. Sagittal position, relation, and shape of maxilla and mandible.
4. Dental relationships.
5. Measurements for facial flatness.

For analysis the roentgenograms were also arranged in seventeen classes, females and males separately, according to age of the individual at the time of examination. Means, standard deviations, and ranges for the various measurements were calculated in each class. The same procedure was also followed for seven combined age classes.

ERRORS OF THE METHOD

The thirty-one reference points were recorded twice for ten roentgeno-grams, one week between the two determinations. The experimental error, a measure of the differences between first and second recordings, was calculated according to the formula $d=\sqrt{i^2/2n}$ (Dahlberg 1940), where i is the difference between first and second determinations and n is the number of double determinations; d was calculated for each point both along the x-coordinate, along the y-coordinate, and along the line going through the two points that represent the x- and y-coordinates for first and second determinations. In general, the error is greater along the y-coordinate than along the x-coordinate and the combined error is within a millimeter. The experimental error has also been used to estimate how much the different linear and angular measurements will vary due to inaccuracy in repeatedly locating reference points.

RESULTS

Midfacial flatness (maxillo-zygomatic line to NSL and maxillo-zygomatic line to the line from nasion to subspinale have been taken as measures of facial flatness) seems to be constant with age. However, in comparison with what Hylander (1972) reported for a precontact skeletal material from the Canadian Arctic, the facial flatness is less pronounced.

Facial convexity is definitely decreasing through the age groups for both males and females. However, even the older groups show more facial convexity than does Hylander's material. In comparison with a much more recent (approximately A.D. 1860) Eskimo skeletal material from Alaska (Dahlberg 1972), the measurements appear to be similar.

The maxillary and mandibular incisors are continuously uprighting, but the adult groups have less upright incisors than the Alaskan skeletal material mentioned above. In the Wainwright population there is notice-able maxillary incisor root resorption in the older groups as compared to the younger.

For the lateral cranial base no intrasample differences can be detected but measurements in general are smaller than those given by Hylander and slightly larger than Björk (1947) reported for Swedish males.

The antero-posterior relation of supramentale and subspinale (ANB-angle, a measure of sagittal apical base relation) is decreasing with a noticeable drop for males in the age range of 16 to 18 years, and the measurements for adult males are approximately one degree which does not differ from the Alaskan skeletal material (Dahlberg 1972).

The facial vertical dimensions are changing in that the ratio between posterior and anterior facial height is increasing with age. The older groups have less anterior facial height than do the younger.

REFERENCES

BJÖRK, A.
1947   The face in profile. *Svenska Tandläkare Tidskrift* 40 (5B).
1960   "The Relationship of the jaws to the cranium," in *Introduction to orthodontics*. Edited by A. Lundström. New York: McGraw-Hill.
DAHLBERG, A. A.
1972   Unpublished data.
DAHLBERG, G.
1940   *Statistical methods for medical and biological students*. London: G. Allen and Unwin.
FEDERAL FIELD COMMITTEE FOR DEVELOPMENT PLANNING IN ALASKA
1969   *Estimates of native population in villages, towns, and boroughs of Alaska.*
HYLANDER, W. L.
1972   "The adaptive significance of Eskimo craniofacial morphology." Unpublished doctoral dissertation, University of Chicago.
LINDEGARD, B.
1953   Variations in human body-build. *Acta Psychiatrica Neurologica* (supplement) 86.
MARGOLIS, H. I.
1947   A basic facial pattern and its application in clinical orthodontics, I: The maxillofacial triangle. *American Journal of Orthodontics and Oral Surgery* 33:631–641.
MOYERS, R. E.
1973   *Handbook of orthodontics* (third edition). Chicago: Year Book Medical Publications.

Odontoglyphics: The Laws of Variation of the Human Molar Crown Microrelief

A. A. ZOUBOV

The masticatory surface of the molars and premolars of humans and primates is covered with an intricate pattern of furrows passing in the intercusp spaces and on the cusps, and separating the elevated sections of the crown one from another. This furrow pattern, on the whole stable but at the same time varying in details, is a valuable and interesting object of morphological study and may form a basis for a whole branch of odontology which, by analogy with dermatoglyphics, may be appropriately called "odontoglyphics." Here we are concerned with the variations of the pattern of the human molar masticatory surface.

Studying the pattern of the masticatory surface of human molars, one will easily see that the number, positions, and shapes of the furrows follow certain laws, so that those who maintain that the number and positions of the furrows are chaotic and random are wrong, their error resulting from a lack of knowledge about the furrows. Even in the case of very tangled patterns, where the masticatory surface is described as "striated," "wrinkled," or with other terms of a similar nature, practically all the furrows can be singled out and identified.

Morphologists usually concentrate on the protruding elements on the masticatory surface of the molars — the cusp and the crest — ignoring the furrow as a passive element formed at the foot of the cusp by two convergent enamel fluxes. This view can be countered in the following manner. First of all, two calcification waves meet in the ontogenesis of the teeth at a definite point, since the growth and calcification gradients of each part of a tooth are genetically fixed. Secondly, the orientation of quite a few principal, if not all, furrows is set prior to the formation of the enamel cap, as is evidenced by our recent observations performed on tooth germs taken from human fetuses of varying ages.

The furrows clearly reflect the number, positions, and boundaries of all independent protruding sections of the molar surface, that is to say the embryonic growth and calcification centers. Another point is that the furrows as depressed sections of the surface are less subject to attrition than the protruding parts and, therefore, are more convenient as an object of study. The crown furrows present a clearly defined system of variations, easily lending themselves to classification, and a great number of morphological features that can be simply and objectively determined.

The pattern of furrowing of the masticatory surface of the teeth is closely associated with the laws of differentiation of the latter. We are of the opinion that the concrescence of tooth germs observed in some animals is not the primary mechanism of formation of the complex multicusp human teeth. Morphological analysis indicates that the entire diversity of human tooth shapes can be accounted for on the basis of differentiation as the main law of tooth morphogenesis with the end result of this differentiation depending on the period and rate of growth of the germ and its components.

According to the most widespread theory of complex tooth formation by way of differentiation (Cope-Osborn tritubercular theory), the various tooth shapes of the mammals originate from the primitive triconical tooth which had developed from the elementary reptilian toothcone. We believe that this kind of differentiation to form three derivative elements is a law of ontogenesis of the teeth of the mammals (at least primates) rather than a chance combination of structures evolved in phylogenesis. At a certain stage of growth of a tooth germ, differentiation sets in. At a sufficiently high rate of growth, each independent growth center tends to branch into three elements which, in turn, are liable to differentiate into three parts.

This assumption is borne out by numerous facts of tooth morphology. These will not be dealt with here specifically since they are outside the scope of this article, but we hope to write a special paper devoted to the morphological proof of the above hypothesis. Suffice it to say that even those formations which are regarded by morphologists as undifferentiated, on reaching particularly large dimensions acquire features of a ternary structure. Thus, we happened to observe a Carabelli's cusp divided into three rudimentary elements. Many other examples of this sort may be observed while studying unstable cusps, such as the hypocone, the sixth cusp, the hypoconulid. These tooth elements, if developed to a considerable degree, as a rule acquire a ternary structure.

The number of tooth elements and the degree of tooth differentiation depend on the length of the period and the rate of growth before the germ begins calcifying, whereas the shape of the tooth depends on the rate of growth to differentiation ratios of the individual parts of the crown-to-be.

In the process of growth, the odontomer (using Bolk's term, this word will designate any independent element having one calcification center) generally differentiates uninterruptedly, which is to say that each of the three elements is liable to be divided into three parts, etc., as a result of which there emerge odontomers of the second order, third order, etc. Differentiation is brought to an end only by the incipient calcification of the germ.

We have theorized at such length about the formation of complex teeth for the sole reason that this process has a direct bearing on the pattern of the crown. Our assumption, which we shall call for the time being "a hypothesis of continuous triple differentiation of the odontomer in ontogenesis," will be used to formulate some rules of odontoglyphics as to the number of furrows and their prediction. In the meantime, however, we shall come back to our main subject — the laws of variation of the molar crown furrows. This discussion is based on material accumulated over several years of work and brought into its final form within the 1967–1971 period.

THE LAWS AND PRINCIPLES OF ODONTOGLYPHICS

1. The furrows of the molar crown can be classified into two major categories: (a) intertubercular (intercusp) or FIRST-ORDER FURROWS deeply clefting the surface and completely isolating the main cusps; and (b) tubercular (cusp) furrows passing over the cusps and providing superficial, incomplete differentiation of the elements. The intertubercular furrows delineate primary odontomers — the main cusps — whereas the tubercular furrows outline the borders of subsequent differentiation, separating from one another the secondary odontomers and their parts (tertiary odontomers).

The intertubercular furrows will be designated by the Roman numerals — I, II, III, etc., while the tubercular furrows will be designated by the Arabic numerals accompanied by the symbol of the cusp on which the furrow is disposed — 2pa, 3pa, etc.

2. Since each odontomer cusp tends to split into three parts, each cusp can be expected to display TWO main furrows — SECOND-ORDER FURROWS (1 and 2), — and reality bears out this assumption. If only one furrow is in evidence, it means that the other is reduced. Examining a certain number of teeth, one will find the theoretically expected furrow. This was invariably the case in our experience.

Besides the two main furrows, there may be additional furrows on each cusp which will be indicative of an incipient further differentiation of the secondary odontomers (THIRD-ORDER FURROWS). The two main cusp furrows of the second order are designated by the numerals 1 and 2, as has been noted above, while the third-order furrows on the same cusp are designated by the numerals 3, 4, and 5. The second-order furrows are characteristically oriented with the central end toward the center of the crown or at any rate toward the median line, whereas the peripheral end is oriented toward the top of the cusp.

As often as not, the peripheral end of the furrow can be traced as far as almost the top of the cusp. At the stage of ontogenesis, the second-order furrow starts evolving immediately after the cusp top has been formed, which is the reason why the peripheral end of the furrow is "tied" to the top of its cusp (a of Figure 1).

3. The two main furrows of each cusp may run parallel or at an angle to each other, falling into different points of the intertubercular furrow system. The point at which the furrows fall into the intertubercular furrow system is designated by the symbol of that intertubercular furrow with which they come into contact (II, III, etc.).

The end of the furrow roughly oriented toward the center of the crown and coming into contact with the intertubercular furrow will be called central for the sake of convenience, while the opposite free end will be referred to as peripheral. Sometimes, two second-order furrows, 1 and 2, fall into one and the same point, thereby forming a single system. If in such a case the furrows have only one common point from which they diverge in two arms, such a system is called a DIRADIUS (b of Figure 1) and is designated by D.

If the furrows have a common segment of a certain length, that is to say a third arm invariably oriented toward the center of the crown (c of Figure 1), the system assumes the aspect of a TRIRADIUS designated T which is analogous to the triradii of the palm skin patterns. The common segment in this case may be referred to as a central radiant. It is always roughly oriented toward the crown center and determines the common point of junction of the whole system. The place where the diradii and triradii fall into the system is designated by the symbol of the furrow or the central pit (fc), for instance, TIII, Dfc.

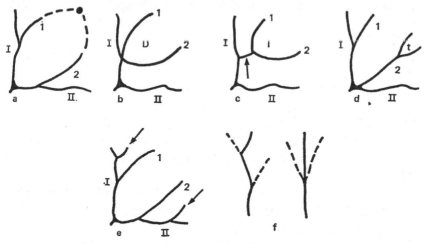

Figure 1. General laws of the tooth furrow pattern formation

4. The tubercular, and in some cases intertubercular, furrows may split into two arms at the peripheral end to form a triradius originating from ONE furrow, as distinct from the above-described *T*, and found on the end of the furrow, which is why it can be called TERMINAL triradius (t) (*d* of Figure 1). Naturally, terminal triradii are third-order elements.

5. There exists an additional kind of differentiation of the crown — "duplication" of the furrow (*e* of Figure 1) or of the entire pattern — sometimes occurring next to the principal furrow. In such a case, there emerges an additional third-order furrow (or several furrows) more or less exactly reproducing the main element.

As a rule, duplication occurs in the intercusp zones which in general are assigned territorially to specific cusps only for the purpose of investigation, being in fact neutral sections having a potential of activity and capable of originating additional interstitial cusps. An additional furrow emerging in such a zone to duplicate one of the second-order furrows on an adjacent cusp is the first step toward a new cusp, a kind of unrealized "claim" for an additional cusp at this point.

6. At a more or less extensive general level of crown reduction, furrows situated close to one another are likely to blend into one, so much so that for certain elements of the human teeth this likelihood

turns into a rule. In such cases, these furrows are seen as separate only on the most differentiated specimens. Sometimes, if furrows are close to one another, they sort of swap their functions: one of them, having acquired an extraordinary length and depth, "assumes" uncustomary functions to become, for instance, a false boundary between two odontomers. In such cases, the true boundary furrow can usually be distinguished by its position. As often as not, this kind of function switching accompanies the emergence and overdevelopment of duplicate furrows.

7. Some third-order furrows look like short fragments which not infrequently serve as crosspieces connecting other larger furrows. These third-order furrows, as distinct from most tubercular furrows, are likely to deviate in their orientation from the habitual axis — from the center to the periphery — to the extent of being perpendicular to this axis.

The position of the crosspiece furrows is generally not as stable as that of the other kinds of furrows. They often serve as connecting elements between first- and second-order furrows, but may also function as independent elements. They often take part in the forming of central cusps, additional odontomers arising outside of the intercusp zones, generally around the crown center. For all their relative instability, these furrows are definitely indicative of crown differentiation and obey their own laws for which in-depth morphological analyses are in order. The case in point is the 3med and 4med furrows.

8. The shape of a furrow depends by and large on the other furrows falling into it: the latter furrows sort of "pull back" the recipient furrow at the point of their junction, forming a bend, a protrusion in the direction of the falling-in furrow (f of Figure 1). This phenomenon is particularly clearly seen on the first-order furrows into which second- and third-order furrows fall on both sides and which accordingly change their orientation as many times. An interesting point is that if two furrows falling from two sides into a third one at a common point fail to reorient it, the "pulling forces" on the two sides seem to cancel out (f of Figure 1). The pattern of the crown resembles a system of taut strands which intertwine and "draw" each other out, forming an intricate lace structure.

THE PATTERN OF THE HUMAN MOLAR CROWN

By studying numerous series of wax prints of teeth (negative prints are more convenient), we have determined the complete pattern of the molar chewing surface shown in Figures 2 and 3, using our numerical system of furrow designation. Since the furrows are the natural borders of all independent elements of the crown, they are very convenient for the description of the microrelief. Any description of a tubercular furrow pattern can by and large be reduced to the symbols of their connecting points.

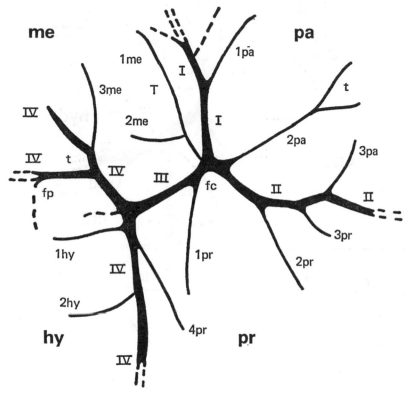

Figure 2. Pattern of furrows of the human upper molar

Such an approach enables even the most complex relief to be expressed by a relatively simple formula. This technique simplifies the descriptive procedure and is applicable to mass studies of the teeth of present-day human populations and fossil hominids. There generally exist only several easily predictable versions of the pattern of the second-order furrows on each cusp. These versions are given in Figure 4 (for the example of a lower molar entoconid). Using our set of symbols, they could be written as follows: 1(IV) 2(III), 1(IV) 2(fc), 1(IV)

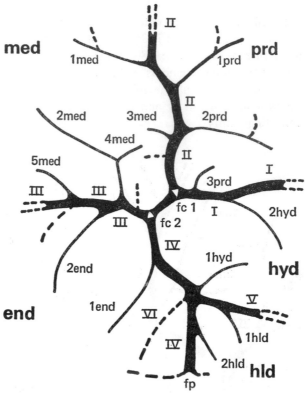

Figure 3. Pattern of furrows of the human lower molar

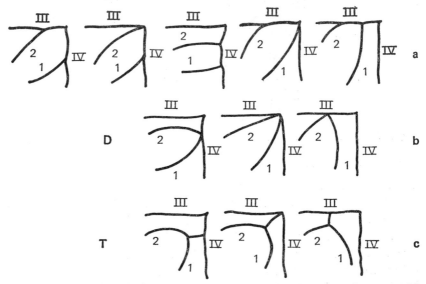

Figure 4. Possible positions of the furrows 1 and 2 (in this case on the entoconid)

2(IV), 1(fc) 2(III), and 1(III) 2(III) for the case of independent furrow orientations (*a* of Figure 4); or DIV, Dfc, and DIII for the case of diradii (*b* of Figure 4); or TIV, Tfc, TIII for the case of triradii (*c* of Figure 4).

Not infrequently, apart from the 1 and 2 furrows, there are also third-order furrows on each cusp. Of these most are duplicating furrows, such as 3pa, 3pr, 3prd or 5med. The greatest number of third-order furrows are found on the lower molar metaconid, which is the reason why the pattern formula of this cusp is the most complicated. Thus, the metaconid pattern of Figure 5 can be represented as follows: 1(II) 2(III) 3(II) 4(2) 5(III). Another prominent third-order element is a terminal triradius, particularly characteristic of the 2pa furrow. Thus, the paracone formula in the presence of the 2pa triradius may be: 1(I) 2t(II).

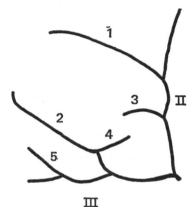

Figure 5. An example of a complicated pattern of the metaconid with the complete set of furrows

For some furrows, along with the points of contact with other furrows, additional characteristics preferably should be given as well. Thus, the 2med and 2prd furrows of the lower molars exhibit a clear system of variations of the following pattern (*a* of Figure 6): type "a," a straight furrow; type "b," a wavy furrow; and type "c," a furrow bend at an angle. The 2pa furrow may be interrupted because of its reduced peripheral end, especially on the second upper molar. Such a case is denoted by an additional symbol "int" (*b* of Figure 6). The kind of pattern given in *b* of Figure 6 may be represented by the formula 1(I) 2 int (II) fa, which, among other things, accounts here for the presence of "a false fovea anterior" (fa).

In some cases, such as on the second molar, the 2pa furrow may be totally lacking, which is represented by the symbol "O". Thus, for example, the pattern of *c* of Figure 6 is given by: 1(I) 2(O) fa. In certain cases, the second-order 1 and 2 furrows are likely to converge with their peripheral ends, rather than their central ends as in the case of a diradius. This phenomenon is most frequently observed on the lower molar hypoconid. For such a case we use an additional symbol "con" (*d* of Figure 6). Then the pattern of *d* of Figure 6 is given by: 1(IV) 2(I) con. Sometimes, certain furrows, mostly of the third order, fall with one end into one furrow and with the other end into another furrow. Then two junctions are to be noted, as for instance, in *e* of Figure 6: 1(I) 2(II) 3(2-II), where the 3pa furrow has two junctions. Two junctions are likewise noted in anomalous triradii having two central radiants (mostly on the metaconid and entoconid), as in *f* of Figure 6: T (II + III). Incidentally, there occurs an opposite version of an anomalous triradius with a reduced central radiant: TO (or "semicircle") in *g* of Figure 6.

Some patterns occur in man more frequently than others, which partly depends on the cusp and the tooth (first and second molars). Thus, triradii occur most often on the metacone and entoconid. The

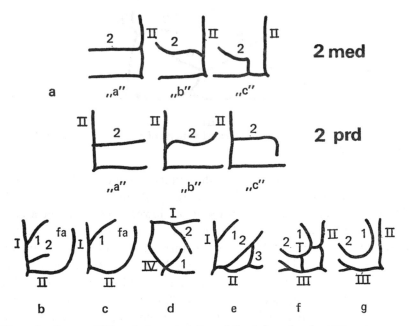

Figure 6. Some additional characteristics of the tubercular furrows
(a) forms of the furrows 2med and 2prd
(b) type "int," (c) type "(O)fa," (d) type "con," (e) double junction of the 3pa, (f, g) irregular triradii in the metaconid

1me furrow on the first molar tends to fall more frequently into the central pit, while on the second molar into the furrow I. The so-called "false fovea anterior" (fa) occurs predominantly on the second molar and extremely rarely on the first one.

In order to give a more detailed and graphic idea about the orientations of the second-order furrows in man, we have prepared charts of rough frequencies of the various versions of orientation of the 1 and 2 furrows, based on the material for the present-day Caucasoid populations (see Figure 7 for the upper molars and Figure 8 for the lower molars). The different hatchings show the frequencies of different second-order furrows (left-hand column) falling into first-order furrows or into the central pit, fc. The last two graphs give an approximate frequency of the diradii and triradii of the 1 and 2 furrows. Figure 9 shows the frequency of certain additional characteristics of the second- and third-order furrows in the present-day Caucasoid groups.

Human populations differ by a considerable margin in terms of the frequencies of different furrow arrangements. Thus, the 2(II) version on the first molar metaconid (i.e. the 2 med furrow falling into the II furrow) is more frequently encountered in the populations of the Europoid race, rather than in Mongoloid groups.

Odontoglyphics seems to be a very promising technique for investigations in anthropogenesis, since standardized microrelief descriptions allow us to objectively compare the structure of the tooth series of the fossil and modern man. The fossil man's molar patterns have specific features distinguishing them from the tooth patterns of modern man, though the general layout of the pattern, described above and shown in Figures 2 and 3, remained unchanged through the various stages of evolution of the hominids.

All fossil hominids differ from modern man by a greater frequency of the third-order elements, particularly terminal triradii, and also by a rare incidence of the *T* triradii formed by the 1 and 2 furrows. And there are other interesting differences inherent in each stage of evolution. It is not impossible either, that odontoglyphics might prove to be useful for solving problems of hominid systematics.

The scholars of our country have already amassed a considerable body of material on the distribution of varying crown patterns by ethnic groups. But as we are concerned here with the general laws of arrangement of the molar crown patterns, as well as with classification and nomenclature of the furrows, we have skipped any mention of the distribution of crown patterns by ethnic groups.

Neither was it possible to include here a well-developed section on premolars which, incidentally, exhibit the same general picture of furrow patterns as the molars, although in a reduced and somewhat distorted form. That is why it is only by means of detailed analysis that each premolar furrow can be identified with its counterpart on the molar and complete analogy of the tooth patterns of these two neighboring classes can be established (certainly, taking into account the fact that some crown elements present on the molars are lacking on the premolars).

FURROWS	I	II	III	fc	D	T
M1						
1pr						
2pr						
1pa						
2pa						
1me						
2me						
M2						
1pr						
2pr						
1pa						
2pa						
1me						
2me						

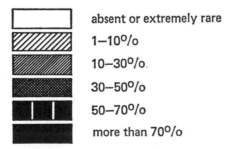

absent or extremely rare
1–10%
10–30%
30–50%
50–70%
more than 70%

Figure 7. Main pattern of the cusps in the human upper molars (approximate frequencies of different types of connection of the furrows 1 and 2 with the intertubercular furrows, diradii and triradii in the modern Caucasoid populations)

Odontoglyphics has been tentatively used for the diagnosis of twins and has given very interesting results. We are tempted to believe that in this field, too, odontoglyphics will prove a valuable complementary technique which will be instrumental in refining the methods of analysis of twins.

We have carried out preliminary experiments in using special measuring points based on the furrow junctions. This method of

FURROWS	I	II	III	IV–V	fc	D	T
M1							
1 prd							
2 prd							
1 med							
2 med							
1 end							
2 end							
1 hyd							
2 hyd							
M2							
1prd							
2prd							
1med							
2med							
1end							
2end							
1hyd							
2hyd							

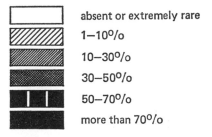

absent or extremely rare
1–10%
10–30%
30–50%
50–70%
more than 70%

Figure 8. Main pattern of the cusps in the human lower molars (approximate frequencies of different types of connection of the furrows 1 and 2 with the intertubercular furrows, diradii and triradii in the modern Caucasoid populations)

measurement provides an objective prerequisite for developing an even more precise technique of crown pattern investigation.

In conclusion, our task here was to expound the substance of the principle of odontoglyphics, and to point to the prospects of its application in various branches of anthropology. The results of investigations using the principle are being published separately.

CHARACTERS	M1	M2
TRIRADIUS OF THE 2pa FURROW	30–50%	1–10%
REDUCED 2pa (TYPE "INT")	absent or extremely rare	30–50%
ABSENCE OF THE 2pa (TYPE "Ofa")	absent or extremely rare	10–30%
PRESENCE OF THE "FALSE fa"	absent or extremely rare	more than 70%
PRESENCE OF THE 3pa	10–30%	30–50%
PRESENCE OF THE 3pr	50–70%	50–70%
PRESENCE OF THE 4pr	30–50%	more than 70%
PRESENCE OF THE 3me	more than 70%	more than 70%
TYPE "a" OF THE 2med	10–30%	50–70%
TYPE "b" OF THE 2med	30–50%	more than 70%
TYPE "c" OF THE 2 med	50–70%	1–10%
PRESENCE OF THE 3med	10–30%	30–50%
PRESENCE OF THE 4med	30–50%	1–10%
PRESENCE OF THE 5med	more than 70%	30–50%
TYPE "c" OF THE 2prd	1–10%	1–10%
PRESENCE OF THE 3prd	10–30%	10–30%
TYPE "con" OF THE hyd FURROWS	10–30%	1–10%

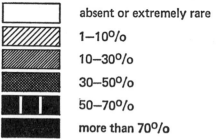

absent or extremely rare
1–10%
10–30%
30–50%
50–70%
more than 70%

Figure 9.   Some additional characteristics of the human molar pattern (approximate frequencies in Caucasoid populations)

An Anthropological Approach to the Study of Dental Pathology

RICHARD T. KORITZER

INTRODUCTION

The term "dental paleopathology" could well be revised so as to indicate coextension with the anthropological field. A more general statement would include connotation of prehistoric, ethnologic, and historic eras. We may then avoid the limitations imposed by using the prefix "paleo-." The diachronic approach required for comparative dental pathology studies would then be free of restriction. Comparative problems also extend to area relations. The notation of geographic extension is not a nomenclature problem as it is generally understood because the discipline title includes no terminologic limitation. Let us remove the terminologic limitation on chronology as well. I would suggest the logical metaphor "dental anthropopathology" to allow more nearly universal description of what people practicing this discipline may do (see Figure 1).

The comparative method can be very effective in developing and testing hypotheses about dental-cultural pathology effects. Such studies fall within the discipline entitled dental anthropopathology. The most common effect recorded by investigators is probably dietary influence on dental pathology incidence resulting from shifting subsistence bases. The influence of economic and political structures as indirect controlling factors of both subsistence base and distribution network seems obvious at this point. These statements nevertheless are mere platitudes without field studies producing hard data suitable for analysis. Before this discipline's work can proceed, a body of theory must be developed and tested. This article is an effort in that direction. Perhaps others may be stimulated to more critical work in this field.

For Plates, see p. xlv, between pp. 330–331.

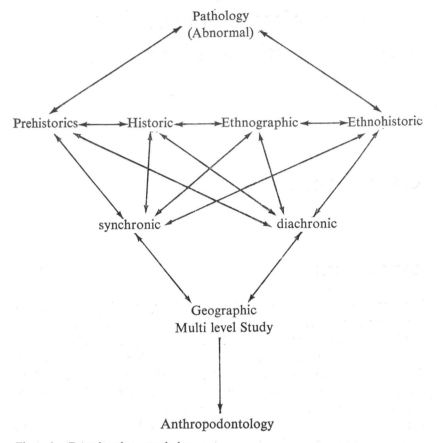

Figure 1.   Dental anthropopathology

There are methodological problems that underlie the present study. The Illinois sample is limited by the whims of the collector who is reputed to have selected for more complete skeletal material. Young individuals are missing. However, no selection on the basis of dental pathology as scored in my measurement system was made. The excavators, not being dentists, had other overriding interests. The same is true of selection for dental phenomena among the Accokeek and Potomac Creek populations. The Angolan sample was randomly selected and included all individuals present in a village at the time of measurement.

The limitations on ossuary material are well known and have been carefully examined by Ubelaker (1973). That any society's burial customs allow direct equation to a natural population is unlikely. The consistency of results within even the limited sample presented here, however, indicates systematic variability allowing comparability.

Another fundamental problem of interest in this article is expressed nicely by Janzen (1973) where he comments on *Amazonian cosmos* by Gerardo Reichel-Dolmatoff:

Cultural anthropologists are finally coming around to confirming what eco-logists have long felt must be true but have not had the data to demonstrate: that where man lives dependent only on the resources within his tribe's home range, his destiny is set by the carrying capacity of that home range, just as it is for other animals. Most recent cultural anthropology either brings its de-scriptive guns to bear on the way the tribe harvests its resources or describes the social glue that holds that resource-harvest machine together. Few studies deal with the co-evolution of the tribe's social institutions and the properties of the resources in the home range.

The relation of home-range carrying capacity and coevolution of dental anthropopathology is a tempting hypothesis. The concept of a social glue holding the resource-harvest machine together suggests dynamic functional interdependencies affecting dental pathology change. A brief description of the populations included in this study is necessary.

CULTURAL DATA

Among the Angolan Herero I examined, millet was the primary cultigen (Urquhart 1963; Herrick et al. 1967). It represented the most important food source for the Zimba subgroup. Milk products are the staple food items among the Himba, who are mainly dependent on herding. Cattle represent their wealth and status, and, while every animal eventually winds up in the pot, slaughtering for food alone is not usual. Goats are also commonly kept. In bad times millet and corn are traded for. I have observed very small amounts of corn added to millet being pounded in wooden mortars with wood pestles. The hard corn kernels were said to aid the milling process. Beer is made from millet and is in constant demand.

Hunting of small antelope is a common side occupation but the spears used are inefficient. The Himba will starve rather than kill their breeding livestock. Gathering of fruit is an occasional occupation based on availability. I have observed use of the pithy portion of baobab tree fruit. Harvesting of wild plant resources such as cooking greens, caper, and *Amaranthus spinosa* occurs. The last may be seeded in old corrals if the spontaneous crop is small. Beeswax and honey are products collected naturally and the use of hives is promoted. Fishing with traps is commonly seen especially at the beginning of the dry season when fish are marooned in pools. A definite division of labor by sex is documented among herders and agriculturists.

The subsistence base of the Angolan natives studied resembles the ethnohistoric Potomac River Valley Indians' subsistence records. Similarities to Illinois Indians' subsistence as intensive hunter-gatherers also emerge. On the other hand, intertribal raiding and active conflict ended by 1920 in this area, and a more consistent resource-harvest machine was possible. However, at the present time, intense drought is an unsettling influence combined with political policies related to land fencing. Unsettling effects of European trading for wine and sundry commodities affect the subsistence base. The extremely low rate of dental disease among this population requires explanation. At this time I wish to display the power of cross-cultural study related to dental anthropopathology as a method of developing testable generalizations.

The provenience of the early Late Woodland, Jersey County, Illinois population in this study is around 600 A.D., established by directly associated pottery. Excavation was by P. H. Titterington. The archaeology of this area has been extensively investigated and is well represented in the literature. I will refer here only to several recent publications establishing support for a dental-cultural hypothesis. I do not wish to survey the literature exhaustively.

Caldwell (1971:361–382) suggests the development in eastern North America of a forest efficiency which slowed further economic innovation, especially adoption of agriculture. Sufficient stimulus for stylistic elaborations and burial complexes existed. In some nuclear civilizations direct progress to sociocultural integration is thought to have occurred. However, in this case a succession of cultural climaxes is postulated, especially as noted in burial practices.

Caldwell speculated that some degree of settled life usually would be a precondition for the acceptance of innovations pertaining to cultivation. Food production, however, among Eastern Woodland Indians, seems never to have provided a complete basis for subsistence. It is suggested that women were more likely the cultivators. As food gatherers their interest in plants would be greater and domestic duties would keep them closer to home. The men were warrior-hunters, or rarely "specialists" of other kinds.

Mobility of people based on hunting opportunities was said by Kroeber to reflect intertribal warfare limiting agricultural adaptation. This further suggests cyclical reversion to a hunting-gathering complex through attritional pressures. Still, Caldwell includes this as speculation without hard archaeological proof, but nonetheless tempting.

Struever (1971:383–390) has used flotation techniques to accumulate evidence of the Lower Illinois Indian diet. His hypothesis suggests a separate center of plant domestication developing in this area. In early Late Woodland this was probably still at the intensive gathering state.

Fowler (1971:391–403) also gives evidence of intensive gathering and shows lack of evidence for maize but possible cultivation of cucurbits in this general Mississippi area. Local traditions are considered to have been basic with only superimposed acquired burial complexes. Fowler (1971: 398) explicitly suggests a cultural decline in terms of sociocultural integration after Hopewell and about one hundred years, more or less, before the period of the Illinois population described here. A period of distinct regional cultures is suggested. Fowler fails to establish evidence of corn cultivation in this area although he suggests it. Griffin (personal communication) has stated that corn was not a significant cultigen at this period in this area. Fowler does not postulate full-scale agriculture until 800 A.D., two hundred years after the dating of this population.

It seems likely when combining Caldwell, Struever, Fowler and others' studies that a combination of forest efficiency and political pressure in terms of warfare operated to control sociocultural patterns in early Late Woodland Illinois.

Let us proceed to a description of the Potomac River Valley situation as gleaned from ethnohistoric sources. North of this area Susquehannocks were found at the contact period (Guss 1883). The area from the Susquehanna River at the head of Chesapeake Bay to below Baltimore was sparsely settled, as Captain John Smith noted (Tyler 1907). Possibly Susquehannock raiding of Indian trade parties contributed to this. The same phenomena existed between Herero areas of Angola prior to 1900. The forest at the Potomac River Valley contact period consisted of great deciduous trees, allowing little sunlight for undergrowth, a poor situation for deer browsing (McGinnes and Reeves 1957).

The Powhatan confederacy seems to have exerted pressure to the north on the Potomac River Valley Indians. They were all, however, Algonquins. Pressure from the Eastern Sioux (Holland 1966) and Iroquois from the west occurred as autumn raids across the Shenandoahs into the coastal plain. Deer-hunting parties from the coastal plain ventured into mountain valley glades created by burning over.

Because at present there are no flotation studies of archaeological vegetal and animal remains from Potomac River Valley sites, such as are available in Illinois (Struever 1971), it is necessary to rely on historical information for resource-harvest information. The ossuary material used in this study dates from about the time of contact, and a reasonable correlation exists. The provenience is established by the artifactual remains (Stephenson, Ferguson, and Ferguson 1963).

Historic knowledge about the Potomac River Valley is limited, and secondary accounts derived from common sources are redundant. Speculation is engaged in by many authors. These addenda may be fabrications based on ethnographic data from other areas or an attempt to impute from the archaeologic to the historic. The gaps most often are filled with untestable rationalizations. The Stephenson, Ferguson, and Ferguson account (1963) of the Accokeek site Piscataways offers a good thumbnail sketch of data available in other secondary reports as well as the primary ones. The Piscataways are reputed to have lived on this site in Maryland for at least 250 years. Four ossuaries were found on the village site numbering altogether a little over 1,300 individuals.

The interaction area for the Piscataways is limited to the southern portion of Prince George County and all of Charles County in Maryland at about 1608.

The Piscataway ossuaries may possibly contain individuals from the entire area of Charles County and southern Prince George County. The ossuaries might be representative of Piscataways in general rather than the Accokeek site specifically (Feest, personal communication). There is one ethnographic source available to us about Hurons in Canada, also an Algonquin group. It was their custom to bury their dead secondarily in ossuaries every four or five years. This burial occasion was held in one of a group of villages, most often a different one each time. The same might be true of the Potomac Indians of Virginia. There is no way with present data to ascertain the true boundaries of Piscataways or Potomacs for 250 years.

It seems reasonable to accept the Potomac river below Washington, D.C. as a geographical barrier. At the time of contact, it is documented as a political barrier among the Indians. Stephenson, Ferguson, and Ferguson (1963) and others seem clear about heavy pressure on the Piscataways from Susquehannocks and Seneca. The villages of the Potomac did not have such pressure from the south. One must conclude that there was a differential pressure on Potomacs and Piscataways. Because they were gathered together in stockaded villages subject to raids, the practice of horticulture may have been often disrupted. This factor, coupled with the availability of wild animals and fish, probably is sufficient cause to postulate different resource harvests by these two groups.

From several sources I have gathered sample lists of the animal and vegetal elements available for resource harvest (Tyler 1907; Semmes 1937; Manakee 1959). Some slight insight into food gathering and preparation

Table 1. Food

Game birds	Animals
Turkey	Deer
Partridge	Dog
Pigeons	Squirrel
Ducks (September – March)	Raccoon
Geese	Beaver
Eggs	Opossum
Swans	Bear
Pheasants	Deer fat — suet
	Buffalo (Kerby 1967)
	Elk
	Hare
	Woodchuck
Vegetables, domestic	*Seafood*
Corn (maize)	Crabs
Pumpkin	Shrimp
Beans	Eels
Peas	Fish
Squash	Oysters
Sunflowers	Clams
	Sturgeon
Wild fruits	*Wild nuts*
Cherries	Acorns
Crab apple	Chestnuts
Grapes	Chinquapins
Persimmons	Hickory nuts
Plums	Walnuts
Huckleberries	
Mulberries	
Strawberries	

technology is also obtained from the assembled lists (see Table 1). Some game birds were indigenous to the Potomac area such as turkey, partridge, and pheasant while others were seasonal migrators. Even today flocks of hundreds of migratory birds can be seen as late as March on the Chesapeake. Early descriptions of large quantities of fowl may be thought by some to be exaggerated, but it is not hard to believe even on contemporary evidence that the small triangular points so common in the Late Woodland period might have been used to shoot birds. Accuracy with bows is described up to forty feet (Manakee 1959).

In various references all of the large and small animals listed turn up. The evidence for elk and buffalo seems highly questionable (Kerby 1967) but the remainder of animals included here are common enough and from many early accounts seem to have been plentiful (Sams 1916).

Seafood was abundant in the Chesapeake area, and accounts refer to fish spawning in the Potomac, very large sturgeon particularly. Oyster heaps such as the one found at Loyola Retreat speak for themselves. Ethnohistoric accounts of large stews containing fish as a major ingredient made by Maryland Indians are reported (Manakee 1959).

The list of wild fruits and berries is probably incomplete. It is common today to find large quantities of these as well as nuts, especially acorns and chestnuts. Preparation of acorns as a major dietary component is not documented ethnohistorically or archaeologically as in Illinois around 600 A.D.

The cultigen list is headed by maize. Most items are common enough

Table 2.   Predators, clothing, and division of labor

Women	Men
Butchers	Hunters
Cooks	Warriors
Tillers of the soil	
Lodge builders (hunting)	
Mat weavers	

Medicaments	*Predators*
Roots	Wolves
Nuts	Eagle
Berries	Hawk
Bark	Goshawk
Leaves	Vulture
	Falcon
	Lanner
	Sparrowhawk
	Marlin
	Heron
	Bittern

Clothing

Deerskin with hair — winter
Deerskin without hair — summer
Fur cloaks   beaver
                    otter
                    mink
Moccasins — skins
Moccasins — woven strips of tree bark
Skin purses
Bone awls — animal sinew thread
Necklaces — drilled sea shells strung on sinew
Decoration — snake rattles, eagle claws, animal teeth, bird wings, turkey feathers, copper beads, copper plate

Clay or grease to protect from insects	Tattoos with dyes
Clay paints to decorate	
Root and seed coloring added	Tobacco pipes
Copper and iron ores used for paints	

but the real question is what diet percentage is attributable to cultigens. The implication of corn in caries susceptibility is very seriously considered by some investigators. A look at farming method (nonplow) and food storage and preparation indicates a laborious process and the necessity for adjustment to seasonal harvest availability. Fishing and hunting technology seem highly developed. The Potomacs and Piscataways probably relied on horticulture for no more than 20 percent of total dietary needs in good times (Feest, personal communication).

The labor division by sex (see Table 2) indicates that males devoted significant time to hunting and indicates that meat protein was a major dietary staple. The possession of a pharmacopoeia along with practical and decorative clothing arts as well as exchange media indicates a well-developed resource-harvest adaptation with variety and surplus. The predators that are listed were in sufficient abundance to be noted by early chronicles and confirm the plenitude of game animals, birds, and fish.

Such a well-adapted economy would be much more sensitive to the pressure of Seneca and Susquehannock raiding than a society less adapted. They possessed something worth raiding for. It seems most likely that the Piscataways absorbed the brunt of attacks while the Potomacs were relatively better off. The Potomacs being south of the river benefited from its geographic protection. The Piscataways had their backs to the river, and raiding between them and the Potomacs on an intermittent basis was sufficient to prevent refuge to the south. I believe that Potomacs and Piscataways had equal access to similar resource harvests. Both had the resource-harvest machine (technology) to use their ecological niches effectively. The one major difference was greater raiding pressure on the Piscataways.

DENTAL DATA

Variations in dental anthropopathology are considered in this study. The measurement method is appended. Total population, age, and sex breakdown are presented in Tables 3 and 4.

Problems arise when unmatched maxillae and mandibles and fragments of these are used. Ossuary materials such as the Potomac Creek and Accokeek samples often consist of skeletons whose burials have been delayed for some time. A specimen ultimately may be represented by only half a jaw or less. These skeletal samples, nevertheless, when interpreted, represent information sources about dental-cultural population conditions.

Table 3.   Breakdown by population and age

	N	Mean age	Standard deviation	Mean age	Standard deviation	Mean age	Standard deviation
			Accokeek				
Whole population	151	25.7	4.79	27.2	5.31	24.1	3.49
Whole skulls with mandible	41	25.2	4.53	26.2	5.24	23.8	2.51
Maxillae	86	25.6	4.67	27.2	4.67	23.9	3.57
Mandible	24	27.0	5.38	30.3	—	24.6	3.35
			Potomac Creek				
Whole population	123	29.4	7.06	30.3	7.17	28.5	7.09
Whole skulls with mandible	27	30.8	9.63	32.8	9.16	29.5	9.72
Maxillae	56	28.0	7.73	28.1	9.11	27.1	—
Mandible	44	28.7	5.48	28.4	6.32	28.4	5.32
			Illinois				
Whole population	101	29.6	7.84	31.7	7.81	26.1	6.23
			Himba				
Whole population	31	26.39	17.88	24.4	223.11	27.3	392.50
			Zimba				
Whole population	34	31.53	16.60	34.7	413.55	30.2	221.96

Table 4.   Breakdown by sex

	Sex ratio male/female	Age range	Age twenty-five or less	Age twenty-six and up
Accokeek				
Whole population	80/71	14–42	80	71
Whole skulls with mandible	25/16			
Maxillae	45/41			
Mandible	10/14			
Potomac Creek				
Whole population	57/66	17–60	45	78
Whole skulls with mandible	11/16			
Maxillae	25/31			
Mandible	24/20			
Illinois	62/39	14–50	42	59
Himba	10/21	4–70	19	12
Zimba	10/24	5–70	15	19

Fragmentary samples are especially difficults. for age and sex estimate Because the study involves dental pathology, only eruptive sequence and morphology may be used for age and sex estimates. Facial and cranial suture closures are of limited accuracy but must be used as part of a very limited record. Qualitative estimates of bone gracility, surface texture, and muscle attachment areas are made. There is also a qualitative sense developed by the investigator, who becomes closely familiar with a sample, and this allows sequential age and sex gradation that may be partly intuitive but is effective in separating young and old, often in less than ten-year increments. Discarding fragmentary material is unjustifiable but when it is used the limitations ought to be carefully stated.

There was no significant difference between the mean ages of the whole skulls with mandible, maxillae, and total population in the sample Accokeek and in the sample Potomac Creek population (P<.01). Mandibles alone in both sample populations were significantly different (P>.01) from the other anatomical categories. This test was based on the underlying assumption that the individuals from the two samples had approximately equal means and standard deviations.

The age range and distribution for the five sample populations may be found in Table 4. Only the Herero samples contain very young or old individuals and because of the small number in these pilot groups the standard deviations of the mean ages are astronomical. It has been suggested that the two populations are sufficiently close genetically (Dr. Gordon Gibson, personal communication) to be combined. From the viewpoint of anthropopathology I have elected to separate them at this time as I look for fine-grain differences suggestive of different subsistence bases.

The age estimates of the Herero individuals are dependable for younger participants. Later evaluation by Gibson, using a historical chronology, resulted in increasing the ages of the older participants. For example one fifty-year-old individual was redetermined at age sixty. The Illinois sample age-determinations are probably most reliable because in many cases postcranial skeletons were available. The dental pathology patterns of the samples presented here are included in Table 5.

Attrition measured in two different ways for the five populations' upper and lower arch dentitions allows comparison of twenty discrete determinations for this trait. The trends suggest Accokeek and Potomac Creek samples are closely related and Himba and Zimba are closely related. The Illinois sample population attrition is highest and the Herero groups lowest. Furthermore, all twenty discrete determinations are consistent with the suggested trend.

Periodontal disease measured qualitatively among the five sample populations' upper and lower dental arches yielded ten discrete values. Accokeek and Potomac Creek determinations are very close to each other as are Himba and Zimba. Illinois is close to the Potomac River Valley groups but still lower than either. All three groups, however, are clearly higher than the Herero groups.

Clinical crown height is greater among Potomac Valley Indians than among Illinois Indians. This is consistent with higher periodontal disease

Table 5.   Dental pathology patterns of samples

	Accokeek	Means Potomac Creek	Illinois Jersey County	Himba	Zimba
Age	25.748	29.423	30.059	26.387	31.529
Upper arch					
Leigh attrition	2.262	2.192	2.654	1.323	1.500
Brothwell attrition	322.248	335.069	449.760	221.774	230.882
Qualitative periodontal measurement	2.847	2.760	2.587	1.419	1.824
Clinical crown height	8.749	8.502	7.874	(2.164)*	(2.161)*
Caries degree	2.221	1.615	1.885	.161	.265
Number of carious teeth	2.073	1.205	1.865	.161	.676
Antemortem tooth loss	.939	.557	1.077	.226	.235
Postmortem tooth loss	7.638	9.910	1.356	—**	—**
Lower arch					
Leigh attrition	2.085	2.225	2.490	1.419	1.618
Brothwell attrition	315.104	350.758	425.721	231.452	258.824
Qualitative periodontal measurement	3.053	3.071	2.558	1.548	1.794
Clinical crown height	8.065	7.715	7.271	(2.499)	(1.977)
Caries degree	2.140	1.972	1.779	.258	.324
Number of carious teeth	2.228	1.746	1.846	.355	.824
Antemortem tooth loss	2.948	1.338	.740	.258	.265
Postmortem tooth loss	6.948	7.817	.981	—	—

*   In living populations depth of periodontal pocket is measured with a calibrated probe. The percent error where pocket depth is one or two millimeters may be 50 percent or more. When pocket depths are much greater, such as five to ten millimeters, the percent error will decline rapidly.

**Obviously postmortem loss is not a confusing factor in live populations.

and lower attrition among Potomac Valley Indians. If an arbitrary 6.5 millimeter addition for average crown height is made to the periodontal pocket depth of Hereros a clinical crown height approximation results. These values are consistent with low attrition and periodontal disease in this sample population. The error in periodontal pocket depth in the Herero sample may be as high as 50 percent. This occurs because the pockets are very shallow. The difference of one or two millimeters measurement error in a pocket of average two millimeters depth is great. The same absolute amount of error in a population with average pocket depth of four millimeters would be one-half the magnitude and at six millimeters only one-third. This was one of the major reasons for using clinical crown height measurement of skeletal material rather than amount of exposed root surface.

By combining caries degree and number of carious teeth, we again acquire a battery of twenty discrete measurements to define caries trends in our five samples. Clearly, the Himba are phenomenally low and consistently so. Zimba are not far behind and are closer to Himba than to the other samples. The Potomac Creek sample is consistently lower than Accokeek with the difference more pronounced on the upper arch. The Illinois Indians seem to fall in between the two Potomac Valley samples, a situation that I cannot explain at this time. The major observations are the similarity of Hereros and the difference among Potomac Valley Indians.

Antemortem tooth loss is exceptionally low for Hereros and at least half of the missing teeth were third molars located in areas of stasis, i.e. areas least subject to physiologic cleansing by materials ingested or normal salivary flow. Lower arch tooth loss seems higher among Potomac Valley Indians. Interarch difference in the other three samples is not large enough to merit comment.

Postmortem tooth loss is high in the Potomac Valley samples because of the fragmentary ossuary material already discussed.

The Himba correlation-coefficient matrix shows a relation of all variables to age ($p < .01$) except caries upper arch ($p < .05$) and the lower-arch caries is uncorrelated. Zimba correlation-coefficient matrix age correlates with all variables ($p < .01$) except number of carious teeth upper arch ($p < .05$). Lower-arch caries indicators are uncorrelated. There is thus reasonable agreement between the two Herero samples for these features.

In the Potomac Creek sample caries is uncorrelated with age and it is also in the Accokeek sample population. This test has not yet been run for Illinois Indians. The trend that has been established, however, is interesting and deserves further study.

Attrition measured by two methods and periodontal disease are correlated ($p < .01$) in all five sample populations except for Himba lower arch periodontal disease significant at ($p < .05$) level. This cross-cultural relation strongly supports an accepted norm in dentistry.

An interesting and tempting situation occurs in that lower arch. Herero caries indicators are uncorrelated with any other variables except each other. A relation between arches does not exist. The Herero eigenvalues also confirm this situation. The lower-arch caries variables appear as the sole significant values in the third eigenvector and appear in no other significant vectors. Assuming that host dentition resistance is uniform in both dental arches, variation in attacking factors seems the most probable explanation. The same situation holds for Potomac River Valley Indians in the correlation-coefficient matrix. The caries eigenvalues in upper and lower arch, however, do occur in the same vectors. Among Illinois Indians caries indicators interarch are correlated ($p < .01$).

CONCLUSION

Many more dental data exist as well as cultural data. This limited presentation is meant only to illustrate a method and model. The concept of dental anthropopathology can be supported, but the relation between cross-cultural and dental observations leaves a gap that must be filled at the microstructural level to prove a statistically acceptable correlation.

A vast physicochemical potpourri is represented by total environment. The ecological niche establishes a set of limitations on environmental utilization. The host dentition susceptibility versus the nature of attacking factors represents a dynamic equilibrium. Some environmental microstructural elements are mandatory components; others may be volitional components. Cultural control of the ultimate mix of attacking versus host factors may exist since change affects the delicate balances between such a multitude of forces.

However, the identity of these changes from the cultural point of view is microevolutionary and the identification of fine-grain differences ought to occur at the microlevel of the host dentition. Statistical limitations on evaluation of gross morphological changes can be overcome by examining differences in microstructure that may be measurable to a higher order of accuracy.

Populations that are culturally closer seem to have less variability in dental pathology. This pattern becomes distinct for more culturally distinct groups and appears to characterize populations. Geographic and chronologic differences are not sufficient to explain the total pattern for dental disease. These conditions fit well the concept that the etiology of dental disease and of caries in particular is multifactorial. Variation of the cultural etiologic factors may alter a population's dental pathology pattern.

APPENDIX

Dental attrition is measured according to a modified Leigh method (Leigh 1925) on a one-to-four scale: (1) enamel only, (2) enamel and dentine light, (3) enamel and dentine heavy, and (4) pulp exposure.

A defect of this system is the fourth category because pulp exposure is dependent on the rate of attrition versus deposition of secondary dentine. Therefore, the actual amount of tooth reduction when pulp exposure occurs may vary significantly and produce inconsistencies.

Attrition is also recorded according to the Brothwell method (Brothwell 1965) of measurement which is applied to molars only. This fails to account for unequal anterior-posterior tooth wear.

We measure periodontal disease qualitatively on a one-to-four scale (Plate 1) based on the amount of exposed root surface. The first category is alveolar crest bone loss not exceeding two millimeters from the cemento-enamel junction. The fourth category is bone loss causing exposure of any molar root furcation or more than one-half of a single root surface. The second and third categories are equally graded between these extremes. There is no zero category because I believe that a totally nonpathologic periodontium is unlikely. In the absence of dental treatment, exposure of a root furcation suggests a negative prognosis for the retention of the tooth.

Clinical crown height (the portion of tooth erupted beyond the alveolar crest) is measured for the buccal and lingual surfaces of all molar teeth and averaged for each dental arch. This was originally thought to be a good quantitative measure of periodontal disease with component of attrition that had resulted in supereruption of the teeth. However, we now feel this measurement is much more complex and will require further in-depth study as a volume of statistical information accumulates.

I measure caries on a one-to-four scale where the first category is a small pit or fissure lesion (Plate 2). The second category is represented by a moderate-sized pit or fissure or a smooth surface lesion up to moderate size. Category three includes any lesion that endangers the pulp and the fourth category is exposure of the dental pulp. Missing teeth are scored in life and from the specimen.

Where judgment is required, individuals are graded for the worst pathology present. If multiple lesions of varying degrees are present the most advanced pathology is graded. Because of this factor, the data presented represent the "maximum" pathologic state of the population studied.

REFERENCES

BROTHWELL, DON R.
  1965   *Digging up bones.* London: British Museum (Natural History).
CALDWELL, JOSEPH R.
  1971   "Eastern North America," in *Prehistoric agriculture.* Edited by Stuart Struever. New York: The Natural History Press.
DENNISTON, EDITH B.
  1948   Food, clothing and shelter of prehistoric Indians of the United States. *Quarterly Bulletin, Archeological Society of Virginia* 3(1).
DUNBAR, GARY S.
  1964   Some notes on bison in early Virginia. *Quarterly Bulletin, Archeological Society of Virginia* 18(4), Part one.

298 RICHARD T. KORITZER

FOWLER, MELVIN L.
　1971　"Agriculture and village settlement in the North American east: the central Mississippi Valley area, a case history," in *Prehistoric agriculture*. Edited by Stuart Struever. New York: The Natural History Press.

GILLIAM, CHARLES EDGAR
　1957　Powhatan religions: title to tribal lands. *Quarterly Bulletin, Archeological Society of Virginia* 12(1).

GLOVER, THOMAS
　1904　"An account of Virginia, its situation, temperature, productions, inhabitants and their manner of planting and ordering tobacco." Reprinted from the Philosophical Transactions of the Royal Society, June 20, 1676.

GUSS, ABRAHAM L.
　1883　*Early Indian history on the Susquehanna*. Harrisburg: Lane S. Hart.

HAMOR THE YONGER, RAPHE
　1615　*A true discourse of the present estate of Virginia*. London: John Beale. Reprinted 1860, Albany: J. Munsell.

HERRICK, ALLISON BUTLER, *et al.*
　1967　*Area handbook for Angola*. Washington, D.C.: U. S. Government Printing Office.

HOBBS, HORACE P., JR.
　1964　Rock dams in the upper Potomac. *Quarterly Bulletin, Archeological Society of Virginia* 18(3).

HOLLAND, C. G.
　1966　Archeology and ethnohistory: an illustration. *Quarterly Bulletin, Archeological Society of Virginia* 21(1).

JANZEN, DANIEL N.
　1973　Social systems, sex, and survival. *Natural History* 82(2).

KERBY, MAUDE LEVEY
　1967　Some notes on bison and elk of the Mississippi River. *Quarterly Bulletin, Archeological Society of Virginia* 21(*2*).

KORITZER, RICHARD T.
　1968　An analysis of the cause of tooth loss in ancient Egyptian populations. *American Anthropologist* 70(3).

LEIGH, R. W.
　1925　Dental pathology of Indian tribes of varied environmental and food conditions. *American Journal of Physical Anthropology* 8:179–199.

LEWIS, CLIFFORD N., ALBERT J. LOOMIE
　1953　*The Spanish Jesuit mission in Virginia 1570–1572*. Chapel Hill: The University of North Carolina Press.

MAC CORD, HOWARD A.
　1957　Indians of Fort Belvoir. *Quarterly Bulletin, Archeological Society of Virginia* 12(1).

MANAKEE, HAROLD R.
　1959　*Indians of early Maryland*. Maryland Historical Society. Baltimore: Garamond Press.

MC CARY, BEN C.
1957 Indians in seventeenth century Virginia. *Quarterly Bulletin, Archeological Society of Virginia* 11(1).

MC GINNES, BURD S., JOHN H. REEVES, JR.
1957 A comparison of pre-historic Indian-killed deer to the modern deer. *Quarterly Bulletin, Archeological Society of Virginia* 12(1).

ROSE, CORNELIS S., JR.
1957 *The Indians of Arlington.* Arlington, Virginia: Office of the County Manager.

SAMS, CONWAY WHITTLE
1916 *The conquest of Virginia: the forest primeval.* New York and London: Knickerbocker.

SCHMITT, KARL, JR.
1965a Patawomeke: an historic Algonkian site. *Quarterly Bulletin, Archeological Society of Virginia* 20(1).
1965b Historical identification and documentation. *Quarterly Bulletin, Archeological Society of Virginia* 20(1).

SEMMES, RAPHAEL
1937 *Captains and mariners of early Maryland.* Baltimore: Johns Hopkins.

SLATTERY, RICHARD G., WILLIAM TIDWELL, DOUGLAS R. WOODWARD
1966 The Montgomery focus. *Quarterly Bulletin, Archeological Society of Virginia* 21(1).

STEPHENSON, ROBERT L., ALICE L. L. FERGUSON, HENRY G. FERGUSON
1963 *The Accokeek Creek site: a middle Atlantic seaboard culture sequence.* Museum of Anthropology, University of Michigan, Anthropological Papers 20. Ann Arbor: University of Michigan Press.

STRUEVER, STUART
1966 The "flotation" process for recovery of plant remains. *Quarterly Bulletin, Archeological Society of Virginia* 20(3), Part one.
1971 "Implications of vegetable remains from an Illinois Hopewell site," in *Prehistoric agriculture.* Edited by Stuart Struever. New York: The Natural History Press.

TYLER, LYON GARDINER
1907 *Narratives of early Virginia.* New York: Charles Scribner's Sons.

UBELAKER, DOUGLAS H.
1973 "The reconstruction of demographic profiles from ossuary skeletal samples: a case study from the Tidewater Potomac." Unpublished doctoral dissertation, University of Kansas.

URQUHART, ALVIN W.
1963 *Patterns of settlement and subsistence in southwestern Angola.* Washington, D.C.: National Academy of Sciences National Research Council.

Morphological Changes in Human Teeth and Jaws in a High-Attrition Environment

WILLIAM L. HYLANDER

INTRODUCTION

The dentition of many human populations is characterized by extensive amounts of wear. An individual will experience, throughout life, the gradual loss of tooth material from both occlusal and interproximal portions of the teeth. Associated with this gradual loss of tooth material are altered anatomical relationships of the teeth and jaws. This study will analyze some of these altered anatomical relationships in an extinct North American Indian population. Particular attention will be focused on the effects (if any) on the dental arch dimensions, vertical facial dimensions, relationships of the maxilla to the mandible, and tooth migration among adults in a high-attrition environment (no distinction is being made here between attrition and abrasion).

While the effects of attrition on individual tooth measurements have been thoroughly discussed (Goose 1963), the morphological changes occurring in the dental arch dimensions are less clear. Although Lundström and Lysell (1953) and Lysell (1958a) were unable to demonstrate a reduction in the arch length in two medieval European populations (Danish and Swedish), Begg (1954) and Murphy (1964a) were able to demonstrate such a reduction among Australian aborig-

I wish to thank Dr. Albert A. Dahlberg for generously supplying the radiographic apparatus that was used for this study. I am also indebted to Tom Muller for computer assistance, and to the Anthropology Department at the University of Kentucky for allowing me to examine, radiograph, and photograph the Indian Knoll skeletal collection. This study was in part supported by USPHS DE173 Training Grant in physical anthropology and by the Department of Anatomy, Duke University.

For Plate, see p. xlvii, between pp. 330–331.

ines. In a later study, Hasund (1965) also demonstrated dental arch length reduction in a medieval population from Oslo.

Begg (1954) states that arch width changes are also associated with increased attrition, although these supposed altered dimensions were not biometrically determined. According to this author, the upper arch increases in width while the lower decreases in width in response to attrition. These observations are in agreement with those of Barrett (1958), who, like Begg, studied Australian aborigines. Lundström and Lysell (1953) and Lysell (1958a), in a biometrical study, did not detect any changes in arch width in two European medieval populations. Murphy (1964a), in one of many biometrical studies on Australian aborigines, did not detect any changes in arch width; however, in a later study (Murphy 1964b), he found that among male Australian aborigines, the mandibular molar arch width increased whiles the maxillary molar arch width remained essentially unchanged. Arch width dimensions among female Australian aborigines were apparently unaffected.

Following occlusal and/or interproximal wear, a tooth responds by moving toward its antagonist and/or toward the adjacent tooth. Apparently in light of this, Gottlieb (1927) proposed the theory of continual tooth eruption and migration. Friel (1945), while studying movements of the dentition, stated that all teeth move in an anterior direction. This has generally been confirmed in the developing dentition (Moss et al. 1959; Latham and Scott 1960). Among young adults, Begg (1954) assumed that all movement in response to occlusal and interproximal wear was occlusal and mesial (thus providing the third molars a larger space in which to erupt). This notion regarding the direction of tooth migration is considered to be correct by most authors (Sicher 1950; Scott and Symons 1953; Schour 1953; Murphy 1964a; Kraus et al. 1969).

Friel states that all teeth move anteriorly, even following the creation of extraction sites. Many workers, however, are in disagreement on this point. Richardson (1965) used metallic implants in *Macaca*, and proved Friel to be wrong. He found that the teeth immediately anterior to an extraction site will occasionally move backward, while the posterior tooth usually moves forward. Lysell (1958b), in studying the movements of teeth following attrition, was unable to detect any mesial movement of the maxillary first molars. However, he did note that the long axis of the central incisors became more vertical with increased attrition, suggesting that the anterior dentition had tipped posteriorly in response to the increased attrition.

Like dental arch length, it would appear that extensive dental attrition also has the potential of reducing vertical facial dimensions. Tallgren (1957) and Murphy (1959) have demonstrated biometrically that vertical facial dimensions are reduced following extensive dental attrition in a European and Australian population, respectively. Other investigators, on the other hand, have made statements to the contrary. Sicher (1950) and Begg (1954) contend that vertical facial dimensions are unaffected by attrition, i.e. passive eruption of the teeth keeps pace with the continual loss of tooth material. These observations, however, were apparently solely impressionistic. Following a biometric analysis, Sarnas (1957) also found that vertical facial dimensions in an extinct North American Indian population were largely unaffected by extensive attrition.

In addition to changes in arch dimensions following attrition, it has generally been recognized that the edge-to-edge bite seen in various human populations is somehow related to tooth migration following interproximal wear (Campbell 1925; Leigh 1929; Begg 1954; Wolpoff 1971; and others), as opposed to being due to intrusive bite forces acting on the anterior dentition (Brace and Mahler 1971). Another (although less plausible) theory views the relationship between the maxillary and mandibular anterior dentition (the edge-to-edge bite as opposed to an overbite) as being strictly genetically determined, unaltered "by the environment or function" (Klatsky and Fisher 1953). According to Murphy (1958), the formation of the edge-to-edge bite is due to attrition, but it is not caused by differential tooth migration, i.e. it is not due to greater anterior migration of the mandibular teeth. Instead it is due to elongation of the mandible as a result of continued bone growth of the mandibular condyle. This additional mandibular growth during adult life is correlated with a more anteriorly positioned mandibular dentition relative to the maxillary dentition. According to Murphy, this condylar growth can take place only following the eradication of the interlocking effect of the tooth cusps by extensive occlusal wear.

While it is generally accepted that arch length is reduced with increased tooth wear, where this reduction occurs — i.e. whether in the anterior or posterior portions — is less clear. This relates to tooth migration and will be discussed below. The apparent disagreement regarding changes in width dimensions is possibly related to the choice of measuring techniques. All of the studies previously discussed have utilized landmarks which are quite unstable because of the effects of attrition. For example, some studies have defined arch width as the distance between the center of the contact point on he right side and the center of the contact point on the left. Others have used minimum or maximum widths obtained by measuring between lingual or buccal surfaces from left to right sides. Contact points and lingual or buccal surfaces are clearly affected by attrition. A better approach would have been to utilize more stable landmarks in the determination of width dimensions. For this important reason, the cementoenamel junction will be used in this study.

Tooth migration and altered relationships between the mandible and the maxilla can be studied best by using a combination of measurements taken directly from the skull, together with measurements derived from radiographs. Radiographs allow one to determine the relationships of various teeth and foramina relative to each other and also relative to various cranial base reference lines. Certain direct measurements also allow one to determine various dental relationships relative to facial foramina. See Moss et al. (1959) and Moss and Greenberg (1967) for theoretical considerations regarding the use of facial foramina as stable reference points.

The present study is concerned with the effects of attrition on the craniofacial complex in an extinct human population. It is thought that a combination of biometric techniques (i.e. both radiographic and direct measurements) will contribute to a better understanding of these altered relationships. As previously mentioned, various hypotheses have been advanced regarding tooth migration, the formation of the edge-to-edge bite, the effects of attrition on vertical facial dimensions, etc. This study is undertaken primarily to test some of these notions.

MATERIALS AND METHODS

Craniofacial alterations in response to attrition were analyzed in the Indian Knoll skeletal population from southwestern Kentucky. This population is characterized by extensive amounts of dental attrition (Snow 1948); it is also large in number and the preservation of the skulls is particularly good. The skeletal material excavated at Indian Knoll is considered to be the remains of an Archaic North American Indian population, presumably about 4,000–5,000 years old (Willey 1966; Winters 1968). This site was excavated in 1939 (Webb 1946) and is presently housed in the Department of Anthropology, University of Kentucky.

A standardized roentgenographic cephalometric technique was employed to analyze biometrically the effects of attrition on the cranio-facial complex. Metric data were also derived directly from the skeletal material. The following procedure was used to select skulls for this analysis: (1) all skulls had to be free of major osteological damage and distortion, (2) all individuals had to be dental adults, i.e. all permanent teeth must have erupted into functional occlusion. In the event that the third molars were congenitally missing or malaligned, the cranial and postcranial material (if present) had to conform to an adult condition. An adult condition of the skull consists of closure of the basioccipital synchondrosis. In the postcranial skeleton, adult condition is defined by closure of all long-bone and pelvic epiphyses. Following the above procedure, eighty-six adult skulls were selected (fifty-one male and thirty-five female) from approximately 1,000 burials. Unfortunately many of the females had either missing mandibles or a mandible that could not be articulated properly with its respective cranium. Therefore, because the female sample size is considered to be inadequate, essentially only the male results will be reported here.

Skull Preparation

Initial preparation of skulls and crania consisted of marking various structures and landmarks with radiopaque materials. Basion, nasion, and anterior and posterior nasal spine were coated with a barium sulfate paste (some of the landmarks were marked for another study) which was prepared by mixing dry barium sulfate with water. The paste was carefully applied to the skull with a glass syringe and a 12-gauge needle. In addition, the left and right mental foramina were marked by inserting lead shot (diameter three millimeters) into each foramen and fixing the shot with a small piece of modeling clay. The skulls were prepared in this manner in order to locate various structures and landmarks on the radiographs more accurately (Björk and Solow 1962).

The skulls and crania were then carefully examined for minor damage. When damage existed, the nature of it was immediately recorded. Damage to the cribriform plate, teeth, and alveolar process was very common in this population. For this reason, many individuals are missing some variable values. As previously mentioned, all warped, distorted, poorly reconstructed, and badly damaged skulls and crania were rejected for this study.

After the radiopaque materials had been applied, the lower jaw (when present) was attached to the skull in centric occlusion. The maxillary and mandibular occlusal planes were carefully checked with regard to any irregularities of the positions of the individual teeth. Such irregularities were usually easily discovered and corrected. In addition to the occlusal relations, the positions of the mandibular condyles to their articular fossae were checked, and then an attempt was made to approximate the thickness of the articular tissue with a shaped piece of soft wax. This step was undertaken to help stabilize the mandibular component. When the proper relationship of the mandible to the maxilla had been determined, the mandible was securely taped to the cranium.

Radiographic Procedure

The skull was inserted into the cephalostat, where its position was carefully checked, particularly with regard to the median sagittal plane. Kodak No Screen X-ray film was then exposed for a period of two to three seconds at ten milliamperes and seventy-five kilovolts. The distances from the X-ray anode and the film to the median sagittal plane were 152 centimeters and approximately 11 centimeters, respectively. By maintaining these constant distances, the linear enlargement was kept at about 5 percent. Because the distance between the midsagittal plane and the film varied, individual correction factors were calculated.

Reference Point Location

After processing, each of the radiographs was securely taped to a sheet of acetate. The necessary contours were traced on the acetate sheets with a 4H (hard) drawing pencil and the reference points or landmarks were located. When reference points were bilateral, the midpoint between the left and right reference points was recorded as the true reference point. Immediately over each reference point, a small hole was punched through the X ray with a sharp stylus. Then the X ray was transferred to an apparatus capable of determining x and y coordinate values. This apparatus was designed and constructed by Dr. A. A. Dahlberg of the Department of Anthropology at the University of Chicago. The x and y coordinates were then determined and recorded for each of the landmarks. All coordinates were recorded to the nearest one-half millimeter. At a later date the coordinate values were transferred to IBM (International Business Machines) computer cards. A program written for the IBM 360 computer at the University of Chicago Computation Center was utilized to generate the various linear and angular measures from the coordinate values.

The Reference Points

All definitions for the radiographic reference points and reference lines were taken from either Björk (1950) or Brown (1965), or were selected and defined by the author.

Ethmoidale (eth): the deepest median point of the anterior cranial fossa in MSP.

Gnathion (gn): the lowest point on the symphysis of the mandible in MSP.

Mandibular Incisor Crown Tip (I_1): the tip of the most anteriorly positioned mandibular central incisor. In worn teeth, this reference point is located by fitting a line to the long axis of the tooth, using the pulp canal as a guide. The point is located at the junction of the fitted line and the incisal tip.

Mandibular Molar Distal Contact (M_2): the most distal contact point of the mandibular second molar.

Maxillary Incisor Long Axis Crown Tip (I^1): after fitting a line to the long axis of the most anteriorly positioned maxillary central incisor, using the pulp canal as a guide, this point is located at the junction of the line and the incisal tip.

Maxillary Molar Distal Contact (M^2): the most distal contact point of the maxillary second molar.

Mental Foramen Point (mf): the center of the mental foramen.

Nasion (n): the most anterior point of nasofrontal suture in MSP.

Sella (s): the center of the bony crypt forming the sella turcica. The center is defined as the midpoint of the greatest diameter from the tuberculum sellae.

The Reference Lines

Figures 1 and 2 demonstrate some of the reference lines used in the radiographic part of this study.

Nasion-Sella Line (NSL): the horizontal line passing through the nasion and sella.

Ethmoid-Sella Line (ESL): the horizontal line passing through the sella and ethmoidale.

Nasion-Sella Perpendicular (NSP): the vertical line passing through the sella and perpendicular to the NSL.

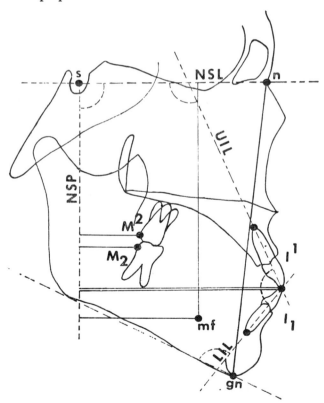

Figure 1.   The radiographic reference points and lines and radiographic variables

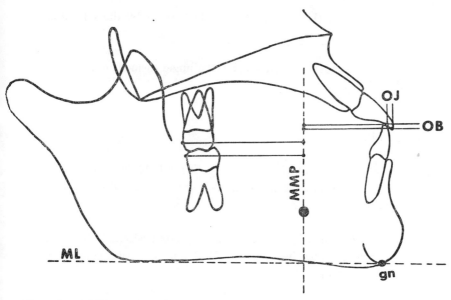

Figure 2. Additional radiographic reference points and lines and radiographic variables

Ethmoid-Sella Perpendicular (ESP): the vertical line passing through the sella and perpendicular to the ESL.

Mandibular Line (ML): the line fitted to the lowest border of the mandibular symphysis and to the lower border of the mandibular angle.

Mandibular-Mental Perpendicular (MMP): the vertical line passing through the mental foramen point and perpendicular to the ML.

Upper Incisor Line (UIL): a line fitted to the long axis of the most prominent maxillary central incisor.

Lower Incisor Line (LIL): a line fitted to the long axis of the most prominent mandibular central incisor.

The Radiographic Variables

The following is a list of the radiographic variables studied (see Figures 1 and 2):

Interincisal Angle (UIL-LIL): the angle formed by the UIL and the LIL.

Maxillary Incisor Angle (UIL-NSL): the angle formed by the UIL and the NSL.

Mandibular Incisor Angle (LIL-ML): the angle formed by the LIL and the ML.

Horizontal Position of the Maxillary Second Molar (NSP-M^2): the perpendicular distance between the NSP and the distal contact of the maxillary second molar.

Horizontal Position of the Mandibular Second Molar (NSP-M_2): the perpendicular distance between the NSP and the distal contact of the mandibular second molar.

Horizontal Position of the Incisal Tip of the Maxillary Central Incisor (NSP-I^1): the perpendicular distance between the NSP and the maxillary central incisor long-axis crown tip.

Horizontal Position of the Incisal Tip of the Mandibular Central Incisor (NSP-I_1): the perpendicular distance between the NSP and the incisal tip of the mandibular incisor.

Horizontal Position of the Maxillary Second Molar Relative to the Mental Foramen (Mental Foramen-M^2): the perpendicular distance between the MMP and the distal contact of the maxillary second molar.

Horizontal Position of the Mandibular Second Molar Relative to the Mental Foramen (Mental Foramen-M_2): the perpendicular distance between the MMP and the distal contact of the mandibular second molar.

Horizontal Position of the Maxillary Central Incisor Relative to the Mental Foramen (Mental Foramen-I^1): the perpendicular distance between the MMP and the maxillary central incisor long-axis crown tip.

Horizontal Position of the Mandibular Central Incisor Relative to the Mental Foramen (Mental Foramen-I_1): the perpendicular distance between the MMP and the incisal tip of the mandibular central incisor.

Inclination of the Lower Jaw Base to the Anterior Cranial Base (ML-NSL): the angle formed between the ML and the NSL.

Vertical Position of the Mental Foramen[1] (NSL-mf): the perpendicular distance between the NSL and the mental foramen.

Vertical Position of the Mental Foramen[2] (ESL-mf): the perpendicular distance between the ESL and the mental foramen.

Horizontal Position of the Mental Foramen (NSP-mf): the perpendicular distance between the NSP and the mental foramen.

Vertical Position of the Lower Symphyseal Border (ESL-gn): the perpendicular distance between the ESL and gnathion.

Craniometric Variables

In addition to the radiographic variables previously listed, many craniofacial variables were measured directly from the skeletal material.

All measurements were taken from the left side, unless the tooth or bony morphological feature was missing or damaged. When damaged, the opposite side was measured. Some variables to be measured required the presence of certain teeth from both the left and right sides. In the event that one or both were absent or damaged, this variable was simply recorded as missing. Before measuring, all preservative was carefully removed from the appropriate teeth with acetone. In addition, all teeth were carefully checked for proper positioning and alignment. When positions were faulty, they were corrected before measuring. When warped and damaged jaws interfered with the accurate recording of a given variable, a missing value for that variable was recorded. All measurements except for the dental arch length perpendiculars and the overbite and overjet values were made directly with a Peacock sliding caliper and were recorded to the nearest one-tenth of a millimeter.

The dental arch length perpendiculars were measured with an instrument that was specially designed by Dr. A. A. Dahlberg. This measuring device is T-shaped, with millimeters marked off along the vertical part of the T. After lining up the horizontal part of the T through the center of the second molar, fourth premolar, or canine distal contacts, the perpendicular distance to the center of the mesial contact point of the central incisor was read directly off the instrument to the nearest one-half millimeter (see Figure 3). The same procedure was used on both the maxillary and mandibular dental arches. Overbite and overjet values were determined according to Lysell (1958a), and were recorded to the nearest one-half millimeter.

Dental Arch Length Variables (Figure 3)

Maxillary Molar-Incisor Perpendicular Distance (M^2-I^1): the midsagittal distance from the center of the mesial contact point of the maxillary central incisor to the center of the distal contact of the maxillary second molar.

Maxillary Premolar-Incisor Perpendicular Distance (P^4-I^1): the midsagittal distance from the center of the mesial contact point of the maxillary central incisor to the center of the distal contact point of the maxillary second premolar.

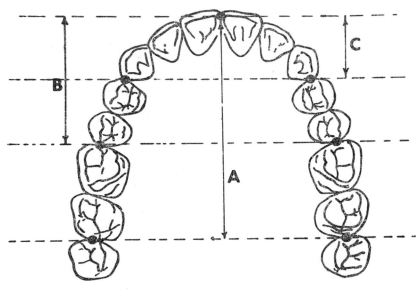

Figure 3.   Dental arch length dimensions

Maxillary Canine-Incisor Perpendicular Distance (C^1-I^1): the mid-sagittal distance from the center of the mesial contact point of the maxillary central incisor to the center of the distal contact point of the maxillary canine.

Mandibular Molar-Incisor Perpendicular Distance M_2-I_1): the mid-sagittal distance from the center of the mesial contact point of the mandibular central incisor to the center of the distal contact of the mandibular second molar.

Mandibular Premolar-Incisor Perpendicular Distance (P_4-I_1): the mid-sagittal distance from the center of the mesial contact point of the mandibular central incisor to the center of the distal contact point of the mandibular second premolar.

Mandibular Canine-Incisor Perpendicular Distance (C_1-I_1): the mid-sagittal distance from the center of the mesial contact point of the mandibular central incisor to the distal contact point of the mandibular canine.

Dental Arch Width Variables (Figure 4)

Maxillary Molar Width (M^2-M^2): the maximum width between the maxillary second molars along the buccal CEJ (cementoenamel junction).

Maxillary Premolar Width (P^4-P^4): the maximum width between the maxillary second promolars along the buccal CEJ.

Maxillary Canine Width (C^1-C^1): the maximum width between the maxillary canines along the labial CEJ.

Mandibular Molar Width (M_2-M_2): the maximum width between the mandibular second molars along the buccal CEJ.

Mandibular Premolar Width (P_4-P_4): the maximum width between the mandibular second premolars along the buccal CEJ.

Mandibular Canine Width (C_1-C_1): the maximum width between the mandibular canines along the labial CEJ.

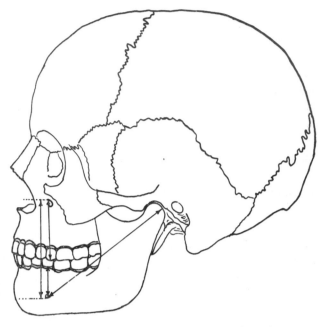

Figure 4.   Dental arch width and vertical dentofacial dimensions

Anatomical and Clinical Crown Height Variables

Maxillary Incisor Anatomical Crown Height (I¹ Anatomical Height): the distance between the incisal tip and labial CEJ of the maxillary central incisor.

Maxillary Incisor Clinical Crown Height (I¹ Clinical Height): the distance between the incisal tip and the labial alveolar margin of the maxillary central incisor.

Maxillary Premolar Anatomical Crown Height (P⁴ Anatomical Height): the distance between the tip of the buccal cusp and the buccal CEJ of the maxillary second premolar.

Maxillary Premolar Clinical Crown Height (P⁴ Clinical Height): the distance between the tip of the buccal cusp and the buccal alveolar margin of the maxillary second premolar.

Mandibular Incisor Anatomical Crown Height (I_1 Anatomical Height): the distance between the incisal tip and the labial CEJ of the mandibular central incisor.

Mandibular Incisor Clinical Crown Height (I_1 Clinical Height): the distance between the incisal tip and the labial alveolar margin of the mandibular central incisor.

Mandibular Premolar Anatomical Crown Height (P_4 Anatomical Height): the distance between the tip of the buccal cusp and the buccal CEJ of the mandibular second premolar.

Mandibular Premolar Clinical Crown Height (P_4 Clinical Height): the distance between the tip of the buccal cusp and the buccal alveolar margin of the mandibular second premolar.

Foramen-Premolar Variables (see Figure 5)

Infraorbital Foramen-Premolar Cusp Tip (Infraorbital Foramen-P^4 Tip): the distance between the superior margin of the infraorbital foramen and the buccal cusp tip of the maxillary second premolar.

Infraorbital Foramen-Premolar CEJ (Infraorbital Foramen-P^4 CEJ): the distance between the superior margin of the infraorbital foramen and the CEJ along the buccal aspect of the maxillary second premolar.

Infraorbital Foramen-Alveolar Margin (Infraorbital Foramen-P^4 Alveolar): the distance between the superior margin of the infraorbital foramen and the alveolar margin adjacent to the maxillary second premolar.

Mental Foramen-Premolar Cusp Tip (Mental Foramen-P_4 Tip): the distance between the inferior margin of the mental foramen and the buccal tip of the mandibular second premolar.

Mental Foramen-Premolar CEJ (Mental Foramen-P_4 CEJ): the distance between the inferior margin of the mental foramen and the CEJ along the buccal aspect of the mandibular second premolar.

Mental Foramen-Alveolar Margin (Mental Foramen-P_4 Alveolar): the distance between the inferior margin of the mental foramen and the alveolar margin adjacent to the mandibular second premolar.

Midsagittal Vertical Facial Dimensions (Figure 4)

Nasion-Maxillary Incisor Tip Height (Nasion-I¹ Tip): the distance between the tip of the maxillary central incisor and the nasion.

Nasion-Maxillary Incisor CEJ (Nasion-I¹ CEJ): the distance between the labial CEJ of the maxillary central incisor and the nasion.

Nasion-Maxillary Incisor Alveolus (Nasion-I¹ Alveolus): the distance between the labial alveolar margin of the maxillary central incisor and the nasion.

Nasion-Mandibular Incisor CEJ (Nasion-I₁ CEJ): the distance between the labial CEJ of the mandibular central incisor and the nasion.

Total Facial Height (Nasion-Gnathion): the distance between the gnathion and the nasion.

Additional Dimensions (Figures 2 and 5)

Infraorbital-Mental Foramen Dimension: the distance between the superior margin of the infraorbital foramen and the inferior margin of the mental foramen.

Mandibular Condyle-Mental Foramen Dimension: the distance between the postero-superior portion of the middle of the mandibular condyle and the antero-inferior margin of the mental foramen (these points are instrumentally determined).

Overjet (OJ): the distance between the labial surfaces of the left maxillary and the mandibular central incisors (parallel to the occlusal plane).

Overbite (OB): the distance between the above point along the labial surface of the mandibular central incisor and the tip of the same tooth.

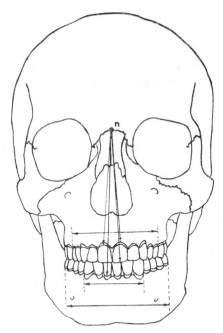

Figure 5.   Additional dentofacial dimensions

Attrition Scores

Following the radiographic and craniometric procedures, each skull was scored as to the amount of attrition present in the molar dentition. Each of the four major cusps of each molar tooth was scored in the following manner:

1 = no attrition
2 = enamel attrition
3 = dentin exposure
4 = cupping
5 = secondary dentin exposed
6 = all cusps coalesced
7 = root attrition

The purpose of the above scoring procedure was to divide the adult Indian Knoll male skulls objectively into a high-attrition group (advanced) and a low-attrition group (moderate). After a visual examination of the attrition scores, it became apparent that most individuals had extensive attrition of the first and second molars. However, the range of attrition scores was much greater on the third molars. Therefore, the attrition scores for the third molar were used to assign each skull to the advanced or moderate attrition group. All skulls with an attrition score of twenty or more (combined score of maxillary and mandibular third molar) were assigned to the advanced attrition group, while all skulls with a score of less than twenty were considered members of the moderate attrition group. This procedure resulted in twenty-four skulls being allocated to the advanced attrition group and twenty-seven skulls to the moderate attrition group.

This cutoff point of twenty results in a fairly clear break in the values of the attrition scores. A two- or three-point shift of the cutoff value in either direction results in lopsided numbers of individuals in the two groups and also in many borderline cases. The selection of the value twenty creates the minimum number of borderline cases and at the same time retains a reasonable number of individuals in each group.

When totaling attrition scores, some individuals were missing either the mandibular or the maxillary third molars. In these situations, the score of the tooth present was simply doubled. In the event that both teeth (maxillary and mandibular) on each side were missing, the state of attrition of the other teeth was taken into consideration, as well as other biological indicators of age (e.g. suture closure).

Statistical Procedure

In the statistical treatment of all linear and angular measures, the advanced and moderate attrition groups were handled separately. The statistical analysis consists of routine descriptive statistics for all variables under consideration. These statistics are the mean, median, minimum and maximum values, skew, kurtosis, and the standard deviation.

Testing for differences between mean values was accomplished by utilizing Student's t-test. The .05 level of confidence was chosen as the level of significance for this study; however, as seen in the various tables and in the results section, the t-values were also tested at other confidence levels (e.g. .01, .001, etc.). Levels not ordinarily considered to be statistically significant were also recorded, but only at the .1, .2, and .3 confidence level. Probability values larger than .3 were simply recorded as not significant. The above procedure has been undertaken primarily because it allows the reader to choose different probability levels regarding the acceptance or rejection of a given null hypothesis. The mean values of a given variable for the two groups were often tested as to whether they were significantly different from one another (two-tailed test). However, in some situations, testing whether mean values are significantly larger or smaller than another mean value was more appropriate (one-tailed test). These situations will be noted when encountered.

Most computations were performed at the University of Chicago Computation Center. A special Fortran IV program was written to derive variable values between *x* and *y* coordinates, and another was written to generate the descriptive statistics. Both of the above programs were written for the IBM 360 electronic computer. The t-values were calculated on a Wang Calculator in the Department of Anatomy, Duke University.

RESULTS AND DISCUSSION

Tables 1 and 2 show the results of the statistical analysis of the dental arch values. All mean values for arch length were tested to determine whether the advanced attrition group had significantly smaller values than the moderate attrition group. As seen in Table 2, all arch length values are in the direction that one might predict, i.e. they are all smaller in the advanced attrition group. All values were significantly smaller, except for the following: the maxillary and mandibular canine-incisor perpendicular values and the mandibular premolar-incisor perpendicular values.

These data support the findings of Begg (1954) and Murphy (1964a), i.e. dental arch reduction occurs following interproximal and occlusal wear. However, it became clear during the data collection portion of this study that Begg's technique in determining the amount of length reduction of the dental arch due to attrition clearly overestimates the amount that actually takes place (at least in the Indian Knoll population). Instead of measuring the dental arch directly, Begg measured individual teeth and then added up the amount of estimated interproximal tooth loss. This sum was considered to represent the amount of length reduction of the dental arch. This sum overestimates length reduction of the dental arch in this population in essentially two different ways: (1) Many of the young individuals of the Indian Knoll population have a rather irregularly aligned dentition (see Plate 1); following wear of the anterior dentition, the teeth can realign themselves without reducing the arch length. (2) Many of the individuals in the advanced attrition group had extensively worn teeth

Table 1. Arch width dimensions

Variable	Attrition	Number	Mean (millimeters)	Standard deviation	Probability
M^2-M^2	Moderate	23	62.7	2.7	NS
	Advanced	16	62.3	1.8	
M_2-M_2	Moderate	20	61.8	2.6	.2
	Advanced	16	63.0	2.2	
P^4-P^4	Moderate	21	52.5	2.0	.3
	Advanced	13	51.6	2.6	
P_4-P_4	Moderate	22	47.5	1.7	NS
	Advanced	20	47.4	1.7	
C^1-C^1	Moderate	18	39.7	1.8	NS
	Advanced	17	39.3	1.5	
C_1-C_1	Moderate	21	30.7	2.3	NS
	Advanced	22	31.3	2.6	

Table 2. Arch length dimensions

Variable	Attrition	Number	Mean (millimeters)	Standard deviation	Probability
M^2-I^1	Moderate	16	43.0	1.8	.005*
	Advanced	13	40.7	2.2	
M_2-I_1	Moderate	18	40.5	2.2	.01*
	Advanced	14	38.1	2.8	
P^4-I^1	Moderate	16	24.0	1.1	.005*
	Advanced	14	22.1	2.3	
P_4-I_1	Moderate	20	19.5	1.8	.1*
	Advanced	19	18.7	1.3	
C^1-I^1	Moderate	14	11.6	1.3	.3*
	Advanced	17	11.1	1.3	
C_1-I_1	Moderate	19	8.4	1.4	NS
	Advanced	17	8.1	1.0	

* One-tailed test.

that had failed to migrate towards adjacent teeth; therefore, inter-proximal and occlusal attrition did not affect arch length dimensions as much as one might initially expect (see Plate 1). The formation of the interproximal spaces in this plate are due, of course, primarily to two factors: (1) the worn teeth have failed to migrate toward adjacent teeth and (2) these teeth continue to undergo occlusal attrition. Wolpoff (1971), however, views the formation of such spaces as due to inter-proximal wear. Clearly, interproximal wear (as opposed to occlusal wear) cannot take place if a tooth has lost contact with adjacent teeth.

The statistical analysis on the arch width dimensions did not reveal any statistically significant differences between the moderate and advanced attrition groups (Table 1). Unlike the situation regarding arch length dimensions, the mean arch width values were tested to determine whether they were significantly DIFFERENT (not larger or smaller) from one another. However, when the female data were included for analysis, a two-way analysis of variance (sex and attrition) showed that the mean values for the mandibular second molar width were significantly different for advanced and moderate attrition groups (p < .002). In both males and females, the mandibular molar arch width increased with the advanced attrition. All other mean differences in arch width using these combined data were not statistically significant. These results tend to support Murphy's data, which show an increase in mandibular molar arch width following extensive attrition among Australian aborigines (1964b).

As previously mentioned, many workers are of the opinion that all teeth migrate anteriorly and toward the midline throughout life (except when continuity of the arch is interrupted by missing teeth). If this were indeed the case, then one would expect to find a DECREASE in arch width dimensions following attrition, particularly in the inter-canine dimensions (see Figure 4). Clearly many factors operate in determining the direction of tooth migration (for a review of such factors, see Graber 1958) and the generalization that all teeth migrate anteriorly and toward the midline certainly does not hold for this population.

The results of the statistical analysis of the various vertical dental and facial dimensions are shown in Tables 3, 4, and 5. As seen in Tables 3 and 4, the clinical and anatomical height dimensions of the second premolars and central incisors are significantly reduced in size following attrition (as expected). However, the vertical relationships of the occlusal and incisal surfaces of the second premolars and central incisors are apparently unaffected by attrition. Unlike the results of other studies (Murphy 1959; Tallgren 1957), passive eruption of the teeth has apparently kept pace with dental attrition in this population. In the premolar region (Table 3), it was found that the distances between (a) the infraorbital foramen and the buccal cemento-enamel junction of the P^4, and (b) the mental foramen and the buccal cementoenamel junction of the P_4, increased with advanced attrition. This, of course, is indicative of continual tooth eruption. In addition, the data also show that the deposition of bone along the alveolar margin continues during passive tooth eruption. The mean values for the distance between the mental foramen and the mandibular second premolar-alveolar margin were not significantly different for advanced

Table 3. Vertical dimensions in premolar region

Variable	Attrition	Number	Mean (milli-meters)	Standard devia-tion	Probability
Maxilla					
P4 Anatomical Height	Moderate	27	6.1	1.5	.0005*
	Advanced	12	3.8	1.4	
P4 Clinical Height	Moderate	25	7.5	1.0	.0005*
	Advanced	20	5.8	2.2	
Infraorbital	Moderate	22	41.0	2.6	NS
Foramen-P4 Tip	Advanced	24	40.3	3.4	
Infraorbital	Moderate	27	34.4	3.5	.005*
Foramen-P4 DEJ	Advanced	12	37.7	1.7	
Infraorbital	Moderate	25	32.9	3.3	.05
Foramen-P4 Alveolar	Advanced	20	34.9	2.1	
Mandible					
P_4 Anatomical Height	Moderate	27	5.7	1.4	.0005*
	Advanced	22	3.5	1.3	
P_4 Clinical Height	Moderate	26	7.2	1.0	.005*
	Advanced	22	5.9	1.7	
Mental	Moderate	22	23.3	2.1	.2
Foramen-P_4 Tip	Advanced	23	22.3	2.1	
Mental	Moderate	27	17.2	2.5	.005*
Foramen-P_4 DEJ	Advanced	21	19.0	2.2	
Mental	Moderate	26	15.6	2.3	.2
Foramen-P_4 Alveolar	Advanced	21	16.5	2.4	

* One-tailed test.

and moderate attrition male groups ($p < .2$). However, again by including the female data, a two-way analysis of variance (sex and attrition) established that both advanced attrition groups had larger mean values that were significantly different from the moderate attrition groups for the mental foramen-alveolar margin dimension ($p < .01$). In addition, the analysis of the female data supported previous conclusions regarding other premolar-facial foramina vertical dimensions among males (Table 3).

In the incisal region (Table 4), the vertical position of the incisal portion of the maxillary central incisor was apparently unaffected by extensive attrition (the mean values for the distance between the nasion and the tip of the maxillary central incisor were not significantly different for the advanced and moderate attrition groups). Like the maxillary premolar region, the position of the cementoenamel junction and the alveolar margin among the maxillary incisors afford evidence for the existence of continual tooth eruption and bone deposition along the alveolus of the erupting tooth. These data are also in

Table 4. Vertical dimensions in incisor region

Variable	Attrition	Number	Mean (milli-meters)	Standard devia-tion	Probability
Maxilla					
I¹ Anatomical Height	Moderate	20	8.6	1.1	.005*
	Advanced	14	5.1	2.4	
I¹ Clinical Height	Moderate	12	10.7	0.8	.01*
	Advanced	17	8.2	3.5	
Nasion — I¹ Tip	Moderate	16	76.0	3.0	NS
	Advanced	17	74.7	4.4	
Nasion — I¹ CEJ	Moderate	18	66.8	3.3	.01*
	Advanced	14	71.5	2.9	
Nasion — I¹ Alveolar	Moderate	11	65.4	2.8	.05
	Advanced	11	67.1	2.3	
Mandible					
I₁ — Anatomical Height	Moderate	25	6.4	1.6	.0005*
	Advanced	16	4.4	1.0	
I₁ — Clinical Height	Moderate	17	9.3	1.2	.005*
	Advanced	10	7.2	2.4	
Nasion — I₁ CEJ	Moderate	19	79.9	4.1	NS
	Advanced	14	79.8	4.1	

* One-tailed test.

Table 5. Vertical dimensions between mandible and cranium

Variable	Attrition	Number	Mean (milli-meters)	Standard devia-tion	Probability
Nasion-Gnathion	Moderate	22	111.9	4.9	NS
	Advanced	23	112.0	5.6	
ESL — Gnathion**	Moderate	22	105.2	5.2	NS
	Advanced	23	105.7	5.8	
NSL — Mental Foramen**	Moderate	22	90.3	4.7	NS
	Advanced	22	90.5	4.7	
ESL — Mental Foramen**	Moderate	22	87.6	5.2	NS
	Advanced	22	87.4	5.0	
Infraorbital — Mental Foramen	Moderate	22	64.2	4.3	NS
	Advanced	20	63.9	4.4	

** Radiographic variable.

agreement with Murphy (1959). The mean values for the distance between the nasion and the cementoenamel junction of the maxillary central incisor and between the nasion and the alveolar margin of the maxillary central incisor are significantly larger in the advanced attrition group. In the mandibular incisor region, only the distance between the nasion and the cementoenamel junction was determined. Determining the distance between the incisal tips afforded great difficulties, and the number of skulls with an intact alveolar margin was too small to constitute an adequate sample size (see sample size for clinical crown height of mandibular incisors in Table 4). The mean values for the distance between the nasion and the CEJ were essentially identical in both groups, suggesting that the amount of passive eruption of the mandibular incisors was negligible.

Unlike the studies on Australian aborigines and Europeans (Murphy 1959; Tallgren 1957), it appears that in the Indian Knoll population there was no loss in vertical facial dimensions due to attrition. Sarnas (1957), after analyzing the distance between the nasion and the gnathion in the Indian Knoll population, came to the same conclusion. In order to confirm this finding, four other measurements that reflect vertical facial dimensions were taken on the Indian Knoll population (see Table 5). The results of this portion of the analysis support the conclusion that vertical facial dimensions in the Indian Knoll population were essentially unaffected by extensive attrition during adult life. Various valid objections might be raised regarding the choice of one or more of these dimensions. However, when considered together, the above conclusion appears reasonably based (Tables 3 and 4 also).

The results of the statistical analysis of the tooth migration data are shown in Tables 6, 7, 8, and 9. Due to occlusal and interproximal wear, the posterior dentition probably migrates anteriorly (mesially). Therefore, using the nasion-sella perpendicular as a reference line, the perpendicular distance between this line and the distal aspect of the maxillary or mandibular second molar should increase with attrition. These dimensions were significantly larger in the advanced attrition group, as predicted by prevailing notions regarding tooth migration (see Table 6).

Based on Lysell's data (1958b) — showing that maxillary incisors become more vertically positioned following attrition — it was hypothesized that the perpendicular distance between the nasion-sella perpendicular and the tip of the maxillary central incisor should decrease following extensive attrition (contra the theory that all teeth migrate anteriorly and toward the midline). Although the mean value for this dimension was smaller in the advanced attrition group, this value was not significantly smaller than the corresponding value in the moderate group.

Murphy (1958) presented evidence for continued condylar growth through adult life, and suggested that the formation of the edge-to-edge bite was related to this horizontal repositioning of the mandible relative to the maxillary teeth (as opposed to the notion of differential tooth migration through alveolar bone). Based on his evidence, it was hypothesized that the perpendicular distance between the nasion-sella line and the tip of the mandibular central incisor should be larger in the advanced attrition group. Although this value is larger in the advanced attrition group, it is not significantly larger than the mean value in the moderate attrition group ($p < .1$). Incisal attrition and posterior tipping possibly have a dampening effect on the enlargement of this dimension (see Table 8). As seen in Table 6, the perpendicular

Table 6. Horizontal position of mental foramen and dentition

Variable	Attrition	Number	Mean (milli- meters)	Standard devia- tion	Probability
NSP — M^2**	Moderate	22	18.5	4.2	.05*
	Advanced	16	20.5	2.8	
NSP — M$_2$**	Moderate	19	17.4	4.2	.005*
	Advanced	17	21.0	3.2	
NSP — I^1**	Moderate	17	58.4	4.7	NS*
	Advanced	16	57.0	4.4	
NSP — I$_1$**	Moderate	19	55.7	4.6	.1*
	Advanced	18	57.5	3.8	
NSP — Mental Foramen**	Moderate	22	33.7	4.8	.025*
	Advanced	22	36.5	3.4	
Condyle — Mental Foramen	Moderate	22	95.8	4.7	.05*
	Advanced	23	98.0	2.5	

* One-tailed test.
** Radiographic variable.

Table 7. Horizontal position of the dentition relative to the mental foramen

Variable	Attrition	Number	Mean (milli- meters)	Standard devia- tion	Probability
Mental Foramen-M^2**	Moderate	22	15.4	3.1	NS
	Advanced	15	15.3	2.6	
Mental Foramen-M$_2$**	Moderate	19	16.7	2.3	.075*
	Advanced	17	15.5	2.5	
Mental Foramen-I^1**	Moderate	17	24.1	2.6	.005*
	Advanced	15	21.1	3.6	
Mental Foramen-I$_1$**	Moderate	19	21.5	2.4	NS
	Advanced	18	21.2	2.8	

* One-tailed test.
** Radiographic variables.

Table 8.   Incisor angulation data

Variable	Attrition	Number	Mean (degrees)	Standard deviation	Probability<
UIL-LIL**	Moderate	16	133.7	9.3	.01*
	Advanced	13	143.9	12.6	
UIL-NSL**	Moderate	17	97.0	6.0	.005*
	Advanced	16	89.6	8.2	
LIL-ML**	Moderate	18	101.9	5.3	.025*
	Advanced	17	97.7	6.0	
ML-NSL**	Moderate	21	27.5	4.8	NS
	Advanced	22	26.1	5.5	

 * One-tailed test.
** Radiographic variable.

Table 9.   Overbite and overjet data

Variable	Attrition	Number	Mean (milli-meters)	Standard deviation	Probability<
Overbite	Moderate	14	.5	0.8	.005*
	Advanced	16	—.1	0.4	
Overjet	Moderate	14	1.8	1.3	.0005*
	Advanced	13	—.2	0.9	

* One-tailed test.

distance between the nasion-sella line and the mental foramen, as well as the actual distance between the mandibular condyle and the mental foramen, support Murphy's notion regarding continual growth and repositioning of the mandible during adult life.

The results of incisor and molar positioning relative to the mental foramen are shown in Table 7. Based solely on the principle of mesial drift, one would expect the horizontal distance between the mental foramen and the molars to decrease in size. Although the mean values between the mental foramen and the maxillary and mandibular second molars are smaller in the advanced attrition groups, only the mandibular molar-mental foramen value approaches statistical significance (p < .075). However, not only are the molars migrating mesially, but the mandible is increasing in length between the mental foramen and the condyle (see Table 6). Therefore, migration of the second maxillary molar cannot be detected using the mental foramen, simply because both structures are migrating anteriorly simultaneously. Analyzing incisor positions relative to the mental foramen is also instructive. The distance between the tips of the mandibular central incisors is essentially unchanged in both the advanced and the moderate attrition groups. However, the position of the maxillary central incisors relative to the mental foramen has changed significantly. This is probably due to two factors: the anterior migration of the mental foramen (associated with compensatory condylar growth) and the more vertical positioning (posterior tipping?) of the central incisors (see Table 8).

Table 8 shows the results of the statistical analysis of the incisor angulation data. Based on observations and also on Lysell's data (1958b), it was hypothesized that maxillary and mandibular incisors become more vertical following extensive attrition. Inclination of the central incisors toward each other and also toward various reference lines indicates that the incisors are significantly more vertical in the high attrition group. As a check on the reference lines used in calculating incisor angulation, it was found that the relationship of the mandibular line to the nasion-sella line is not significantly different for the moderate and the advanced attrition groups.

Lastly, the overbite and overjet values were calculated and it was found that these values were significantly smaller in the advanced attrition group (Table 9). These data confirm earlier impressions regarding the reduction of overbite and overjet with increasing age, i.e. the gradual formation of the edge-to-edge bite. Most values for overbite and overjet in the advanced group were recorded as zero, although a few individuals actually had small negative values for these dimensions. This accounts for the small negative mean values in the advanced attrition group.

CONCLUSIONS AND SUMMARY

Craniofacial alterations, presumably due to extensive dental attrition, were investigated in an adult male North American Indian skeletal population (Indian Knoll). As expected, reduction of the length of the dental arch was associated with an increase in attrition. The only change in arch width dimensions following attrition was a widening in the mandibular second molar region. It is generally acknowledged that tooth migration is normally anterior and toward the midline. Although the Indian Knoll population exhibited extensive occlusal and interproximal wear, the width dimensions did not support the notion that all teeth (e.g. the canines) migrate in this manner. In addition, incisor angulation data suggest that the maxillary central incisors were possibly being tipped posteriorly.

The data on vertical facial dimensions suggest that although this population is characterized by extensive dental attrition, vertical facial dimensions are unaffected. Apparently, unlike certain European and Australian human populations, passive eruption of the teeth in this population kept pace with occlusal and incisal wear.

Many workers have noted the correlation between attrition and the edge-to-edge bite. One notion considers the formation of the edge-to-edge bite to be due to differential tooth migration, i.e. the mandibular teeth undergo more mesial drift than the maxillary teeth (Begg 1954). The data from this study do not support this hypothesis. Instead, they support the hypothesis that the edge-to-edge bite is in part formed by continued compensatory condylar growth of the mandible during adult life (Murphy 1958). Continued elongation of the mandible is associated with a more anterior positioning of the mandibular dentition. Another possible factor in edge-to-edge bite formation is the tipping and uprighting of the maxillary incisors following interproximal and incisal wear. As the maxillary incisors tip posteriorly, they are brought into more of an edge-to-edge relationship with the mandibular incisors. Mandibular incisors are also tipped more vertically following attrition, but to a lesser degree.

REFERENCES

BARRETT, M. J.
   1958   Dental observations on Australian aborigines. *Australian Dental Journal* 4:39–52.
BEGG, P. R.
   1954   Stone Age man's dentition. *American Journal of Orthodontics* 40:298–312, 373–383, 462–475, 517–531.
BJÖRK, A.
   1947   The face in profile. *Svensk Tandläkare Tidskrift* 40 (supplement 5B). Lund: Berlingska Boktryckeriet.
   1950   Some biological aspects of prognathism and occlusion of teeth. *Acta Odontologica Scandinavica* 11:111–128.
BJÖRK, A., B. SOLOW
   1962   Measurements on radiographs. *Journal of Dental Research* 41: 672–683.
BRACE, C. L., P. E. MAHLER
   1971   Post-Pleistocene changes in the human dentition. *American Journal of Physical Anthropology* 34:191–203.
BROWN, T.
   1965   *Craniofacial variations in a Central Australian tribe, a radio-*

graphic investigation of young adult males and females. Libraries' Board of South Australia, Adelaide, Australia.

CAMPBELL, T. D.
1925 *Dentition and palate of the Australian aboriginal.* Adelaide: Universiy of Adelaide Press.

FRIEL, SHELDON
1945 Migration of teeth following extraction. *Proceedings of the Royal Society of Medicine* 38:456.

GOOSE, D.
1963 "Dental measurement: an assessment of its value in anthropological studies," in *Dental anthropology.* Edited by D. Brothwell. New York: Pergamon Press.

GOTTLIEB, B.
1927 The gingival margin. *Proceedings of the Royal Society of Medicine* 20:51–54.

GRABER, T. M.
1958 Extrinsic factors. *American Journal of Orthodontics* 44:26–45.

HASUND, A. P.
1965 Attrition and dental arch space. *Transactions of the European Orthodontic Society,* 121.

KLATSKY, M., R. L. FISHER
1953 *The human masticatory apparatus.* London: Henry Kimpton.

KRAUS, B. S., R. E. JORDAN, L. ABRAMS
1969 *Dental anatomy and occlusion.* Baltimore: Williams and Wilkins.

LATHAM, R. A., J. H. SCOTT
1960 Confirmed mesial migration of teeth by using implants in monkeys. *Transactions of the European Orthodontic Society,* 199–203.

LEIGH, R. W.
1929 Dental pathology of aboriginal California. *Dental Cosmos* 71: 756–767.

LUNDSTRÖM, A., L. LYSELL
1953 An anthropological examination of a group of medieval Danish skulls, with particular regard to the jaws and occlusal conditions. *Acta Odontologica Scandinavia* 11:111–128.

LYSELL, L.
1958a A biometric study of occlusion and dental arches in a series of medieval skulls from northern Sweden. *Acta Odontologica Scandinavica* 16:177–203.
1958b Qualitative and quantitative determination of attrition and the ensuing tooth migration. *Acta Odontologica Scandinavica* 16:267–292.

MOSS, M., S. GREENBERG
1967 Functional cranial analysis of the human maxillary bone: I, Basal bone. *Angle Orthodontist* 37:151–164.

MOSS, M., S. GREENBERG, C. R. NOBACK
1959 Developmental migration of mandibular buccal dentition in man. *Angle Orthodontist* 29:169–176.

MURPHY, T.
1958 Mandibular adjustment to functional tooth attrition. *Australian*

Dental Journal 3:171–178.

1959   Compensatory mechanisms in facial height adjustment to functional tooth attrition. *Australian Dental Journal* 4:312–323.

1964a Reduction of the dental arch by approximal attrition. *British Dental Journal* 116:483–488.

1964b A biometric study of the helicoidal occlusal plane of the worn Australian dentition. *Archives of Oral Biology* 9:255–267.

RICHARDSON, M. E.

1965   The directions of tooth movement subsequent to the extraction of teeth in the Rhesus monkey. *Transactions of the European Orthodontic Society*, 133.

SARNAS, K. V.

1957   Growth changes in skulls of ancient man in North America. *Acta Odontologica Scandinavica* 15:213–273.

SCHOUR, I.

1953   *Noyes' oral histology and embryology.* Philadelphia: Lea and Febiger.

SCOTT, J. H., N. B. B. SYMONS

1953   *Introduction to dental anatomy.* Edinburgh and London: E. and S. Livingstone.

SICHER, H.

1950   *Oral anatomy.* St. Louis: C. V. Mosby.

SNOW, C. E.

1948   Indian Knoll skeletons of site OH2 Ohio County, Kentucky. *Reports in Anthropology* 4:381–554.

TALLGREN, A.

1957   Changes in the adult face height. *Acta Odontologica Scandinavica* 15 (supplement 24).

WEBB, W.

1946   Indian Knoll site OH2 Ohio County, Kentucky. *Reports in Anthropology* 4:115–364.

WILLEY, G. R.

1966   *An introduction to American archaeology*, volume one: *North and Middle America.* Englewood Cliffs, N. J.: Prentice-Hall.

WINTERS, H. D.

1968   *The Riverton culture.* Springfield: Illinois State Museum.

WOLPOFF, M.

1971   Interstitial wear. *American Journal of Physical Anthropology* 34: 205–225.

Plates

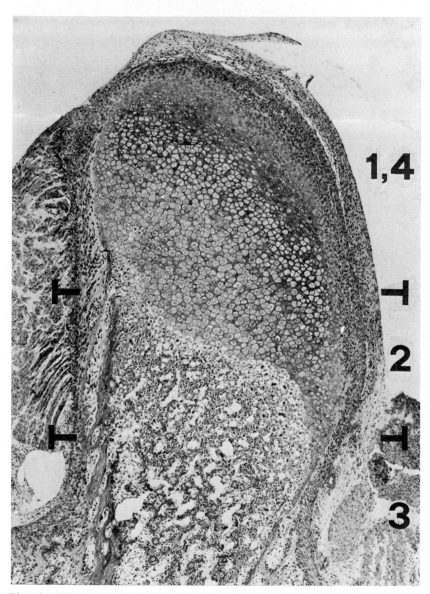

Plate 1.   The condyle of a five-day-old rat, sagittal view. The approximate boundaries of the four types of transplants are indicated; the numbers correspond to those in the text

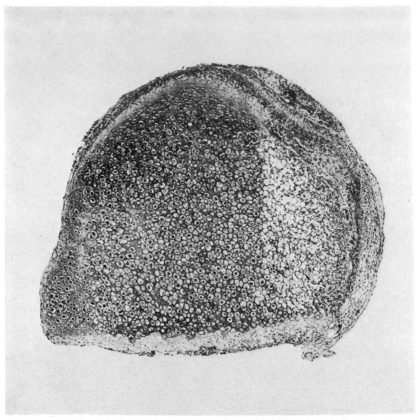

Plate 2.   A condylar cartilage after five days of transplantation in the brain tissue; note the erosion which has already destroyed one-third of the cartilage

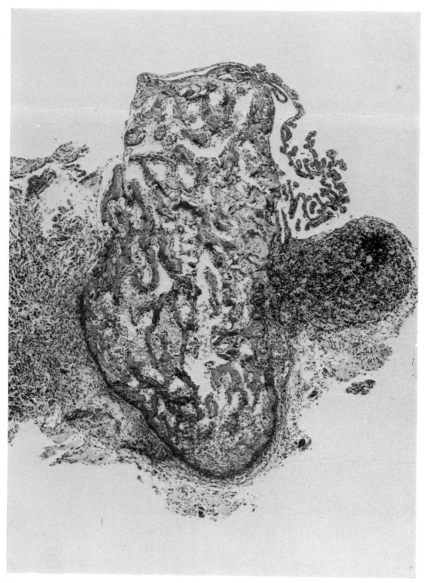

Plate 3. A condylar cartilage plus disc transplant after ten days in the brain tissue; the cartilage has been substituted by woven bone

Plate 4.   The major part of a type 3 condylar cartilage plus bone transplant after thirty days in a subcutaneous site. Note the presence of cartilage in the "upper" end of the transplants, and the amount of woven bone, which gives the transplant a length of nine millimeters, or threefold the original length

Plate 5. The cranial base of a five-day-old rat, sagittal view. The approximate boundaries of the three types of transplants are indicated; the numbers correspond to those in the text

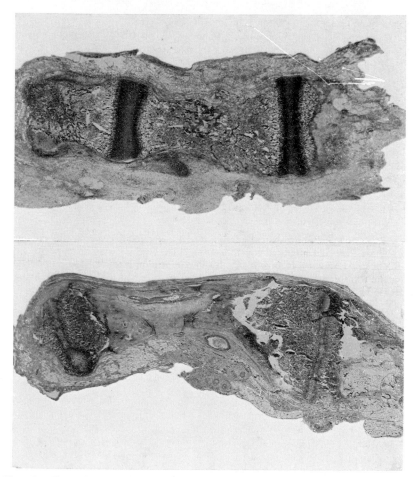

Plate 6. Central parts of whole cranial base transplants from subcutaneous sites, the upper after two, the lower after sixty days; note the increase in the inter-synchondroseal distance

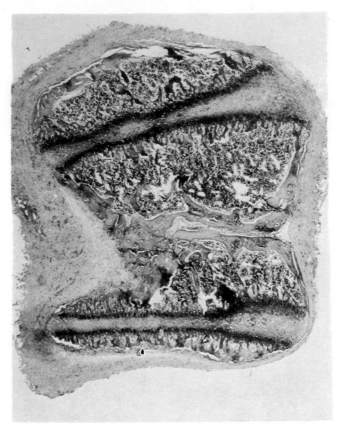

Plate 7.   Two synchondrosis transplants, type 1, after sixty days in a subcutaneous site, where they had migrated together from their original sites on opposite sides in the host. Although it is most likely that the migration has occurred immediately after the transplantation, both transplants have maintained their integrity; a slight increase has taken place

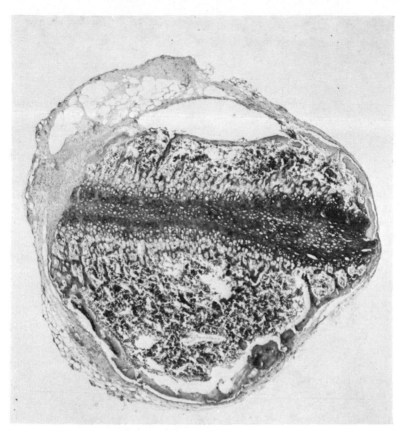

Plate 8. A synchondrosis transplant, type 2, after thirty days in a subcutaneous site; no increase in size

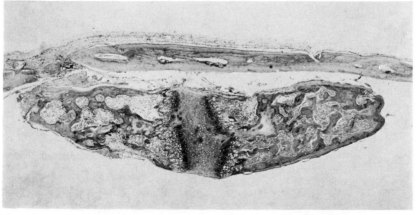

Plate 9. A synchondrosis transplant, type 2, after thirty days in the brain tissue, attached to the calvarial bone and about twice the original length

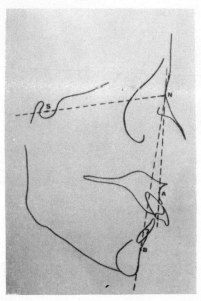

Figure 1. Diagram demonstrating the placement and relation of cephalometric landmarks Point A (maxilla) and Point B (mandible). The ideal ANB angle is two degrees, placing the mandibular basal bone slightly posterior to the maxillary

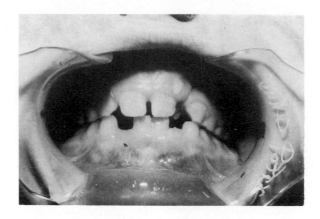

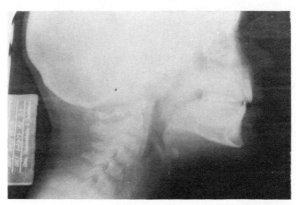

Plate 1.   (a) Intraoral view of the patient at seven and one-half years (D.P.). No orthodontic treatment has been done on this patient to date. Note the lack of anterior crossbite of the central incisors and the maintenance of good buccal segment alignment. (b) Cephalometric radiograph (D.P.), showing good overall basal relations of the maxilla and mandible

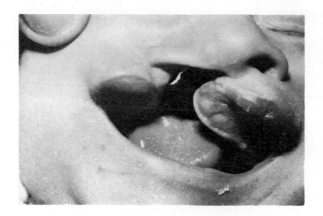

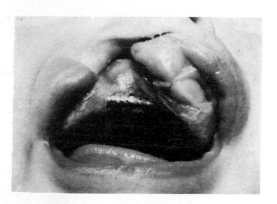

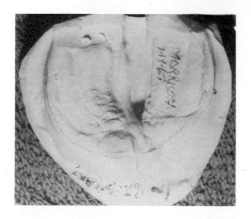

Plate 2.   (a) Frontal view of the patient (R.M.) at birth, before lip closure (above) and placement of maxillary orthopedic appliance to help guide molding of segments after lip closure (below). (b) View of maxillary arch alignment (R.M.) approximately one month post graft

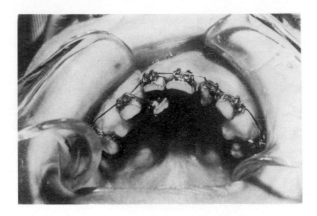

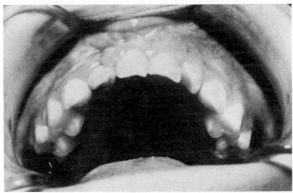

Plate 3.   (a) Intraoral view of maxillary dentition (R.M.) just after placement of orthodontic edgewise appliance in the primary dentition. (b) Alignment of maxillary dentition (R.M.) just after the first phase of orthodontic treatment.

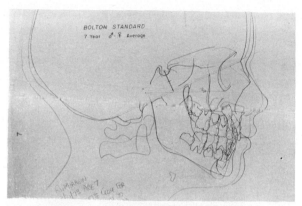

Figure 2. Superimposition of cephalometric tracing of the patient (R.M.) on a "standard" from the Bolton Case-Western-Reserve growth study, demonstrating "normal" maxillo-mandibular relation and lack of growth attenuation

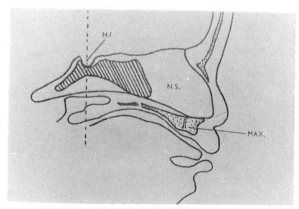

Figure 3. Midline section of a full-term human fetus to show the size and relationship of the nasal septum (N.S.) to the maxilla. The superimposed, shaded area represents the size of the septum at four and a half months' fetal life. Note: the endochondral ossifications of the basiocciput and the basisphenoid have been omitted for clarity as has also the vomer. H.f. is the hypophysial fossa (Burston 1959)

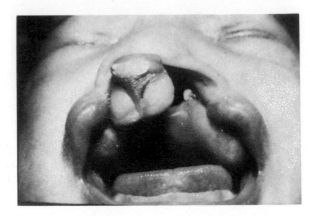

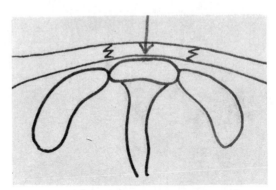

Plate 4.   Placement of a maxillary orthopedic appliance prior to lip closure (above) to maintain position of lateral segments while the premaxilla repositions itself after lip closure (below)

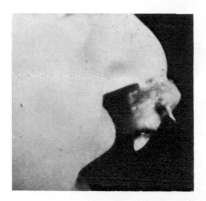

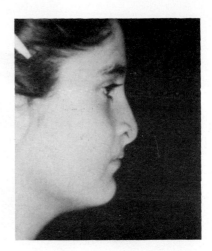

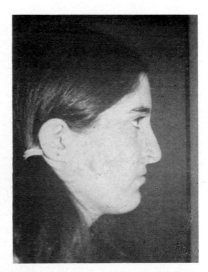

Plate 5.   (a) Lateral facial view of the patient (M.S.) prior to lip closure. (b) Prior to revision of the columella and orthodontic treatment. Age eleven years. (c) Four years after columellar revision and orthodontic treatment. Age fifteen years. (d) Profile view of patient at eighteen years of age

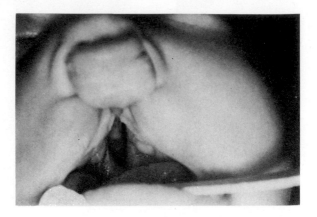

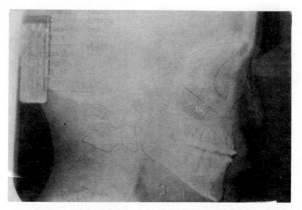

Plate 6.   (a) Intraoral view of the newborn (M.N.) with protrusion of the pre-maxilla. A septum setback was done. (b) Lateral cephalometric radiograph of the same patient at eleven years, nine months. At termination of orthodontic treatment, note the minimal overjet of the maxillary anterior teeth. The mandibular point is ahead of the maxillary point. Note the apparent maxillary attenuation in the profile

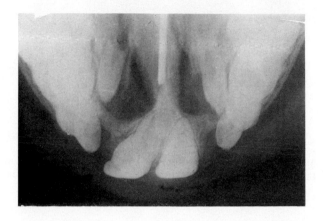

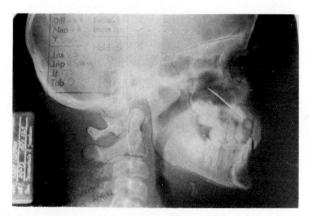

Plate 7.   (a) Occlusal radiograph of the patient (W.E.), showing firm bony union and stabilization of the premaxilla, five years after bone graft. (b) Lateral cephalometric radiograph and tracing (W.E.) at twelve years, nine months. Note the anteroposterior relation of maxilla and mandible as compared to the previous case

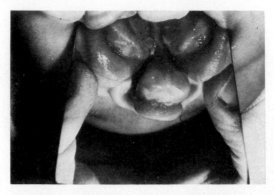

Plate 8.   An example of lateral maxillary segments relating well to the mandibular arch, but presenting a large and anteriorly placed premaxillary segment

Plate 1.
Dentin of gorilla M^1. 50×

Plate 2.
Dentin of chimpanzee M_1. 50×

Plate 3.
Dentin of chimpanzee M_1
with broad area of interglobular
dentin near dentoenamel
junction. 50×

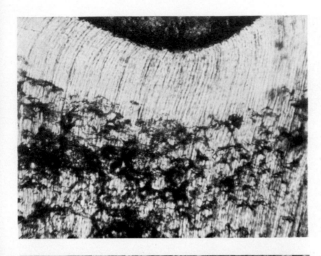

Plate 4.
Dentin of human M_1 with broad
area of interglobular dentin near
dentoenamel junction. 50×

Plate 5.
Dentin of chimpanzee M^1
with well-defined incremental
lines of von Ebner. 50×

Plate 6.
Dentin of gorilla M^1 with
faintly defined incremental
lines of von Ebner. 50×

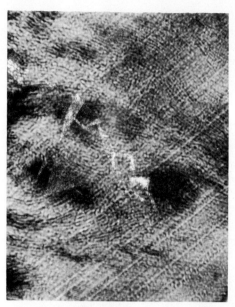

Plate 7.   Enamel of gorilla M^1 with very irregular—even circular—rod direction (gnarled enamel). 50×

Plate 8.   Enamel of human M^1 with extensive hypoplasia and broad distinctive striae of Retzius. 50×

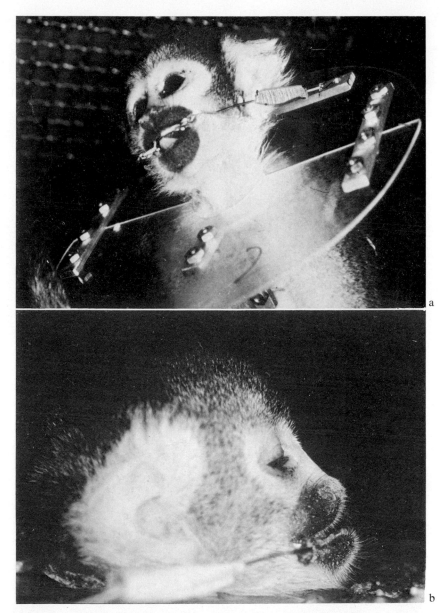

Plate 1. (a) *Saimiri sciureus* monkey, with restraining collar and bilateral spring-traction appliance in place. The coil springs are attached to a pivoting posterior anchor bar, which permits the monkey to turn his head. The plastic collar prevents digital manipulation of the appliance. (b) Monkey with springs still attached, showing mid-face deficiency (see Plate 3(b) for skin stripped away). This is after three months of restrictive traction

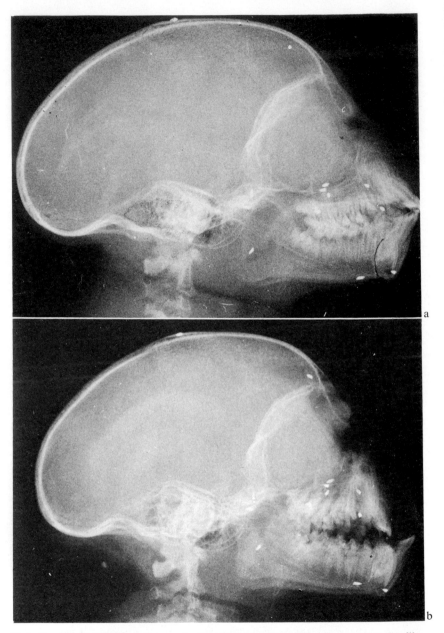

Plate 2. Monkey M-3, before and after three months of traction against maxilla.
Implants appear as white hash marks. Note severe retrognathism of maxilla in 2(b)

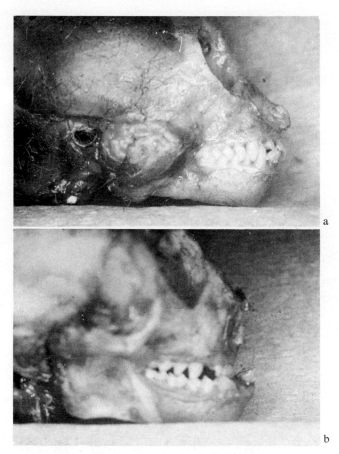

a

b

Plate 3. Control *Saimiri sciureus* (top) and monkey M-3 after ninety days restraining traction against maxilla. Skin has been stripped away on both animals to show contrasting dental relationships. The maxilla in (b) is posteriorly placed by the width of three cusps

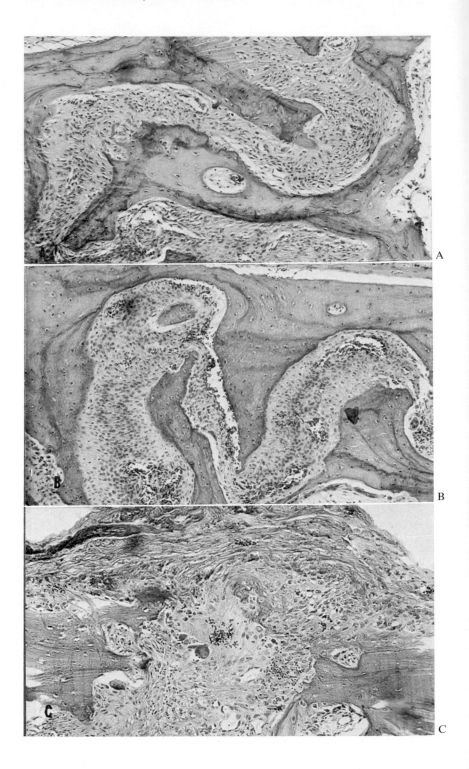

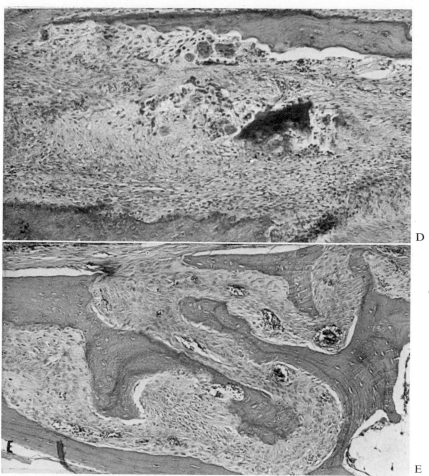

D

E

Plate 4. Pterygopalatine suture (hematoxylin-eosin), × 65. Monkey M-4 (control monkey) vertical section through pterygopalatine suture. This untreated specimen shows a regular pattern. The capsular zone in the middle of the suture consists of dense, regular connective tissue and blood vessels. The adjacent intermediate zone is much looser in texture and more cellular. It is composed largely of immature precollagenous fibrils. As these fibrils approach the sutural surface, they thicken to become coarse collagenous fibers of the border zone. In B, Monkey M-1, treated fourteen days, shows the same general pattern, but with beginning osteoclastic activity in some areas. In C, Monkey M-2 has had maxillary orthopedic restraint for thirty days, and shows a major change in size and pattern. The width of the suture is trebled and there is great cellular activity, with cells and fibrils running in all directions. Note numerous osteoclasts on the bone surface. In D, Monkey M-3, which has been subjected to orthopedic restraint on the maxilla for ninety days, shows a pattern similar to B, above, with much less activity than in C. The three zones seem to be forming again in some areas, reorganization has started and cellular activity is reduced. Osteoblasts are lining up on the bone margin, indicating new bone formation. Osteoclasts are also still active. In E, taken from Monkey M-5, untreated for ninety days, the configuration is the same as in A, above

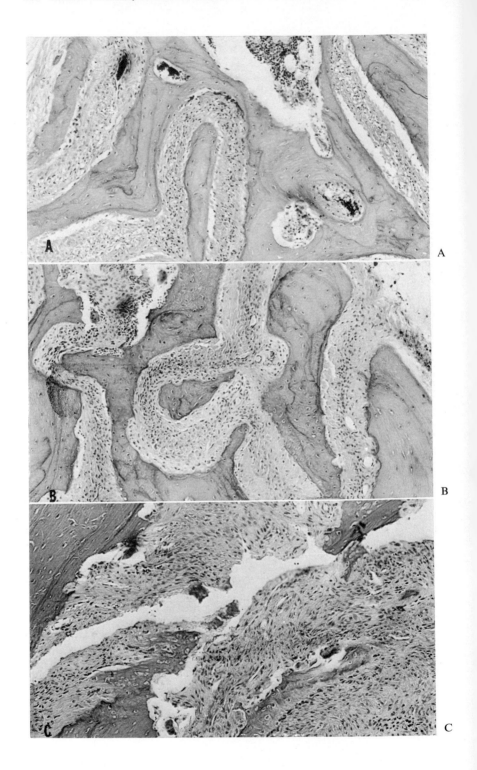

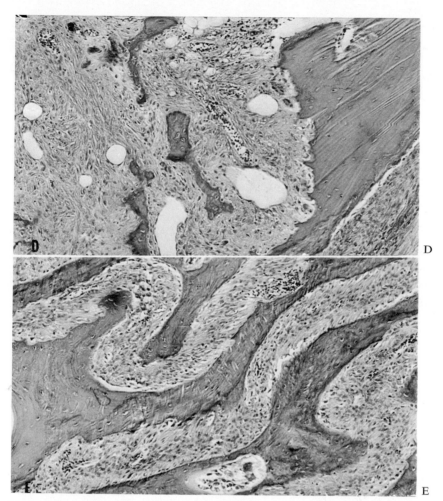

D

E

Plate 5. Zygomatico-maxillary suture (hematoxylin-eosin) × 65. A through E are from the same monkeys as in Plate 4, same time of death, but with sections taken from the zygomatico-maxillary instead of pterygopalatine suture. Findings are similar to those observed in Plate 4. The significant observation made is the change from a regular serpentine pattern to an irregular, wide suture. This snake-like configuration returns again in 5-E

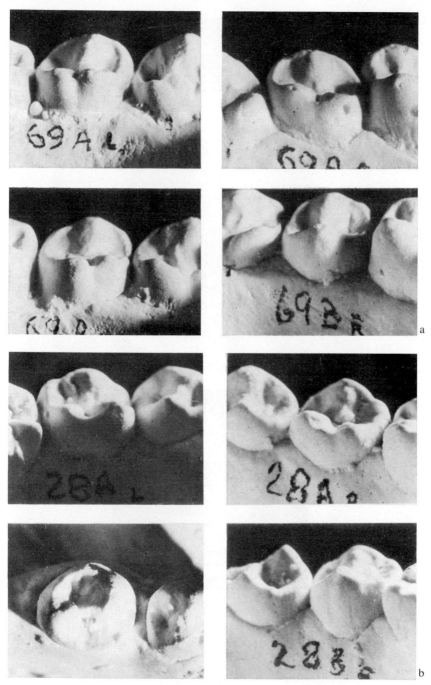

Plate 1a, b.   Lower second premolars in two pairs of twins, diagnosed as monozygotic (Lundström 1963)

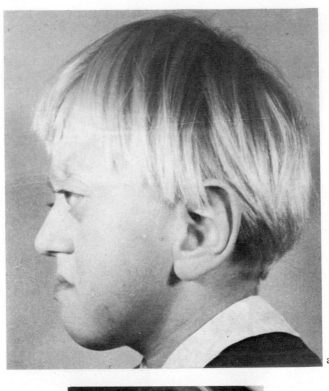

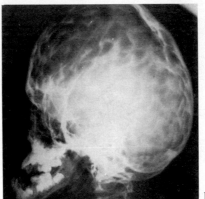

Plate 2a, b.   Photo and lateral head-plate for a case with craniofacial dysostosis Crouzon

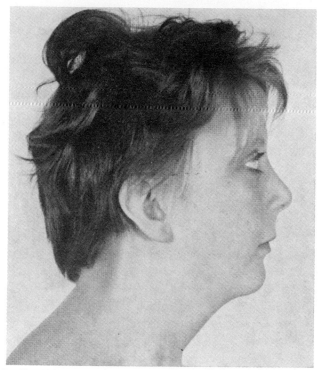

Plate 3.   Profile of the head in a case of Turner's syndrome (Filipsson et al. 1965)

Plate 1. Soapstone carving from the Canadian Arctic; note the use of the "third hand" in lifting the seal. (Courtesy of Dr. John T. Mayhall)

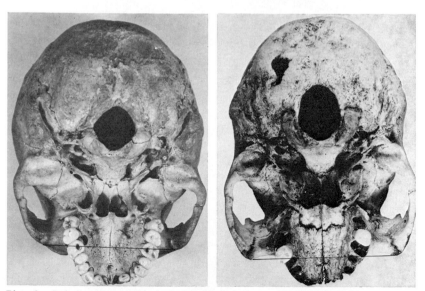

Plate 2. Inferior view of the skull. (L) Adult male from Indian Knoll (University of Kentucky 24–409). (R) Adult male Canadian Thule Eskimo (Silumiut 24)

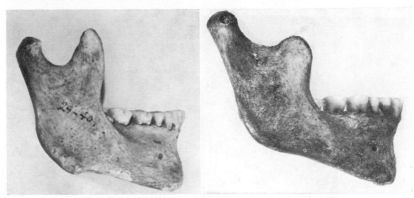

Plate 3.   Lateral view of the mandible. (L) Adult male from Indian Knoll (University of Kentucky 24–409). (R) Adult male Canadian Thule Eskimo (Silumiut 24)

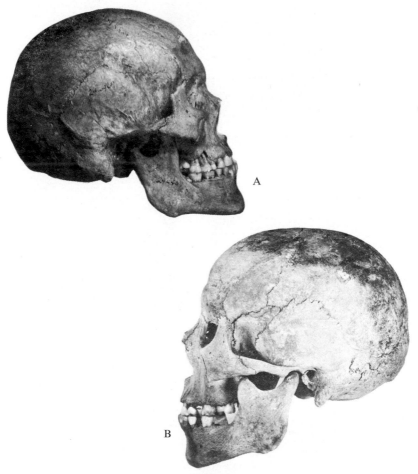

Plate 4.   Lateral view of the skull. (A) Adult male from Indian Knoll (University of Kentucky 24–409). (B) Adult male Canadian Thule Eskimo (Silumiut 24)

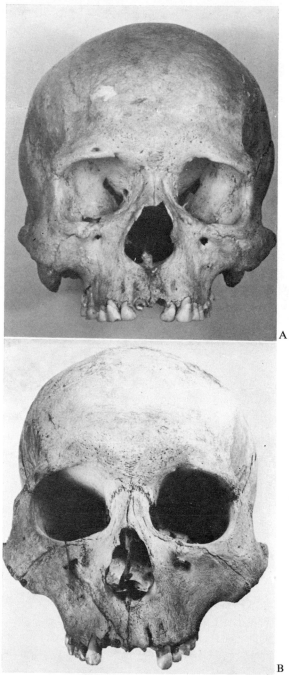

Plate 5.   Frontal view of the skull. (A) Adult male from Indian Knoll (University of Kentucky 24–409). (B) Adult male Canadian Thule Eskimo (Silumiut 24)

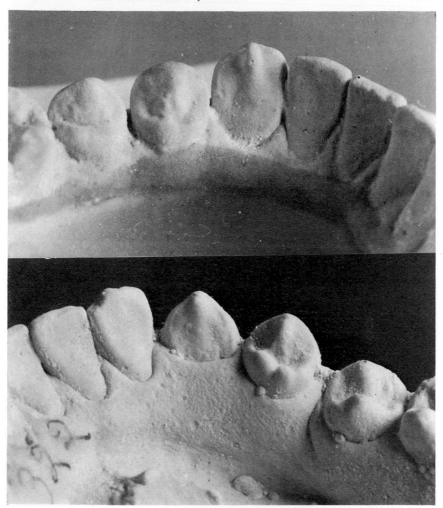

Plate 1 (a, b). Male (above) and female (top) canine teeth showing difference in occlusal outline

Plate 2. Occlusal surfaces of teeth showing occlusal tubercles

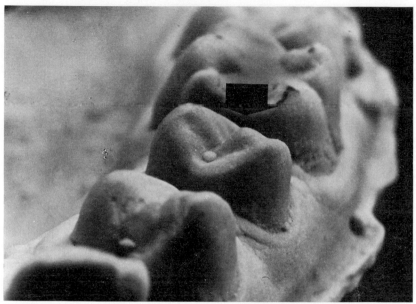

Plate 1. Bulging of the lingual aspect of the buccal cusp on a maxillary second premolar

Plate 2. A lingual view of a maxillary permanent canine with reduced mesial lobe

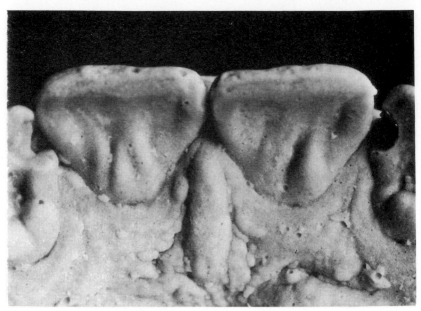

Plate 3. Expressions of lingual tubercles on maxillary permanent central incisors

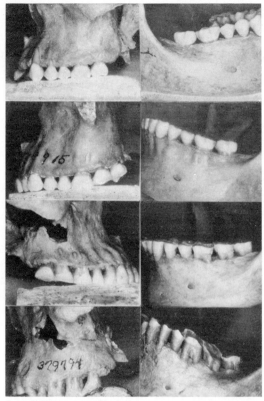

Plate 1.   Periodontal disease standard

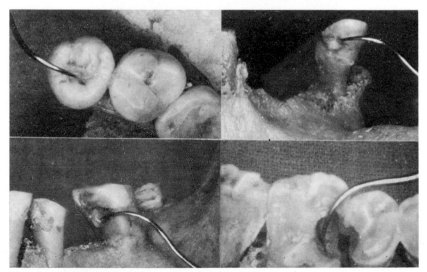

Plate 2.   Caries standard

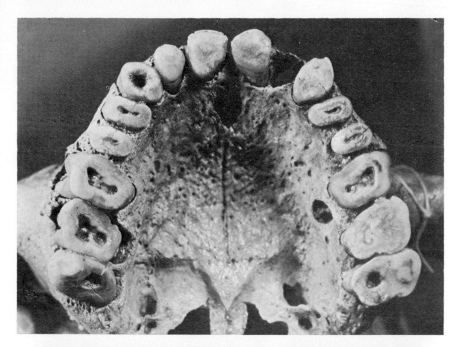

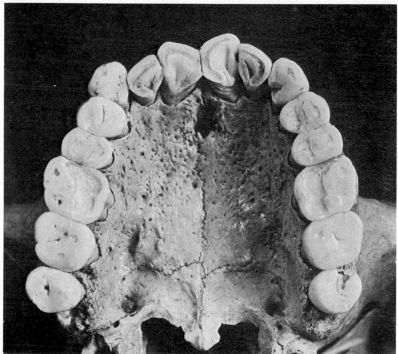

Plate 1. Severely (above) and moderately (below) worn dentitions from Indian Knoll

Appendix: Abstracts

Editor's Note: At the Pre-Congress Symposium on Oral Growth and Development and Dental Anthropology, several papers were presented without a publishable text. The following two items were the abstracts submitted by the authors.

"The Histogenetic Specificity of Meckel's Chondrocytes" *by Clarke L. Johnson*

The ability of embryonic cells liberated by enzymatic digestion to aggregate and organize into tissues is well established. When differentiated cells from two dissimilar tissues are liberated, mixed, and aggregated, the cells will segregate according to tissue type. Chimeric aggregates of embryonic chick and mouse Meckel's chondrocytes combine homogeneously to form a common tissue fabric. A similar result is observed with the mixture of hind limb chondrocytes. Limb and Meckel's chondrocytes, however, will segregate when aggregated, suggesting a histogenetic difference within a morphologically similar cell type on the basis of derivation from cranial neural crest or somite mesoderm. This confirms and extends earlier reported findings of differential fusion of amphibian cartilage fragments derived from somite mesoderm and cranial neural crest. Confrontations of liberated embryonic limb or vertebral chondrocytes with Meckel's whole cartilage fragments reveal a clefting or separation of the cell groups. Clefting was not observed when dissociated Meckel's chondrocytes were confronted with Meckel's whole cartilage fragments.

Dissociation and aggregation of the embryonic chick mandible prior to the onset of ossification reveals that the Meckel's chondrocytes quickly reorganize to form cartilage tissue. It is the only clearly defined tissue present in 3-day cultured aggregates. The competence of Meckel's chondrocytes to reorganize may reflect the role of Meckel's cartilage in the early organization and growth of the mandible.

"Toothless Albino Rats" *by William R. Cotton and James F. Gaines*

Clinically toothless rats occurred as a spontaneous mutation in the Osborne-Mendel strain from apparently normal parents. The F_1 generation consisted of 12 offspring including 2 females and 1 male, each with the absence of teeth, and 3 females and 6 males with normal dentition. The original dam, mated with the affected F_1 male, produced 3 affected females, 1 affected male, and 7 normal offspring, including 2 normal males and 5 normal females. The affected rats exhibited a reddish brown periorbital encrustation, apparently due to aberrations of the lacrimal apparatus, without nasal exudate or signs of respiratory disease. The hair coat was coarse and dry, with small areas of alopecia. Microscopically the affected hair showed some loss of birefringency and an increase of crenate scales. The normal litter mates did not show changes in hair or lacrimal apparatus. Skeletal remains of the F_1 male and a F_1 female revealed 1 or 2 partially erupted vestigial maxillary and/or mandibular molars, which had erupted through the bone but not through the gingiva. The latter teeth were conical in shape, lacking definitive cusp formation. In addition to the partially erupted molars, mineralized molars were radiographically visible embedded within the mandibles and maxillae. There was no evidence of maxillary or mandibular incisors by radiographic or gross examinations of the skeletal remains. At the site of the incisors a patent opening was present, or the area was fused over. The affected rats manifested retarded growth compared to their normal litter mates, most likely due to difficulty in eating. The affected animals are presently maintained on a water mixture of sucrose-free 2000 diet supplemented with fatty acids. The oligodontia and the unerupted and malformed molars appear to be an autosomal recessive hereditary characteristic, possibly associated with the observed changes in the lacrimal apparatus and hair. The development of a clinically toothless rat colony would offer a significantly new animal model for dental and craniofacial research.

Biographical Notes

LASSI ALVESALO (1939–   ) is Special Lecturer (Docent) of Dental Genetics at the University of Turku, Finland. He received his Ph.D. (D. Odont.) from the University of Turku in 1971, and in the years 1972 to 1974 he was senior investigator at the University of Wisconsin, Department of Anthropology, working on a dental-genetic research project. His special research interest is focused on sex-chromosomal influence on quantitative structures, especially human teeth.

BRUCE J. BAUM (1945–   ) received a B.A. from the University of Virginia in 1967, a D.M.D. from Tufts University in 1971, and a Ph.D. in Biochemistry from Boston University in 1974. He was recently a Dental Research Officer at the Naval Medical Research Institute and is presently a Senior Staff Fellow at the National Heart, Lung and Blood Institute at Bethesda, Maryland. His research interests include salivary gland and connective tissue biochemistry.

ROBERT H. BIGGERSTAFF (1927–   ) was born in Richmond, Kentucky. He received his B.S. (1951) and D.D.S. (1955) degrees from Howard University. After practicing dentistry for eight years, he studied physical anthropology at the University of Pennsylvania and received his M.S. (1966) and Ph.D. (1969) degrees. He is currently an Associate Professor and Chairman of the Department of Orthodontics at the University of Kentucky. He received his certificate in orthodontics at the University of Kentucky in 1973. His research interests include the analysis of human dentitions and the applications of physical anthropology methodologies for resolving orthodontic questions related to the growth and development of the human cephalofacial complex.

ROBERT CEDERQUIST (1938–   ) graduated from the Faculty of Odontology, University of Lund, in 1964. He did his graduate training at the Department of Orthodontics of Northwestern University, 1966–1968, and at the Department of Anthropology, University of Chicago, from 1972 to the present. Since 1972 he has been a Fellow in Orthodontics at the University of Chicago.

M. MICHAEL COHEN (1905–   ) was born in Boston, Massachusetts. He received his dental degree from the Tufts University School of Dental Medicine in 1928. He taught at Tufts University from 1928 to 1971 and was retired as Professor Emeritus in both Pediatric Dentistry and Oral Pathology. At present he is a Lecturer on Oral Pathology at the Harvard School of Dental Medicine. He is the author of two textbooks and numerous scientific articles.

WILLIAM ROBERT COTTON (1931–   ) was born in Miami, Florida, and attended the University of Miami from 1949 to 1951. He received his D.D.S. from the University of Maryland in 1955. He entered the U.S. Navy that year and advanced through the ranks to his present rank of Captain in 1972. He received postgraduate training at the U.S. Naval Dental School at Bethesda, Maryland, in 1960. Following two years aboard the aircraft carrier *U.S.S. Roosevelt*, he attended Northwestern University, Chicago, and received an M.S. degree in Anatomy. He began his research career at the Naval Medical Research Institute at Bethesda, Maryland, in 1963. In 1967 he returned to sea aboard the submarine tender. *U.S.S. Fulton.* In 1969 he returned to research as Chief, Histopathology Division, Naval Dental Research Institute, Great Lakes, Illinois, where he ultimately became Deputy Commanding Officer. During this period he earned a M.A. degree in Education from Roosevelt University, Chicago. In 1976 he assumed his present position as Chairman, Dental Sciences Department, Naval Medical Research Institute, Bethesda, Maryland. His special research interests are biology of the dental pulp and mechanisms of bone resorption related to the *tl* rat.

ALBERT A. DAHLBERG (1908–   ) graduated from Loyola University with a B.S. and D.D.S. in 1932. His research interests are in dental genetics and morphology. He is Research Associate and Professor in both the Zoller Memorial Dental Clinic and the Department of Anthropology, University of Chicago, and has done field research among Amerinds and circumpolar peoples. He is a Fellow of the American

College of Dentists and of the International College of Dentists, has been awarded the Japanese government's decoration Order of the Rising Sun, and is an honorary corresponding member of the Finnish Dental Society, membre honoraire of the Groupement Internationale de Recherche en Stomatologie, member of the American Dental Association and of the International Association for Dental Research, and author of numerous books and articles on dental evolution, genetics, and morphology.

HELMUT DROSCHL (1942–) was born in Graz, Austria. He studied at the University of Graz Medical School and got his M.D. in 1966. He later received his dental education at the Dental Clinic of the University of Graz and subsequently went into orthodontics at that clinic. In 1971 he did research at the Department of Orthodontics at the University of Chicago. He then returned to Austria and was appointed Head of the Department of Orthodontics at the Dental Clinic of the University of Graz in 1974.

JAMES F. GAINES (1938–) was born in the District of Columbia. He received his D.V.M. from the University of Georgia in 1962 and his M.S.C. in Laboratory Animal Medicine from Texas A & M University in 1972. He was Board Certified by the American College of Laboratory Animal Medicine in 1974. He is a Major in the United States Air Force and has served as Chief of Veterinary Services at various Air Force bases both in the United States and abroad. His current position is Chief of the Veterinary Sciences Division, Naval Dental Research Institute, Great Lakes, Illinois, where he has been since 1972. He is a member of the American Association for Laboratory Animal Science and the American Association of Zoo Veterinarians.

STANLEY M. GARN (1922–) was born in New London, Connecticut, and received his A.B., A.M., and Ph.D. from Harvard College and Harvard University. He has been Chairman of the Department of Growth and Genetics at the Fels Research Institute and is a Fellow of the Center for Human Growth and Development, University of Michigan, Professor of Nutrition in the School of Public Health, and Professor of Anthropology. He is the author of over five hundred papers, monographs, and publications.

DENYS H. GOOSE (1923–) studied dentistry and anatomy at Birmingham University (B.D.S., 1945; B.Sc., 1950) and -worked in public health service for ten years. He then joined the staff of the School of Dental Surgery of Liverpool University, receiving his M.D.S. in 1961 for an anthropological dissertation. He is now Reader in Children's Dentistry and is continuing his research into dental anthropology and genetic studies.

T. M. GRABER (1917–) is Professor of Biological Sciences, Pediatrics, and Anthropology at the University of Chicago. His major research thrust has been in craniofacial growth and development, with the emphasis on congenital defects of the face, i.e. cleft lip and palate. Specifically, his work called attention to the growth arrest effects of early and traumatic surgery. He has continued his research on the orthopedic effects of extraoral force on the face and jaws and in roentgenographic cephalometrics. As Chairman of the Department of Orthodontics at the University of Chicago, he has directed a number of research projects in the field. His numerous publications include works in craniofacial anomalies, cephalometrics, clinical orthodontics, and dental education. He has received the highest honors in the field of orthodontics, the Albert H. Ketcham and the Distinguished Service Awards.

KAZURO HANIHARA (1927–) was born in Tokyo, studied physical anthropology at the University of Tokyo, and received a Doctor of Science degree in 1958. During the period between 1956 and 1972 he gave lectures on anthropology and legal medicine at Sapporo Medical College, and since 1972 he has been Professor of Anthropology at the University of Tokyo. He also gave lectures at the Department of Anthropology of the University of Chicago in 1959–1960 and 1967, and was invited to the University of Adelaide, Australia, in 1969 to investigate Australian Aboriginal dentition. His research has been concentrated on dental and skeletal anthropology.

WILLIAM L. HYLANDER (1938–) is Associate Professor of Anatomy and Anthropology at Duke University. He received a D.D.S. from the University of Illinois in 1963 and a Ph.D. in Anthropology from the University of Chicago in 1972. His current research efforts are directed towards analyzing the evolutionary and functional morphology of the craniofacial region in primates. This includes characterizing patterns of *in vivo* facial bone strain in both prosimians and anthropoids during ingestion and mastication. In addition, he is an Associate Editor for the *American Journal of Physical Anthropology* and holds a Research Career Development Award from the National Institutes of Health.

BAILEY N. JACOBSON (1934–), a native Chicagoan, completed his studies at Northwestern University. He received his D.D.S. in 1957, and his M.S. in Orthodontics in 1961. At present he is an Associate Professor of Clinical Orthodontics at both Northwestern University Dental School and the University of Detroit Dental School. He has worked in cleft lip and palate habilitation since his specialization and is presently an Attending Orthodontist on the team at Children's Memorial Hospital in Chicago, Illinois. His special interest at this time is a study of the efficacy of early maxillary orthopedics and bone grafting procedures in the cleft lip and palate patient as performed by the plastic surgery and orthodontic sections of the team at Children's Memorial Hospital.

CLARKE L. JOHNSON. No biographical data available.

MARKKU KARI (1947–) was born in Turku, Finland. He studied at the University of Turku and graduated (Licentiate in Dentistry) in 1971. Since 1972 he has been an Instructor at the Department of Pedodontics and Orthodontics of the Institute of Dentistry, University of Turku. His interests include dental genetics.

PENTTI KIRVESKARI (1940–) is Assistant Professor at the Institute of Dentistry, University of Turku, Finland, where his teaching responsibilities include functional disorders of the stomatognathic system. He is a graduate of that institute (1964) and received his doctor's degree at the University of Turku in 1974 with a thesis entitled "Morphological traits in the permanent dentition of living Skolt Lapps." He was Visiting (Assistant) Professor at Northwestern University Dental School in Chicago in 1968–1970, and in 1970–1972 he did most of the analysis work of the Lapp dentitions at Odontologiska Kliniken, University of Gothenburg, Sweden, where he also taught prosthetic dentistry. His research interests are centered in dental anthropology.

RICHARD THOMAS KORITZER (1926–) was born in Baltimore, Maryland. He received a D.D.S. from the University of Maryland in 1962, a Master of Liberal Arts from Johns Hopkins University in 1967, and a Ph.D. in Anthropology from the American University in 1976. He has had a general practice in dentistry located in Glen Burnie, Maryland, since 1962. He is Clinical Associate Professor of Crown and Bridge at Georgetown University School of Dentistry and Research Associate at the Smithsonian Institution. His publications include works on general dentistry and dental anthropology. He is a member of numerous organizations including the ADA, WSDS, ADSA, AAAP, and AGP; affiliate member of the AMA; Fellow of the American Anthropological Association and the American Association for the Advancement of Science.

KALEVI KOSKI (1921–   ) was born in Helsinki. He graduated from the Institute of Dentistry, University of Helsinki (L. Odont. 1945) and received his doctoral degree from the same university (D. Odont. 1948). He joined the faculty of the Helsinki dental school in 1946 and was Head of the Department of Orthodontics from 1950 to 1959. There followed a short spell in anatomy, and since 1962 he has been Professor of Pedodontics and Orthodontics at the University of Turku. He has also spent several years at a number of institutions in the United States. His research has been mainly on aspects of postnatal growth, especially on dental eruption and craniofacial development.

PIERRE LE BOT (1935–   ) is Assistant of Biology at the Faculté de Chirurgie Dentaire, Université Paris V. He is primarily concerned with the study of dental anthropology and genetics, at the Laboratoire d'Anthropologie Biologique, Université Paris VII. He is General Secretary of the Société Française d'Anthropologie et de Génétique Dentofaciales and a Docteur en Sciences Odontologiques.

ANDERS LUNDSTRÖM (1916–   ) is Professor of Orthodontics at the Karolinska Institute, Stockholm. His research has primarily been concerned with the role of genetic factors in the etiology of facial variation and malocclusion of the teeth, which he first studied on twins. His doctoral thesis, "Tooth size and occlusion in twins," in 1948 has been followed by numerous publications in this and adjacent fields.

JOHN T. MAYHALL (1937–   ) is Assistant Professor in the Faculty of Dentistry and a Research Associate in the Department of Anthropology of the University of Toronto. He received his B.A. from DePauw University in 1959 and his D.D.S. from Indiana University in 1963. After practicing dentistry in Alaska, he enrolled at the University of Chicago where he studied dental anthropology (M.A., 1968; Ph.D., 1976). He has been a resident of Canada since 1970 and has been involved with oral epidemiology, dental morphology, and the dental growth and development of the Inuit (Eskimo) and Indians of North America.

STEPHEN MOLNAR (1931–) is Associate Professor and Chairman of Anthropology, Washington University, St. Louis. He received a Ph.D. in Anthropology from the University of California at Santa Barbara in 1968. His research interests are in orofacial biomechanics and stress analysis of masticatory forces. Recently he has been doing comparative work in primate dental histology. A recent publication describing this work appeared in *American Journal of Physical Anthropology* 43(3).

HERROLD M. NAGY. No biographical data available.

RICHARD H. OSBORNE. No biographical data available.

CARLOS H. OSORIO. No biographical data available.

SHELDON W. ROSENSTEIN (1927–) was born in Chicago. He graduated from Northwestern University Dental School in 1951, with a D.D.S. He continued his studies at Northwestern and received an M.S.D. in Orthodontics in 1955. His special interests are in the fields of cleft lip and palate, and growth and development of the cranial complex. He is co-editor of the book *Cleft lip and palate* (1971) and has recently authored a chapter on craniofacial anomalies and their treatment in the forthcoming text, *Pediatric dental medicine* (1977). At present, he is Professor of Orthodontics at Northwestern University Dental School, Chicago; Clinical Professor of Orthodontics, St. Louis University Medical School, Graduate Department of Orthodontics, St. Louis; and Attending Orthodontist, Children's Memorial Hospital, Chicago, Illinois.

G. RICHARD SCOTT (1946–) is Associate Professor of Anthropology at the University of Alaska, Fairbanks, where he also serves as Associate Editor for the University of Alaska Anthropological Papers. He helped organize the Alaska Anthropological Association by serving as its first President. He has carried out anthropological work in Arizona and Alaska. His doctoral studies at Arizona State University, Tempe, considered the ways in which dental crown morphology might be inherited as well as assessing the biological significance of dental variation in western American Indians. He has recently begun (in Switzerland) a study of Bering Sea Eskimo dentition.

PATRICIA SMITH (1936–) was born in London and studied dentistry at the London Hospital Medical College, obtaining her degree in 1961.

After carrying out fieldwork in Israel on dental epidemiology, she continued her studies in Anthropology at the University of Chicago, obtaining her Ph.D. in Physical Anthropology in 1970. She is now Senior Lecturer in the Department of Anatomy and Embryology at the Hebrew University Hadassah Schools of Medicine and Dental Medicine. Most of her work to date has been related to genetic and epidemiological factors associated with evolution and variation in dentition.

CHRISTY G. TURNER, II (1933–) is Professor of Anthropology and Associate Dean of Graduate College, Arizona State University, Tempe. His doctoral research at the University of Wisconsin evaluated dental variation of Aleuts, Eskimos, and Indians of Alaska, Canada, and Greenland for microevolutionary and genetic considerations. His physical anthropological and archaeological studies in Arizona, Utah, New Mexico, Hawaii, Alaska, Taiwan and Japan have resulted in more than fifty articles and monographs. His present dental anthropological studies are concerned with the origins and peopling of the New World and the Pacific basin and with reconstructing the evolution of Mongoloids. He is presently completing a monograph on the dentition of the Shang Dynasty Chinese from An-yang China.

GEOFFREY WALKER (1920–) was born in New Zealand and studied dentistry in New Zealand and Australia, and anthropology and computer sciences in the United States. Currently, he is Director of the Biometrics Laboratory at the University of Michigan Dental School. An initiator of quantitative cephalometrics using a computer-oriented method, he is primarily interested in development anatomy and the variation of cephalofacial parameters within population groups. His present research is related to the quantification and analysis of human growth, and its simulation and projection using biostatistics and computer graphics. His numerous publications include works on facial growth, computer graphics, computer-aided diagnosis, and the physical anthropology of the face and jaws.

ALEXANDER A. ZOUBOV (1934–) graduated in 1960 from Moscow University in Biology, specializing as a physical anthropologist. In 1964 and 1970, he received his candidate's and doctor's degrees. He is presently in charge of the Department of Physical Anthropology at the Ethnography Institute of the Academy of Sciences of the U.S.S.R. and is Lecturer in Dental Morphology at Moscow University. He has been an initiator of the research work in dental anthropology in the

U.S.S.R., in particular of the extensive investigation of different dental types of different human populations after a standard program. He has more than forty publications on dental morphology and human evolution, including two books (in Russian) — *Anthropological odontology* (1968) and *Ethnic odontology* (1973) — and has worked out a new classification of the morphological details of the masticatory surface of human molars (odontoglyphics). He has also participated in numerous anthropological expeditions to different parts of the U.S.S.R. and to other countries (Finland, India, Peru).

Index of Names

Index of Subjects